This volume of essays by a leading scholar of Victorian intellectual history reflects research, teaching, and writing carried out over more than twenty years. Five of the essays are new; seven, although published previously, have been revised for this collection. The essays cover an extremely wide spectrum of Victorian thought, including the issues of secularization, cultural apostasy, the crisis of faith, Victorian scientific naturalism, the conflict between science and religion, the relationship of science and politics, and the Victorian attitudes towards the ancient world. Taken as a whole the essays constitute a major revisionist overview of the Victorian intellectual enterprise which will be of interest to scholars in a wide variety of fields.

A theme that runs throughout the volume is the manner in which various groups within the Victorian intellectual elite attempted to wrest or to protect cultural dominance for their particular professions, academic disciplines and philosophical outlooks. The author is concerned with the manner in which these struggles determined the social organization of British thought, education, and general intellectual endeavour. He draws important parallels between developments in fields as different as Victorian science and classical studies. In that regard the essays are designed to speak to one another and to draw the reader into frequently unfamiliar byways of Victorian thought.

CONTESTING CULTURAL AUTHORITY

CONTESTING CULTURAL AUTHORITY

AUTHORITY

Essays in Victorian Intellectual Life

FRANK M. TURNER

John Hay Whitney Professor of History, Yale University

CAMBRIDGE
UNIVERSITY PRESS

Published by the Press Syndicate of the University of Cambridge
The Pitt Building, Trumpington Street, Cambridge CB2 1RP
40 West 20th Street, New York, NY 10011-4211, USA
10 Stamford Road, Oakleigh, Victoria 3166, Australia

© Cambridge University Press 1993

First published 1993

Transferred to digital printing 1999

Printed in the United Kingdom by Biddles Short Run Books

A catalogue record for this book is available from the British Library

Library of Congress cataloguing in publication data

Turner, Frank M. (Frank Miller), 1944–
Contesting cultural authority: essays in Victorian intellectual
life / Frank M. Turner.
p.   cm.
ISBN 0 521 37257 7 (hard)
1. Great Britain–Intellectual life–19th century. 1. Title.
DA533.T86 1993
941.081′08′631–dc20   92–20887 CIP

ISBN 0 521 37257 7 hardback

For
Michael Finnerty
Terry M. Holcombe
Charles H. Long
Dorothy K. Robinson
Sheila W. Wellington

Friends and Colleagues in Good Causes

Contents

Preface

The essays in this volume, composed over a period of twenty years, reflect portions of my exploration of Victorian intellectual life. I commenced that effort as a graduate student suspicious that many of the categories used to understand the Victorians were inadequate and misleading. As I read further Victorian writers, I repeatedly encountered passages that did not fit the patterns of interpretation that then generally predominated. As time passed, I came to the firmer conviction that the history of the nineteenth century whether in Great Britain or elsewhere was still to be written. So long as Victorian scholars tended to interpret their field largely according to the categories and values bequeathed them by Victorian writers themselves, the scholarly enterprise could not extend beyond the intellectual and cultural boundaries established by the nineteenth-century writers for their own purposes. Those boundaries have now begun to shift as new categories have been introduced, as Victorians previously unread by scholars have become read, and as the contemporary polemical purposes of Victorian writers have been recognized. As a consequence, the experience of the Victorians and their intellectual activity can no longer be regarded as unproblematic, inevitable, or quaint.

A theme that unites virtually all of these essays is the attempt of various groups of Victorian intellectuals to establish foundations for new mental outlooks, to challenge existing cultural authorities, to propose themselves as new authorities, or to resist the challenge of newcomers and to preserve earlier ideas and values in novel guises and institutional arrangements; hence the title of the collection. By the close of the century a remarkable diversity of intellectual outlooks existed in Great Britain within a wide variety of institutional settings. Such had not been the case in 1800. At that date science was suspect; Roman Catholicism was regarded with both suspicion and prejudice; the study of the ancient world upheld a conservative social and intellectual order. The thought of both Germany and France had made only marginal impact. The major intellectual authorities remained overwhelmingly Anglican. Much of the history of Victorian intellectual life, as has become evident through the research of the past quarter century, was embodied in the process whereby groups advocating different ideas came to the fore, claimed the right to be heard, and established institutions that fostered their own ideas and values. Those who sought to preserve more traditional ideas and values did likewise. It is this process as manifested in a variety of situations that I have addressed in these essays.

My own research has probed two apparently diverse arenas – the relationship of religion to more advanced modes of thought and the Victorian encounter with the cultures of ancient Greece and Rome. Although these appear disparate and unrelated, I have found them to be mutually illuminating. The former obviously deals with ideas directly associated with modern thought. Paradoxically, classical scholarship does also because it provided a vehicle for debating modern developments and introducing modern or advanced ideas into the educational curriculum and the larger culture. The disparate paths of science and the classics also illustrate the manner in which the social organization of intellectual life influenced the dispersion of particular ideas.

I have divided the essays somewhat arbitrarily into three sections illustrating separate though not wholly unrelated themes. In Part I, I examine some of the categories through which scholars have explored Victorian intellectual life and the manner in which categories employed by the Victorians themselves to interpret their world changed in their own hands. Part II examines aspects of Victorian scientific naturalism and the manner in which Victorian advocates of science challenged both clerical and liberal democratic culture. In Part III, I provide four studies of the uses to which the Victorians put the ancient world and the manner in which those discussions permitted debate over modern or contemporary topics several of which relate to issues in Part I and II. Another theme that unites several of these essays is the manner often unrecognized by historians in which idealism and religious categories persevered throughout much of the century.

Five of the essays in this volume are new though two of those draw extensively on ideas and research that I have published previously in different contexts. The other seven essays have been previously published, but appear here in somewhat revised and updated versions. I have attempted to remove passages that would be repetitive to the reader who wishes to read the volume from start to finish rather than selecting individual essays. I have also consolidated and somewhat condensed the footnotes, removed many secondary references which are still available to scholars in the original formats of the essays, and attempted to provide references to more recent historical literature on the various issues examined.

During the two decades that witnessed the writing of these essays I have accumulated a number of scholarly debts. All of my work is rooted in the teaching and intellectual friendship that I received from Franklin Le Van Baumer. No graduate student ever encountered a better teacher and no young scholar, a better friend. During a time when most of my energies were devoted to academic administration, my wife Professor Nancy Rash encouraged me to pursue the publication of this volume so I might not forget the larger scholarly purposes that lie behind administering a university. As a help in preparing my previously published essays for revision and publication, Professor Bernard Lightman generously reread and criticized them. He was also responsible for organizing conference sessions in which several essays originated as papers. His own scholarship has been important in reshaping my understanding of Victorian agnosticism and other forms of unbelief. At various times Professor Jeffrey Von Arx provided important conversations as did Dr David Spadafora. Over the years colleagues Donald Kagan, Steven Ozment, Jaroslav Pelikan, Joseph Hamburger, Gordon Williams, John Herrington, Sidney Eisen, Peter Gay, Linda Peterson, Bernard Semmel, Arnold Thackray, Ramsay MacMullen, Hugh Lloyd-Jones, Harry Stout, Lee Wandel, Martha Garland, James Livingston, Lori Ann Farrell, and Cyrus Vakil offered advice on one or more of these essays. The editors of the journals in which several of these essays originally appeared as well as their anonymous readers improved the early drafts.

I am indebted to conferences or lecture invitations at the Yale Center for British Art, the University of Leicester, the National University of Australia, Drew University, Boston University, the City University of New York, the University of Toronto, the University of Wisconsin, and Tulane University for the opportunity to work through ideas that later appeared in these chapters. Sessions at the American Historical Association, the Conference on British Studies, the Virgilian Society of North America, and the Northeast Victorian Studies Association provided other venues for the presentation of papers.

Research for these essays was made possible by the generous leave policy of Yale University, grants from the Griswold Fund of Yale University, and fellowships from the National Endowment for the Humanities and the Guggenheim Foundation.

I would also like to thank Josie Broude and Donna Del Buco for help in the preparation of the manuscript and for good humour and warm friendship along the way.

F.M.T.

I

Shifting boundaries

CHAPTER I

The religious and the secular in Victorian Britain

During the 1880s R. W. Dale, the leading British Congregationalist clergyman of his day, published an essay entitled, 'Every-day business a divine calling'. Portraying the world as the creation of God in which the divine will was to be realized through all vocations, Dale observed, 'It is convenient, no doubt, to distinguish what is commonly described as "secular" from what is commonly described as "religious". We all know what the distinction means. But the distinction must not be understood to imply that in religious work we are doing God's will, and that in secular work we are not doing it.'[1] Dale thus rejected boundaries in the conceptualization of social life that might have permitted his contemporaries to shy away from particular moral duties. As a Christian minister, Dale was unwilling to allow the members of his prosperous middle-class Birmingham congregation or his readers to divide their lives into conveniently distinct religious and secular arenas in which the values of the former did not inform the activities of the latter. Religious convictions were to result in civic action as well as in personal morality and piety.

For much of this century historians of Victorian intellectual and social life have had difficulty accommodating themselves to figures such as Dale and have resisted such rejection of boundaries between religious and secular activity. There long existed a general agreement among historians and literary scholars of Victorian Britain that secularization or the movement from a culture in which theological thinking, religious activity, and clergy were important or dominant to one in which they were much less important explained many of the most significant religious and intellectual developments of the era. This interpretation left little room for the likes of R. W. Dale or

[1] R. W. Dale, *Laws of Christ for common life*, 7th edn (London: Hodder and Stroughton, 1903), pp. 3–4.

his assertion that the religious and the secular might blend into and overlap each other.[2] Nor could that secular interpretation easily accommodate itself to the Victorian Nonconformist and Roman Catholic revivals, the political and spiritual resurgence of the Church of England, the liveliness of religion in both Ireland and Scotland, the strong religious alignments in nineteenth-century British politics, or the ongoing religious forces of the first decade of the twentieth century which manifested themselves in the struggle over the Education Act of 1902, the Welsh tax strikes, and Welsh disestablishment. Furthermore, that interpretation could not account for the enormous drive toward churchbuilding throughout the nineteenth century and the erection of the Roman Catholic Cathedral in Westminster or the Anglican Cathedral in Truro.

Yet despite these explanatory shortcomings, the chief interpretive framework for both Victorian and general modern European intellectual history has remained the emergence of a secular world view replacing a religious world view. As Rodney Stark and William Sims Bainbridge have asserted, 'At least since the Enlightenment, most Western intellectuals have anticipated the death of religion as eagerly as ancient Israel awaited the messiah.'[3] Following this general interpretation, intellectual and cultural historians of Victorian Britain for most of this century have portrayed religious thought and activity in a critically negative light while favourably presenting secular intellectual activity as progressive and desirable. The demise of religion according to numerous intellectual historians and other commentators opened the way for a better, truer life of the mind embodied in the work of secular intellectuals and quite often university-based scholars.[4] For most historians the undermining of the influence of both the Church of England and the Nonconformist denominations as well as the erosion of religious faith and conviction among the educated classes by modern intellectual forces seemed

---

[2] Only Asa Briggs in *Victorian cities* (London: Oldhams Press, 1963) seriously attempted to draw the Nonconformist clergy deeply into Victorian social history.

[3] Rodney Stark and William Sims Bainbridge, *The future of religion: secularization, revival and cult formation* (Berkeley: University of California Press, 1985), p. 1. See also, Franklin L. Baumer, *Religion and the rise of scepticism* (New York: Harcourt, Brace and World, Inc., 1960); Owen Chadwick, *The secularization of the European mind in the nineteenth century* (Cambridge: Cambridge University Press, 1975), pp. 1–18.

[4] See A. J. Engel, *From clergyman to don: the rise of the academic profession in nineteenth-century Oxford* (Oxford: Clarendon Press, 1983), for a treatment of the subject that despite its title employs less than the usual self-congratulation.

almost inevitable and unproblematic. Those developments were certainly rarely if ever the occasion for regret or criticism.

This complacently approving attitude toward the demise of religious influences stood in sharp contrast to the outlooks exhibited by social and economic historians toward other nineteenth-century developments that contributed to the emergence of modern British society. Many of the latter historians directed critically and even harshly probing questions toward the contemporaneous emergence of British industrial society. Indeed, providing a critique of industrial society became as much a part of the vocation of mid-twentieth-century scholars as did the championing of the emergence of secular intellectual life.

This situation reflected a general division of labour that emerged during the middle of this century between British and American scholars of Victorian Britain. The former tended to be concerned with economic and social developments whereas the latter addressed themselves to questions of intellectual and cultural history.[5] This division of labour in turn reflected the political and cultural situations of the two scholarly communities after the end of World War II. Many British historians living through the first Labour government, the return of the Conservatives, and the various strains of the mid-century associated with the retreat from empire continued the over half-century-old tradition of associating a socialist or radical political agenda with a critique of the nineteenth-century industrial experience as well as of liberal politics. American historians and literary scholars, for their part, similarly pursued an earlier tradition of working out their own cultural vocation through reference to British intellectuals. The discrepancy in the two national research agendas occurred without planning and provoked little or no significant notice or comment.

The secular interpretation of Victorian and general nineteenth-century intellectual life very much reflected the concerns of mid-twentieth-century American university intellectuals. In the United States the study of intellectual history by historians, philosophers,

---

[5] There are notable exceptions to this generalization as witnessed by the work of Noel Annan, Basil Willey, Raymond Williams, and John Burrow. On the general absence of a role for intellectual history or the history of ideas in Great Britain, see Noel Annan, *Our age: English intellectuals between the world wars, a group portrait* (New York: Random House, 1990), pp. 247–79.

and literary scholars constituted in part an attempt at a self-definition of American intellectual life, vocation, and values. Intellectual history devoted in large measure to the study of the development of liberalism, secularism, rational science, psychoanalysis, socialism, and other progressive, non-religious outlooks, as well as to the emergence of critical and liberal theology, provided secular university scholars with a history of their own past and of the values that they and their institutions were to epitomize. Intellectual history set forth a spectrum of opinions within which scholarly, cultural and political debate might properly or wisely take place. Alternatively, certain intellectual outlooks received relatively little attention or friendly analysis. These included romantic and early Victorian science that did not fit the positivistic mould, popular pseudo-sciences, radical politics, Communism (as opposed to versions of Marxist humanism), European conservative politics, post-tridentine Roman Catholicism, and Judaism, each of which received only modest scholarly attention during the middle years of this century. Through these omissions intellectual history became in no small measure an approving account of the emergence of Protestantism, the subsequent secularization of the Protestant vision, and the social and intellectual displacement of Protestant clergy by lay academics in universities or by lay intellectuals in the society at large.

During most of the third quarter of this century accepting some version of the secular interpretation of modern life became almost a rite of passage, though often an unconscious one, for historians entering the academic profession. From the 1930s through the 1970s many American university scholars genuinely believed (the wish perhaps being father to the thought) that institutional religion would no longer constitute a major factor in modern society. Many students entering graduate school knew from their own childhoods that religion was an important and significant human activity and that it was alive and well in various parts of the world or at least in the worlds where they had come of age. Those were the worlds of small, largely Protestant towns or of urban Roman Catholic and Jewish communities where religion provided a significant part of the basis for the social structure and for social cohesion. Students generally entered graduate school just as they were finally separating from those communities to which they may have retained significant ties during the undergraduate years. Universities, especially those with the leading graduate schools, had and have little or no place for religion. Such was also true of the academic profession as it had established itself by the 1960s. To enter the academic profession was to take one's place alongside the secular clerisy who upheld what were regarded as the best values of the liberal democratic tradition and who attempted to draw those values from literature and philosophy. Such professional scholars generally embraced cultural relativism and a somewhat unarticulated new orthodox belief that in the future there must be no orthodoxies.[6] Consequently, it seemed a natural course of personal maturation and professional development for young scholars to look to non-religious values, ideals, and institutions to shape their own era and scholarship and to interpret past ages.

It is worth noting that this secular outlook toward contemporary culture and historical change persisted among academic historians and other university scholars at the very time when the Roman Catholic Church experienced a major expansion in the non-Western world, Judaism displayed new vitality throughout the Western world, American evangelicalism grew in political and social influence unrivalled since the 1920s, the Black Church provided the leadership to the American civil rights movement, and the Islamic revival transformed the political and social face of Asia and Africa.[7] These various developments have by the last two decades of this century directly, if perhaps imperceptibly, begun to change the attitude of historians to religion in the past as well as in the present. What sustained university academics in their adherence to a belief in the inevitable movement of secular forces was the actual decline of the major mainline liberal Protestant denominations in the United States which in the parochialism of their own religious experience many academics (still overwhelmingly Protestant at mid-century) equated with the totality of religious life.

All of these contemporary mid-twentieth-century scholarly outlooks came to influence the treatment of the religious and the secular in Victorian Britain. During the third quarter of this century young professional scholars and teachers of Victorian Britain generally

---

[6] I am indebted to Professor Martha Garland for the insight of the general rejection of orthodoxy as such.

[7] One of the notable exceptions to this generalization was Sidney Ahlstrom in *A religious history of the American people* (New Haven: Yale University Press, 1972), pp. 1079–96.

accepted several more or less given truths about nineteenth-century British intellectual history. There had been a sharp, necessary conflict between science and religion. The logic of scientific, rationalistic, and critical historical thought had driven men and women from their traditional Christian faith and from adherence to the authority of scripture. Darwinian natural selection and a thoroughly naturalistic science had displaced virtually all science that retained supernatural, animistic, or idealist elements. Darwin's burial in Westminster Abbey symbolized the acceptance of his theory. John Stuart Mill despite his posthumous essays on nature and religion had been a rationalist and secular thinker. Those same scholars learned and taught a good deal about substitute secular religions of the nineteenth century such as St Simonianism, positivism, the religion of humanity, nationalism, socialism and the like. They tended to concentrate on the emergence of philosophical theology and paid relatively little attention to advances in biblical study except to the extent that those changes were destructive to earlier interpretations of scripture. Versions of post-Kantian idealism, perhaps the most pervasive outlook of the century, stood virtually ignored except as certain strains related to the emergence of Marxism.

This reading of nineteenth-century intellectual life, which illustrated what W. L. Burn in another context termed 'selective Victorianism', served to support many of the vocational ideals of the mid-century academic community of the United States.[8] American scholars simply accepted often at face value the reading and self-explanation of a relatively limited number of Victorian authors and then tended to use them as guides to their own cultural situation. This practice in large measure replicated the nineteenth-century situation when many educated Americans had looked to Britain for cultural guidance and had in turn provided a major publishing market for many of the Victorian sages, commencing with Thomas Carlyle. The major Victorian writers, who generally had seen themselves as separating from contemporary religious life, provided a pattern for mid-twentieth-century American academics who were seeking to forge a place for themselves in a liberal democratic society where previously many intellectuals including those in the academy had been clerics or laymen with strong religious values. As applied to the twentieth century, the nineteenth-century secular hypothesis

[8] W. L. Burn, *The age of equipoise: a study of the mid-Victorian generation* (London: G. Allen and Unwin, 1964), p.36.

served to confirm the vocation of mid-twentieth-century American academicians based on the various nineteenth-century concepts of intellectual elites.[9]

By taking upon themselves the role of a Coleridgean clerisy and an Arnoldian cultural elite, American academics at mid-century could also tackle two other immediately pressing threats in their culture. First, they could present a set of non-Christian humanistic moral values drawn from the Western tradition that were opposed to the secular values of mid-twentieth-century Communism. Second, by championing Darwin and the advanced groups in the Victorian scientific community, they could continue to fight a rearguard action against religious fundamentalism and other modes of anti-intellectualism in American life – the demise of which was more a wish than a reality in the America of the fifties and sixties.[10]

The division of nineteenth-century intellectual and social activity into generally distinct religious and secular spheres that mid-twentieth-century scholars imposed upon British, European, and American Victorians was not a wholly false view; and it was certainly not implausible. But to revert to an Arnoldian term, it was not really adequate to an historical understanding of the Victorian age. The most significant issues that mid-twentieth-century scholars did not really probe deeply were the actual, specific, concrete character of nineteenth-century religion and nineteenth-century secular developments. Rather they allowed a positivist concept of science derived from Comte and Mill to provide the undergirding for their definition of the secular. Similarly they adopted a generally romantic concept of religion, which meshed well with the mid-century desire of American intellectuals to withdraw from institutional and denominational religion, to evaluate nineteenth-century religious developments. Both conceptual approaches, rooted in a single tradition of Victorian scientific philosophy on the one hand and a single tradition of religious thought on the other, prevented scholars from confronting in a direct manner the full spectrum of the secular and the religious as the latter concretely manifested them-

---

[9] It was probably no accident that Lionel Trilling's first book was *Matthew Arnold* (New York: W. W. Norton, 1939). See also, Ben Knights, *The idea of the clerisy in the nineteenth century* (Cambridge: Cambridge University Press, 1978)

[10] Richard Hofstadter's *Social Darwinism in American thought* (Philadelphia: University of Pennsylvania Press, 1944) and *Anti-intellectualism in American life* (New York: Knopf, 1963) symbolized these attitudes. Many scholars of Victorian Britain drew their interpretive categories from such treatments of American intellectual history.

selves in nineteenth-century life and crossed over the twentieth-century conceptual boundaries.

My own doubts about the adequacy of the bipolar interpretation of Victorian intellectual life emerged rather slowly. My first book, written during the late sixties and early seventies as my doctoral dissertation, explored the lives and thought of six late nineteenth-century thinkers who had undergone a double loss of faith.[11] Each had first abandoned Christianity and embraced science with considerable confidence and then in turn abandoned that latter faith. In rejecting scientific naturalism, each had sought some kind of religious dimension in life through pursuit of spiritualism, psychical research, metaphysical speculation, or idealism. By their adulthood they could be regarded neither as traditional religious thinkers nor as fully secular writers. While preparing that volume, I had assumed my protagonists were personally rather confused and even atypical. I later came to recognize, as did numerous other scholars working in other areas of Victorian life, that the situation of my protagonists was not untypical of many British, European, and American intellectuals during the last forty years of the century.[12] The book, I believe, proved useful to later scholars because it had opened the door, however hesitantly, to consideration of figures who did not fit neatly into what had previously seemed to be regarded as exclusively scientific or religious outlooks. Without fully understanding at the time, I had begun to reject the conceptual categories then widely accepted in the historical literature because those categories simply could not encompass nineteenth-century intellectual life as I found it.

More serious doubts emerged in my thinking as I began to teach and undertake further research. I soon reached the conviction that intellectual historians had for many years approached the field with far too much emphasis on the *intellectual* and with an inadequate appreciation for the *historical*. Intellectual historians had too often regarded their vocation as a subset of philosophy or of the history of

---

[11] Frank Miller Turner, *Between science and religion: the reaction to scientific naturalism in late Victorian England* (New Haven: Yale University Press, 1974).

[12] See particularly Janet Oppenheim, *The other world: spiritualism and psychical research in England, 1850–1914* (Cambridge: Cambridge University Press, 1985); James T. Kloppenberg, *Uncertain victory: social democracy and progressivism in European and American thought, 1870–1920* (New York: Oxford University Press, 1986); Charles D. Cashdollar, *The transformation of theology, 1830–1890: Positivism and Protestant thought in Britain and America* (Princeton: Princeton University Press, 1989), as well as the more recent works on Darwin and evolution in n. 26 below.

philosophy. Ideas were assumed to have a life of their own (which in a very real sense they do) and their fate to be largely oblivious to the world about them.[13] Important documents of intellectual history were treated not only outside any social or political context but also outside the immediate intellectual context. Not only secondary thinkers had been ignored but also important figures and schools of thought whose fame or influence had declined. Foremost among such ignored intellectuals were those whose ideas had opposed or been unrelated to the emergence of a progressive, secular, critical, scientific, naturalistic, or rational world view.[14] The most significant subgroup among these were Roman Catholic intellectuals and theologians. There was also little or no appreciation for the manner in which popular interest in magic, superstition, religious ritual, mesmerism, and spiritualism could shade into science or respectable religion.[15]

The roots of this largely Whiggish approach to the historical account of intellectual activity lay in the origins of intellectual history. Many intellectual historians in the past consciously or unconsciously took as their model histories of religious doctrine or sectarian religious struggle. Almost invariably those works had cast their narratives into struggles between truth and error or orthodox and unorthodox doctrines. The history of doctrine and sectarian conflict tended to be seen as the triumph of truth through combat with error. The later secular historical philosophies embodied in the works of the Enlightenment, Hegelian philosophy, Comtean

[13] Quentin Skinner during the 1970s was constructing a widely discussed theoretical approach to this problem which, I must confess, never seemed particularly useful to my own concerns. The most important of his statements was Quentin Skinner, 'Meaning and understanding in the history of ideas', *History and Theory*, 8 (1969), 3–53. For a recent criticism of Skinner's views which includes references to the general dispute, see David Spadafora, *The idea of progress in eighteenth-century Britain* (New Haven: Yale University Press, 1990), pp. 417–24.

[14] Both the political and scientific philosophy of Karl Popper were instrumental in leading to these views. *The open society and its enemies* (London: G. Routledge and Sons, Ltd, 1943) associated totalitarian thought with modes of idealist political philosophy. In turn this analysis meshed with that of nineteenth-century philosophers of science, such as John Stuart Mill, who had attacked philosophic idealism in the latter parts of his autobiography. The major exception to this ignoring of non-rational thought was Isaiah Berlin's various essays; see in particular Isaiah Berlin, *Against the current: essays in the history of ideas* (New York: Viking Press, 1980), and *The crooked timber of humanity: chapters in the history of ideas* (New York: Alfred A. Knopf, 1990).

[15] Some of the earliest works to remedy this omission were Robert Young, *Mind, brain, and adaptation in the nineteenth century: cerebral localization and its biological context from Gall to Ferrier* (Oxford: Clarendon Press, 1970); James Obelkevich, *Religion and rural society: South Lindsey, 1825–1875* (Oxford: Oxford University Press, 1976); and Robert Darnton, *Mesmerism and the end of the Enlightenment in France* (Cambridge, Mass.: Harvard University Press, 1968).

positivism, and Marxism partook in differing ways of these originally religious paradigms of intellectual development and in turn deeply informed later intellectual history. The various divisive schisms in turn arising from those modern ideologies served to undergird the truth-vanquishing-error model of intellectual history. Many of the earliest classics of intellectual history quite consciously adopted the stance of truth supplanting falsehood whether they were histories of science, theology, or socialism. Paradoxically, the errors generally receiving correction were the reigning orthodoxies of a previous era. During the middle of this century both the conflict surrounding the Cold War and the tensions in American culture between liberal progressive thought and various modes of conservative thought further encouraged this bipolar approach to intellectual activity to continue.

This bipolar analysis resulted in significant gaps of historical understanding. In particular there existed virtually no account of the difficulties experienced by Enlightenment ideas during the late eighteenth and early nineteenth centuries. Romanticism and especially romantic epistemology embodied in romantic literary criticism received considerable attention as a reaction against Enlightenment thought, but little research confronted the difficulties encountered by the Enlightenment in its own day or during the century thereafter.[16] This problem presented itself to me specifically when I discovered that over a century after David Hume had ridiculed the miraculous in his destructive chapter 'Of miracles' (1748), scientific writers throughout Europe found themselves required to refute arguments defending supernatural occurrences, such as claims for healing through prayer in Great Britain and the cult of Lourdes in France.[17]

---

[16] M. C. Abrams, *The mirror and the lamp: romantic theory and the critical tradition* (New York: Oxford University Press, 1953), represented a brilliant analysis of romantic aesthetics and its criticism of Enlightenment epistemology. But Abrams was not concerned about the larger intellectual and historical context. As a literary critic, that may or may not have been his task. However, intellectual historians used his important volume and generally did not attempt to supply the missing analysis. Jerome McGann has recently sharply attacked this approach to romanticism and demonstrated the manner in which it reflects a selective reading of romantic writers themselves in *The romantic ideology: a critical investigation* (Chicago: University of Chicago Press, 1983).

[17] See chapter 6 in this volume and Harry Paul, *The edge of contingency: French Catholic reaction to scientific change from Darwin to Duhem* (Gainesville, Fla.: University of Florida Press, 1979); T. A. Kselman, *Miracles and prophesies in nineteenth-century France* (New Brunswick, N.J.: Rutgers University Press, 1983); Margaret Lavinia Anderson, 'Piety and politics: recent work on German Catholicism', *Journal of Modern History*, 63 (1991), 681–716.

The widespread view of the historically unproblematic secularization of thought in the nineteenth century provided no explanation
for the outburst of the miraculous in the midst of the unprecedented nineteenth-century advance in scientific knowledge and
technology.

Like thousands of other American students in the 1950s and
1960s, I had encountered Hume's discussion of miracles in a
philosophy course. There Hume appeared as a forerunner of modern
analytic philosophy. To the extent that contemporary objections to
his thought were examined, they involved consideration of Kant's
response. Intellectual historians had not gone much further than had
the ahistorical philosophers of the mid-century to explain the reasons
why the influence of Hume's thought underwent a demise in the late
eighteenth and early nineteenth centuries. Neither intellectual historians nor philosophers pointed to the Scottish School of Common
Sense philosophy and the determination of its proponents to refute
Hume's epistemology and scepticism. This neglect arose from the
general demise of Common Sense philosophy in American and
British universities and more important from a reluctance on the
part of mid-twentieth-century intellectual historians to investigate
philosophers, such as Thomas Reid and William Whewell, who were
regarded as mistaken opponents of early modes of analytic philosophy. Intellectual historians during the third quarter of the century
were equally unsympathetic to idealist philosophical thought. What
was disliked or held in intellectual disdain at mid-century quite often
received little or no research and analysis lest guilt by association be
the result.

There existed very considerable reluctance on the part of mid-
twentieth-century scholars to admit that conservative religious
ideas and institutions could under certain circumstances do effective battle with the forces of progressive, secular thought. This
attitude meant that intellectual historians neglected late eight-
eenth- and early nineteenth-century religious issues and thereby
ignored the problematic character of the emergence and assimilation of secular Enlightenment ideas in the public forum over
time and especially in competition with religious ideas or conservative political ideology. In regard to Hume's influence and
that of the Enlightenment generally there existed no systematic
historical account, such as Richard Sher would later provide, of the
changes that occurred in the religious climate and structures of

Scotland.[18] Nor did intellectual historians address themselves to the Roman Catholic religious revival throughout Europe predating and then encouraged by the reaction to the French Revolution.[19] Nor was the extremely religious and conservative character of romanticism broadly explored except for reference to Friedrich Schleiermacher who stood at the fountainhead of liberal Protestant theology.[20]

My initial teaching experience led me to a second difficulty with the secular thesis. My graduate study had been in Victorian intellectual history, but my first full-time teaching assignment required a lecture course on Victorian political and social history. Few of the books I read or historical issues I encountered during my lecture preparations meshed with the general view among intellectual and literary historians that religion had undergone decline in the nineteenth century and that secular forces were the most important factors of the day. By contrast, George Kitson Clark in *The making of Victorian England* (1962) presented considerable evidence to support a view of the century as a time of immense religious activity. The same image of Victorian society emerged in Peter Marsh's *The Victorian Church in decline* (1969) and Kenneth Inglis's *The churches and the working class* (1963). Even E. P. Thompson's *The*

---

[18] Richard Sher, *Church and university in the Scottish Enlightenment: the moderate literati of Edinburgh* (Princeton: Princeton University Press, 1985). See also John Gascoigne, *Cambridge in the age of the Enlightenment: science, religion and politics from the Restoration to the French Revolution* (Cambridge: Cambridge University Press, 1989), pp. 237–69; Peter Harrison, '*Religion*' and the religions in the English Enlightenment (Cambridge: Cambridge University Press, 1990); A. M. C. Waterman, *Revolution, economics and religion: Christian political economy, 1798–1833* (Cambridge: Cambridge University Press, 1991).

[19] An important exception to this generalization was Klaus Epstein's *The genesis of German conservatism* (Princeton: Princeton University Press, 1966). For a more recent treatment, see Robert M. Berdahl, *The politics of the Prussian nobility: the development of a conservative ideology, 1770–1848* (Princeton: Princeton University Press, 1988).

[20] During the third quarter of the century there was a general tendency to concentrate on the more radical romantic writers or to portray romantic politics as a rejection of the new industrial order. Romantic writers also tended to be portrayed as rejecting the alleged shallowness or reductionism of the Enlightenment, rather than as leading a full frontal assault on many enlightened writers. Even conservative figures who did receive attention, such as Samuel Taylor Coleridge, often had their thought cast into a progressive mould. In this regard, Coleridge was seen as an innovative critic of literature and as a theologically liberal reader of scripture. See I. A. Richards, *Coleridge on the imagination*, 2nd edn (New York: W. W. Norton, 1950); Thomas McFarland, *Coleridge and the pantheist tradition* (Oxford: Clarendon Press, 1969); Basil Willey, *Samuel Taylor Coleridge* (London: Chatto and Windus, 1972); E. S. Shaffer, '*Kubla Khan*' and the fall of Jerusalem: the mythological school in biblical criticism and secular literature, 1770–1880 (Cambridge: Cambridge University Press, 1975). For a correction of this view see Marilyn Butler, *Romantics, rebels, and reactionaries: English literature and its background, 1760–1830* (Oxford: Oxford University Press, 1981).

making of the English working class (1963) for all of its animus toward Methodism made a powerful case for the ongoing influence of religion among the working classes of the nineteenth century.[21] G. I. T. Machin's *The Catholic question in English politics, 1820 to 1830* (1964) put religious concerns directly into the realm of high politics and the political events leading to the First Reform Bill. It was also clear that Roman Catholicism had played an enormous role in the various later Irish political crises. Even a modest knowledge of Gladstone's political career required recognition of the intensity of his religiosity and its impact on his politics. The Nonconformist denominations seemed ubiquitous in their activity. It was in the course of this lecture preparation that I first encountered in Asa Briggs's *Victorian cities* (1963) the redoubtable R. W. Dale and his determination not to surrender the world of daily life and business to secular values.

My puzzlement arising from research in one field of Victorian studies and teaching in another reflected a structural division among Victorian scholars that was in turn indicative of similar divisions within the entire historical profession. During the late 1960s and most of the 1970s there existed a compartmentalization of social and intellectual history from each other and a similar compartmentalization of popular and elite cultures. An historian could study elite or popular culture, but the two cultures and the historians of each rarely intermixed.

Indeed for about two decades there existed a mutual disregard and perhaps even distrust between the two groups of historians. Many intellectual historians quite frankly did not want to explore the emerging social history even when it addressed issues of religion. Many historians of the working class or popular culture especially

---

[21] E. P. Thompson's *The making of the English working class* (London: Victor Gollancz, 1963) played a paradoxical role. Thompson argued that Methodism had served to repress revolutionary tendencies among the working class. But he and his followers so clearly disliked Methodism and religion generally that they did not explore the manner in which it had or had not continued to play a role in later nineteenth-century working-class developments. The logical conclusion of Thompson's analysis was that labour historians should pay very considerable attention to religion, but almost none of them did so. Bernard Semmel presented a refutation of Thompson in *The Methodist revolution* (New York: Basic Books, 1973). Not, however, until the late 1970s and after with J. F. C. Harrison, *The second coming: popular millenarianism, 1780–1850* (New Brunswick, N.J.: Rutgers University Press, 1979); Julia Stewart Werner, *The primitive Methodist connexion: its background and early history* (Madison: University of Wisconsin Press, 1984); and Deborah Valenze, *Prophetic sons and daughters: female preaching and popular religion in industrial England* (Cambridge, Mass.: Harvard University Press, 1985) did careful studies of early nineteenth-century working-class religion appear.

during the 1970s emphasized their disdain for elite culture. Further-more, many of the first generation of post-war social historians held publicly articulated left-wing political opinions which included a general disliking for religion in both the past and the present. The teaching assignments of social and intellectual historians rarely required them to integrate the two fields or even to read widely outside their own particular areas of research. Had my own early teaching assignments been different, so also no doubt would have been my thinking about the Victorians and about the realms of the religious and the secular.

During the last decade or so the situation has changed markedly in the writing of intellectual history. The new sensibilities arising from social history have led to a serious questioning of the secular thesis. No intellectual historian trained during the past ten or perhaps fifteen years has been able to escape the influence of the various modes of social history. Historians daily cross the boundaries between elite and popular culture. Intellectual historians no longer believe they can discuss their concerns in terms of clashing epistemologies without reference to the intricacies of gender relationships, family concerns, social structure, and political milieu. There has also arisen, from sources that are less clear but perhaps a reflection of the changing political and cultural climate in both the United States and other areas of the world, a new appreciation for the influence of religion in history and for the role of ideas that are not wholly of the critical, rationalist, scientific, progressive mode.

As a result of these new sensibilities, Victorian intellectual histor-ians have rather quietly and quite unconsciously embraced an outlook about the connection of religious ideas and society that John Henry Newman enunciated almost a century and a half ago. In his *Essay on the development of Christian doctrine* (1845), Newman con-tended,

When an idea, whether real or not, is of a nature to interest and possess the mind, it is said to have life, that is, to live in the mind which is the recipient of it ... [W]hen some great enunciation, whether true or false, about human nature, or present good, or government, or duty, or religion, is carried forward into the public throng and draws attention, then it is not only passively admitted in this or that form into the minds of men, but it becomes a living principle within them, leading them to an ever-new contemplation of itself, an acting upon it and a propagation of it... It will, in proportion to its native vigour and subtlety, introduce itself into the framework and details of social life, changing public opinion and supporting or undermining the foundations of established order . . . This process is called the development of an idea . . . And it has this necessary characteristic, – that, since its province is the busy scene of human life, it cannot develop at all, except either by destroying, or modifying and incorporating with itself, existing modes of thinking and acting. Its development then is not like a mathematical theorem worked out on paper, in which each successive advance is a pure evolution from a foregoing, but it is carried on through individuals and bodies of men; it employs their minds as instruments, and depends upon them while it uses them.[22]

It is particularly significant that Newman thought the power of an idea lay not in its correctness or truth content, but rather in its power to assimilate itself within institutions of human society or 'the busy scene of human life'. It is such bracketing of the issue of the truth content of ideas and ideological movements that has led to new departures for intellectual history. Historians remain concerned about the truth or falsehood of ideas, but the truth or falsehood of a set of ideas espoused by an individual thinker or a group no longer constitutes the basis for determining whether the history of that intellectual activity is worthy of investigation and analysis. In particular, this new outlook has led to a rethinking of the character of the secular and the religious in the nineteenth century and of developments between and within both spheres.

In the history of Victorian science the new thinking about the secular and the religious has occurred through a quite self-conscious abandonment of the equating of scientific activity with the nineteenth-century positivistic definition of that activity associated with John Stuart Mill, Auguste Comte, Claude Bernard, and the advocates of scientific naturalism.[23] Historians had once generally regarded science that followed this positivistic model as good and correct whereas they neglected or condemned as non-progressive scientific activity related to popular culture, natural theology, or

---

[22] John Henry Newman, *An essay on the development of Christian doctrine* (London: Penguin Books, 1974), pp. 97–9.

[23] See Peter Allan Dale, *In pursuit of a scientific culture: science, art, and society in the Victorian age* (Madison: University of Wisconsin Press, 1989), pp. 3–85, 102–28; and Sally Shuttleworth, *George Eliot and nineteenth-century science: the make-believe of a beginning* (Cambridge: Cambridge University Press, 1984). D. G. Charleton had outlined many of the difficulties of adhering to a positivist version of science in *Positivist thought in France during the second empire, 1852–1870* (Oxford: Clarendon Press, 1959). The initial impulse to this new approach to the history of science, of course, originated in the work of Thomas S. Kuhn and most importantly in *The structure of scientific revolutions* (Chicago: University of Chicago Press, 1962).

idealistic philosophies of science. Historians of science have come to doubt that the history of scientific activity broadly conceived primarily constitutes the record of the emergence of the cutting 'Edge of Objectivity' or the record of truth, especially scientific truth, displacing error, especially religious error. This is not to say that historians do not believe in scientific truth and error, but they see the relationship in any given era being related to matters extending beyond narrow issues of epistemology. Increasingly historians of science have become concerned with the particular social setting of scientific activity and the manner in which that milieu has affected the ideology surrounding that activity. This changing attitude among historians of science and intellectual historians generally has produced remarkable reevaluations of the relationship of science and religion in Victorian thought.

In no other area of Victorian intellectual history has there occurred so extensive a revision in attitudes toward the relative importance of religious and non-religious strains of thinking as in Darwin studies. Certainly if one message tended to come through much of the work surrounding the centenary of *On the origin of species*, it was the generally positivistic character of Darwinian science.[24] Darwin was regarded as having sought to displace science imbued with natural theology and to replace it with a firmly positivist mode of analysis. With the exceptions of Louis Agassiz, Asa Gray, and St George Jackson Mivart, the scientists who criticized Darwin received little attention or intellectual respect. The presence of Lamarckianism in the post-Darwinian world received virtually no consideration.

During the decade of the 1980s a new generation of young scholars – almost the contemporary equivalent of the aggressive mid-Victorian scientists whom Leonard Huxley once dubbed 'the young guard of science'[25] – transformed the face of Darwin studies so that lively debate now centres on whether or not Darwin was the last of the great natural theologians. James Moore, Dov Ospovat, J. H. Brooke, Neal Gillespie, David Kohn, and others have implicitly asked how

---

[24] There were notable exceptions: Maurice Mandelbaum, 'Darwin's religious views', *Journal of the History of Ideas*, 19 (1958), 363–78; John C. Greene, 'Darwin and religion', *Proceedings of the American Philosophical Society*, 103 (1959), 716–25, and *Darwin and the modern world view* (Baton Rouge: Louisiana State University Press, 1961); and Walter (Susan F.) Cannon, 'The bases of Darwin's achievement: a revaluation', *Victorian Studies*, 5 (1961), 109–34.

[25] Leonard Huxley, *Life and letters of Sir Joseph Dalton Hooker* (London: John Murray, 1918), I, 541.

secular was Darwin's thought and they have answered that it was not nearly so secular or positivistic as historians had previously contended. That is to say, Darwin certainly did wish to displace the theological apparatus of natural theology and resisted the cultural pressures of ecclesiasticism. Yet many of his moral motives and many of his categories of thought as well as problems that he believed he must address and carry to satisfactory solutions through the concept of natural selection derived from natural theology.

This modified image of Darwin has led to the possibility of much more subtle interpretations of the reception of *On the origin of species* and of evolutionary thought in general as seen in the work of Adrian Desmond, James Moore, Jon Roberts, and Peter Bowler. Desmond has demonstrated the manner in which Darwin's thought associated him with radical circles in the London medical community. Roberts has shown that by no means all of the American religious reaction was hostile. The abandonment of the positivist approach to Darwin and natural selection has allowed historians such as Bowler with good conscience and better understanding to speak of the 'eclipse of Darwinism' without any fear that such an expression indicates sympathy for biblical literalism.[26] Having forced Darwin out of his role as the white knight of positivistic science triumphing over the dark knight of natural religion, historians can actually look at the general disarray of evolutionary biological thought at the turn of the century. In turn this process has allowed Ronald Numbers to raise important new questions about the character of the American fundamentalist and creationist challenge to evolutionary thought in the 1920s and then in our own day.[27]

[26] James R. Moore, *The post-Darwinian controversies: a study of the Protestant struggle to come to terms with Darwin in Great Britain and America, 1870–1900* (Cambridge: Cambridge University Press, 1979); Jon H. Roberts, *Darwinism and the divine in America: Protestant intellectuals and organic evolution, 1859–1900* (Madison: University of Wisconsin Press, 1988); Peter J. Bowler, *The eclipse of Darwinism: anti-Darwinian evolution theories in the decades around 1900* (Baltimore: Johns Hopkins University Press, 1983); Adrian Desmond, *The politics of evolution: morphology, medicine and reform in radical London* (Chicago: University of Chicago Press, 1989); and Adrian Desmond and James R. Moore, *Darwin* (New York: Warner Books, Inc., 1991). Alvar Ellegard, *Darwin and the general reader: the reception of Darwin's theory of evolution in the British periodical press, 1859–1872* (Chicago: University of Chicago Press, 1990; originally published 1958), pioneered all such studies. Although Ellegard made many of the mid-century assumptions about a necessary conflict between religion and science, his volume was among the most open-minded publications at the time of the centenary.

[27] Ronald L. Numbers, 'The creationists', in David C. Lindberg and Ronald L. Numbers, eds., *God and nature: historical essays on the encounter between Christianity and science* (Berkeley: University of California Press, 1986), pp. 391–423, and Ronald L. Numbers, *The creationists* (New York: Alfred A. Knopf, 1992).

In even the most familiar scenes of the clash between Darwinian truth and religious falsehood historical interpretation has shifted. T. H. Huxley, Darwin's most vociferous public defender, has become known to thousands of students as 'Darwin's Bulldog'. Yet Huxley himself did not accept natural selection as a fully adequate explanation of evolution. He wished to push for the acceptance of evolution and leave the battle over the adequacy of natural selection per se for separate consideration. Huxley's letters on this matter had long been public, but this side of his scientific personality received full attention only long after the Darwin centenary. Once Huxley's partial scepticism is admitted, then the question emerges as to what the battle over evolution was really about and why Huxley supported evolution in the first place and then hesitated fully embracing natural selection in the next. The answer has something to do with scientific knowledge and something to do with the place of science and scientists in Victorian society and intellectual life. The immediate social implications of the acceptance of evolution were more important to Huxley than agreement about the mechanism. Huxley acknowledged as much to Darwin.[28]

Bernard Lightman's studies of agnosticism provide a second example within the world of Victorian scientific naturalism of the new landscape that emerges when an historian actually reads the Victorians without forcing them into distinctly separate religious and secular roles.[29] Lightman has read the agnostics without scorn or fervour and has taken them at their word. His work makes a convincing case that far from spurning religion, many agnostics actually sought to set forth a serious new, non-clerical religious synthesis. Agnostics in Lightman's view obviously pursued genuine religious goals and not merely the substitution of something secular for something religious. No less important and ironic so far as the distinction between the religious and the secular is concerned, Lightman has located the origin of agnostic epistemology within the thought of the high churchman H. L. Mansel. In doing so, Lightman has begun to cast light on the large, neglected subject of why so

[28] Michael Bartholomew, 'Huxley's defence of Darwinism', *Annals of Science*, 32 (1975), 525–35; Peter J. Bowler, *Evolution: the history of an idea*, revised edn (Berkeley: University of California Press, 1989), pp. 194–6; Moore, *Post-Darwinian controversies*, pp. 176–7; Bowler, *The eclipse of Darwinism*, p. 187; Mario A. di Gregorio, *T. H. Huxley's place in natural science* (New Haven: Yale University Press, 1984), pp. 60–8.
[29] Bernard Lightman, *The origins of agnosticism: Victorian unbelief and the limits of knowledge* (Baltimore: Johns Hopkins University Press, 1987).

many nineteenth-century observers regarded the ideas emerging from the Oxford Movement as potentially sceptical.

Similarly Ruth Barton has presented a convincingly revisionist reading of physicist John Tyndall's Belfast Address. When delivered in 1874 to the British Association for the Advancement of Science, this address gave Tyndall a lifelong reputation as a thoroughgoing materialist and stirred an enormous Victorian controversy over the alleged materialism of science. Barton has very carefully examined Tyndall's concept of matter and discovered that Tyndall's matter was very much a metaphysical and almost mystical intellectual construct that held very real pantheistic and transcendental possibilities.[30] In that sense, Tyndall's matter resembled a kind of stream of spiritual possibilities that recalled the oversoul of Emerson and the natural supernaturalism of Carlyle, both of which writers he deeply admired.[31]

The rejection of the alleged sharp distinction between religion and secularism allowed Jack Morrell and Arnold Thackray in *Gentlemen of science* to explore the social and ideological dimension of the religious impulse that lay behind the appeal of early Victorian scientists to natural theology.[32] Their analysis of the early years of the British Association for the Advancement of Science demonstrated two important points. First, most of the early leaders of Victorian science did sincerely believe the various arguments associated with natural religion. Second, the public cloaking of the early Victorian scientific enterprise in the garments of natural religion served a very important secular ideological function. The appeal to natural theology allowed scientists and interested laymen of different religious outlooks and denominations to work together. No less important, the appeal to natural theology protected the scientists' endeavour from accusations of materialism, atheism, and the like which the political rhetoric stemming from the reaction to the French Revolution had associated with science.

Just as the use of a generally nineteenth-century positivistic concept of science confused mid-twentieth-century views of Victorian scientific activity, the simultaneous acceptance of the nineteenth-century romantic assertion of the spiritual inadequacy of Victorian

---

[30] Ruth Barton, 'John Tyndall, pantheist: a rereading of the Belfast address', *Osiris*, 2nd ser., 3 (1987), 111–34.
[31] See chapter 5 in this volume.
[32] Jack Morrell and Arnold Thackray, *Gentlemen of science: early years of the British Association for the Advancement of Science* (Oxford: Clarendon Press, 1981).

religion similarly confused Victorian religious history and our understanding of the secular and the religious in Victorian culture. This situation can be illustrated by examining a passage from Ralph Waldo Emerson's *English traits* (1856) in which he recounted his impressions of religion in England during the 1830s and 1840s. Drawing upon his visits to the country, Emerson commented,

The national temperament deeply enjoys the unbroken order and tradition of its church; the liturgy, ceremony, architecture; the sober grace, the good company, the connection with the throne and with history, which adorn it ... No church has had more learned, industrious or devoted men ... But the age of the Wicliffes, Cobhams, Arundels, Becketts; of the Latimers, Mores, Cranmers; of the Taylors, Leightons, Herberts; of the Sherlocks and Butlers, is gone. Silent revolutions in opinion have made it impossible that men like these should return, or find a place in their once sacred stalls. The spirit that dwelt in this church has glided away to animate other activities, and they who come to the old shrines find apes and players rustling the old garments. The religion of England is part of good-breeding ... Their religion is a quotation; their church is a doll; and any examination is interdicted with screams of terror.[33]

Emerson continued his indictment observing the inadequate pay of the poor clergy, the aristocratic social connections of the bishops, the lack of clerical learning in German theology, and the inability of the Anglican Church to include the Nonconformists about whom he also did not have a particularly high opinion. For Emerson, English religious institutions were not really religious or genuinely spiritual because they were wealthy, established, socially respectable, relatively powerful, and theologically complaisant. They allegedly embodied a religion devoid of subjective feeling and a theology devoid of criticism or science. They were insufficiently poor to meet the standard of true Christian piety.

Similar criticisms of the Anglican Church and the major Nonconformist denominations appeared in the pages of Thomas Carlyle, F. D. Maurice, Francis Newman, Mark Rutherford, and many of the other romantic, liberal critics of nineteenth-century Christianity.[34]

---

33 B. Atkinson, ed., *The selected writings of Ralph Waldo Emerson* (New York: The Modern Library, 1968), pp. 640-2.
34 Basil Willey in both *Nineteenth century studies, Coleridge to Matthew Arnold* (London: Chatto and Windus, 1949) and *More nineteenth century studies, a group of honest doubters* (London: Chatto and Windus, 1956) analysed numerous Victorian unbelievers and religious doubters in a manner that made their unbelief largely a matter of having questioned the sincerity of the Victorian Church of England. Virtually all of his subjects emerged from his analysis as profoundly religious if also profoundly unorthodox. In effect he judged all of his protagonists by the values of romantic religion and liberal theology.

The largely unquestioning acceptance of such contemporary critiques as descriptively correct led many intellectual historians until recently to ignore or to deprecate a vast amount of religious activity in the nineteenth century and even more perhaps in the eighteenth. Having decided at the instigation of romantic critics that real or truly spiritual religion is subjective, personal and philosophical rather than biblical, and largely non-institutional, historians and literary scholars decided that virtually all of the activity in what the Victorians called the 'religious world' was not really, truly, sincerely, or authentically religious. In effect scholars adopted a prophetic or antinomian stance toward organized religion. From this prophetic standpoint, scholars criticized the Victorian priests (both Anglican and Nonconformist) on the one hand for failing to embrace prophetic religion and on the other for letting priestly organized religion diminish. Historians tended to suggest that the decline and diminishment of that false or inadequate religious activity were the result of its moral and intellectual failures. Yet in point of fact its difficulties may be seen, as Jeffrey Cox has argued, as arising first from an organizational failure to sustain exceedingly high levels of recruitment and second from a well-intentioned but mistaken strategy of urging the state to assume social welfare functions once performed by religious groups.[35]

The idea that genuine religion is subjective, non-biblically oriented, based on feeling, and only moderately institutional made historians inevitably uncomfortable with the Victorian religious scene. The foremost characteristic of Victorian religion was its unabashed, unapologetic denominationalism exhibited in the conflict between the Church of England and the Nonconformists and in the struggle among the various versions of Anglicanism. Mid-twentieth-century scholars were themselves living in an unprecedented ecumenical period of Christian history and following the lead of Victorian writers who had abandoned denominational affiliations and embraced more philosophically oriented religion or simply abandoned religious observance. These scholars perhaps not surprisingly treated nineteenth-century denominational religion with its

[35] Jeffrey Cox, *The English churches in a secular society: Lambeth, 1870–1930* (Oxford: Oxford University Press, 1982). Gertrude Himmelfarb has also pointed to the enormous moral concern about poverty that arose in the late nineteenth century which provided a larger ethos for the substitution of social work and awareness for more traditional religious activity. See Gertrude Himmelfarb, *Poverty and compassion: the moral imagination of the late Victorians* (New York: Alfred A. Knopf, 1991).

disputes over biblical studies, liturgy, and ecclesiastical organization as something unclean or distasteful or not authentically religious.

Anyone who has read deeply in such denominational literature discovers that indeed it is often most unpleasant, but that unpleasantness does not mean it is any'less religious. No sixteenth-century historian would deny that the polemics of the Reformation and Counter-Reformation are religious, but historians of the Victorian era did so when confronted by the polemics of nineteenth-century denominationalism. Historians and literary scholars accepted the Arnoldian critique of the cultural vulgarity of Nonconformists and low Anglicans and dealt with those figures accordingly. Indeed, major scholars and university presses published anthologies of Victorian religious writings in which the denominationally polemical passages were simply excised.[36] This tactic constituted the parallel in religious history of reading or citing only the positivistic passages from Darwin and other Victorian scientists. Historical distortion was the result in both cases.

The kind of openness and sensitivity to the social dimension of intellectual life that has occurred in the recent writing of the history of Victorian science needs to be carried into the history of Victorian religion. It is necessary to reexamine Victorian religion by probing its relationship to the secular areas of Victorian society. Historians of Victorian intellectual life have long pursued the thought and activity of persons involved in secular religions, such as the religion of humanity. What has not been equally recognized or researched is the thought and action of persons involved in what might be regarded as *religiously secular activities*.

Until recently in discussions of the secular and the religious in the nineteenth century no single topic received so little attention or full recognition as the relationship between politics and religion. Political and social historians generally concentrated on issues of class, party formation, cabinet arrangements, electoral reform, working-class activity, urban issues, social justice, distribution of goods, and the emergence of an industrial society. To the extent that religion

---

[36] B. M. G. Reardon, ed., *Religious thought in the nineteenth century* (Cambridge: Cambridge University Press, 1966); Owen Chadwick, ed., *The mind of the Oxford movement* (Stanford, Calif.: Stanford University Press, 1960); Eugene R. Fairweather, ed., *The Oxford movement* (New York: Oxford University Press, 1964); John Henry Newman, *Essays and sketches*, ed. C. F. Harrold, new edn, 3 vols. (New York: Longmans, Green, 1948). Reardon pursued a similar non-denominational approach to religious thinking in *From Coleridge to Gore: a century of religious thought in Britain* (London: Longman, 1971).

entered their considerations, it was largely whether or not Methodism led to social and political acquiescence or how the Anglican Church responded to challenges directed against its various privileges or how Nonconformists penetrated the political arena. The polemical accusations of one group against another were often taken at face value. Consequently, the religious statements of political leaders were generally discounted as opportunistic or insincere or, as with Lord Shaftesbury and Gladstone, extreme and eccentric.

For their part religious and intellectual historians examined issues of ecclesiastical and doctrinal disputes, the loss of faith, anti-Catholicism, science, utilitarianism, economic thought, historical writing and political philosophy. They generally avoided the rough and tumble political and social worlds in which the ideas they studied were enunciated and championed – Newman's 'busy scene of human life'. There were a few notable exceptions, for example G. I. T. Machin's initial survey of early Victorian politics and religion and Richard Soloway's work on the social thought of Anglican bishops. But since these works crossed the religious–secular divide and quietly challenged existing historical assumptions, they did not exert widespread influence upon either political or intellectual history. Similarly Emmett Larkin's vast survey and important articles on the interaction of Roman Catholicism and politics in Ireland failed to be assimilated into the broader interpretations of British political and intellectual life.[37] As a consequence of this situation scholars of both political and intellectual history neglected the intense politicization of British religion and the increasing religiosity in British politics from the late 1820s onward when every Prime Minister from Wellington through Asquith, with the exceptions of Aberdeen, Derby, and Palmerston, had to confront major political crises at the centre of which lay religion.

In the last decade historians have begun to bring religious issues directly into the analysis of political matters and the reverse. Richard Brent has reinterpreted the religious concerns of the Whigs

[37] G. I. T. Machin, *Politics and the churches in Great Britain, 1832–1868* (Oxford: Clarendon Press, 1978), followed by *Politics and the churches in Great Britain, 1858–1921* (Oxford: Clarendon Press, 1987); Richard Allen Soloway, *Prelates and people: ecclesiastical social thought in England, 1783–1852* (London: Routledge and Kegan Paul, 1969); Emmett Larkin, *The historical dimensions of Irish Catholicism* (Washington, D.C.: Catholic University of America Press, 1984), reprints his most important individual essays, but see also *The making of the Roman Catholic Church in Ireland, 1850–1860* (Chapel Hill: University of North Carolina Press, 1980) and *The consolidation of the Roman Catholic Church in Ireland, 1860–1870* (Chapel Hill: University of North Carolina Press, 1987).

of the 1830s. Perry Butler has provided a serious interpretation of
Gladstone's early religious and political development. Walter Arnstein has demonstrated the centrality of anti-Catholicism in political
and social life. J. P. Parry has cogently argued for the disruptive
influence of religious issues and religious orientation in British
political life from the sixties through the eighties. Jeffrey Von Arx
has demonstrated how profound fears of a mass Irish democratic
politics led by Roman Catholic priests abroad and apprehensions
over a ritualist-dominated church education system at home spurred
the actions of numerous agnostic writers during the 1870s.[38] These
historians have been able to open these new paths because they were
willing to reject the division of Victorian political, social, and
intellectual life into secular and religious spheres. They have recognized that those spheres were overlapping in the lives of most
Victorians.

Two examples drawn from the extremes of the British religious
spectrum will further illustrate the inadequacy of previous analysis
of Victorian intellectual life and culture in categories of the secular
and the religious. They are the Oxford Movement and the Nonconformists. In the former case activity traditionally viewed as spiritual
may be seen to have been deeply political in nature; in the other,
political activity may be seen to have had genuinely religious roots.

Historians have long viewed the Oxford Movement as the most
important religious event in the century and as a reaction by a group
of high church clergy against the reform of the Church first by the
Whigs and later by the Tories following the First Reform Act.
Theologically the Oxford Movement has been seen as an attempt by
clergy to return the Church of England to the Catholic faith of the
fourth century. Its greatest leader John Henry Newman emerged as
a key spiritual figure for both modern Anglicanism and modern
Roman Catholicism and became identified with a general resistance
to political and theological liberalism. Also not unimportantly his
Apologia pro vita sua and *The idea of a university* became widely read at

---

[38] Richard Brent, *Liberal Anglican politics: Whiggery, religion, and reform, 1830–1841* (Oxford:
Clarendon Press, 1987); Perry Butler, *Gladstone: church, state, and tractarianism: a study of his
religious ideas and attitudes, 1809–1859* (Oxford: Clarendon Press, 1982); Walter Arnstein,
Protestant versus Catholic in mid-Victorian England: Mr. Newdegate and the nuns (Columbia, Mo.
University of Missouri Press, 1982); J. P. Parry, *Democracy and religion: Gladstone and the liberal
party, 1867–1875* (Cambridge: Cambridge University Press, 1986); Jeffrey Paul Von Arx,
Progress and pessimism: religion, politics, and history in late nineteenth century Britain (Cambridge,
Mass.: Harvard University Press, 1985).

the middle of this century in American university literature classes whereas his opponents were generally ignored.

Yet a closer examination of the Oxford Movement casts considerable doubt upon its fundamental spirituality. The doctrine espoused by its leaders in 1833 over all others was that of apostolic succession. They emphasized this doctrine in order to deny authentic clerical status to the Nonconformist clergy and thus to retain the traditional social status of Anglican clergy. Addressing the very first of the tracts to the clergy and playing upon their social anxieties, Newman asked them,

Should the Government and Country so far forget their GOD as to cast off the Church, to deprive it of its temporal honours and substance, on what will you rest the claim of respect and attention which you make upon your flocks? Hitherto you have been upheld by your birth, your education, your wealth, your connexions; should these secular advantages cease, on what must CHRIST's Ministers depend? Is not this a serious practical question? We know how miserable is the state of religious bodies not supported by the State. Look at the Dissenters on all sides of you, and you will see at once that their Ministers, depending simply upon the people, become the creatures of the people. Are you content that this should be your case? ... Surely it must not be so; – and the question recurs, on what are we to rest our authority, when the State deserts us?[39]

Newman responded that Church of England priests must henceforth emphasize the spiritual authority that they received through their ordination by bishops who stood in direct descent from the original apostles. This apostolic succession assured the Anglican priests of a supernatural authority which Nonconformist clergy lacked. Furthermore, it assured the Anglican clergy that their authority and status rested upon the authority of the bishops rather than the goodwill of the congregations.

The Tractarians also emphasized the role of the sacraments in religious life for similar clerical political ends. Baptism, which according to the Tractarians could under ordinary circumstances only properly be administered by a priest ordained by a bishop, constituted the effective vehicle for the transmission of regenerative grace. The Tractarian doctrine of the Eucharist stressed the real presence and the spiritual union of the partaker with Christ which

[39] [J. H. Newman], *Thoughts on the ministerial commission*, 9 September, 1833, reprinted in *Tracts for the times by members of the university of Oxford* (London: J. G. and F. Rivington, 1834), pp. 1–2.

again could be achieved only through the actions of a properly
ordained Anglican priest.[40] Behind their doctrine lay a very clear
and distinctly articulated social and political agenda as the Tractarians repeatedly declared that Nonconformist clergy lacking proper
episcopal ordination could not administer sacraments informed by
genuine spiritual efficacy. The Tractarians, therefore, did appeal to
a thoroughly supernatural mode of religion, but they did so at least
in part for clearly secular political and social reasons.

The Tractarian appeal to the authority of the fourth century and
their emphasis on church tradition also led to paradoxical situations
wherein religious ends and secular means became confused or
conflated. The Tractarians viewed church tradition as a source of
Christian truth standing on a level equal to that of scripture. In
Tract 85, *Lectures on the scripture proof of the doctrines of the Church* (1838)
Newman sought to vindicate the necessary role of the Church, and
especially of its clergy, as an institution required to transmit, define,
and teach correct doctrine. To support this contention, Newman
presented a major critique of the historical character of the scriptures
and their adequacy as a vehicle for transmitting and defining
doctrine. The means for his vindication of the necessity of the
Church was a tract filled with irony toward the scriptures and with
destructive scepticism worthy of an Enlightenment author. Indeed
so extreme was Tract 85 that Huxley almost half a century later
claimed that virtually all of his own criticism of the scriptures could
have been taken from Newman's teaching.[41] The difference was
that Huxley emphasized scepticism toward the scriptures to move
people away from the authority of the Church; Newman emphasized
scepticism to draw people toward the necessary authority of the
corporate Anglican Church and to turn them away from voluntary
Nonconformist congregations. But in either case the result could be
simple scepticism leading to loss of faith.

There existed still another more subtle secular political element in
the polemics of the Tractarians. They resented the role of Nonconformists in the reformed Parliament and the possible extension of
further civil liberties to Nonconformists. From the earliest tracts the

[40] Alf Hardelin, *The Tractarian understanding of the Eucharist* (Uppsala: Almquist and Wiksells,
1965). R. C. K. Ensor also noted that the emphasis on the sacraments served to enhance the
social and professional status of Anglican priests though he made too little distinction
between the Tractarians and the later Ritualists. See R. C. K. Ensor, *England, 1870–1914*
(Oxford: Clarendon Press, 1936), p. 141.
[41] Lightman, *The origins of agnosticism*, pp. 114–15.

Oxford writers presented both Nonconformist Protestantism and Anglican evangelicalism as potentially leading to the doctrines of Socinianism. Read in isolation those theological charges indicate a concern over the doctrine of the Trinity, but those accusations also resonated as part of a longstanding tradition of Anglican political polemic. Unitarians and Unitarian clergy had been active in late-eighteenth-century radical politics, and the Unitarian Richard Price had provided the occasion for Burke's *Reflections on the revolution in France*. From the time of that tract and well before the French Revolution, Anglican writers had associated Socinianism and Unitarianism with political radicalism and social disruption.[42] Thereafter, much of the British ideological resistance to the French Revolution had taken the form of a defence of religion in general and of Anglicanism in particular. Consequently, for the Tractarians to brand their opponents as actual or more often potential Socinians was to make not only a theological charge but also a political one that raised the spectre of radicalism and social turmoil.

Just as the religious or spiritual interpretation of the Tractarian movement concealed secular elements, the political interpretation of the Nonconformists that arose from Anglican polemics concealed religious factors in Nonconformist life. Following the Anglican lead, historians and literary scholars long regarded the activities of the Nonconformists as political in character rather than religiously or spiritually motivated. This attitude received much support during the mid-twentieth century when Matthew Arnold's criticism and religious writings received widespread attention by American scholars who were critical of American fundamentalism which may have become conflated in their minds with English Nonconformity. Arnold's relentless attacks on Nonconformists in *Culture and anarchy* and his later prose works represented a mid-Victorian version of

---

[42] J. C. D. Clark, *English society, 1688–1832: ideology, social structure and political practice during the ancien regime* (Cambridge: Cambridge University Press, 1985), pp. 279–348; J. A. W. Gunn, *Beyond liberty and property: the process of self-recognition in eighteenth-century political thought* (Kingston and Montreal: McGill-Queen's University Press, 1983), *passim*; H. T. Dickinson, *Liberty and property: political ideology in eighteenth-century Britain* (London: Weidenfeld and Nicholson, 1977), pp. 195–269; Robert Hole, *Pulpits, politics and public order in England, 1760–1832* (Cambridge: Cambridge University Press, 1989); John Gascoigne, 'Anglican latitudi-narianism and political radicalism in the late eighteenth century', *History*, 71 (1986), 22–38; Isaac Kramnick, 'Religion and radicalism: English political theory in the age of revolution', *Political Theory*, 5 (1977), 505–34; Isaac Kramnick, *Republicanism and bourgeois radicalism: political ideology in late eighteenth-century England and America* (Ithaca: Cornell University Press, 1991).

rather standard Anglican condescension. The Nonconformists appeared as a selfish, politically motivated group who spurned good manners in everyday life and higher culture in the life of the mind. Enunciating similar Anglican views in the late 1850s about the manner in which Nonconformists had allegedly segregated themselves from the broader culture of the nation, the historian William Stubbs wrote to E. A. Freeman, 'I do not believe that a Dissenter could write a history of England.'[43]

Once a modicum of scepticism is directed toward the Anglican interpretation of Nonconformity, still another reversal of the traditional secular–religious dichotomy in Victorian life presents itself. From at least the 1770s increasing numbers of English Nonconformists had believed that to achieve religious liberty it was necessary to combine their campaign for religious equality with the demands of political radicals for political equality. As the Unitarian David Williams explained to fellow Nonconformists in the late eighteenth century,

Your very existence depends on your changing the reason of your dissent, which used to be an opinion of superior orthodoxy and superior purity of faith and worship, for another which is the only rational and justifiable reason of dissent – the inalienable and universal right of private judgement, and the necessity of an unrestrained enquiry and freedom of debate and discussion on all subjects of knowledge, morality, and religion. This may be called Intellectual Liberty. This should be the general reason of dissent.[44]

The radical political and intellectual paths thus became during the late eighteenth century vehicles for the realization of suppressed Nonconformist religious and ecclesiastical convictions. Thereafter, until at least World War I English Nonconformity was a major factor in British radical and liberal political life.

Once various Nonconformist leaders had directly adopted political tactics to achieve their religious ends and to challenge Anglican exclusivity in political life and privilege in other areas of society, Anglican commentators, such as the Tractarians, sought to divide Nonconformists between *Political Nonconformists* who were bad, religiously insincere, and unwilling to accept civic disabilities and *Conscientious Nonconformists* who were good, religiously sincere, and prepared to accept a position of second-class citizenship as a result of

---

[43] Quoted in Philippa Levine, *The amateur and the professional: antiquarians, historians and archaeologists in Victorian England, 1838–1886* (Cambridge: Cambridge University Press, 1986), p. 3.
[44] Quoted in Dickinson, *Liberty and property*, p. 202.

their beliefs. In other words, Anglicans presented conscientious Nonconformists as truly religious and political Nonconformists as less than truly religious. The litmus test was whether the Nonconformist was sufficiently sincere in religion to be supine in politics. This Anglican polemical analysis in a somewhat diluted form with rare exception has been implicitly, if not always explicitly, accepted by both political and intellectual historians very few of whom have had much good to say about the Nonconformists.[45]

Throughout much of the Victorian era Nonconformists experienced the Church of England as a genuinely repressive institution in areas such as free expression, taxation, education, and burial privileges.[46] The Nonconformist drive for political and civic equality constituted an effort to achieve fundamental religious liberty and equality through secular means which included attempts to remove the direct influence of the state Church from various areas of daily social life. The device advocated was often removing the disputed issue from the authority of the Anglican Church and investing it in the secular state. For example, the requirement of marriage registration was transferred from the parish church to a government registrar in 1836 in order to overcome the humiliation experienced by Nonconformists who had previously been required to be married in the Anglican parish church or who might be refused marriage if they had not been baptized by an Anglican priest.

Similarly, in the third quarter of the century significant groups of

[45] In this respect, it should be noted that throughout the historiography of Victorian intellectual and religious life there continues to exist a vast lacuna in regard to theological or even ecclesiastical thought of Nonconformists. They remain portrayed even by the few sympathetic observers as primarily a political constituency. The intellectual life of Nonconformity quite simply has not been probed. Yet their clergy wrote extensive treatises in virtually all areas of theology and biblical studies. Little or nothing is known of this work including that of writers of international standing such as the Unitarian James Martineau. It is not insignificant that Walter Houghton in *The Victorian frame of mind, 1830–1870* (New Haven: Yale University Press, 1957) virtually ignored the role of Nonconformity; and even when quoting Nonconformists, he did not attempt to explore the manner in which their particular ideas and attitudes reflected or articulated their problematic situation in Victorian society and intellectual life.

[46] The published studies of Victorian Nonconformity remain very few in number. See Alan Everitt, *The pattern of rural dissent: the nineteenth century* (Leicester: Leicester University Press, 1972); Stephen Koss, *Nonconformity in modern British politics* (London: Batsford, 1975); A. D. Gilbert, *Religion and society in industrial England: church, chapel and social change, 1740–1914* (London: Longmans, 1976); Clyde Binfield, *So down to prayer: studies in English Nonconformity, 1780–1920* (London: Dent, 1977); D. W. Bebbington, *The Nonconformist conscience: chapel and politics, 1870–1914* (London: Allen, 1982). There are also important observations in Neil J. Smelser, *Social paralysis and social change: British working-class education in the nineteenth century* (Berkeley: University of California Press, 1991).

Nonconformists championed purely secular education without religious instruction in order to remove Anglican priests as religious instructors. The attack on Anglicanism often assumed a distinctly anti-clerical tone which probably increased over the course of the century with the growing clerical pretensions arising from the Tractarian movement. That the major examples of English anti-clericalism are to be found among Protestant Nonconformists who saw Anglican priests as a threat to their social lives and to the truth necessary for the salvation of their souls rather than among secular or even secularist writers clearly illustrates the historical inadequacy of dividing Victorian intellectual or social life into distinctly religious and secular categories.[47]

There can be little doubt that the drive for Nonconformist civil rights, education reform, disestablishment in England, Ireland, and Wales, as well as the sharp Nonconformist anti-clericalism contributed to the emergence of a secular society, but it is a highly questionable proposition to see such a society as the goal of the Nonconformists. At the time, many Victorian Christians conceived secular solutions as a device to realize distinctly religious goals and indeed to Christianize the nation. That those goals were denominational does not necessarily make them any less really religious any more than the theological language of the Anglicans made their goals less political.

The denominational character of Nonconformist activity explains why their leaders did not see themselves or their agenda as posing a danger to religious life. From the thirties through at least the seventies, the non-Anglican denominations including Roman Catholics were growing. They assumed that such growth and recruitment would continue and that the institutions of religion, which also included a resurgent Anglican Church, could successfully fend for themselves and Christianize the nation. Freed of the difficulties of civic inequality, Nonconformists believed that they, both Roman Catholic and Protestant, could remake significant portions of British society into their own religious image and that a world of genuine, free, voluntary Christian commitment would supplant a world of corrupt Anglican domination.

47 Susan Budd, *Varieties of unbelief: atheists and agnostics in English society, 1850–1960* (London, 1977), pp. 43–8. For an example of the manner in which earlier religious disputation led to unexpected secular results, see Alan Charles Kors, *Atheism in France, 1650–1729: the orthodox sources of disbelief* (Princeton: Princeton University Press, 1990).

For the Nonconformists denominationalism was intrinsically related to their theological understanding of the spiritual life. The character of one's denominational community was as much a part of one's religious life as was one's thought about the nature of God, the role of revelation, or the Eucharist. It was an issue that in their minds far transcended the rivalry between themselves and the Anglicans. For example, R. W. Dale once contrasted the position of his denomination to that of the Methodists for whom he had much personal respect:

Methodism is simply anxious to make men Christians: Congregationalism is anxious that men who are Christians should realise in their church life Christ's own conception of what their church life should be; and we believe that only by restoring the true conception of the Christian Church is there any chance of Christianising the English people, and that the Church exists at once for the discipline of Christian perfection and evangelisation of mankind. We believe, moreover, that knowledge of the higher forms of Christian life is only possible in a church communion of the kind which the Lord Jesus Christ Himself intended to establish.[48]

Dale's religious critique of the Church of England which unlike Methodism possessed all manner of political privileges would have been all the stronger. He and other Protestant Nonconformists deeply believed that religion must be a matter of individual decision freely exercised and realized through freely chosen religious association which did not carry social and political disabilities.

In the past it has been difficult for historians to take the Nonconformists' political activities seriously as part of their religious life or to see how religion and politics meshed. Dale himself was one of the most politically active Nonconformists of the second half of the century, and for that he was ridiculed by Matthew Arnold. Dale was also a prolific writer on serious theological topics including both the atonement and interpretation of scripture. He was active in educational reform and in theological education. He was a leading spokesman for the municipal gospel which urged civic activity on Christian grounds. Regarding the world as an arena of human action wherein the will of God was to be realized through all vocations, he refused to divide human life into secular and religious realms. In a sermon of 1873 he directly presented participation in political life as a mode of Christian activity:

[48] A. W. W. Dale, *The life of R. W. Dale of Birmingham*, 3rd edn (London: Hodder and Stroughton, 1899), pp. 352–3.

Politics un-Christian! Why, the emancipation of the slaves in the West
Indies was a political act, and it was done mainly by Christian people in
direct obedience to Him who, according to the old prophecy, was to listen
to the cry of the oppressed, and to break in pieces the oppressor. The repeal
of the Corn Laws was a political act, and it was almost a repetition of the
miracle of Christ when He multiplied the loaves in the wilderness, because
the people were faint from want of bread. Christ is the King of our political
life, and in that, as in every other province of our activity, we have to serve
and to honour Him. It was a miracle of mercy when He laid His hand on
those struck by fever, and cured them; and by going on to Boards of Works
and into Town Councils, and improving the drainage of our great towns,
and removing the causes of fever, men are but following in Christ's
footsteps. To make men sober is a Christian work ... To have your own
house governed honestly, and to have it kept clean and wholesome, is a
Christian duty; and to get your city honestly governed, and kept clean and
wholesome, is a Christian duty.[49]

For such a Nonconformist the world of secular society and politics
was the venue for Christian action and personal Christian commitment and fulfilment.

   Similar social and political actions undertaken by the evangelical
Lord Shaftesbury or the muscular Christian Charles Kingsley or
ritualist priests would have been seen as exemplifying the impact of
Victorian Christianity on politics. Yet Dale and other Nonconformists like him have tended to be forgotten or written off as clergyman-
politicians, while the ever politically active Anglican bishops and
local Anglican parsons still tend to be viewed as spiritual leaders
first and political figures second. The overwhelmingly conservative
political commitment of the Church of England, long considered
the Tory Party at Prayer, did not carry over to a dismissal of the
religious character of the Anglican Church as did the liberal political
activities of its Nonconformist denominational counterparts. For
example, the late Victorian and Edwardian Baptist minister John
Clifford, who vociferously resisted payment of taxes to support
Anglican religious activities, stands regarded as a bit of a radical
crank while the Edwardian Archbishop of Canterbury Randall
Davies, who actively participated in the partisan political struggles
of the day, retains his stature as a major spiritual leader and, in the
House of Lords crisis of 1911, as a national statesman.

   If historians of Victorian Britain were to draw Ireland more fully
into their field of vision, the categories of the secular and the religious

---

[49] Dale, *Laws of Christ*, pp. 167–268.

would become even more confused and congruent. From one point of view Irish disestablishment stands as a clear case of secularization. The Church of Ireland lost its privileges and much of its property.[50] Yet the Church of Ireland retreated in the face not only of Irish nationalism but more important in the wake of the great mid-century Irish Catholic revival. Anglicanism in Ireland gave way to resurgent Roman Catholicism and Irish Protestantism. There can be no question that Ireland after disestablishment was more intensely religious in every aspect of life than before disestablishment.

Religion is a far more many splendoured thing than most of us who pursue intellectual history have tended to recognize. Victorian religion was a matter of existential belief about eternal things and personal moral behaviour, and it provided spiritual aid through the passages of life. But for both Church and Chapel Victorian religion in practice and doctrine also involved political agendas and established social parameters for interacting with other classes and denominations. Those intellectuals about whom historians have written understood the denominational, social, and political inter-connectedness of religion and thought. Historians must recapture that world of concrete social reference that informed both religious and non-religious intellectual life and exchange. When that world of concrete specificity is recovered for Victorian religious life as it has been for Victorian science, the categories of the religious and the secular as generally understood at present will largely dissolve.

A generation ago scholars clearly found the distinction between the secular and the religious in nineteenth-century life useful. Although the words *secular* and *religious*, as well as the concept of *secularization*, remain and intellectual historians, including myself, will continue to employ them, those terms and the often unexamined assumptions that may lie behind them no longer in and of themselves provide an adequate analytic framework for probing the Victorian age. That secularization of English and British culture occurred is true, but the occurrence was anything but inevitable, unproblematic, or systematically steady. Like all broad interpretive frameworks, the secularization thesis smoothed the intellectual landscape in hopes of finding a clearer path to understanding. It may very well have aided American scholars in defining for a time their own cultural aspirations, but the costs were very considerable for under-

[50] P. M. H. Bell, *Disestablishment in Ireland and Wales* (London: SPCK, 1969).

standing both the twentieth and the nineteenth centuries. The secularization thesis left twentieth-century intellectuals unprepared for the religious resurgence of the late twentieth century. The same thesis left Victorian scholars unprepared to confront both the religious and the non-religious intellectual activities of the nineteenth century in all of their fulsome complexity. The experience with both past and present suggests that new interpretive frameworks must be sought, ones rooted in a deep appreciation of the intricacies of social and religious life rather than in the self-referential cultural aspirations of our contemporary scholarly community.

The problems relating to the self-referential cultural aspirations of scholars today are different from those of scholars at the mid-century, but they may still obscure our pathways to understanding. Each discipline in the humanities has undergone a remarkable splintering and has witnessed the rapid expansion of new areas of methodology and specialization often in conflict both with past research agendas and with each other. In the historical profession the process of changing the categories, terms, and frameworks of interpretation has given rise not unexpectedly to the desire to provide different names to the various kinds of history being pursued. John Morley once caustically observed, 'Labels are devices for saving talkative persons the trouble of thinking.'[51] The danger of that loquacious pitfall exists today. Far too much academic energy in recent years has been devoted to quarrels over nomenclature the point of which has been to exclude, displace, or discredit the work of colleagues or to achieve a redirection from one arena to another of the financial resources that undergird academic and intellectual life. The use of labels and the separation of historical research into mutually suspicious or even hostile camps that only rarely communicated to or with each other accounted, as I indicated earlier, in large measure for the confusion about the character of the religious and the secular in the Victorian age.

The achievement of a more nearly complete and adequate understanding of the past must always involve a catholic approach to human experience and to the various tools that may open that experience to the historian. The historical profession collectively might well take to heart the belief, described by Walter Pater as the

[51] John Morley, *Nineteenth-century essays*, ed. Peter Stansky (Chicago: University of Chicago Press, 1970), p. 36.

essence of humanism, 'that nothing which has ever interested living men and women can wholly lose its vitality – no language they have spoken, nor oracle beside which they have hushed their voices, no dream which has once been entertained by actual human minds, nothing about which they have ever been passionate, or expended time and zeal'.[52] It is such inclusiveness of interest and breadth of appreciation of the past that the rise of increasing numbers of professional subdisciplines and subspecializations endangers. Even the expansion of areas of research that claim to open to exploration previously unexamined groups will ironically narrow our vision of the past if their advocates seek to close research on areas that have already attracted much attention. Fields once abandoned or demeaned by scholars frequently come in time to be reclaimed and transformed, reinvigorated and redirected. Most assuredly such will be the situation confronting virtually all British and European history intellectual and otherwise as the European world enters what is most assuredly a new epoch that will demand fundamental rethinking about the past and reconsideration of the categories that have informed so much twentieth-century analysis of earlier thought.

[52] Walter Pater, *The renaissance: studies in art and poetry*, 1893 text (Berkeley, Calif.: University of California Press, 1980), p. 38.

CHAPTER 2

Cultural apostasy and the foundations of Victorian intellectual life

No other group of major British intellectual and cultural figures still seems to appear so much as insects trapped in amber as do the Victorians. We repeatedly acknowledge the striking transformations that occurred in nineteenth-century political, social, and economic activity, but we have too rarely analysed in a distinctly historical fashion changes that occurred in Victorian intellectual life or the manner in which they took place. Ironically, until very recently we tended to analyse the two or three intellectual generations that carried the concept of evolution to the forefront of Western thought in distinctly non-evolutionary terms. We often write about Victorian intellectuals as if they existed outside time. We rarely imagine them as young or as changing or as developing. We forget that John Keats and Thomas Carlyle were born in the same year: the one remaining ever young, the other seeming ever grizzled. Nor do we often regard the Victorians as having been perhaps fundamentally unconventional. How could we? Were they not the people who forged the conventions against which rebellion in this century from Bloomsbury onward has been and continues to be a cultural cottage industry? Despite enormous strides in the scholarship of the past quarter century we too often continue to view and treat Victorian intellectuals as historical figures who did not themselves develop historically. In that respect, we approach Victorian intellectual and literary life as some nine-teenth-century scriptural geologists viewed the layers of geological strata. We consider and discuss the now cold, solid fossil remains of Victorian intellectual enterprise, but we fail to recognize that the strata in which they lie embedded were once hot, moving, molten.[1]

[1] Samuel Hynes, *The Edwardian turn of mind* (Princeton: Princeton University Press, 1968); Martin Green, *Children of the sun: a narrative of 'decadence' in England after 1918* (New York: Basic Books, 1976); Robert Skidelsky, *John Maynard Keynes: hopes betrayed, 1883–1920* (New York: Elizabeth Sifton Books Viking, 1986); Jonathan Rose, *The Edwardian temperament* (Athens,

The reasons for this persistent, static approach to Victorian intellectual life are many and complex. First, the single most influential modern study of Victorian intellectual history, Walter Houghton's *Victorian frame of mind* (1957), despite its multifold virtues presented a generally static and largely ahistorical portrait of the Victorian intellectual and cultural arena.[2] Houghton forged a brilliant synthesis from which scholars will continue to profit for years to come, but it was a work with profound historical shortcomings. Houghton rescued the Victorians from the clutches of Lytton Strachey and the condescension of Strachey's camp followers, but Houghton did not transform the Victorians into creatures of history. He quoted widely and brilliantly but sought to portray psychological rather than historical categories. He paid little attention to the details of chronology or institutions. He avoided exploration of the varied and various microcosms of Victorian intellectual life. He rarely distinguished a Nonconformist from a Tractarian. He ignored the intricacies and politics of the learned societies. He paid little or no attention to the institutions of education or the structures of publication.

It would, however, be unfair to press upon the shortcomings of Houghton's volume. It was by no means the sum of his scholarship. In the great monument of his scholarly life, *The Wellesley index to Victorian periodicals*, he provided all later scholars with the fundamental tools to delineate a sharply different portrait of the Victorian intellectual landscape. In that seminal work of reference upon which all future studies of the Victorian age must stand grounded Houghton provided the pathway to the very kind of particularistic study of the century that he had not presented in his own synthesis. Consequently Houghton in the course of his life and labours brought one era of Victorian scholarship to an end and opened a new one.

The absence of a genuinely historical analysis of Victorian intellectual life is also the result of a virtual missing generation of Victorian intellectuals so far as the scholarly community has been concerned. Very considerable information and research have existed in regard to early Victorians who lived long into the century or late

Ohio: Ohio University Press, 1986); Perry Meisel, *The myths of the modern: a study in British literature and criticism after 1850* (New Haven: Yale University Press, 1987); Noel Annan, *Our age: English intellectuals between the world wars, a group portrait* (New York: Random House, 1990), pp. 3–65.

[2] Walter Houghton, *The Victorian frame of mind, 1830–1870* (New Haven: Yale University Press, 1957).

Victorians who survived into the twentieth century. Yet only recently have serious studies commenced about intellectual figures whose active careers occurred during the first fifty or sixty years of the century. With the notable exceptions of Thomas Arnold, Thomas Babington Macaulay, and Charlotte Brontë very few of the major figures of British intellectual life including theologians who were active primarily between 1825 and 1865 received distinguished contemporary biographies. The lives and careers of such notables as William Whewell, Edward Copleston, Charles Babbage, Archbishop Sumner, Bulwer Lytton, Harriet Martineau, Archbishop Whately, Bishop Connop Thirlwall, Adam Sedgwick, and George Grote, even if recorded in modest nineteenth-century biographies, did not become well known. Except within a relatively small radical circle the reputation of so important a figure as John Stuart Mill underwent serious decline after his death in 1873. Only Alexander Bain's small volume commemorated his life.

The Victorians who became most familiar in the twentieth century were those who lived till at least the 1870s and 1880s and who not incidentally often had developed significant audiences in America. These included Carlyle, Darwin, Newman, Tennyson, Ruskin, Spencer, George Eliot, Arnold, Huxley, Jowett, and Browning. The early biographers and historians of this Victorian cultural elite frequently encountered them personally or by reputation only after they had become elderly or when they were already well-established cultural authority figures rarely associated with major contemporary religious or intellectual controversy. Furthermore, many of their biographers interpreted the lives and thought of these eminent Victorians in terms of the secular or at least non-Christian *Sage* whose cultural role had emerged as an ideal type of intellectual in the pages of the Victorian writers themselves.[3] In that sense the Victorian authors' own timeless and largely ahistorical critical categories served to interpret their lives. This situation received a new lease on life in the middle of the present century when, in reaction to the destructive and hostile Edwardian treatment of Victorian intellectual life, scholars, such as Houghton, Basil Willey, and Dwight Culler, again discovered Victorian intellectuals and treated them somewhat as fixed stars of spiritual or cultural wisdom.

---

[3] George P. Landow, *Elegant Jeremiahs: the sage from Carlyle to Mailer* (Ithaca: Cornell University Press, 1986); John Holloway, *The Victorian sage: studies in argument* (Hamden, Conn.: Archon Books, 1962; originally published 1953).

In seeking to understand the ahistorical approach to Victorian culture, it is also important not to underestimate the impact made on later generations by the large, well-bound sets of collected works of major Victorian writers. It was through those sets that most scholars, then as now, became acquainted with the documents of Victorian intellectual history. Those sets themselves stood as static, sometimes impenetrable, monuments that 'contained' the intellectual life of the age. G. B. Tennyson has explored the manner in which on a much smaller scale over the decades John Keble's single-volume *The Christian year* came as a published book eventually to resemble a devotional missal.[4] The multivolume works of later Victorian writers similarly took on a published life of their own.

Those great collected sets which one still finds as scholarly treasures in used book shops more often than not concealed two major historical realities. First, in most cases the versions of books or articles published in those sets represented the final revision rather than the original edition. Sometimes revisions were minor. On other occasions the revisions were substantial and the details of revision often remained unnoted by the revising author or editor. In Newman's case the identity of the original author became virtually transformed as the later Roman Catholic Newman commented on and revised the work of the younger Anglican Newman. Second, the bound collected sets by their very format hid from readers and later scholars the original format of works that had first appeared as tracts, pamphlets, or journal articles. Frequently, the materials that finally came to lodge in the great bound sets had initially seen the light of published day in a world of rapid, sharp polemical exchange. The initial publication, which usually created the major contemporary impact, may have been little more than a rough draft which became subject to later revision and polishing for a second or third publication setting. No less important, when republished in a set of collected works, the other side of the original debate was naturally almost invariably omitted. In some cases, original introductions and conclusions were removed and what had first appeared as a polemical article stood republished in a revised format as a reflective essay. In such instances, quite literally the context had been changed, hidden, and concealed. Or when the collected works contained a final revision as with the sixth edition of Darwin's *On the origin of*

---

[4] G. B. Tennyson, *Victorian devotional poetry: the Tractarian mode* (Cambridge, Mass.: Harvard University Press, 1981), pp. 75–93, 226–32.

species, the original statement of the thesis and previous revisions remained on the shelves of those persons who possessed the earlier editions but were inaccessible to the possessors of the final version. All of these problems became further compounded when selections of Victorian prose were anthologized for purposes of university teaching.

Newman along with other older, eminent Victorians, such as Carlyle, Darwin, Tennyson, Arnold, Spencer, Huxley, and George Eliot illustrates a third reason why historical analysis has been lacking from consideration of Victorian culture. None of these figures during the most influential periods of their lives were (or in Newman's case remained) Anglican clergy. For just that reason they were of special interest to late nineteenth-century, Edwardian, and mid-twentieth-century critics. The eminent late Victorian intellectual elite represented a cultural coterie who had been dependent on neither the Anglican Church nor the aristocracy for patronage and career advancement. They stood as examples of the self-fulfilment of the various concepts of a secular clerisy that had been set forth so often during the nineteenth century and to which in large measure twentieth-century intellectuals saw themselves as heirs. They were especially useful to American critics and academics who saw themselves as successors in American culture to the clergy.

Newman poses a more difficult case, but he stood as a Roman Catholic whose prose and whose views on the liberal education made him acceptable to Protestant scholars throughout the English-speaking world. Newman's *Apologia pro vita sua* by the power of its rhetoric, its narrative structure, and its argument of a person defending his honesty against misrepresentation succeeded in achieving a place of literary respect among American non-Catholic scholars as it had among English non-Catholics. In America Newman exemplified a learned Roman Catholic who was English rather than Irish. Furthermore, among Roman Catholics he represented a theologically liberal direction of thought in regard to church authority as did Lord Acton, the other much-quoted Victorian Roman Catholic. Both appeared to later observers to stand at the fountain-head of Catholic modernism and were thus more acceptable to secular university scholars than were exemplars of Victorian Roman Catholic orthodoxy, such as W. G. Ward or Cardinal Manning.

The fascination in both Britain and the United States from the late nineteenth to the mid-twentieth century with the secular or non-

Anglican Victorian sage resulted in a major distortion of historical understanding. The emphasis on the sagelike figures in Victorian life fostered a lack of sensitivity to the profoundly Anglican and often clerical culture of the early nineteenth century into which virtually all of those figures had been born. To the extent Anglican culture was recognized prior to the last decade of scholarship its adherents or representatives were often demeaned or seen as intellectually retrograde or as religiously inadequate. They were associated with the old unreformed and hence illiberal universities. They embodied spiritually and intellectually the allegedly inadequate religion against which Tractarians, evangelicals, secularists, as well as agnostics alike revolted. It was from their fold that the opponents of Darwin and other scientific advances had emerged. Since so much intellectual history has been written as the story of the movement from illiberal to liberal ideas or from reaction to progress, Anglican culture represented the negative pole in the bipolar analysis.

Recent studies have just begun to correct this older teleological approach, but much remains to be done. Most important, historians need to think more clearly and critically about the transition from the older Anglican culture to the mid- and late-Victorian one in which Anglicanism existed as only one of many strains of thought and values. Historians of politics, economics, diplomacy or society have long recognized that history is contingent and that what happened did not necessarily have to have happened or to have happened in the manner that it did. Intellectual and cultural historians have too rarely begun their work from that standpoint. There has existed a residual Whiggishness and concern for modern relevance or correctness in their historical evaluation of nineteenth-century ideas.[5]

---

[5] Examples of this tendency were long dominant in the history of Victorian science. Walter Cannon's perceptive analysis of the affinities of Darwinian thought with natural theology met considerable resistance. Robert Young's emphasis on the importance of phrenology has only recently begun to receive its due regard. Martin Rudwick's *Devonian controversy*, which presented a dispassionate analysis of a major geology debate, represented an important turning point as has the more recent Darwin literature associated most particularly with James Moore and Peter Bowler. The pitfall confronting some more recent studies is that of the older Whiggish tendencies being replaced by the pursuit of a different kind of contemporary social relevance pursued through a radical political approach to the history of science. Walter (Susan F.) Cannon, 'The bases of Darwin's achievement: a reevaluation', *Victorian Studies*, 5 (1961), 109–34; Robert Young, *Mind, brain, and adaptation in the nineteenth century: cerebral localization and its biological context from Gall to Ferrier* (Oxford: Clarendon Press, 1970); Martin J. S. Rudwick, *The great Devonian controversy: the shaping of scientific knowledge among gentlemanly specialists* (Chicago: University of Chicago Press, 1985); James R. Moore,

The question that needs to be addressed is how British intellectual life marked by a predominance of Anglican institutions, ideas, and ideology in 1830 moved by 1870 to a culture in which Nonconformists and Roman Catholics played an important part and one in which scientific naturalism had replaced natural theology, bold experiments such as Pre-Raphaelitism had begun to influence art, aestheticism had challenged all the neoclassical literary and artistic verities, socialism had begun to present a serious critique of political economy, and one in which there was so much confusion that Arnold could equate it with anarchy and prescribe as the remedy a concept of culture that itself closely resembled a secularized Anglicanism. What has been forgotten is that the high Victorian culture of the third quarter of the century – thirty years later embodied in leather bound sets – was lively, rebellious, irreverent, and demanding of change at every turn. In effect, the Victorian era was intellectually an age of transition because many people wanted it to be so.

A concept that may contribute to a clearer historical sense of the foundations of high Victorian culture is that of *cultural apostasy*. A very significant group of those intellectuals who by the end of the century had become 'the Victorians', recognized for their staid, conventional qualities, commenced their careers in the 1840s as cultural apostates whose thought (rather than personal social behaviour) challenged one or more widely held cultural or moral assumptions associated with the Anglican world. Elite high Victorian intellectual life emerged as the product of a mode of cultural rebellion far more profound than that which the Edwardians saw themselves carrying out against the Victorians. This reality long lay concealed in and by the static conceptual categories through which first the Edwardians and then later mid-twentieth-century scholars analysed the Victorians.

Cultural apostasy was different from the direct social and political protests of the 1840s that arose from the Owenites, the Chartists, radical Dissenters, Irish Nationalists, or the Anti-Corn Law League. Those organized groups whose ideas were often rooted in the radicalism of the eighteenth century were attempting directly to change the configuration of social, economic, and political forces. In

The post-Darwinian controversies: a study of the Protestant struggle to come to terms with Darwin in Great Britain and America, 1870–1900 (Cambridge: Cambridge University Press, 1979); Peter J. Bowler, *The eclipse of Darwinism: anti-Darwinian evolution theories in the decades around 1900* (Baltimore: Johns Hopkins University Press, 1983).

contrast to these direct challengers of the early Victorian political and social structures who were frequently themselves outsiders, the cultural apostates rebelled from within the core of Anglican culture. The cultural apostates actually shattered the presuppositions of Anglican culture more fully than its external enemies and critics because they challenged it on its own terms and then undertook radically new intellectual and cultural initiatives. The Anglican intellectual elite had to pay attention to them because they were of it and like it. They could not be dismissed as troublesome outsiders though they might be forced to leave Anglican institutions or find themselves denounced by fellow Anglicans. The cultural apostates whose thought would so inform high Victorian intellectual life wanted not to change what other Anglicans thought, but rather to transform the very way that they conceived thinking about problems and major cultural forces in their lives. Once they had publicized the intellectual fruits of their apostasy and their ideas worked their way through Anglican-dominated institutions, the remaining framework of Anglican culture stood shattered beyond repair. In different ways, the cultural apostates lost confidence in the existing Anglican intellectual culture in the same manner that many political Tories had somewhat earlier lost confidence in the unreformed political system after the passage of Catholic Emancipation, then out of frustration overturned the Wellington ministry, and thus opened the way for new elections, a Whig ministry, and the Reform Bill.

The cultural apostasy of the 1840s was directed primarily against modes of thought that had come to dominate English culture during the last forty years or so of the seventeenth century and that had become rigidified during the eighteenth century and more particularly during the decades of reaction to eighteenth-century radicalism and the French Revolution. The late seventeenth century had seen the consolidation of a distinctly Protestant (though not Puritan) version of Anglicanism, the triumph of a Newtonian world view and with it a version of natural religion that was distinctly English, and the promulgation of classicism in the arts and letters. As the cultural apostates of the 1840s challenged these outlooks, they produced enormous controversy and actually undermined the Anglican cultural ideals that had been institutionalized during the early decades of the nineteenth century. It was this destruction of the major presuppositions of Anglican culture from within that made possible the eventual creative tumult of high Victorian culture.

Until the recent work of Thackray, Morrell, Garland, Clark, Corsi, Waterman, and Rudwick, and the earlier research of Cannon and Soloway, most of early nineteenth-century Anglican culture remained unexplored.[6] There was, of course, no single Anglican culture; but there did exist a series of widely shared intellectual or cultural assumptions within the Anglican-dominated portion of the English intellectual community that gave it a mode of self-definition. These had originally been connected with the exclusively Anglican political monopoly that originated in the late seventeenth century and that had been reasserted during the years of reaction to the French Revolution.

Anglican culture first and foremost rested upon a religious definition of cultural identification and political outlook.[7] From the Restoration through the battles over Catholic Emancipation and after, spokesmen for the Anglican monopoly had defined their character and that of the political and social culture that they defended in terms of the dual opposition to Roman Catholics and Protestant Nonconformists. Roman Catholicism was identified with tyranny, potential domination by a foreign prince, superstition, idolatry, and Ireland. Nonconformity was identified with Puritanism, the political turmoil of the seventeenth century, religious enthusiasm, and from the third quarter of the eighteenth century onward with politically radical Unitarianism. Conversely, in the early decades of the nineteenth century Anglicanism became almost entirely associated with Protestantism and loyalty to the political status quo. The key element in this Anglican self-definition was the Thirty-Nine Articles. Until the repeal of the Test Act in 1828 and the enactment of Catholic Emancipation in 1829 the Articles had provided a generally effective, if not total, barrier against non-Anglican participation in national politics. Thereafter, the Articles were expected to constitute an ongoing means of maintaining the evangelical and Protestant character of the Church of England and

---

[6] Jack Morrell and Arnold Thackray, *Gentlemen of science: early years of the British Association for the Advancement of Science* (Oxford: Clarendon Press, 1981); Martha McMackin Garland, *Cambridge before Darwin: the ideal of a liberal education, 1800–1860* (Cambridge: Cambridge University Press, 1980); Pietro Corsi, *Science and religion: Baden Powell and the Anglican debate, 1800–1860* (Cambridge: Cambridge University Press, 1988); Susan F. Cannon, *Science in culture: the early Victorian period* (New York: Science History Publications, 1978); Richard Allen Soloway, *Prelates and people: ecclesiastical social thought in England, 1783–1852* (London: Routledge and Kegan Paul, 1969).

[7] J. C. D. Clark, *English society, 1688–1832: ideology, social structure and political practice during the ancien regime* (Cambridge: Cambridge University Press, 1985).

with it dominance of Anglican religious and social culture. The Articles served successfully to define and to maintain Anglican social exclusivity as when Parliament refused in 1834 to modify oaths regarding the Articles so as to open the universities to Dissenters.

Anglican culture as it touched upon the larger intellectual life of the nation and in particular the pursuit of science was very closely associated with expositions of natural religion. Again, the roots of this outlook lay in the seventeenth-century achievements of the Royal Society among whose members natural religion stood as one of the intellectual and cultural bulwarks against the alleged materialism of Hobbes and others and the religious enthusiasm of Puritans and later Nonconformists. Natural religion was used to uphold the centrality of a reasonable religion embodied in the faith and liturgy of the Church of England.

During the early decades of the nineteenth-century natural religion, as will be more fully discussed in a subsequent chapter, provided a theodicy that explained or a veil that concealed the pain of nature and the malfunctioning of the social order.[8] Thomas Malthus in his *Essay on the principle of population* (1798) first portrayed a world of nature at war with itself as the superfecundity of humankind and other animals outstripped the food supply. Then in the closing chapters he retreated from that image by providing a brief theodicy in which the sufferings in nature served to spur human beings to industry and to a moral concern with the hereafter. In his *Natural theology* of 1802 Archdeacon Paley repeatedly defended the sufferings revealed in nature by appealing to their utilitarian functions. The Bridgewater treatises of the 1830s and 1840s similarly set forth expositions of the natural order that led to acquiescence in the trials of the social order. Recently, George Levine has drawn a brilliant parallel between the prose of William Whewell's Bridgewater treatise and the manner in which it concealed potential discord in nature and the novels of Jane Austen in which potential moral discord was similarly muted.[9]

The link between early Victorian scientific endeavour and natural religion became virtually institutionalized in the founding and early

---

[8] For the most recent discussion of these developments, see A. M. C. Waterman, *Revolution, economics and religion: Christian political economy, 1798–1833* (Cambridge: Cambridge University Press, 1991).

[9] George Levine, *Darwin and the novelists: patterns of science in Victorian fiction* (Cambridge, Mass.: Harvard University Press, 1988), pp. 24–119.

activity of the British Association for the Advancement of Science. As Morrell and Thackray have so convincingly contended, the scientists who founded the British Association carefully and persistently argued that scientific pursuits necessarily supported natural religion in order to alleviate the association between science and materialism and thus disorder that had arisen from Burke's attack on French thought.[10] For the first thirty years of the life of the British Association every presidential address included reference to the religious function of scientific investigation.

Although there is less firm ground to discuss the presence of an Anglican aesthetic, there existed in the writings of the late seventeenth century through the mid-eighteenth a deep suspicion of subjectivity and individualism in art. It was assumed that part of the role of art was prescriptively moral and that its goal was to restrain. A conservative or neoclassical outlook most clearly associated with Sir Joshua Reynolds's *Discourses* tended to prevail. The models for paintings were the old masters and most especially Raphael, Claude, and Poussin. There had arisen from the mid-eighteenth century onward a vast outpouring of new criticism of both poetry and art, but no single theory had come to predominate or to displace neoclassicism as a cultural norm.[11] Romantic theory remained suspect within Anglican culture at the very time that Anglicans as well as others read deeply and widely in romantic poetry. However, all such theory continued to be regarded suspiciously in the exclusively Anglican universities and parsonages. The models for painting which young artists should emulate were the Old Masters.

Such was the culture into which many young writers of the 1840s who two decades later became the high Victorians were normally educated, pursued their early careers, and then rejected and challenged in profound ways. The character of this apostasy from Anglican culture and its opening of enormous cultural fissures stand exemplified in the intellectual transformation forged in different arenas of intellectual life during the late 1830s and early 1840s by Charles Darwin, John Henry Newman, and John Ruskin. By the close of the century, each of them had become quintessential high Victorian intellectuals and dominant cultural figures whose works

[10] Morrell and Thackray, *Gentlemen of science*, pp. 224–9.

[11] See John Barrell, *The political theory of painting from Reynolds to Hazlitt: 'the body of the public'* (New Haven: Yale University Press, 1986), for a discussion of some of the pressures against Reynolds within late eighteenth- and early nineteenth-century aesthetics.

had been issued in uniform editions. In the eyes of their own contemporaries and later observers the thought of each writer had become regarded as one of the monuments of the age. Toward the close of the third decade of the nineteenth century their situation was quite different. Each stood encapsulated by the forces of Anglican culture, and each was about to break through those cultural boundaries.

In the opening years of the 1840s Newman, Darwin, and Ruskin produced major statements that constituted cultural apostasy, though to be sure Darwin did not go public for almost twenty years. Between 1837 and 1845 John Henry Newman challenged the Protestant interpretation of the Thirty-Nine Articles of the Church of England; Charles Darwin questioned the fixed character of species; and John Ruskin drew into question the prescriptive adequacy of the classical portrayal of nature in the paintings of Poussin and Claude and the aesthetic authority of Joshua Reynolds. The cultural apostates of the 1840s did not provide new answers to questions; they posed old questions in a new manner and thereby shifted the entire centre of intellectual discourse. Moreover, as they set forth those doubts, criticisms, and new interpretations, they redefined intellectual questions in a profoundly open-ended fashion. Thereafter, the kind of gloss that had been applied to the texts of Anglican religious faith, physical nature, and the plastic arts became transformed. By the third quarter of the century in one arena of intellectual endeavour after another Victorians confronted their cultural texts without a traditional gloss or interpretation to guide them. The old gloss no longer held sway. Traditionally minded Victorians found themselves in that near anarchic world to which Matthew Arnold would in vain seek to restore order and authority.

To the extent that such intellectual disarray characterized Victorian intellectual life in the second half of the century it was the direct result of the cultural apostasy of the 1840s. Indeed the seeds of the intellectual subjectivism and independence that so disturbed Arnold and led to the impulse of 'doing as one likes' lay in the intellectual activity of the late 1830s and 1840s which spilled over and broke through the internal boundaries of Anglican culture. The apostasy of Newman, Darwin, and Ruskin in the 1840s meant that the Victorian culture of the 1860s had to deal directly with those forces of Roman Catholicism, naturalism and materialism, and romantic subjectivism that early nineteenth-century Anglican culture had by definition and design excluded.

In February 1841, John Henry Newman published anonymously Tract 90 entitled *Remarks on certain passages in the Thirty-Nine Articles.* The Church of England would never be quite the same again. For almost a decade Newman and the small group of Oxford-related clergy had been publishing the *Tracts for the times* and other works in which they had demanded the ecclesiastical autonomy of the Anglican Church and protested against virtually all forms of Erastian interference with that autonomy. They had also during that period entered upon an extensive religious and devotional experiment in which they sought to revive the role of tradition in Anglican religious life and to displace the evangelical emphasis on scripture. They looked to the Christian Church of the fourth century and to tradition for their religious models and guides rather than to either the New Testament Church or the Protestant Reformation. The teachings toward which they aspired they called *Catholic*, but they differentiated them from Roman Catholicism.

By the opening of the 1840s certain of Newman's colleagues and younger followers had begun to fear that the doctrines of the Church of England were incompatible with Catholic tradition. They were dissatisfied with the traditional English Protestant interpretation of the Thirty-Nine Articles then being reasserted through the impulse of evangelicalism. Most of these young Anglo-Catholics were either already Anglican priests or prospective candidates for the Anglican priesthood. In Tract 90 Newman attempted to address the doubts of this small group and to assure them that there existed no necessary discrepancy between Catholic teaching and the devout, honest subscription to the Thirty-Nine Articles required of Anglican priests. To that end, Newman radically reinterpreted the character of the doctrinal teachings of the Church of England.

Throughout the tract Newman played upon what he regarded as deep inner tensions in the teachings of the Church of England as embodied in the Articles, the Prayer Book, and the Homilies. He contended that in point of fact the Thirty-Nine Articles were not a Protestant statement of faith. The purpose of this argument was to assure his troubled Anglo-Catholic colleagues that subscription to the Articles did not require subscription to a strictly Protestant and hence unCatholic faith. Therefore, they could in good conscience as Anglo-Catholics remain among or enter the ranks of Church of

England clergy. To provide that assurance for a tiny group of troubled Anglo-Catholics, Newman had to offend the much larger group of Anglicans who believed the entire purpose of the Thirty-Nine Articles was to establish a doctrinal and cultural boundary that distinguished the Anglican Church from the Roman Church. Such Protestant Anglicans did not in most cases distinguish between a Catholic and a Roman Catholic tradition.

Newman pointed to the disunity that currently prevailed within the Anglican Church divided as it was among evangelicals, moderates, high churchmen, Tractarians, and Anglo-Catholics. He thought such disunity would not be overcome by 'ordinary political methods' of a religious sort, but rather required heartfelt agreement achieved through time by 'a supernatural influence'. In the meantime members of the Church of England must endure a situation of less than clear religious direction and teaching. He described this situation which he regarded as one of spiritual ambiguity in terms that were deliberately offensive to all but a handful of Tractarian supporters:

Till her members are stirred up to this religious course, let the Church [of England] sit still; let her be content to be in bondage; let her work in chains; let her submit to her imperfections as a punishment; let her go on teaching with the stammering lips of ambiguous formularies, and inconsistent precedents, and principles but partially developed.[12]

So far as Newman was concerned, the Church of England in its present state was not a fully developed religious institution but rather one of imperfect and imprecise teachings and ambiguous formularies.

Directly attacking the Reformers and relishing the confusions of the age of the Reformation, Newman declared that he intended his criticism 'to show that, while our Prayer Book is acknowledged on all hands to be of Catholic origin, our Articles also, the offspring of an uncatholic age, are, through GOD's good providence, to say the least, not uncatholic, and may be subscribed by those who aim at being catholic in heart and doctrine'.[13] Through this contorted rhetoric Newman contended that the Prayer Book was directly part of

[12] John Henry Newman, *Tract ninety or remarks on certain passages in the Thirty-Nine-Articles*, ed. A. W. Evans (London: Constable and Co., Ltd, 1933), pp. 5–6. This is the most readily available edition of the original tract. Newman revised it slightly in a second edition which circulated more widely.
[13] Ibid., p. 6.

Catholic (though not Roman Catholic) tradition and that the Articles were not wholly dissociated from that tradition. In other words, the Articles were not wholly Protestant, but permitted an interpretation at one with the Catholic tradition which most early Victorian Anglicans conflated with Roman Catholicism against the corruptions of which they believed the Articles had long provided a bulwark.

Newman's contentions were repugnant in the extreme to virtually all adherents to early Victorian Anglicanism except the small party surrounding the Tractarians in the early 1840s. High churchmen, moderates, and evangelicals regarded the Articles as defining the Church and its witness in a fundamentally clear manner despite the possibility of dispute over particular matters in the Articles. To them the idea of the Articles as 'stammering lips' and 'ambiguous formularies' was repugnant both religiously and socially. Newman's interpretation, if accepted or left unchallenged, meant for most readers that the Articles no longer served to define the character of the Church of England and Anglican culture by the exclusion of Roman Catholics. That the Articles could be interpreted to include under their umbrella an undefined group of clergy and their followers designated as Catholics was no less unwelcome to most Anglicans than would have been the inclusion of Unitarians.

In the more detailed arguments of Tract 90 Newman contended that the Thirty-Nine Articles of the Church of England were open to a Catholic interpretation that was not necessarily distinct from that of the Roman Catholic Church. He emphasized the role of the Church and tradition over scripture and private judgement. He stressed baptismal regeneration over justification by faith. Most controversially he attempted to distinguish between Roman Catholic and primitive church teachings on matters such as purgatory, pardons, worshipping and adoring relics, and invoking saints. According to Newman, the Articles condemned the Roman teaching on these matters but not the primitive. In particular he urged that the Anglican Articles did not condemn Tridentine Roman Catholicism since they had been written before the promulgation of the decrees of the Council of Trent. Newman further sought to dissociate Tridentine Christianity from the popular Roman Catholic devotional practices most offensive to Protestants. Other of Newman's arguments were more technical but no less distasteful to other Anglicans.

It was well known that the Articles had been written in the sixteenth century to allow the widest possible religious comprehension within the Elizabethan Church. Nonetheless, from the Restoration through the Revolution of 1688, and then in the major commentaries on the Articles such as that of Bishop Burnet, there had existed a virtually universal Protestant interpretation of the Articles, an interpretation that had been rigidified during the late eighteenth century onward by the impact of the Evangelical Awakening on the Church of England. In the face of that century and a half of Protestant interpretation Newman contended that the Articles had originally been written to comprehend within the Anglican Church persons whose attachment to Protestantism did not go so far as that of the framers of the Articles and by implication not so far as the later upholders of a Protestant ascendancy in Britain. He claimed the Anglo-Catholics of the 1840s as the natural successors of those Elizabethan Catholics who had been so comprehended by the framers:

The Protestant Confession was drawn up with the purpose of including Catholics; and Catholics now will not be excluded. What was an economy in the reformers, is a protection to us. What would have been a perplexity to us then, is a perplexity to Protestants now. We could not then have found fault with their words; they cannot now repudiate our meaning.[14]

Newman was demanding that those who regarded themselves as Catholic and who adhered to practices that most of their fellow churchmen regarded as Roman Catholic could properly and in good conscience remain in the Church of England and more important serve as its clergy.

The publication of Tract 90 was as much an act of cultural apostasy as it was of religious daring. Tract 90 constituted a remarkable attempt to redefine the terms of discourse within the English Church and English culture. In this tract Newman in the most pointed fashion of all his Anglican writings changed the boundaries of religious orientation. He removed all the traditional Anglican signposts according to which the Articles had generally been interpreted for decades. Newman set out to include within the compass of the Articles various beliefs and practices associated with the Roman Catholic Church which mainline Anglican Protestants and even traditional high churchmen regarded as reprehensible.

14 Ibid., pp. 101–2.

Newman's 'Church' as envisioned in Tract 90 was not the Anglican
Church experienced or acknowledged by most of its adherents in
1841; rather it was the Church Catholic defined according to his
own mode of reading history and theology. He transformed the
meanings of the Articles interpreting them from their silences,
quoting them only in part, and resorting to his own sources without
any sense of historical or theological context.

Authorities at Oxford and bishops across the Anglican theological
spectrum condemned Tract 90. Newman himself eventually
resigned from St Mary's and later converted to Rome, again an act
as much of cultural as of religious apostasy in the England of the
1840s. But the creatively destructive legacy of Tract 90 remained. As
James Anthony Froude wrote many years later, Newman broke 'the
back of the Articles'.[15] For the rest of the century the Church of
England was torn asunder over the question of the ethics of belief.[16]
What did it really mean for a candidate at ordination to say to a
bishop or other church authority, 'I accept or believe the Thirty-
Nine Articles?' Those articles as a device defining and sustaining
Anglican culture as the dominant culture of England in opposition
to Roman Catholicism and Nonconformity could no longer function
satisfactorily. The impact of Tract 90 by shattering the prevailing
cultural function and doctrinal interpretation of the Articles shifted
the arena of religious controversy from outside the Church of
England to combat within the Anglican Church itself. The pluralism
initially demanded to accommodate Anglo-Catholicism was claimed
within a few years by liberals, as the young A. P. Stanley in 1841
realized would be the case. Those internal quarrels became no less
important than the longstanding quarrel between Anglicans and
Nonconformists. Anglican culture itself became more diverse. Its
members also became for several generations deeply distrustful of
each other as no one could quite be certain to what kind of Christian
faith another actually adhered when subscribing to the Articles.

The rejection of Newman's interpretation of the Articles also led a
number of Anglicans to convert to the Roman Catholic Church.
Their presence in that communion gave it a higher social standing

[15] James Anthony Froude, *Short studies on great subjects*, new impression (London: Longmans,
   Green, and Company, 1898), IV, 308.
[16] Frank M. Turner and Jeffrey Von Arx, 'Victorian ethics of belief: a reconsideration', in
   W. Warren Wagar, ed., *The secular mind: transformations of faith in modern Europe* (New York:
   Holmes and Meier, 1982), pp. 83–101; James C. Livingston, *The ethics of belief: an essay on the
   Victorian religious conscience* (Tallahassee, Fl.: American Academy of Religion, 1974).

and wider cultural impact than at any time prior to the Reformation. After the conversions of the mid-century, Roman Catholics could no longer be ignored or automatically demeaned in English cultural and intellectual life. Anglicans now had to deal with people socially exactly like themselves who now followed the faith of the Roman Church.

There exists an interesting and significant chronological parallel between the development of Darwin's thought and that of Newman. Between 1836 and 1844 Darwin moved from the last vestiges of a traditional creationist view of nature through adoption of a transmutationist outlook in 1837 to the formulation of the theory of natural selection in 1838 culminating in his first written sketch of the theory in 1842 and his much more extensive essay of 1844 that set forth a wholly evolutionary theory of nature. During exactly the same years Newman moved from a sharp defence of the Articles in the Hampden Crisis of 1836 through private criticism of the Articles and public exploration of Anglo-Catholic religious ideas to the publication of Tract 90 in 1841 and the formulation of a developmental view of the emergence of Christian doctrine which he wrote in 1844 and published after his conversion in 1845. The ideas that Newman published during these years brought disorder to the Anglican Church; the ideas that Darwin developed during the period but delayed publishing for almost twenty years brought disorder to the world of British science in the 1860s and 1870s and helped to shatter the early Victorian alliance of science and moderate Anglicanism.

For the purposes of this essay, the important issue is not the well-elaborated, if still debated, path of Darwin's discovery and formulation of natural selection but rather the manner in which Darwin saw his intellectual activity as socially and culturally dangerous and subversive within the world of early Victorian science.[17] During his years on *The Beagle* the organization of British science had undergone a significant change. The British Association had firmly established itself as the major voice for the scientific community. Its leadership included a number of liberal Anglican clergymen-scien-

[17] The literature on the movement of Darwin's thought toward the formulation of evolution by natural selection is by now vast. The best guides are the bibliography in Peter J. Bowler, *Evolution: the history of an idea*, revised edn (Berkeley: University of California Press, 1989), and the footnotes in David Kohn, ed., *The Darwinian heritage* (Princeton: Princeton University Press, 1985).

tists including several of Darwin's former teachers from Cambridge. The leaders of the Association carefully identified the pursuit of science with support for the political and social status quo, a broad tolerant mode of Anglicanism, a traditional version of natural religion, and the avoidance of any connection of respectable science with either political radicalism or philosophical materialism. Darwin's thinking upon his return led him in directions very different from those of the emerging Anglican scientific establishment.

Consequently, between 1836 and 1844 Darwin pursued two quite divergent scientific and cultural paths. On the one hand he forged for himself a successful scientific career with all of the necessary respectable social and intellectual linkages. These activities included cultivating his old Cambridge connections, building friendships in the major London scientific societies, carrying out a wide correspondence in regard to his collections from *The Beagle*, publishing articles and books, and through his marriage to Emma Wedgewood establishing his family. On the other hand, during the same period through his reading and private notebook speculations, Darwin explored the writings of political economists and statisticians, probed the problem of the origin of species, examined the thought of his grandfather Erasmus who had been a friend of the radical Unitarian Joseph Priestley, became deeply impressed with the ideas of Auguste Comte, adopted a deterministic and materialistic view of both man and nature, and privately moved steadily toward a transmutationist position. In effect during these years two souls struggled within the being of Charles Darwin: the public Darwin of Anglican social respectability and the private Darwin of intellectual radicalism and cultural apostasy.

After the publication of *On the origin of species* (1859) there was no question of the fundamentally radical implications of Darwin's thought for both science and religion. Various entries in Darwin's notebooks from the late 1830s and early 1840s clearly indicate that beginning with his earliest speculations Darwin himself quite consciously perceived how profoundly his thinking ran against the grain of contemporary Anglican thought.[18] He also understood that his

---

[18] The most recent and extensive exploration of the radical cultural associations of evolution during the 1830s is Adrian Desmond, *The politics of evolution: morphology, medicine, and reform in radical London* (Chicago: University of Chicago Press, 1989). In regard to this volume see also, Phillip R. Sloan, 'Deconstructing evolution', *History of Science*, 28 (1990), 419–28. Peter Bowler emphasizes the scientifically radical character of Darwin's thought in his provoca-

potential offence lay not with any single theory but with the general frame of mind in which he approached issues touching upon religion, human nature, and metaphysics. In Darwin's private notebook musings and early draft essays of his theory of natural selection there resided the seeds of virtually all of the ideas associated with Victorian scientific naturalism – the tendency toward determinism, the questioning of orthodox religion and traditional natural religion, the emphasis on evolution, and a naturalistic view of both organic nature and human nature.[19] When these ideas came to the fore of Victorian scientific life in the 1860s, the house of science so carefully constructed by the primarily Anglican founders of the British Association collapsed as did the tradition of British natural theology that had flourished for two centuries.

Very early in the course of his private notebook speculations Darwin grasped that his theories and the conclusions derived therefrom would challenge the image of God associated with both mainline Anglican theology and natural religion. The issue at hand was the character rather than the existence of the deity. Throughout these speculations, as Ospovat argued, Darwin was seeking to account both for the manner in which the idea of God evolved among humankind and for the character of that idea.[20] Darwin believed that the natural theology then currently so intermeshed with science led to an unworthy image of God. For example, in Notebook B, Darwin wrote, 'Has the Creator since the Cambrian formations gone on creating animals with same general structure – miserable limited view.'[21] Darwin believed that a truly powerful and creative God might be expected to enlarge upon and improve the structures that he had first constructed. The concept of God creating beings that underwent no significant change appeared to Darwin as unworthy of a divine being.

tive volume, *The non-Darwinian revolution: reinterpreting a historical myth* (Baltimore: Johns Hopkins University Press, 1988).

[19] Frank Miller Turner, *Between science and religion: the reaction to scientific naturalism in late Victorian England* (New Haven: Yale University Press, 1974), pp. 8–37.

[20] Dov Ospovat, 'God and natural selection: the Darwinian idea of design', *Journal of the History of Biology*, 13 (1980), 171–83. For further considerations of the moral problems that Darwin associated with creationism, see Neal C. Gillespie, *Charles Darwin and the problem of creation* (Chicago: University of Chicago Press, 1979).

[21] Paul H. Barrett, Peter J. Gautrey, Sandra Herbert, David Kohn, Sydney Smith, eds., *Charles Darwin's notebooks, 1836–1844* (Ithaca: Cornell University Press, 1987), B., 216, p. 224. Hereafter notes will indicate the letter notebook and page of Darwin's manuscript and the page on which it is reprinted.

In another passage of his notebooks, which anticipated the closing paragraph of *On the origin of species*, Darwin explained how much more grand was the image of nature conceived as emerging from lawful natural causes than from creation:

What a magnificent view one can take of the world Astronomical ⟨& unknown⟩ causes, modified by unknown ones. cause changes in geography & changes of climate superadded to change of climate from physical causes. – these superinduce changes of form in the organic world, as adaptation. & these changing affect each other, & their bodies, by certain laws of harmony keep perfect in these themselves. – instincts alter, reason is formed, & the world peopled ⟨⟨with Myriads of distinct forms⟩⟩ from a period short of eternity to the present time, to the future – How far grander than idea from cramped imagination that God created. (warring against those very laws he established in all ⟨nature⟩ organic nature) the Rhinoceros of Java & Sumatra, that since the time of the Silurian, he has made a long succession of vile Molluscous animals – How beneath the dignity of him, who ⟨⟨is supposed to have⟩⟩ said let there be light & there was light. – ⟨⟨bad taste {whom it has been declared 'he said let there be light & there was light'. – ⟩⟩[22]

Here as elsewhere in the notebooks one finds hints of Darwin's later effort to provide a concept of God both more dignified and moral than that associated with traditional Christianity.[23] Darwin believed that God must have a different, higher character than the God of natural theology and scripture and that his own speculations could in effect lead to a better and higher view of God. Furthermore, he contended that creationist science provided a demeaning image of God.

Darwin's speculations on human nature were no less offensive to Anglican culture than were his views of God. Although in *On the origin of species* Darwin very carefully avoided the topic of human nature, quite early in his notebook speculations he realized that all his ideas would require a fundamental rethinking of the subject. In Notebook C, Darwin engaged in a lengthy meditation on the possibility that man was one of many intelligent beings and not the

---

[22] Ibid., D., 36–7, pp. 342–3.
[23] For an important discussion of Darwin's deep personal concerns about morality and the Christian God, see James R. Moore, 'Of love and death: why Darwin "gave up Christianity" ', in James R. Moore, ed., *History, humanity and evolution: essays for John C. Greene* (Cambridge: Cambridge University Press, 1989), pp. 195–230. Darwin's concern about the morality of the Christian God was at one with others of his intellectual generation, see Howard R. Murphy, 'The ethical revolt against Christian orthodoxy in early Victorian England', *American Historical Review*, 60 (1955), 800–17.

sole possessor of reason and intellect. He rejected the idea that human beings in contrast to animals could take pride in their ancestry:

Let man visit Ourang-outang in domestication, hear expressive whine, see its intelligence when spoken; as if it understood every word said – see its affection. – to those it knew. – see its passion & rage, sulkiness, & very actions of despair; ⟨⟨let him look at savage, roasting his parent, naked, artless, not improving yet improvable⟩⟩ & then let him dare to boast of his proud preeminence. – ⟨⟨not understanding language of Fuegian, puts on par with Monkeys⟩⟩[24]

Darwin observed the similarity of human beings and animals and rejected the traditional manner in which human beings proclaimed their superiority to the latter:

It is our arrogance, to raise on the same shelf – to (look at common ancestor,(scarcely[)] conceivable in savages) Has not the white Man, who has debased his Nature ⟨⟨& violates every best instinctive feeling⟩⟩ by making slave of his fellow black, often wished to consider him as other animal – it is the way of mankind. & I believe those who soar above Such prejudices, yet have justly excalted [*sic*] nature of man. like to think his origin godlike, at least every nation has. done so as. yet. – [25]

In this passage Darwin directly challenged the mode of anthropological thought that had characterized Britain since the close of the eighteenth century when anthropology became used to establish the cultural superiority of Christian and genteel civilization.[26] Darwin confessed his own belief a few pages later, 'Man in his arrogance thinks himself a great work. worthy the interposition of a deity, more humble & I believe true to consider him created from animals.'[27] All of these comments on human nature flew in the face of an Anglican view of human nature as having a special place in the universe and the providence of God. Not until the appearance in 1871 of *The descent of man* would Darwin dare to voice these views publicly.

Finally, in by now well-known and much-analysed notebook passages, Darwin readily admitted that there existed a clear materialistic drift to his speculations. At one point in Notebook C while writing about heredity and habit, he chastised himself, 'Thought (or

[24] Darwin, C., 79, p. 264.   [25] Ibid., C., 154, p. 286.
[26] George W. Stocking, Jr, *Victorian anthropology* (New York: The Free Press, 1987), pp. 8–46.
[27] Darwin, C., 196, p. 300.

desires more properly) being heredetary⟨)⟩. – it is difficult to imagine it anything but structure of brain heredetary,. analogy points out to this. – love of the deity effect of organization. oh you Materialist!' A few lines later he pondered, 'Why is thought. being a secretion of the brain, more wonderful than gravity a property of matter? It is our arrogance, it our admiration of ourselves.' In Notebook N he went so far as to assert, '– the mind is function of body'. Darwin clearly saw affinities between the determinism in his own thought and that of Auguste Comte whose work he knew through a review by David Brewster. Darwin commented, 'M. le Comte argues against all contrivance – it is what my views tend to.' Darwin believed that both his ideas and Comte's suggested that animals were a product of their physical organization and further implied a determinism that 'would make a man a predestinarian of a new kind, because he would tend to be an atheist'.[28]

Darwin clearly recognized that his thought had drifted toward a position that most of his contemporaries would have called materialistic and therefore regarded as socially and intellectually dangerous. Such materialism linked him to the disreputable social and intellectual radicalism associated with French thought, philosophically advanced London medicine, and phrenology. To have marked himself publicly in that fashion would have put him at odds with the early Victorian scientific establishment as epitomized in the British Association and its kindred respectable London scientific societies with which he was at that time seeking to establish his credentials. As David Kohn has contended, Darwin received ongoing reminders of the potentially disruptive character of his thought from his wife who read his work and often suggested changes in language which Darwin followed.[29] Those social concerns and professional ambitions prevented Darwin from publishing his early essays on natural selection which he had penned in 1842 and 1844 contemporaneously with Newman's separating himself from Anglicanism.

Darwin like Newman was initially led into cultural apostasy as much by probing the ambiguities of certain important foundations of Anglican culture as by directly rejecting them. Images of a

[28] Ibid., C., 166, p. 291; N., 5, p. 564; M., 69–70, p. 535; M., 74, p. 536. Brewster's article on Comte appeared in the *Edinburgh Review*, 67 (1838), 271–308.
[29] Darwin, M., 57, pp. 532–3; Roger Cooter, *The cultural meaning of popular science: phrenology and the organization of consent in nineteenth-century Britain* (Cambridge: Cambridge University Press, 1984); David Kohn, 'Darwin's ambiguity: the secularization of biological meaning', *British Journal for the History of Science*, 22 (1989), 215–39.

thoroughly disharmonious nature lay poorly veiled in the works of Malthus and Anglican natural theology which Darwin knew intimately. His cultural apostasy occurred as he studied those works without accepting the particular theological interpretation which their authors put forth to rationalize the struggle, conflict, pain, and competition.[30] Darwin accepted the Malthusian war of nature and the Paleyan vision of pain and suffering in the natural order without recourse to a higher theological rationalization. Newman played upon the ambiguities of the Articles and indeed upon certain insecurities felt by mainline Anglicans about the character of their formularies so as to include within their compass modes of religious faith that most members of the Church of England believed the Articles had been constructed to exclude. Darwin similarly probed the literal statements of Malthus and Paley about the disharmony of nature, embraced that confusion, and then discerned order arising naturalistically from that very discord.

There was another link between the cultural apostasy of Darwin and that of Newman during the 1830s and 1840s despite the obvious profound differences in their thought and intellectual experience. Newman pressed for an open-ended and indeterminate view of the character of scripture, as well as the Articles, which was analogous to Darwin's approach to nature. Darwin approached nature directly by the close of the 1830s having rejected the systematic interpretation of nature implicit in Anglican natural theology. He could interpret nature differently only as he freed himself from that previous system which provided rationalizations for the pain and waste in the natural order. Simultaneously Newman approached the Bible having rejected the systematic exposition of that text printed at the bottom of the page in annotated Bibles such as that of Thomas Scott and inherent in evangelical theology that rationalized moral and historical discrepancies in the Bible. Newman could lead his readers and followers to a dogmatic view of the authority of the Church only when he had destroyed their confidence in the evangelical interpretive framework of the Bible. Newman interpreted the Bible as a work without clear divinely predetermined content in the

[30] In passages in the concluding chapter of *On the origin of species* Darwin does tend to construct a type of secular theodicy whereby he claims that all changes ultimately work toward the perfection of the species. However, there is little or no evidence of such a theodicy in his notebooks or the early sketches of his theory of natural selection. See Gillespie, *Charles Darwin and the problem of creation, passim,* and Chapter 4 of this volume.

same fashion that Darwin interpreted nature without divinely predetermined pattern. The former outlook dissolved the Anglican evangelical reading of scripture; the latter outlook dissolved the Anglican reading of nature.

Newman during the 1830s polemicized against the sufficiency of the authority of the Bible for Christian religious life as read by individuals according to the system of evangelical exposition. He pursued this polemic by setting forth arguments of a highly sceptical character in regard to scripture. In Tract 85, *Lectures on the scripture proof of the doctrines of the Church*, published in 1838 two years after Darwin returned from the *Beagle* voyage, Newman argued that there was no reason to regard the Bible as more than it appeared to be, that is, a collection of diverse writings composed by many different authors for a variety of purposes. The formal doctrines of the Church existed only latently in scripture as 'by a sort of accident' and could not be clearly discerned by a single individual's reading of scripture.[31] The general purpose of Newman's tract was to argue that a Christian must accept the superior authority of the Church over that of his or her own individual discernment of doctrine in scripture. Newman's tactic was to present the fragility and totally unsystematic character of scripture and to emphasize its character as a collection of disparate writings bound by particular historical experiences. The authoritative discernment of purpose or doctrines in those unsystematic ancient writings was the function of the dogmatic teaching of the Church. Reading scripture by itself without the aid of tradition could not properly illuminate those dogmatic truths since the scriptures themselves did not present a clear statement of doctrine.

Newman wished to displace one religious authority, that of a private individual reading and interpreting scripture, with another, that of an authoritative Church. His tactic was to urge that scripture was such a confused collection of ancient texts that only an external divine authority could find sense and purpose in them. Scripture did not explicate itself. In setting forth these arguments, which often very closely replicated eighteenth-century anti-Christian attacks on the authority of scripture, Newman commented,

God effects His greatest ends by apparent accidents. As in respect to this earth, we do not find minerals or plants arranged within it as in a cabinet –

---

[31] [John Henry Newman], *No. 85. Lectures on the scripture proof of the doctrines of the Church* (London: J. F. and G. Rivington, 1840), p. 34.

as we do not find the materials for building laid out in order, stone, timber, and iron, – as metal is found in ore, and timber on the tree, – so we must not be surprised, but think it great gain, though we find revealed doctrines scattered about high and low in Scripture, in places expected and unexpected. It could not be otherwise, the same circumstances being supposed. Supposing fire, water, and certain chemical and electrical agents in free operation, the earth's precious contents *could* not be found arranged in order and in the light of day without a miracle; and so without a miracle (which we are no where told to expect) we could not possibly find in Scripture all sacred truth in their place, each taught clearly and fully, with its suitable prominence, its varied bearings, its developed meaning, supposing Scripture to be, what it is, the work of various independent minds in various times and places, and under various circumstances.[32]

In this remarkable passage Newman approached scripture in a manner not unlike that which Darwin in the privacy of his notebooks and early sketches of natural selection was contemporaneously approaching nature. Darwin saw nature, as Newman did scripture, as an unsystematic arrangement in which order emerged through accidents or as Darwin would eventually say chance or random occurrence.

The purpose or divine ends that expositors discerned in scripture or nature depended upon the presuppositions they brought to each. Newman believed that without assuming the presence external to scripture of the divinely guided expository authority of the Church or some other presupposed external interpretive system one could not find systematic doctrines present in scripture. Similarly Darwin believed the ends of nature discerned by the natural theologians were present only if one approached nature with their external theological presuppositions. Remove those presuppositions, and neither scripture nor nature taught what contemporary Anglican theologians claimed them to teach.

Newman throughout his adult life found neither natural theology nor individual reading of scripture persuasive. He escaped the religious scepticism inherent in his position by resorting to the authority of first the Anglican and then the Roman Catholic Church. His particular concept of Anglicanism isolated him within that communion; his conversion to Rome isolated him within English culture. Both isolations emerging from his search for an authoritative Church were the result of his cultural as well as religious

[32] Ibid., pp. 33–4.

apostasy from the reading of scripture embraced to a greater or lesser degree by most Anglicans. Darwin for his part accepted intellectually the scepticism inherent in his own analysis of nature. He did, however, for many years pull back from publishing it because he very clearly understood the implications of that scepticism for English cultural values and the potential social isolation that he and his family might encounter.[33]

During the same years that Newman publicly challenged the traditional gloss on the Articles and the evangelical interpretation of scripture and Darwin privately pondered materialism and transmutation, John Ruskin commenced his career as the most important Victorian critic of art and architecture. Just as the Protestant gloss on the Articles had circumscribed English religious life and the gloss of natural theology had limited speculation about nature, the critical gloss set forth in Sir Joshua Reynolds's *Discourses* and prescriptively exemplified in the landscapes of Claude and Poussin had established limits of expression for artists. In the first two volumes of *Modern painters*, John Ruskin challenged the contemporary boundaries of art and laid the foundations for a radically subjective and amoral aesthetic that would become fully realized only during the third quarter of the century. Ruskin's later social and economic radicalism has paradoxically served to obscure the aesthetic radicalism of his earlier writings.

When publishing the first volume of *Modern painters* in 1843, Ruskin identified himself only as 'An Oxford Graduate'. That designation associated the work with one of the conservative ancient universities and the respectability accruing therefrom. The ideas contained in *Modern painters* were anything but ancient, conservative, or respectable. The book was very much the work of a young author sure of his message for the world. Ruskin's later reputation as a sage and authority of taste concealed the extreme headiness and boisterous confidence of his first work. Ruskin by the end of his life became transformed into an institution, first by the various societies

---

[33] The theme of isolation among Victorian intellectuals is one that might well be pursued further. James Secord has made interesting suggestions in regard to Robert Chambers. Alfred Russel Wallace articulated his version of evolution through natural selection while in Malaysia when he was unmarried with virtually no family responsibilities. See James A. Secord, 'Behind the veil: Robert Chambers and *Vestiges*', in Moore, ed., *History, humanity and evolution*, pp. 165–94; H. Lewis McKinney, *Wallace and natural selection* (New Haven: Yale University Press, 1972); Malcolm J. Kottler, 'Charles Darwin and Alfred Russel Wallace: two decades of debate over natural selection', in Kohn, ed., *The Darwinian heritage*, pp. 367–434.

founded around his teachings, and then by the careful management of his declining years by the Severns. To the extent that he was regarded as radical it was in the arena of social thought rather than aesthetic criticism.

Furthermore, within a decade of his death, the great thirty-nine-volume edition of his collected works appeared, and 'Ruskin' came to be equated with those heavy volumes. As other scholars have pointed out, the magnificent multivolume edition of Ruskin's works conceals the truth that many of his writings were published in small volumes, articles, and pamphlets. The urgency and dynamic energy of Ruskin stood rigidified. The great bound volumes hindered seeing the differences between the contents of the various books and essays, the time elapsing between their composition, and the tension existing between those publications and the cultural context in which they appeared. In particular, the youthful audacity of the early achievements became obscured. Ruskin the widely admired cultural sage eclipsed Ruskin the cultural apostate. Consequently, *Modern painters* came to be interpreted from the reputation of the elderly Ruskin rather than from the subversiveness of the young Ruskin.

As the young writer of 1843, Ruskin forcefully championed modern painters and most especially J. M. W. Turner against the ancient painters of the seventeenth century and the aesthetics of Reynolds. Ruskin cast himself in the role of aggressive spokesman for modern art and for art that broke with what he regarded as a bad tradition. He portrayed Turner as a modern protagonist who had overcome the burden of the past. Ruskin's championing of Turner in 1843 foreshadowed his championing of the Pre-Raphaelites a decade later. In both cases he emphasized the modern and the innovative against artists who adhered to older traditions approved by Reynolds.

Ruskin, drawing upon the romantic tradition, demanded that the particular beauties of nature itself be portrayed. He repeatedly criticized and excoriated the seventeenth-century landscape painters for deviating from a truthful representation of real, actual nature. Just as Newman was rejecting the glosses on the Thirty-Nine Articles and Darwin the gloss of natural theology on the interpretation of nature, Ruskin similarly argued that to portray the beauty of nature, it must be understood directly in terms of immediate sensations rather than Platonically or through the traditional artistic modes provided by the Old Masters. This outlook associated Ruskin with romantic critics, such as Blake, who stood outside the circle of Anglican respectability in a manner similar to the Roman Catholics who attracted Newman and the radical transmutationists whose thought bore affinities with Darwin's. Ruskin's aesthetic was one that broke through traditional boundaries instead of reinforcing them.

In the initial volume of *Modern painters* Ruskin raised the most profound kind of questions about the prescriptive adequacy of the classical landscapes of Poussin and Claude and the adequacy of Reynolds's aesthetics. Reynolds, in the tradition of Bellori, had spoken of the artist seeking to express a beauty he had not and would never see. Throughout *Modern painters*, volume 1, Ruskin attacked and rejected convention in art as he unremittingly criticized Reynolds's injunction to copy the masters. Ruskin for his part urged the artist to look directly at nature rather than at the paintings of the past. The role of artists was that of 'followers and historians of nature', and their rank should be established according to the success with which they achieved those ends.[34]

Ruskin demanded that artists conceive of and express beauty in its earthly rather than in its intellectual manifestations. In his notebooks Darwin at one point commented, 'When we talk of higher orders, we should always say, intellectually higher. – But who with the face of the earth covered with the most beautiful savannahs & forests dare to say that intellectuality is only aim in this world.'[35] Ruskin would have sympathized with that outlook and in particular would have agreed with Darwin that nature must be confronted on its own terms and not in terms of intellectual beauty or conventional artistic norms of beauty. No less important, he transformed artists into real, concrete human beings who were part of historic communities and who expressed the character of those particular communities rather than some mode of Platonic knowledge.

The beauty that Reynolds praised and believed the best artists might attain was a highly intellectualized beauty toward which the artist might strive but never actually achieve. In contrast, Ruskin's was a moral beauty achieved through the subjective transformation of the artist's own personal experience of physical nature. The landscape artist first faithfully reproduced nature but then guided

34 E. T. Cook and Alexander Wedderburn, *The works of John Ruskin* (London: G. Allen, 1903), III, 130.
35 Darwin, B., 252, p. 233.

the viewer toward genuinely worthy objects and allowed the viewer to share his thoughts. Ruskin declared that

in attaining the second end, the artist not only *places* the spectator, but *talks* to him; makes him a sharer in his own strong feelings and quick thoughts; hurries him away in his own enthusiasm; guides him to all that is beautiful; snatches him from all that is base; and leaves him more than delighted, – ennobled and instructed, under the sense of having not only beheld a new scene, but of having held communion with a new mind, and having been endowed for a time with the keen perception and the impetuous emotions of a nobler and more penetrating intelligence.[36]

Whereas Reynolds and earlier writers had seen the painter as aspiring to an intellectual and necessarily partial experience of beauty, Ruskin concentrated on the relationship of the spectator and the painter and a shared subjective experience:

We do not want his [the artist's] mind to be like a badly blown glass, that distorts what we see through it, but like a glass of sweet and strange colour, that gives new tones to what we see through it; and a glass of rare strength and clearness too, to let us see more than we could ourselves, and bring nature up to us and near to us.[37]

In these and other comments Ruskin was transfiguring the usual meaning of knowledge in painting. The sign of the presence of such new knowledge was not the following of convention but rather brilliance, vigour, and even strangeness because what previous critics would have called audacity Ruskin called knowledge. Even more important, Ruskin transformed the morality associated with the observation of art from the pursuit or experience of an objective transcendental moral ideal into the subjective moral perception of the individual artist who through his personal genius possessed the capacity to provide moral instruction. Artistic antinomianism replaced the pursuit of Platonic ideals.

This rejection of any kind of objective moral or artistic truth permeated the first as well as the subsequent volumes of *Modern painters*. Ruskin repeatedly criticized the ideal of the representation of general truth. No injunction had been so dear to the voices of neoclassical criticism in all fields as this pursuit of general truth. Ruskin caustically commented that

---

[36] Cook and Wedderburn, *The works of John Ruskin*, III, 133–4.
[37] Ibid., 137.

it is carelessly and falsely said that general ideas are more important than particular ones; carelessly and falsely, I say, because the so-called general idea is important, not because it is common to all the individuals of that species, but because it separates that species from everything else. It is the distinctiveness, not the universality of the truth, which renders it important. And the so-called particular idea is unimportant, not because it is not predicable of the whole species, but because it *is* predicable of things out of that species. It is not its individuality, but its generality, which renders it unimportant. So then truths are important just in proportion as they are characteristic; and are valuable, primarily, as they separate the species from other created things; secondarily, as they separate the individuals of that species from one another.[38]

Within this attack on the prescriptive character of the general lay a radical emphasis on the particular that could lead to the dissolving of boundaries whether natural, social, or moral. Inherent was a thoroughgoing individualism that derived from Ruskin's emphasis upon the subjective genius and power of the individual artist. All convention was to fall before the particular moral insights of the individual. It was that same rejection of conventional reading of the Articles, scripture, and nature that had informed the radical thought of Newman and Darwin.

In addition to this rejection of convention and general truth, Ruskin decried the role of repetition. He regarded the painting of nature as an infinite series of opportunities to experience and then replicate the individual truths of nature. His description of the process undermined all convention, emphasized process, and left neither the artist nor the viewer with any certain ground:

The teaching of nature is as varied and infinite as it is constant; and the duty of the painter is to watch for every one of her lessons, and to give . . . those in which she has manifested each of her principles in the most peculiar and striking way. The deeper his research and the rarer the phenomena he has noted, the more valuable will his works be; to repeat himself, even in a single instance, is treachery to nature, for a thousand human lives would not be enough to give one instance of the perfect manifestation of each of her powers; and as for combining or classifying them, as well might a preacher expect in one sermon to express and explain every divine truth which can be gathered out of God's revelation, as a painter expect in one composition to express and illustrate every lesson which can be received from God's creation.[39]

[38] Ibid., 152.   [39] Ibid., 156–7.

The prose in this passage stands as a forecast of Pater's later infamous 'Conclusion' to *The renaissance: studies in art and poetry* (1873) with its description of failure as the formation of habits and the injunction to pursue rare and exotic moments of experience. With Ruskin as with Pater's later aesthetic decadence the experience of nature has become a flux.

Virtually all of Ruskin's contentions in volume 1 of *Modern painters* point toward that later more radical aesthetic in which convention and objective morality dissolve in the pursuit of the momentary subjective experience. Nothing could have been further from the mainline aesthetic and artistic theories and opinions of the first four decades of the century. The view of beauty derived from Reynolds and from Bellori before him was an austere intellectual beauty associated with the emanation of the One and available only to certain artists. Ruskin's beauty was visible throughout the world in a variety as infinite as the infinity of God in his creation. For Ruskin, beauty resided not in the conventional rendering of an intellectual insight that builds upon similar insights of previous artists but rather in the precise rendering of a single subjective experience from an infinite number of such experiences of physical nature. Indeed, Ruskin contended, 'All really great pictures ... exhibit the general habits of nature, manifested in some peculiar, rare, and beautiful way.'[40] Ruskin condemned the Old Masters as 'prodigals, and foolish prodigals in art' because 'they lavish their whole means to get one truth, and leave themselves powerless when they should seize a thousand'.[41] This outlook rendered the aesthetic experience virtually open-ended, grounded in the experience of physical nature with few, if any, limits or bounds.

In the long, important preface to the second edition of the first volume of *Modern painters*, published in 1844, Ruskin in attempting to clarify a number of his ideas expressed them in a far more radical manner. Although knowledge of earlier art protected artists from being 'swept away by the rage of fashion, or lost in the glare of novelty', they still retained the right to advance beyond the accomplishments of the past.[42] Ruskin declared, 'Any given generation has just the same chance of producing some individual mind of first-rate calibre, as any of its predecessors; and ... if such a mind *should* arise, the chances are, that, with the assistance of experience and

[40] Ibid., 157. [41] Ibid., 262. [42] Ibid., 11.

example, it would, in its particular and chosen path, do greater things than had been before done'.[43] A young artist should suspect those who would have him simply reject the past, but he must be no less suspicious of those whose emphasis on the past would 'fetter his strength from all advance, and bend his eyes backward on a beaten path; who would thrust canvas between him and the sky, and tradition between him and God'.[44] Ruskin reminded such artists that 'all that is highest in art, all that is creative and imaginative, is formed and created by every great master for himself, and cannot be repeated or imitated by others'.[45] Ruskin's rejection of prescriptive tradition and his antinomian emphasis on the role of individual artistic genius represented the rejection in an aesthetic arena of the conservative emphasis on tradition that would politically have been associated with Burke, Coleridge, and similar spokesmen for the traditionalism of Anglican culture or what Paul Fussell in a different context termed 'Augustan humanism'.[46]

By 1846 when Ruskin published volume II of *Modern painters*, his attitude had become even more culturally subversive. In describing the advance of the imaginative artist, he insisted,

He owns no laws. He defies all restraint, and cuts down all hedges. There is nothing within the limits of natural possibility that he dares not do, or that he allows the necessity of doing. The laws of nature he knows; these are to him no restraint. They are his own nature. All other laws or limits he sets at utter defiance; his journey is over an untrodden and pathless plain. But he sees his end over the waste from the first, and goes straight at it; never losing sight of it, nor throwing away a step. Nothing can stop him, nothing turn him aside; falcons and lynxes are of slow and uncertain sight compared with his.[47]

Here was a manifesto of cultural apostasy reflecting Carlyle's hero that when carried to its limits would lead to the cultural anarchy against which two decades later Matthew Arnold would rail. Ruskin's artist further prefigures in the aesthetic realm the general role John Stuart Mill assigned to the intellectual genius in *On liberty* (1859). Throughout the first two volumes of *Modern painters*, there runs an appeal to the subjective and unconventional that as early as his important prefaces of the 1850s Arnold combated. Indeed part of

---

[43] Ibid., 12.   [44] Ibid., 12.   [45] Ibid., 12.
[46] Paul Fussell, *The rhetorical world of Augustan humanism: ethics and imagery from Swift to Burke* (Oxford: Oxford University Press, 1965).
[47] Cook and Wedderburn, *The works of John Ruskin*, IV, 239.

Arnold's agenda during the 1860s and 1870s was to reestablish Anglican culture on new grounds. The subjectivism of Ruskin like the radical individualism of Mill was the great enemy to that culture.

Ruskin's aesthetic presented an open-ended path for the development of art beyond existing conventional boundaries that was paralleled in Darwin's image of a nature similarly evolving in yet to be determined directions. Ruskin's emphasis on the individual artist forging his own tradition also in many respects paralleled Newman's thought of the 1840s. Although Newman presented himself as reasserting the role of ancient religious tradition, in both his rejection of the longstanding reading of the Articles and his eventual conversion to Roman Catholicism, his thought and actions actually flowed from radically subjective and individualistic readings of religious traditions and history. He approached religious life and tradition with little less than the aesthetic radicalism of Ruskin's artist. For all of his appeal to tradition Newman's religious journey was paradoxically a distinctly modern one. His *Essay on the development of Christian doctrine* (1845) constituted a vindication of the spiritual validity of the modern Roman Catholic Church as a legitimate development of the Church of earlier times and a rejection of the Protestant position that the Church must resemble the ancient original New Testament institution.

When Newman asserted in 1845 that 'to live is to change and to be perfect is to have changed often', he pointed to a pattern that the lives of many of his contemporaries would trace.[48] The changes that they wrought in their own personal intellectual lives began to link them to areas of English culture that had previously been either suspect or anathema to Anglicans. Newman himself drifted into Roman Catholicism. Darwin's thought led him toward the ideas associated with radicals and Nonconformists in the London medical and scientific community. Ruskin's aesthetic lay deeply rooted in romantic theories that were suspect in the eyes of upper-class Anglicans.

Yet these and other examples of cultural apostasy during the late 1830s and early 1840s provided the foundation stones for the major elements of high Victorian culture. Newman's cultural apostasy

---

[48] John Henry Newman, *An essay on the development of Christian doctrine* (London: Penguin Books, 1974), p. 100.

fostered the radical high church movement, the claims to inclusion in the Church by liberal Anglicans, and the mid-century second spring of Roman Catholicism. Darwin's thinking explored the most radical strains of thought associated with Victorian scientific naturalism and its claims to scientific autonomy from theology and religious cultural authority. Ruskin sowed the seeds of the extreme subjectivity of Victorian aestheticism. High Victorian intellectual life from the mid-sixties through the mid-eighties would not have been what it was without the impact of the cultural apostasy of the 1830s and 1840s. By the 1860s elite Victorian intellectual life had begun to domesticate many of those strains of thought that Anglican culture had rejected or sought to insulate itself against three decades earlier. Ruskin's subjective aestheticism remained the most difficult for Victorians to assimilate as witnessed by the harsh criticism encountered by Pater, Swinburne, and Wilde. Yet even as early as 1877 the aesthetes found their way into the conversations of W. H. Mallock's *The new republic*.

The foundation of high Victorian culture and intellectual life lay grounded in a series of deeply personal fallings away from the major ideals of early nineteenth-century thought and values and most particularly those associated with Anglicanism. The leaders of high Victorian intellectual life who became the eminent Victorians of the close of the century had lost faith in one culture and forged the sinews of another based on naturalism, religious experiment, and subjective aesthetic response. They had been rebels and intellectual revolutionaries, but most fundamentally they had been cultural apostates. It was their experiences of cultural apostasy that explains historically why the Victorian thought of the 1860s and 1870s differed so sharply from that of the decade just before and after Victoria's ascension to the throne. Other Anglicans felt they must come to grips with those dangerous ideas and must attempt to refute them lest their culture be endangered by such apostasy. It was as much from that intra-Anglican cultural struggle as from the response to hostile external non-Anglican critics that the Victorian culture of the third quarter of the century emerged with all of its pluralism and frequent intellectual conflict.

CHAPTER 3

The crisis of faith and the faith that was lost

A more familiar feature of Victorian intellectual life than the cultural apostasy of Anglicans turning against their cultural setting are the cases of individuals who experienced a loss of faith in Christianity. In the past scholars have generally regarded the situations involving such Christian faith in crisis as primarily an intellectual experience. They have tended to point to works of dissolvent literature associated with Enlightenment rationalism, the higher criticism of the Bible, or new theories of physical science as the chief causes for particular persons modifying or rejecting the faith of their childhoods. The nineteenth-century documents recording the loss of faith experience in no small measure themselves led to that conclusion. In their autobiographies Victorian doubters and un-believers often recalled the impact of advanced works of science, biblical criticism, or history upon their religious thought and then recounted the manner in which those new ideas had led them to renounce major Christian doctrines, to stop attending church, to change denominations, to leave the Christian ministry, or to em-brace atheism, agnosticism, or some other substitute for traditional Christianity. Many of the loss of faith novels, such as *The autobiography of Mark Rutherford* (1881) and *Robert Elsmere* (1888), embodied this same scenario. Furthermore, the earliest histories that examined the rise of religiously dissolvent literature, such as *A critical history of free thought* (1862) by A. S. Farrar, *History of rationalism* (1867) by J. F. Hurst, and *The history of English rationalism in the nineteenth century* (1906) by A. W. Benn set forth this intellectualist analysis. Twen-tieth-century historians and literary scholars generally pursued a

From Richard J. Helmstadter and Bernard Lightman, eds., *Victorian faith in crisis: essays on continuity and change in nineteenth-century religious belief*, with permission of the publishers, The Macmillan Press Ltd, and Stanford University Press. © 1990 Richard J. Helmstadter and Bernard Lightman.

similar mode of analysis. They rather uncritically assumed that intellectual factors or motivations alone must have moulded actions claimed by the Victorians to have been taken for intellectual reasons.

In recent years somewhat new outlooks have come to inform the historical, religious, and literary considerations of Victorian faith in crisis.[1] Scholars from various fields now regard the Victorian crisis in faith as a *problematical* occurrence. That is to say, they no longer regard it as the inevitable and virtually self-explanatory result of the expansion of progressive historical and scientific knowledge. They have stopped reading the documents recording and analysing changes in faith at face value. James Moore's important analysis of the military metaphor in the debates over the relationship of science and religion has alerted Victorian scholars to the subtle and powerful polemic that may reside in what appear to be non-polemical, rather matter of fact figures of speech.[2] Recent literary criticism has awakened a new awareness of the manner in which setting personal experiences into a narrative format, such as the autobiography, reshapes the experiences so narrated, brings them under control, and provides outer ordered form to what was a more formless and much less orderly subjective experience. Narrative may in that manner render a fearful experience into a more nearly safe and familiar one. Consequently, the content of a narrative almost inevitably constitutes only a portion of the experience narrated and cannot be regarded as an unproblematic record. Finally, even the barest acquaintance with psychology leads the scholar to understand that behind intellectual and intellectualized experiences reside non-rational and non-intellectual forces of feeling and emotion which may both mask and manifest themselves in rational appearances.

Without intending to deny the power of the printed word on the mind or the efficacy of ideas on actions, scholars now feel that it is necessary to think more critically and sensitively about the social and cultural functions and meanings of that Victorian behaviour traditionally subsumed under the terms 'loss of faith' or 'crisis of

[1] Helmstadter and Lightman, eds., *Victorian faith in crisis: essays on continuity and change in nineteenth-century religious belief* (London: Macmillan, 1990); on the American side see James Turner, *Without god, without creed: the origins of unbelief in America* (Baltimore: Johns Hopkins Press, 1985).

[2] James R. Moore, *The post-Darwinian controversies: a study of the Protestant struggle to come to terms with Darwin in Great Britain and America, 1870–1900* (Cambridge: Cambridge University Press, 1979), pp. 19–76.

faith' or 'faith in crisis'. Why did the loss of faith as an observable and much discussed cultural phenomenon commence in the 1840s rather than in the immediate wake of the rationalist writings of the eighteenth-century Enlightenment which would seem to have provided more than enough critical ideas to shake religious faith if ideas alone were the crucial motivating factor? Were there elements in the religious life of the nineteenth century rather than in the dissolvent literature itself that contributed to the loss of faith or determined the course of its occurrence? Why did unorthodox or advanced dissolvent religious ideas find in certain cases a mind or heart prepared to receive them? To what extent were the actions of some persons who experienced a loss of faith related to areas of their lives that were distinct from religion proper? Did their turmoil and apostasy in regard to the Christian supernatural allow them in some manner to deal with natural modes of personal human development that might have been even more painful and traumatic if confronted directly than if mediated through the obviously (indeed necessarily obviously) painful experience of loss or change of faith? In other words, what can be understood about the loss of faith phenomena if scholars regard them as something that did occur in the middle and late years of the nineteenth century rather than as something that necessarily had to occur simply as the result of the march of mind? Finally, what new insights into the Victorian crisis of belief can be achieved if scholars regard religious behaviour as a product of social and psychological interaction among human beings rather than as a manifestation of the interaction of human beings with the divine which has remained the often unstated working assumption of much previous scholarly literature on the subject?

A remarkable and virtually unnoticed irony lies at the very heart of the problem of nineteenth-century religious doubt, unbelief, and scepticism. Victorian faith entered crisis not in the midst of any attack on religion but rather during the period of the most fervent religious crusade that the British nation had known since the seventeenth century, indeed during the last great effort on the part of all denominations to Christianize Britain. The religion that was rejected, modified, and transformed in the lives of generally young intellectuals was not some mode of staid long-established Christianity (whatever that may be) but rather a recently intensified faith associated with militant Christian institutions. In this regard it seems virtually certain that the personal criticism of ecclesiastical institutions arose less from dissolvent, sceptical literature than from a Christian faith that had become overbearingly intense on the personal and vocational levels and shamelessly embittered through inter- and intra-denominational conflict on the political, educational, and social scenes.

Broadly speaking, three basic interrelated factors led to this intensified religious life. First, the political reaction to the French Revolution brought religion to the forefront of public life.[3] Many of the policies of the revolution were anti-clerical, and others, distinctly anti-Christian. Edmund Burke's counterrevolutionary polemic blamed the turmoil in France on atheistic and materialistic writers. He further linked his criticism of France to the alleged danger of radical domestic political change posed by Protestant Nonconformists in general and the rationalist Unitarians in particular. In Burke's mind and that of others the ongoing resistance to the revolution assumed the character of a crusade to protect religion. As Britain assumed the leadership of the counterrevolutionary coalition against France the protection of religion in turn became increasingly associated with the preservation of the existing social and political structures. For all the propertied classes religion in general and Anglicanism in particular came to have a new importance and became something that required fostering. One manifestation of that public support for the Church of England was the post-Waterloo parliamentary grant for the building of new churches in London.

Also directly related to the anti-revolutionary political polemic was what can only be described as a revival in publications expounding natural religion. The connection between the pursuit of science and natural religion was, of course, a longstanding one, but a new intensity came to that viewpoint at the turn of the century as the religiosity of the anti-revolutionary ideology required British intellectuals working in and near scientific and rational thought to reassert their own orthodox religious commitment. From the publication of Paley's *Natural·theology* (1802) onward one work of natural theology after another fell from British printing presses with the Bridgewater treatises being the most famous. Two strategies

---

[3] Robert Hole, *Pulpits, politics and public order in England, 1760–1832* (Cambridge: Cambridge University Press, 1989); Ursula Henriques, *Religious toleration in England, 1787–1833* (Toronto: University of Toronto Press, 1961), pp. 99–135; Michael R. Watts, *The dissenters: from the reformation to the French revolution* (Oxford: Clarendon Press, 1978), pp. 478–90; V. Kiernan, 'Evangelicalism and the French Revolution', *Past and Present*, 1 (1952), 44–56.

were in operation. Clergymen appealed to natural theology to refute the alleged materialism, scepticism, and atheism of radical religious, philosophical, or scientific writers and also the problems inherent in Malthus's view of nature.[4] Scientists, who were of course also often clergymen, in turn appropriated a new emphasis on natural theology to demonstrate that science and rational thought correctly understood would lead not to materialism, atheism, and revolution as in France but rather to reverence for God and support for the existing political and social order. The leadership of the British Association for the Advancement of Science (1831) consciously used natural religion both to protect science from dangerous political associations, previously embodied by the radical Unitarian scientist Joseph Priestley, and to advance the cause of science among the propertied classes during the era of reform.[5]

The second factor leading to an intensified religious life arose from the attack on, and demise of, the exclusive Anglican confessional state. The undermining of the Anglican religious-political monopoly had begun in earnest with the late eighteenth-century drive by Protestant Nonconformists to secure broader civil rights and later became most fully realized in the repeal of the Test Act, the passage of Catholic Emancipation, the restructuring of the finances of the Church of England, and eventually in the disestablishment of the Anglican Church in Ireland and Wales. In the face of these destructive reforms and the unrelenting Nonconformist attacks and institutional growth, the Church of England found that it must henceforth compete as a denomination in the religious marketplace. Such competition required Anglicans to define themselves theologically, and that process in turn, especially as a result of the Tractarian movement, generated competing parties within the Established Church. Consequently, one result of the Anglican loss of political privilege was a marked resurgence in the religious activity of the Church of England as well as new political actions to preserve its

---

[4] A. M. C. Waterman, *Revolution, economics and religion: Christian political economy, 1798–1833* (Cambridge: Cambridge University Press, 1991), pp. 114–36.
[5] Jack Morrell and Arnold Thackray, *Gentlemen of science: early years of the British Association for the Advancement of Science* (Oxford: Clarendon Press, 1981), pp. 224–45; Nicolaas A. Rupke, *The great chain of history: William Buckland and the English school of geology (1814–1849)* (Oxford: Clarendon Press, 1983), pp. 29–34, 209–18; 231–74; Henriques, *Religious toleration in England*, pp. 206–59.

surviving advantages or to recapture lost ones. Furthermore, in addition to this resurgence of Anglican activity there occurred further new religious activity and denominational competition resulting from the Great Disruption in the Church of Scotland, the expansion of the Protestant Nonconformist denominations, the Roman Catholic revival in Ireland led by Paul Cullen, and the restoration of the Roman Catholic hierarchy in England under Nicholas Wiseman.[6]

The third significant manifestation of new intensity in British religious life was the late eighteenth- and early nineteenth-century evangelical revival. Evangelical Christianity was an intensely personal religion grounded in subjective religious experience which could and often did lead to intense introspection. Evangelical Christians spurned nominal Christianity that allegedly involved the outward forms without the inner experience confirming the presence of real Christian faith. Evangelicals were also Christians of the Bible as read (by no means always literally) and interpreted by individual believers. Evangelicals thus tended to put much more emphasis on the role of the laity rather than of the clergy and regarded the visible church as less important than the eternal, invisible church. For evangelicals faith did come by hearing the preaching of the word and responding to that preaching, but faith also came and received nurture through reading the word and through reading devotional works about the Bible and the Christian faith, many of which were authored by laymen. Finally, evangelicals were quite concerned with the teaching of particular crucial doctrines of which the efficacy of Christ's redemptive atonement was perhaps the most important. The centrality of the atonement led them to emphasize the Trinity. Thus, any tendency toward a Unitarian view of Christ as a noble, but less than fully divine, person was theologically no less pernicious

---

[6] Owen Chadwick, *The Victorian Church* (New York: Oxford University Press, 1966), I, 7–66; P. T. Marsh, *The Victorian Church in decline* (London: Routledge and Kegan Paul, 1969); Kenneth Inglis, *The churches and the working classes in Victorian England* (London: Routledge and Kegan Paul, 1963); George Kitson Clark, *The making of Victorian England* (Cambridge, Mass.: Harvard University Press, 1962), pp. 147–205; J. Edwin Orr, *The second evangelical awakening in Britain* (London: Marshall, Morgan, and Scott, 1949); Olive J. Brose, *Church and parliament: the reshaping of the Church of England, 1828–1860* (Stanford: Stanford University Press, 1959); G. I. T. Machin, *Politics and the churches in Great Britain, 1832–1868* (Oxford: Clarendon Press, 1978); Henriques, *Religious toleration in England*, pp. 1–174; Jeffrey Cox, *The English churches in a secular society: Lambeth, 1870–1930* (Oxford: Oxford University Press, 1982), pp. 3–47.

in the eyes of evangelicals than were radical Unitarian political ideas.[7]

Political reaction, denominational rivalry, and evangelicalism expanded the arena of religion in terms of both personal belief and social behaviour far beyond the normal existential and tragic dilemmas of life and death that seem always to arouse religious sentiments. In so doing, these forces of intensified religiosity sowed the dragon teeth that generated the soldiers of unbelief. By the end of the third decade of the century British Christianity was neither institutionally passive nor spiritually nominal. The sphere of religion during these years and after touched upon more and more personal and public concerns. This expansion and intensification of personal and public religious life transformed religion into a significant and problematic burden. Increasing numbers of people for a variety of reasons had to define or redefine their thinking about the nature and meaning of religious activity.

Paradoxically a religion that is not oppressive, intrusive, or demanding of substantial time and attention or one that remains more or less compartmentalized from other social and intellectual concerns, as would seem to have been the case with both eighteenth-century Anglicanism and Nonconformity, does not generate personal crisis and inner conflict. In such a circumstance there exists no fervent faith to be lost or to assert its presence in some other kind of problematical manner. Such times of quiescent or cold faith seem to generate revivals instead of doubt. By contrast it is expansive, intensified religion, as in this case fostered theologically first by Methodism and the evangelical revival and later by the Oxford Movement, that establishes a faith to be lost. Only a person with a firm faith can lose it in a problematical fashion, and he or she will lose it in a manner directly related to the character and expectations of the faith itself. In that respect the loss of faith or the modification of faith are inherently religious acts largely conditioned by and channelled through the spiritual categories and social expectations

[7] Geoffrey Best, 'Evangelicalism and the Victorians', in Anthony Symondson, ed., *The Victorian crisis of faith* (London: Society for Promoting Christian Knowledge, 1970), pp. 37–56; Geoffrey Best, 'The evangelicals and the established church in the early nineteenth century', *Journal of Theological Studies*, 10 (1959), 63–78; F. K. Brown, *Fathers of the Victorians* (Cambridge: Cambridge University Press, 1961); Ian Bradley, *The call to seriousness: the evangelical impact on the Victorians* (London: Jonathan Cape, 1976); Elizabeth Jay, *The religion of the heart: Anglican evangelicalism and the nineteenth-century novel* (Oxford: Clarendon Press, 1979); Boyd Hilton, *The age of atonement: the influence of evangelicalism on social and economic thought, 1785–1865* (Oxford: Clarendon Press, 1988).

of the original community of faith. To the extent that an intensified religion has attached itself to modes or institutions of normal personality development, it may find itself challenged as individual personalities achieve maturation. Finally, to the extent that intensified religion has made extensive cultural or moral claims, those who reject it may do so on the grounds that other sets of beliefs or other ideas appear better able to fulfil those goals.

The character of evangelical religion determined many of the forms and categories through which the protagonists of unbelief felt they must explain or give voice to the experience. The key validation of evangelical Christian faith was the subjective experience of conversion to which the believer afterwards offered witness in terms of actual verbal testimony and through the high moral quality of his or her subsequent personal life. The wrongs, evils, sins, and moral inadequacies of the old life and the shallowness of any previous faith had to be recounted and the joys, benefits, and sincere moral and spiritual earnestness of the new faith presented. One of the chief vehicles for the presentation of this conversion experience had been the spiritual autobiography that portrayed the passage from one life to another.

From the time of Carlyle's *Sartor resartus* (1833–4) onward Victorians who encountered a crisis of faith also often resorted to the literary genre of the autobiography or autobiographical novel.[8] That they adopted this genre is not surprising since it was the literary vehicle that had long been established to present a change in the direction of one's life and to assert the sincerity of that change. Evangelicals had directed their autobiographies toward former friends in an effort to persuade them of the desirability of the new Christian life. Victorians who lost faith in the Christianity of their childhood or who wished to change religious belief in some substantial manner similarly attempted to demonstrate their former religious orientation to have been morally and intellectually inadequate. Just as the evangelical conversion involved passage from a scene of worldly pleasures and easy friendships to one of spiritual rigour, so also did the loss of faith experience. Doubters and

---

[8] M. Maison, *The Victorian vision: studies in the religious novel* (New York: Sheed and Ward, 1961); R. L. Wolff, *Gains and losses: novels of faith and doubt in Victorian England* (New York: 1977); A. O. J. Cockshut, *The art of autobiography in nineteenth and twentieth century England* (New Haven: Yale University Press, 1984); Linda Peterson, *Victorian autobiography: the tradition of self-interpretation* (New Haven: Yale University Press, 1986).

unbelievers repeatedly presented their new lives pursued without the
solace and support of their original faith as more difficult, rigorous,
and in a sense less worldly than their earlier lives as conforming
Christians. They had left the way of easy faith for a more arduous
path. They had passed from a nominal religious life to a real one and
in the process they had moved from an intellectually and morally
inadequate position to one that accorded with the real, fundamental
truth of morality, history, and nature.

There were other evangelical resonances within those autobiographies or other autobiographical accounts of change in faith. The
importance attached by unbelievers to having heard particular
rationalist, secularist, or scientific lecturers followed the pattern of
evangelicals emphasizing having listened to particularly persuasive
preachers. The evangelical emphasis on the benefits of key works of
devotional literature found its equivalent in the new emphasis on the
power of certain texts of dissolvent scientific or historical scholarship.
Most important, the doubters and sceptics upheld the centrality of
the Bible for the experience of unbelief. With the unbeliever as with
the evangelical the reading of the scriptures led to the seeking of a
new life and a real faith. But what the unbelievers encountered in the
Bible were moral and intellectual difficulties that transformed the
greatest of all evangelical and Christian texts into a dangerous book
leading to doubt and scepticism rather than to faith and belief.
Finally, doubters of virtually all varieties claimed the moral high
ground. They contended that the doctrines of the atonement and
hell were immoral and that their abandonment in favour of melior-
istic, secular moralities was good for all concerned. Furthermore,
in the hands of a brilliant polemicist, such as W. K. Clifford, the
intellectual basis as well as the substance of what could and could
not be believed became a moral issue of the highest significance with
the true moral benefits flowing to those who rejected theology.[9]

In their critique of ecclesiastical institutions and doctrines Victorian unbelievers and agnostics pursued a path of lay religious
advocacy, criticism, and authorship pioneered two generations
earlier by the evangelicals. Evangelicalism in both its criticism of
nominal religion and in its devotional and organizational life had
been an overwhelmingly lay movement. Its founding text, William
Wilberforce's *Practical view of the prevailing religious conceptions of*

9 James C. Livingston, *The ethics of belief: an essay on the Victorian religious conscience* (Tallahassee,
   Fl.: American Academy of Religion, 1974).

professed Christians in the higher and middle classes in this country contrasted with real Christianity (1797) was the work of a layman. In such books and other polemics against the complacency of late eighteenth-century religion the evangelicals had provided a pattern for sharp criticism of ecclesiastical institutions on the basis of their inadequate moral, intellectual, and spiritual life. The unbelievers repeatedly echoed those charges.[10]

The activities of the advocates of scientific naturalism during the third quarter of the century in particular illustrate the actions of engaged laymen criticizing the adequacy of religion in a manner reminiscent of evangelicalism. Their attack pitted what they regarded as real religion, honest in thought and morally beneficient in action, against the nominal religion of the Anglican Church and to a lesser extent of the Church of Scotland. The Church of England had defended its position intellectually as upholding a learned theology that resisted the extremism of religious antinomianism on the one hand and the dangers of Roman Catholicism on the other. Anglican clerical scientists and other interested clergy had claimed to resist the inroads of materialism, which was regarded as a political and social as well as a spiritual danger, through their previously mentioned advocacy and support of natural theology. The scientists and scientifically minded philosophers associated with scientific naturalism sought to beat the Church of England at its own cultural game.

Like the evangelicals of an earlier day, the honest doubters and advocates of scientific naturalism demanded a truer and more genuine religion that was not an intellectual, moral, and political scandal. First, in their metaphysics despite their rather loose and continuously misunderstood polemical vocabulary Spencer, Tyndall, Huxley, and others of the camp of scientific naturalism presented themselves as opponents of any form of reductionist materialism. That is one reason why their adopting the name *agnostic* rather than *atheist* was an important political as well as intellectual move. In works, such as Spencer's *First principles*, and in philosophies, such as Tyndall's transcendental materialism, these publicists set forth new versions of generally evolutionary natural religion to replace those associated with the devout Anglican scientists. Second, the scientists attempted to present themselves as advocates of a

[10] Howard R. Murphy, 'The ethical revolt against Christian orthodoxy in early Victorian England', *American Historical Review*, 60 (1955), 800–17.

moderate religious stance in contrast to the revivalism, bibliolatry, superstition, and ritualism rampant within the contemporary Church of England. In the sixties and seventies it was by no means clear whether the ecclesiastical establishment could or even wanted to control extreme religious actions while it was clear that it wanted to silence advanced learning in the Church and the universities. The ineffectiveness of the attack by Anglican leaders on Anglo-Catholic ritualism even through parliamentary legislation only served to highlight the success of the vendetta against the authors of *Essays and reviews*.

Finally, the advocates of scientific naturalism moved to the fore as major public opponents of Roman Catholicism. Indeed, anti-Catholicism marked their polemics in a number of key documents – Huxley's speeches to the London School Board and his attacks on St George Jackson Mivart, Tyndall's Belfast Address, Spencer's and Edward Tylor's attacks on priestcraft, Clifford's aggressive anti-clericalism, and Leslie Stephen's reviews of English religion in American journals. The significance of their anti-Catholic polemic is that it occurred at the very time when the Anglican Church was becoming increasingly *Anglo-Catholic*. The scientists and agnostics clearly attempted to raise doubt as to whether the Anglican faith could or would remain the certain buttress of the true Protestant faith and a firm block against the onrush of Roman Catholics who had restored the hierarchy in England and led the great revival in Ireland.[11]

In the context of the third quarter of the century the proponents of scientific naturalism, as well as the spokesmen for other new theologies or new reformations, could in many respects seem to have been claiming the traditional mantle of the Anglican Church. Their cultural claims constituted a virtual mirror image of those of the Established Church. They were restoring real religion in place of the nominal religion of a divided, strife-torn Anglican Church. The new theologies could now successfully oppose materialism, religious enthusiasm, and the resurgence of Roman Catholicism. Furthermore, they could embrace new learning and knowledge. They alone were the protectors of stability, moderate religion, and Protestantism. And in the context of the debates of the 1870s those claims were intended to establish the scientists and secular laymen as the natural

11 Jeffrey Paul Von Arx, *Progress and pessimism: religion, politics, and history in late nineteenth century Britain* (Cambridge, Mass.: Harvard University Press, 1985).

successors to the Church of England as the proper educators of the nation.

Just as evangelicalism had at its inception been a faith of social action and reform, so also were the new secular faiths. In numerous cases the scientists and the unbelievers adopted the earlier evangelical role of advocacy for social reform. The fictitious Robert Elsmere pursued that path as did scores of other young men who passed through Toynbee Hall.[12] Often philosophic idealism provided a non-theological ideology for such action, but the advances of science and technology provided new tools for moral reform. Scientists, many of whom had been initially spurred to social action by reading Carlyle, saw the discoveries of science and technology as providing a powerful technological infrastructure leading to better housing, improved food, more effective medicine, and purer water that could improve not only the material but also the moral lives of their fellow citizens.

Thus far considerations of the affinities of the crisis of faith with the faith that was lost have been drawn from the public sphere of autobiographical publication and scientific polemic. In those areas unbelievers and honest doubters repeatedly mimicked the actions and cultural agendas of believers. But there were other, deeper and more intimate ways in which evangelical religion and the general intensification of religious life not only had provided modes of actions and moral expectations for unbelievers but also may actually have unintentionally caused persons to experience loss of faith and to feel the necessity of making changes in personal religious behaviour. Certain of the very successes of evangelical religion contributed directly to unbelief in ways that no evangelical and perhaps no unbeliever actually understood.

The most important but neglected private context for those Victorians whose faith entered a time of crisis or change was the family. The primacy of the family setting for nineteenth-century British Christianity was again a direct result of evangelical religion. During the late eighteenth and early nineteenth centuries evangelicals seeking to affirm real religion through emphasis on lay activity had discovered the efficacy of numerous institutions outside the Church proper for spreading their beliefs and sustaining their faith and values. The most famous of these were the various evangelical

---

[12] Standish Meacham, *Toynbee Hall and social reform 1880–1914: the search for community* (New Haven: Yale University Press, 1987).

societies directed toward reform of manners and morals. But the most powerful of these institutions was the family.

For evangelical religion the family, far more than the Church, constituted the centre of Christian nurture. Parents and devout relatives were the chief Christian teachers of their children. The household was the scene of family prayers and devotions. The Bible along with evangelical devotional literature provided the text for family-oriented religious training. The image of domestic evangelical Christian piety was frequently associated with the pious mother. It was also generally accepted that women, whether mothers, grandmothers, or aunts, would be very active in the process of Christian education. Indeed, the maintenance of a Christian home, the education of Christian children, and the sustenance of a Christian husband constituted a major part of the gender-defined social role for evangelically reared women. In some cases there also existed a darker side to this family faith. It might involve harsh discipline, personal physical and psychological mortification, and no doubt frequent psychological conflation between God the Father and the father of the household. Many British Christians whose own personal theology did not mesh with those of evangelicals nonetheless still embraced the model and social expectations of the evangelical family.

By having transformed the family into a major religious institution, the evangelical revival ironically also transformed religion into a vehicle whereby young persons could establish some personal psychological independence through modifying that family religion. In a very real sense the religious character and role of the evangelical family in and of itself fostered spiritual crisis because the usual familial tensions arising from normal personality development toward the achievement of autonomous adulthood could be and in some cases were mediated through religious categories that had been grafted on to family life. One of the most striking features of both the autobiographical and fictional accounts of transformation of religious belief or practice is the recognition on the part of the protagonist of the pain and turmoil that his or her action will cause for the family. A person's change or loss of faith inevitably disrupted the family community that was sustained in part on the basis of religion and provoking such disruption was one of the inner psychological reasons for undertaking the modification of faith. In other words, some people experienced loss of faith and all the pain and anguish accompanying it quite simply because they wished to grow up and thus consequently and necessarily break out of their original family circle.

Loss of faith almost always occurred in late adolescence or early adulthood. The disruptions of family expectations and interpersonal relationships that they involved was part and parcel of the normal and necessary achievement of personal independence and autonomy of a child from a family. Often the change in religious opinion occurred at the university where not only new intellectual influences impacted on the young man but novel personal loyalties as well. New friends and teachers brought about the acceptance of new ideas. Furthermore at the university, then as now, young men of firm religious backgrounds discovered peers who had been reared with different moral and religious expectations. The letters of John Henry Newman and John Ruskin from their university days indicate the kinds of unexpected temptations confronted by the evangelical youth in Oxford colleges.[13] Simply by virtue of growing up and attending the university the young person had begun to disrupt the family community of childhood. So closely related to the family was evangelical religion that virtually any intellectual or moral independence indicating normal maturation of personality was likely to touch some aspect of that faith. The religious and intellectual changes were further indications of that movement toward adult independence and toward the inevitable necessity of choosing which values, expectations, and role models drawn from parents would direct the young man's own life and which of those values would come from other sources.

The frequent reports of the very real emotional pain involved in change of religious belief may indicate the close relationship between loss of faith and the achievement of personal adult autonomy. George John Romanes expressed such despair anonymously in *A candid examination of theism* (1878). After having previously written an undergraduate essay on the efficacy of prayer, Romanes, a young scientist becoming warmly embraced by the Darwin circle, completed a second book in which he denied the validity of traditional

[13] Ian Ker and Thomas Gornall, eds., *The letters and diaries of John Henry Newman* (Oxford: Clarendon Press, 1978), I, 66; V. A. Burd, *The Ruskin family letters: the correspondence of John James Ruskin, his wife, and their son, John, 1801–1843* (Ithaca: Cornell University Press, 1973), II, 421–674; Jeffrey L. Spear, *Dreams of an English Eden: Ruskin and his tradition in social criticism* (New York: Columbia University Press, 1984), pp. 25–9.

natural religion that assured the presence of God behind the appearances and operations of nature. At the conclusion he complained,

I feel it desirable to state that any antecedent bias with regard to Theism which I individually possess is unquestionably on the side of traditional beliefs. It is therefore with the utmost sorrow that I find myself compelled to accept the conclusions here worked out; and nothing would have induced me to publish them, save the strength of my conviction that it is the duty of every member of society to give his fellows the benefit of his labours for whatever they may be worth ... And for as much as I am far from being able to agree with those who affirm that the twilight doctrine of the 'new faith' is a desirable substitute for the waning splendour of 'the old', I am not ashamed to confess that with this virtual negation of God the universe to me has lost its soul of loveliness; and although from henceforth the precept to 'work while it is day' will doubtless but gain an intensified force from the terribly intensified meaning of the words that 'the night cometh when no man can work', yet when at times I think, as at times I must, of the appalling contrast between the hallowed glory of that creed which once was mine, and the lonely mystery of existence as now I find it, – at such times I shall ever feel it impossible to avoid the sharpest pang of which my nature is susceptible.[14]

Romanes's voicing of the difficulty he confronted in reaching this conclusion served in part to manifest his sincerity and to indicate that he had not undertaken religious change from base motives. Such statements were common among unbelievers, but they may have served other functions deeper than that of demonstrating sincerity.

Romanes's pain may well have reflected not only religious loss but also through the intellectual and emotional category of religion the even more genuine anguish of the psychological process of achieving non-dependent relationships to his family, part of which involved his movement into a warm personal relationship with Darwin and other evolutionary scientists, the desire for whose approval and affection was displacing that which Romanes felt toward his original family. To a young man of science rejection of traditional natural religion may have seemed a useful way to bond himself to the advocates of scientific naturalism in place of previous family ties and loyalties. His angst over the prospect of a godless nature may have arisen from both the guilt aroused by wishing such independence and the simultaneous sorrow of losing the support and consolation of his first family. The despair over the disappearance of God indicates at least in part both the fear of the removal of a parent and the simultaneous wish for that removal. The manner of the expression of the sadness similarly suggests both the wish for and the fear of independence, as well as the desire to reject the parent without at the same time injuring the parent or withholding love. In that sense to some extent – and there is no desire to reduce the loss of faith only to a familial dimension – the experience and the recounting of the loss or change of religious faith and the vanquishment of the traditional evangelical god served to displace the tensions and conflict necessarily involved with the achievement of normal personal psychological autonomy. Painful and difficult as were the changes in religious belief and practice, they were less painful than the confrontation that might have arisen or that the protagonists feared would arise from the direct manifestation of their deepest residual childhood feelings toward their families in general and most particularly toward their parents. Religion could serve such a mediating role because of the close link established by evangelical Christianity between religion and family life.[15]

There may well have been another psychological dimension to this sense of loss so commonly voiced by new unbelievers. The feelings about the inadequacy of the childhood faith, the anguish and suffering experienced, and the sense of near despair over the prospect of a godless world may also have arisen in Romanes and other protagonists of unbelief from the recognition that many of the wishes that they had hoped to achieve as children within their families and through their parents had not been and would not ever be fulfilled. To become an adult requires in some measure this very recognition so that new goals and personal aims may be developed in

[15] It is worth noting the example of a major Victorian writer who grew up in a liberal rather than evangelical Christian family and who did not undergo a personal crisis of faith. Matthew Arnold encountered the higher criticism of the scripture within his immediate family circle and among many of Thomas Arnold's closest friends. The younger Arnold's own path toward independent selfhood was in part mediated by religion in particular through his attraction to Tractarians who had criticized his father, but it was not mediated through a crisis in theological belief. See Ruth ap Roberts, *Arnold and God* (Berkeley: University of California Press, 1983), pp. 56–79.

place of those of childhood and be fulfilled in a context other than
that of one's original family. For a previously devout young Victorian to encounter a universe without a God who renders it meaningful was not unlike confronting life and adulthood without parents
who determine meanings, establish expectations, and assure safety.
The expressed fear or hesitant acceptance of a godless world suggests
the hesitance of a child actually confronted with undirected or
undetermined choices to be made. The statements of simultaneous
wishes to retain faith and to assert intellectual independence replicate the very kind of emotional pulls experienced between wishes to
retain and to fulfil the hopes of childhood and wishes to establish
independent personal goals for one's life.

The close line between family life and religion could serve to
channel several kinds of evangelical child–parent confrontations
that fostered pain, disappointment, and anxiety as the child attained
maturity. Bonds between parents and children and parental goals
for their offspring were often profoundly rooted in religious expectations. After all, one of the signs of successful evangelical parenting
was the rearing of a child who would experience conversion and
acceptance of faith in Christ and then lead a Christian life that
would result in a similar nurturing of a succeeding generation. A
child in late adolescence or early adulthood might very well decide
that he or she entertained other aims in life and might feel that the
only way they could achieve sufficient independence to attain those
personal goals was to challenge the religious faith of their parents. A
challenge to the faith was less fearful than the more direct challenge
to parental authority. The process was still painful because the
children's rejecting or substantially modifying that parental faith
could be viewed or they could view themselves as imposing a sense of
failure on their parents.

In Edmund Gosse's *Father and son* (1907), one of the most familiar
loss of faith texts, the father upon the death of his first wife sets an
immense personal emotional stake on his very young son's being
accepted into the Plymouth Brethren congregation and being admitted to communion at an uncommonly early age. The father was
understandably enough seeking to establish a closer bond between
himself and his son as well as demonstrating to the religious
community his own success as a Christian parent. The son's eventual
movement away from the faith of his father clearly meant that he
had deeply disappointed and frustrated the father's expectations of

his own parenting. The novel also clearly indicates that the son's loss
of religious faith involved a simultaneous loss of faith and confidence
in his father and a distinct movement toward personal psychological
independence since religious acquiescence was the single way in
which the father continued to demand parental obedience and
allegiance from the son.[16]

Other children in both fiction and life employed conflict with
parents over religion or over expectations of a clerical career to
mediate their way to independent adulthood. Change in faith and
consequent rejection of the clerical career served to reject parental
hopes and expectations. This could be a very painful process for all
concerned because it indicated to the parent both less than successful
religious nurturing and loss of parental control over the child. There
was for the child potential guilt for leaving the faith and causing
turmoil in the family fold. Certainly these latter problems emerged
in the exchange of letters between young Samuel Butler and his
clergyman-father over the former's vocational choice. The debate
and discussion over the clerical vocation, in which the younger
Butler not insignificantly raised questions about theological doctrines relating to free will and which ended in his decision to try his
fortune outside the ministry and far away from home in New
Zealand, directly mediated and channelled the tensions over his
personal independence from a very dominant father and from the
values that father had fostered in his family.[17]

Even those relatively rare cases of substantial change of faith
during early middle age also seem to have involved a rejection of
family ties and parental domination. The most memorable example
of such late loss of Christian faith is that of John Ruskin. Although
his religious opinions had shifted somewhat over the years, he
remained a devout moderate evangelical until 1858. In that year, as
he later recounted, he visited a Waldensian church in Italy and upon
leaving the service found he was no longer a believer. That experience, which no doubt was the culmination of much more complex
inner psychological activity, occurred chronologically very near to
his completion of the final volume of *Modern painters*, the work that
from the beginning he had seen himself writing for his father and
largely under his father's aegis. Thereafter, becoming much more

---

[16] Edmund Gosse, *Father and son* (New York: Penguin Books, 1982), pp. 208–24.
[17] Arnold Silver, ed., *The family letters of Samuel Butler, 1841–1886* (Stanford: Stanford
University Press, 1962), pp. 59–90.

independent of his father, who died in 1864, Ruskin set out upon his crusade for social reform much of which he directed at criticism of the commercial middle-class structure that his merchant father had epitomized at its best. Imperfect as was Ruskin's eventual passage to adulthood, his religious crisis and his independence from parental dominance and expectations were closely associated factors in that maturation process.[18]

The relationship between independence in personality development and religious doubt seems to have been especially close in those few cases about which we have significant information in which women experienced modifications in religious faith and practice. Because women did not go to universities and normally remained geographically close to their families even if not necessarily residing in the same household, they tended to confront religious scepticism while still near or within the confines of the family circle. Since relationships to men and most particularly to their fathers determined so much in the lives of women, their personal independence, if achieved at all, almost invariably involved direct confrontations with their fathers and the rejection of the traditional female evangelical social role. Furthermore since no major religious denomination provided a significant role for women either preaching or administering the sacraments, to engage in serious religious thought leading to modification of faith required women to challenge the limitations set by contemporary religion on their lives and actions.

The personal religious development of the young Marian Evans, later in life to become the novelist George Eliot, provides a well-documented instance of the passage of a woman from faith to doubt and illustrates its ramifications for her family environment. Although Evans once claimed to have entertained doubts near the age of twelve about the tenets of evangelicalism according to which she had been reared, her real crisis occurred during her late teens and early twenties. She was then living near Coventry looking after the household of her father Robert Evans, her mother having been dead for several years and her sister and brothers having established their own homes. She had begun to read widely in advanced theology and critical religious history and had become close friends with local Unitarians. Regarded as physically unattractive, she

[18] Tim Hilton, *John Ruskin: the early years, 1819–1859* (New Haven: Yale University Press, 1985), pp. 253–79; George P. Landow, *The aesthetic and critical theories of John Ruskin* (Princeton: Princeton University Press, 1971), pp. 265–93.

seemed to have little prospect of making a marriage. Consequently, she had failed to fulfil her father's expectations in terms of her religious faith, her social acquaintances, and her eventual role as wife and mother. Early in 1842 Marian Evans, as a result of her reading and conversations among Unitarians, refused to go to church with her father. Normal family interchange came to a virtual halt as each week her father noted in his diary his solitary attendance at the local Anglican services. The silent strife became so consider-able that Marian resorted to writing a long letter to her father in an effort to assuage his anger and disapproval.

That letter of 28 February 1842 is a most remarkable Victorian document. Evans brought to the fore of her father's attention substantive comments about religion, relationships to men, and money as she made a virtual declaration of independence from paternal domination. Evans explained to her father that she did not, as he apparently had feared, intend to join a Unitarian congre-gation. However, she also indicated she no longer adhered to important evangelical beliefs. She wrote of the scriptures 'as histories consisting of mingled truth and fiction' and explained that while admiring the moral teaching of Jesus, she considered 'the system of doctrines built upon the facts of his life and drawn as to its materials from Jewish notions to be most dishonourable to God and most pernicious in its influence on individual and social happiness'.[19] One of Marian Evans's biographers has expressed surprise that she had reached the age of twenty-two before rejecting evangelicalism.[20] That astonishment arises from understanding the process of loss of faith as primarily intellectual when in point of fact the renunciation of evangelicalism on the part of a woman involved the rejection of a parent and the rejection of the expected vocations of dutiful, obedient daughter and future pious wife. For both young women and men such intellectual religious scepticism served to establish emotional and psychological detachment from family as they set off into the years of normal sexual activity which itself invariably involves in some manner upsetting the previous family community.

In her letter of 28 February 1842, Marian Evans made clear that all of these associations were very much present in her mind. In the

[19] Gordon S. Haight, ed., *The George Eliot letters* (New Haven: Yale University Press, 1954), I, 128.
[20] Gordon S. Haight, *George Eliot: a biography* (New York: Oxford University Press: 1968), p. 40.

same paragraph in which she had indicated her intellectual difficulties with Christianity, she addressed the issue of the impact of her
new beliefs on her personal religious conformity and on her prospects
for marriage. She told her father, 'I could not without vile hypocrisy
and a miserable truckling to the smile of the world for the sake of my
supposed interests, profess to join in worship which I wholly
disapprove. This and *this alone* I will not do even for your sake –
anything else however painful I would cheerfully brave to give you a
moment's joy.'[21] Later in the letter she indicated that she had no
hope of convincing her family of the sincerity of her new-found
religious opinions and that she clearly recognized the difficulty they
might pose to her prospects for marriage. She explained,

From what my Brother more than insinuated and from what you have
yourself intimated I perceive that your establishment at Foleshill is regarded
as an unnecessary expence – having no other object than to give me a centre
in society – that since you now consider me to have placed an insurmount-
able barrier to my prosperity in life this one object of an expenditure held by
the rest of the family to be disadvantageous to them is frustrated – I am glad
at any rate this is made clear to me, for I could not be happy to remain as an
incubus or an unjust absorber of your hardly earned gains which might be
better applied among my Brothers and Sisters with their children.[22]

In effect, Marian Evans, while expressing her change in religious
faith, also clearly and expressly declared that she would not depend
upon her father for encounters with men. She also not very subtly
indicated an awareness of jealousy and rivalry with her sisters and
brothers as a result of the cost of providing her with a place to meet
suitable men. She closed the letter by indicating her love for her
father, her willingness to continue to care for him, and her willingness to forego any economic provision he may have made for her
future.

Shortly after writing this extraordinary letter, Marian Evans went
to live for a brief time with her brother. She then returned to her
father's household and resumed Anglican church attendance but
apparently on the grounds that she would think her own thoughts in
church. She cared for her father until his death in 1849. However,
while dwelling in his household, she continued to read widely in
philosophy and theology and persevered in her friendships with local
theological radicals. In 1846 she published her important translation

[21] Haight, ed., *The George Eliot letters*, I, 129.   [22] Ibid.

of David Friedrich Strauss's *Life of Jesus* then regarded as the most advanced and destructive theological work of the day.[23]

There can be no question that Marian Evans genuinely suffered pain, embarrassment, and humiliation at the hands of her family. Her plight became a public one in the neighbourhood. But it is equally clear that she used (consciously or unconsciously) her new religious convictions combined with new social relationships to assert and to achieve personal, sexual, and vocational independence from her family. It also seems possible that her later ongoing search for an acceptable intellectual substitute for Christianity which carried her through a number of close relationships with men associated with particular advanced creeds manifested in part a desire to achieve once more the closeness to a man of strong opinions that as a young child she had experienced with her evangelical father and for which as an adult she may still have unconsciously yearned despite her stronger conscious desire for independence.

Frances Power Cobbe, the Irish-born early British feminist, provides another reasonably well-documented case of a woman's loss of faith and its relationship to family. In a passage from her autobiography resonating with the tensions raised by the attempt to achieve personal independence within and from the confines of family, Cobbe vividly recalled the occasion of her first inklings of religious doubt in the evangelical home of her youth:

The first question which ever arose in my mind was concerning the miracle of the Loaves and Fishes. I can recall the scene vividly. It was a winter's night; my father was reading the Sunday evening sermon in the dining-room. The servants, whose attendance was de rigueur, were seated in a row down the room. My father faced them, and my mother and I and my governess sat round the fire near him. I was opposite the beautiful classic black marble mantelpiece, surmounted with an antique head of Jupiter Serapis (all photographed on my brain even now), and listening with all my might, as in duty bound, to the sermon which described the miracle of the Loaves and Fishes. 'How did it happen exactly?' I began cheerfully to think, quite imagining I was doing the right thing to try to understand it all. 'Well! first there were the fishes and the loaves. But what was done to them? Did the fish grow and grow as they were eaten and broken? And the bread the same? No! that is nonsense. And then the twelve basketfuls taken

[23] For a discussion of the entire incident of Marian Evans's rebellion against her father, see Haight, *George Eliot*, pp. 32–67; Haight, ed., *The George Eliot letters*, I, 124–51; and John W. Cross, *George Eliot's life, as related in her letters and journals* (New York: Harper and Brothers, n.d.), I, 61–106.

up at the end, when there was not nearly so much at the beginning. It was not possible!' O Heavens! (was the next thought) *I am doubting the Bible!* God forgive me! I must never think of it again.[24]

Cobbe states that she was twelve years old at the time of this remembered experience.

What seems so significant about her recollection of first questioning the Bible are the details of the scene she paints rather than the content of her sceptical thoughts. Those details record the memory and consequent associations of a woman in her early seventies. The doubt may or may not have occurred when she was twelve, but she remembered and portrayed the experience as a personal subjective disruption, and one recognized as such, of family worship, social hierarchy, and her father's dominant religious role. The image of the dark pagan Jupiter presiding over the scene almost as a rival to her father suggests in addition to the rejection of the Christian dispensation for the pagan a sense of apprehension of the danger to the family circle and its faith posed by awakening sexuality and the spectre of independent personal action.

Although Cobbe indicates that she recoiled from doubting the Bible, she may rather have recoiled from the fear of doubting not the Bible but rather the parents and other figures, such as the governess, who had taught her to trust the Bible. Religious scepticism involved the rejection either halting or assertive of parental expectations and values. Frances Power Cobbe's early inner questioning of the miracle of the loaves and fishes presents a child's early attempt at independent thought and the child's almost immediate recognition that such thoughts will bring it into collision with the opinions and authority of its parents and may consequently also risk the loss of parental love and the encounter with personal emotional disorientation.

Cobbe also recounts that she later underwent a conversion experience in her mid-teens as was expected of evangelically reared children. Then in her late teens and early twenties she began four years of soul searching and religious pilgrimage at the conclusion of which she no longer believed in the divinity of Christ or the inspiration of the scriptures. While both of her parents still lived, she continued to attend Anglican services but did not take communion. Upon her mother's death she told her father of her new religious

---

[24] Frances Power Cobbe, *The life of Frances Power Cobbe by herself* (Boston: Houghton, Mifflin, and Company, 1894), I, 75–6.

opinions. Upon hearing them he sent her from her home for almost a year which she spent in the country with her brother. Thereafter she returned to her father's household where she lived for another eight years attending neither church nor family prayers. While living in these circumstances, she published with Longmans in 1855 a book on ethics that was deeply informed by the thought of liberal theologians whose opinions she had embraced at such high personal cost. Her father died in 1857, and Cobbe thereafter set out on her career in journalism and liberal political and religious causes.[25]

Still other family-related issues came to the fore of the loss of faith experience on the part of a man if it took place after his marriage. Should the wife be told? Could a godly Christian woman who had married a then Christian man continue in that close intimate relationship when the man was no longer a Christian? Would the children be reared in the faith? Furthermore, the change in the husband's beliefs and vocation could undermine his wife's personal vocational expectations. If she were the wife of a clergyman who lost faith, her prestigious social role in the parish would be almost immediately transformed into a kind of marginal existence. As the spouse of a publicly unbelieving layman, she might experience social discrimination. But whether the wife of a doubting cleric or the wife of an assertive lay unbeliever, her gender-determined role as the religious teacher and model of piety in the family would become problematical. She might in effect stand robbed of her vocation and at the same time appear to be intellectually weaker or more backward than her husband if she persisted in her faith. Similar difficulties of personal vocation and decisions about childrearing had to be confronted by women who freely entered into marriage with avowed unbelievers. In the past the concerns and difficulties of the wives of doubters, unbelievers, and agnostics have elicited condescension but little or no understanding on the part of scholars who have assumed any interference with the attainment and manifestation of a rationalistic and scientific outlook was undesirable and

---

[25] Ibid., 70–196. Cobbe's account presents an interesting confirmation of the family dimension of loss of faith on the part of women in regard to her comments on Marian Evans. Cobbe had read the Cross biography of George Eliot which did *not* include the important letter of February 1842 discussed in this essay. In her autobiography Cobbe (ibid., 81) indicates her envy and implied puzzlement at Marian Evans's apparently easy and entirely intellectual movement out of evangelicalism. Such was the manner in which Cross's narrative and selection of documents portrayed the event, and it was exactly that intellectualist portrayal that disturbed Cobbe when comparing her own experience to Evans's.

fundamentally contemptible. Such a Whiggish intellectualist position has ignored the family dynamic involved in the lives of unbelievers as well as the relatively few resources available to women in asserting a position of influence in family life.

In point of fact, many wives seem not to have reacted passively to being or becoming the spouse of a doubter. Rare was the male unbeliever within the professional classes who actually reared his children with no religious training or no religious sacraments. The determination of wives to set some rules in the family circle and to realize their own social hopes and expectations seems to have established limits to the expression of their husbands' unbelief. Such family considerations seem to have particularly circumscribed the unbelief of scientists. Thomas Henry Huxley thoroughly disliked the Church of England, but he permitted his children to be baptized into the Anglican fold as did many other agnostics.[26] Joseph Dalton Hooker, distinguished botanist and Keeper of Kew Garden, once complained to Huxley that Alfred Russel Wallace, then unmarried, did not understand the constraints that family considerations set on the expression of one's opinions:

> It is all very well for Wallace to wonder at scientific men being afraid of saying what they think – he has all 'the freedom of motion in vacuo' in one sense. Had he as many kind and good relations as I have, who would be grieved and pained to hear me say what I think, and had he children who would be placed in predicaments most detrimental to children's minds by such avowals on my part, he would not wonder so much.[27]

George John Romanes while still unmarried had published the aforementioned *Candid examination of theism* (1878). He published the work anonymously, but within months of its publication he began to back away from that book and its arguments when he decided to marry a woman who was a devout high Anglican. Indeed, the story of Romanes's intellectual movement away from *A candid examination of theism* and toward his posthumous *Thoughts on religion* (1895), edited by his wife, is in large measure the narrative of loss of faith outside marriage and imposition of faith within marriage.[28]

[26] Leonard Huxley, *The life and letters of Thomas Henry Huxley* (New York: D. Appleton and Co., 1900), I, 240.
[27] J. D. Hooker to C. Darwin, 6 October 1865, in Leonard Huxley, *Life and letters of Sir Joseph Dalton Hooker* (London: John Murray, 1918), II, 54.
[28] Turner, *Between science and religion*, pp. 134–63. This previous discussion of Romanes on my part does not reflect the family dynamic and would be subject to some revision in light of the present essay.

Scholars have viewed male unbelievers thus constrained as buf-
feted or wrongly pressured by their devout and insufficiently intellectual wives, but in doing so they have ignored the character of the
family dynamic. Wives and the situation of marriage seem to have
reestablished for the male unbeliever certain familial religious
constraints previously associated with parents. In the relationship of
the doubter or agnostic to both parents and wives one of the chief
issues was that of family community and family bonds of affection
and dependence. With his parents a male doubter's unbelief may
have served to establish separation. However, in the case of his wife
and children family considerations limited the husband's unbelief
because he wished to establish with them a new family life and
community. The very movement to adult psychological independence and autonomy that initially led to unbelief as a mediation of a
man's rejection of his parents and original family later led to an
acceptance of constraint on unbelief in the effort to establish his
marriage and new family.

It is also necessary to note that the challenge to family through the
categories of religion did not always lead to a loss of faith but
sometimes to a much more moderate religious change within a
distinctly Christian setting. For example, William Gladstone moved
from evangelicalism to high Anglicanism. Sometimes the modification of religion actually led to more religious conviction rather than
less. F. D. Maurice converted from Unitarianism to liberal
Anglicanism. There were also undoubtedly family dimensions yet to
be researched and explored in the numerous conversions from the
Church of England to Roman Catholicism as in the case of the
children of the evangelical William Wilberforce. Again in the
conversion to Roman Catholicism the tendency was from less to
more religion. In the case of persons who made those conversions,
which were perhaps the most frequent mid-century change in
religious faith, the departure quite literally led the protagonists to a
new mother in the form of the Roman Church or the Virgin who
would intercede with God the Father and a new father in the form of
the priest who possessed the capacity to accept and to forgive.
Finally, it is important to observe that modification or rejection of
the faith of one's childhood was by no means a certain path to
personal autonomy as witnessed by the personal and religious
development of Francis Newman and Arthur Hugh Clough. Nor
was all religious scepticism necessarily related to independence from

family as with the thought of Herbert Spencer whose condescension toward ecclesiastical institutions retained much continuity with his Nonconformist family's resentment of the Established Church of England.[29]

Victorian scholars have had little difficulty accepting family dimensions to John Stuart Mill's 'loss of faith' and mental crisis in regard to the strict utilitarian creed of his childhood and his hesitant movement toward romantic literature and acceptance of a role for feelings in his personal life. Indeed virtually no historian or literary scholar would examine Mill's intellectual development without consideration of the expectations of his father.[30] Nor would they chart his subsequent intellectual development without attention to the influence of his relationship to Harriet Taylor. Yet scholars of Victorian religious life have tended to limit the analysis of their materials strictly to intellectual and theological categories. The utilitarianism that James Mill imposed on his son was not unlike the total evangelical environment that many Christian parents imposed on their children. Both Mill and evangelical parents dedicated their children to the service of a particular faith or creed and saw their success as parents closely related to the child's fulfilment of that role in life. In both cases the creed and associated expectations placed on the children were intimately related to parental authority and served as boundaries to the development of the children's personal independence. Just as the achievement of personal autonomy on the part of evangelical children might have been forged in terms other than those of religion had the faith not been so closely grafted on to the family, no doubt so would John Stuart Mill's had his father been less determined to link his utilitarian creed so intimately to the parenting of his eldest child.

Near the time that so many English were about to enter a time of

[29] Perry Butler, *Gladstone: church, state, and Tractarianism: a study of his religious ideas and attitudes, 1809–1859* (Oxford: Clarendon Press, 1982); Frederick Maurice, *The life of Frederick Denison Maurice* (New York: Charles Scribner's Sons, 1884), I, 22–60; David Newsome, *The Wilberforces and Henry Manning: the parting of friends* (Cambridge, Mass.: Harvard University Press, 1966); Evelyn Barish Greenberger, *Arthur Hugh Clough: the growth of a poet's mind* (Cambridge, Mass.: Harvard University Press, 1970).

[30] A. W. Levi, 'The "mental crisis" of John Stuart Mill', *Psychoanalytic Review*, 32 (1945), 86–101; Michael St J. Packe, *The life of John Stuart Mill* (London: Becker and Warburg, 1954); Bruce Mazlish, *James and John Stuart Mill: father and son in the nineteenth century* (New York: Basic Books, 1975). It should also be noted that scholars have also quite often criticized the role of the politically and philosophically radical Harriet Taylor in Mill's intellectual life as they have similarly criticized the role of devout wives in the intellectual lives of Victorian agnostics.

religious crisis, Ralph Waldo Emerson confided to his notebook, 'What we say however trifling must have its roots in ourselves or it will not move others. No speech should be separate from our being like a plume or a nosegay, but like a leaf or a flower or a bud though the topmost & remotest, yet joined by a continuous line of life to the trunk & the seed.'[31] Historians of Victorian faith in crisis must begin to take a similar stance to the subject of their research. They must look at the social and psychological as well as the intellectual being of those Victorians who transformed their religious faith. Scholars must admit that matters of intellect pertain not to reason alone, and must become sceptical and curious about why these transformations were and have continued to be so frequently portrayed in strictly rational and intellectualist terms. They must also comprehend that the intensified modes of Christianity that penetrated so deeply into the personalities and social and political milieu of early nineteenth-century Britain may well have been the most important factors leading to change in faith, determining the manner of those changes, and establishing the expectations of the new faiths and theologies. For to adopt Emerson's metaphor, the trunk and the seed of the Victorian crisis of faith were nurtured and sustained in and by the faith that was lost.

[31] Joel Porte, ed., *Emerson in his journals* (Cambridge, Mass.: Harvard University Press, 1982), p. 84.

CHAPTER 4

The secularization of the social vision of British natural theology

The classical age of British natural theology extended from its rise in the middle of the seventeenth century through its general, though not complete, demise toward the close of the nineteenth. Scientific workers and their supporters in the seventeenth century had originally appealed to natural theology to assure potential critics that science or natural philosophy implied a religious and eternal rather than a secular or time-limited frame of reference. Simultaneously, natural theologians had also located inside this framework of eternal values and providential purposes the society within which that early science flourished. The secularization of British science – that is, the establishment of science within the saeculum or within history rather than within eternity – required the separation of *both* the subject matter of science and its social venue from reference to the eternal and providential backdrop provided for two centuries by natural theology. The first of those separations has received much historical analysis. The second separation whereby scientists and scientific publicists ceased to use religious values in general and natural theology in particular to provide a moral justification or theodicy for the kind of society to which British science contributed and from which it received support has received very little attention. It may very well be that only as a secular or temporal theodicy replaced the religiously grounded social vision associated with traditional natural theology could scientists pursue the investigation of nature without reference to the divine.

From the very beginning British natural theology had addressed itself to both nature and society. The seventeenth-century virtuosi embraced natural theology in order to defend science from association with contemporary atheism or materialism that was believed to foster social turmoil or political absolutism. Natural theology was also supposed to inhibit religious enthusiasm which might spawn

civil upheaval. In the process, natural theologians explicitly associated the cause of science or natural knowledge with maintaining
the contemporary social status quo as understood by moderate
Anglicans.[1] Natural theologians of the era of Boyle and Newton
directly encouraged the economic exploitation of the earth and
rationalized the human suffering and social inequality that might
result therefrom in a manner that clearly embraced the economic
and social values of Locke's *Second treatise of civil government*. The
natural theologians specifically transferred the divine teleology
associated with nature to contemporary commercial arrangements.
This support of commercial life did not exclude charity and benevolence, but those virtues existed as a force to temper excesses within
the larger commercial framework. These prescriptive teachings in
favour of economic development and commercial life remained for
two centuries as much an articulated article of faith in natural
theology as did the argument from design.

John Ray's *The wisdom of God in the creation* (1691) represented one
of the most important and widely read works of late seventeenth-
century natural theology.[2] In his *Synopsis Stirpium Britannicarum*
(1690) Ray had strongly supported William and Mary and thus
identified himself with the new regime and its policies of commercial
growth. The theme of the propriety and righteousness of human
economic expansion associated with their reign permeated Ray's
natural theology. Ray contended that human beings completed the
original creative labour of God by discovering and bringing into
conscious use the otherwise hidden or latent utility of the various
parts of nature such as fire, stone, timber, and metal. Since the
potential for that utility existed anterior to the application of 'the wit
and Industry of an intelligent and active Being', its presence
suggested to those who believed in God that such materials had been

[1] Richard S. Westfall, *Science and religion in seventeenth-century England* (New Haven: Yale
University Press, 1958); Margaret C. Jacob, *The Newtonians and the English revolution* (Ithaca:
Cornell University Press, 1976); Steven Shapin and Simon Schaffer, *Leviathan and the air-
pump: Hobbes, Boyle and the experimental life* (Princeton: Princeton University Press, 1985);
Keith Hutchison, 'Supernaturalism and the mechanical philosophy', *History of Science*, 21
(1983), 297–323; John Gascoigne, 'From Bentley to the Victorians: the rise and fall of
British Newtonian natural theology', *Science in Context*, 2 (1988), 219–56; James R. Jacob and
Margaret C. Jacob. 'The Anglican origins of modern science: the metaphysical foundations
of the Whig constitution', *Isis*, 71 (1980), 251–67.
[2] Neal C. Gillespie, 'Natural history, natural theology, and social order: John Ray and the
"Newtonian ideology" ', *Journal of the History of Biology*, 20 (1987), 1–49; Charles E. Raven,
John Ray Naturalist: his life and works (Cambridge: Cambridge University Press, 1942).

created intentionally for human uses.[3] In other words, God placed human beings on earth to realize or exploit the potentialities that inhered in the rest of the creation.

Ray taught that by providing such materials, the Almighty had in effect declared that humankind stood placed in the world 'to exercise and employ' their 'Art and Strength'. By creating a landscape for cultivation, plants and seeds for human nourishment, and materials for housing human beings and animals, God had implicitly commanded humankind to exploit the earth for their own benefit. In making human beings social creatures, God had in effect told them to

build ... large Towns and Cities with streight [*sic*] and well paved Streets, and elegant rows of Houses, adorned with magnificent Temples for my Honour and Worship, with beautiful Palaces for ... Princes and Grandees, and with stately Halls for public meetings of the Citizens and their Several Companies, and the Sessions of the courts of Judicature, besides public Porticos and Aquaeducts.[4]

Here and elsewhere Ray quite specifically suggested that God had commanded humankind to establish a society with virtually all the features characteristic of contemporary Europe in general and late-seventeenth-century England in particular.

Throughout *The wisdom of God in the creation* Ray presented as clear signs of divine providence the manner in which the natural creation made possible extensive trade and sound commercial transactions. He claimed that God had furnished materials for shipbuilding and had implanted in humankind a desire to see foreign lands and to advance knowledge by searching out the world for plants, fruits, and minerals so as 'to benefit and enrich' their 'Country by encrease of its Trade and Merchandise'. By arming humankind with courage and assisting it with the knowledge of the compass, God had commanded humankind, 'Go thither for the Purposes before mentioned, and bring home what may be useful and beneficial to thy Country in general, or thy Self in particular.' God had created a vast array of differences in the human face because without such facial diversity 'Confusion and Disturbance' and 'Uncertainty in all Sales and Conveyances, in all Bargains and Contracts' would ensue. Without

---

[3] John Ray, *The wisdom of God manifested in the works of the creation* (1691; New York: Garland Publishing Inc., 1979), p. 113.
[4] Ibid., pp. 114, 115–16.

such differences in the faces of human beings, there would occur
'Frauds and Cheats and suborning of Witnesses' and 'a subversion of
all Trades and Commerce' as one person could easily pass himself off
as another without the possibility of easy detection. Furthermore, all
judicial proceedings would be cast into doubt over absence of clear
personal identity based on physical appearance. Ray concluded,
'Many other inconveniences might be instanced in: So that we see
this [variety of faces] is no contemptible Argument of the Wisdom
and Goodness of God.'[5]

From the days of John Ray through those of the Bridgewater
authors, natural theologians contended that the manner in which
Europeans and more particularly the British could exploit the earth
for its own benefit provided evidence of God's providential care for
human beings and his approval of a competitive, commercial society
tempered by benevolence. Since natural theology directed itself
against atheists and intellectual enemies whose ideas allegedly
endangered the social order, natural theologians functioned as much
as defenders of contemporary social arrangements and their underlying values as they did of science. They sought to demonstrate not
only that science did not endanger religion but also that science and
natural theology positively embraced contemporary commercial
values. Science provided evidence of God's existence and also new
means to make nature useful to human beings and profitable to
commercial trade and other economic activity. Natural theology
thus brought nature, science, and contemporary British society into
the embrace of divine purpose. Science and natural theology supported each other and in turn the social order.

Had intellectual or philosophical arguments alone sustained natural theology in its relationship with science, David Hume's *Dialogues
concerning natural religion* published in 1779 should have provided
more than enough destructive content.[6] The separation of natural
theology from science, however, involved more than logical argument. Hume's reputation as a sceptic was enough to prevent many

---

5 Ibid., pp. 116–17, 117, 168, 169.
6 Significantly, Hume though sceptical about natural theology was a firm supporter of
   commercial society. His own arguments for commercial society like those of the other
   Scottish writers tended to emphasize the social benefits that came from it and the politeness
   that it fostered in contrast to military society. In that regard, like the Victorian writers
   discussed later in this chapter, Hume attacked natural religion but only while bolstering
   commercial society and the general social status quo on other grounds. See John Hedley
   Brooke, *Science and religion: some historical perspectives* (Cambridge: Cambridge University
   Press, 1991), pp. 181–9.

people from contending seriously with his arguments. Furthermore, as Richard Sher, George Stocking and John Gascoigne have recently argued and as Klaus Epstein argued a generation ago, enlightened and rationalist thought during the last quarter of the eighteenth century confronted enormous new opposition from the forces of the religious revival that swept across Britain and Europe. These were seized upon by the opponents of social and political change both before and after the events of the French Revolution. Natural theology along with other religious viewpoints participated in and benefited from that religious revival and conservative political and social resurgence. At the same time it should be noted that evangelical writers during that revival sensed the lack of vital religiosity in natural theology.

During the late 1780s and 1790s science in Britain became associated with certain radical or potentially radical thinkers such as Joseph Priestley, Erasmus Darwin, and James Hutton. Priestley as a Unitarian and political radical became a special target with his home and laboratory in Birmingham being destroyed in 1792 by a Church and King mob. The polemics against the revolution in France and against both moderate and utopian reform at home associated domestic radical politics with French political, scientific, and mathematical thought. New proponents of natural theology came to the fore, as had occurred in the midst of the political turmoil at the end of the previous century, to demonstrate that the natural and social orders understood within a religious or eternal framework ordained political and social passivity and that scientific knowledge both natural and economic was politically and socially inoffensive. As in the past, the protection of science was in a very real sense secondary to the protection of the social and political status quo and to the theological defence of the Christian deity from guilt associated with the apparent evils in either nature or society.[7]

It was in that climate that in 1802 William Paley published his influential *Natural theology*.[8] He had previously published works on

---

[7] A. M. C. Waterman, *Revolution, economics and religion: Christian political economy, 1798–1833* (Cambridge: Cambridge University Press, 1991), provides an important revisionist discussion of this broad phenomenon including important material on both Malthus and Paley.

[8] Neal C. Gillespie, 'Divine design and the industrial revolution: William Paley's abortive reform of natural theology', *Isis*, 81 (1990), 214–29; D. L. LeMahieu, *The mind of William Paley: a philosopher and his age* (Lincoln, Nebr.: University of Nebraska Press, 1976); John Gascoigne, *Cambridge in the age of the Enlightenment: science, religion and politics from the Restoration to the French Revolution* (Cambridge: Cambridge University Press, 1989), pp. 241–7.

social philosophy and Christian evidences widely read and assigned to students at Cambridge. He regarded the volume on natural theology, though written last, as the proper opening volume of his studies. Yet it is not insignificant that the theological arguments underpinning his social and political views appeared in print only after the other writings on those subjects as if to justify what had come earlier. Indeed, he reiterated the views from his *Principles of moral and political philosophy* (1785) in the concluding chapters of his *Natural theology* so that his mechanistic, utilitarian image of nature led in that volume quite directly toward his conservative view of society.

Robert Young among others has seen the social passivity and rationalization of suffering in nature present in Paley's *Natural theology* as defending the emerging industrial order.[9] Yet Paley's injunctions to social acquiescence, illustrated in his *Principles of moral and political philosophy* and 'Reasons for contentment, addressed to the labouring part of the British public' (1792) as well as in his *Natural theology*, should not be seen as an ideological justification of industrial society of which only the smallest beginnings existed in his day. Rather Paley's defence of hierarchy and commerce echoed numerous eighteenth-century political works that predated the arrival of any significant industrialism. Paley's *Natural theology* along with his other writings emerged as part of the more general eighteenth-century defence of modern commercial society against various country-party writers who had nostalgically championed the civic virtue of landed society. Within the context of natural theology the roots of Paley's social vision clearly existed in Ray. Writing a century apart, Ray and Paley sought to place Anglican theology as well as science on the side of material and economic progress and social stability. Paley, like both Ray before him and other natural theologians after him, saw his work as contributing toward conserving order in British society then threatened by economic change and political and religious radicalism.

Paley's famous, if anachronistic, appeal to the watch metaphor and his general bedazzlement by contrivance in nature reflected the eighteenth-century fascination with machinery that was appearing

9 Robert M. Young, *Darwin's metaphor: nature's place in Victorian culture* (Cambridge: Cambridge University Press, 1985), pp. 27–31, 189–92; A. M. C. Waterman, 'The ideological alliance of political economy and Christian theology, 1798–1833', *Journal of Ecclesiastical History*, 34 (1983), 231–44.

in so many different areas of Britain. Paley's nature was a realm of such machinery writ large. Through his memorable arguments about natural mechanical contrivances, Paley attempted to prove the existence of an 'intelligent, designing author'.[10] As if in anticipation of Feuerbach's contention that all theology is anthropology, Paley transformed his deity into a skilled and ingenious English engineer. The archetype of Paley's Creator-designer was the human designer or human mechanic. If one understood good human engineering, one understood God. In that respect, Paley's God was indeed an Englishman – an Englishman who was a mechanical genius. The social vision that his prose reflected and defended was that of the commercial exploitation of all available natural resources through machinery and commerce.[11]

It was necessary to his goal of countering social utopians and political radicals for Paley to assert that the designer God was a beneficent creator of nature. In a passage wherein he had pointed to many of the difficulties of nature and the painful competition fostered by the superabundance of living things, Paley declared in conclusion, 'It is a happy world after all. The air, the earth, the water, teem with delighted existence.'[12] Evils or examples of suffering in nature stood rationalized on utilitarian grounds. Paley then transferred that complacency into his analysis of the social order as well. The wisdom of God evident in the useful, if sometimes painful, contrivances of the natural order first prevented the atheist from using science to sow mischief in the social order. Second, the wisdom of God displayed in the utility of contemporary social arrangements, which like certain paradoxes of nature appeared evil

[10] William Paley, *Natural theology* (Houston: St Thomas Press, 1972), p. 314.
[11] Josiah Tucker, writing a few years before Paley, once praised the machinery of England in the following manner: 'Few countries are equal, perhaps none excel, the English in the number of contrivances of their Machines to abridge labour. Indeed, the Dutch are superior to them in the use and application of Wind Mills for sawing Timber, expressing Oil, making Paper and the like. But in regard to Mines and Metals of all sorts, the English are uncommonly dexterous in their contrivance of the mechanic Powers; some being calculated for landing the Ores out of the Pits, such as Cranes and Horse Engines; others for draining off superfluous Water, such as Water Wheels and Steam Engines; others again for easing the Expense of Carriage such as machines to run on inclined planes or Roads downhill with wooden frames, in order to carry many Tons of Material at a Time. And to these must be added the various sorts of Levers used in various processes . . . Yet all these, curious as they may seem, are little more than Preparations or Introductions for further Operations . . . [We] may aver with some confidence that those parts of England in which these things are seen exhibit a specimen of practical mechanics scarce to be paralleled in any part of the world.' Josiah Tucker, *Instructions to travellers* (London, 1757), p. 20.
[12] Paley, *Natural theology*, p. 340.

until properly interpreted, undergirded the correctness of the British social order and similarly foiled the mischief of social critics.

Paley warmly defended the hierarchical character of English society, urging, 'The distinctions of civil life are apt enough to be regarded as evils, by those who sit under them: But, in my opinion, with very little reason.' Paley commended distinctions in social rank and station because they called forth work and competition on the part of those who would rise in life. He observed, 'It is not ... by what the Lord Mayor feels in his coach, but by what the apprentice feels who gazes on him, that the public is served.' The privileges and advantages of the propertied over the unpropertied 'so long as they are unaccompanied by privileges injurious or oppressive to the rest of the community, are such, as may, even by the most depressed ranks, be endured, with very little prejudice to their comfort'. Still later Paley defended the morality of fortunes falling by chance to persons born into prosperous families. The laws that protected such large and growing fortunes equally protected holders of much smaller amounts of property. Paley portrayed money as the wise vehicle for softening potential social conflict observing,

It is not necessary to contend, that the advantages derived from wealth are none, ... but that they are not greater than they ought to be. Money is the sweetener of human toil; the substitute for coercion; the reconciler of labour with liberty. It is, moreover, the stimulant of enterprise in all projects and undertakings, as well as of diligence in the most beneficial arts and employments.[13]

Paley also defended the general poverty of the vast majority of the population as being the spur that induced them to work.

The keystone to Paley's conception of the social and moral order and to that of other natural theologians was human immortality. Paley contended that the lives of individuals on earth must be regarded as probationary for a life to come in which rewards and punishments would be meted out. Admitting that there seemed to be much injustice and suffering on earth, he argued, 'When we let in religious considerations, we often let in light upon the difficulties of nature ... In a religious view ... privation, disappointment, and satiety, are not without the most salutary tendencies.'[14] This appeal to immortality, based upon faith in revealed religion, suggests that Paley actually found his assertion of the utility of social inequality

[13] Ibid., pp. 374, 375, 376, 374.   [14] Ibid., p. 392.

morally unconvincing despite its important functional role in his general philosophy. The significance he attached to immortality also indicated that the utilitarian social philosophy which his natural theology supported made real sense only in the context of a society that lay in the embrace of things eternal. If contemporary social life occurred only within history rather than within eternity, even Paley implicitly understood that the plight of most people was difficult, unjust, and unacceptably evil.

Paley was not alone in this situation of recognizing the need for a theodicy to justify the contemporary social situation. Malthus had concluded his *Essay on the principle of population* in 1798 with a theodicy.[15] In those chapters Malthus attempted to make sense of the frightful disparity between the ratios of arithmetic expansion of food production and geometric expansion of the human population and the consequent human suffering. He explained the difficulties arising therefrom as functioning to make human beings industrious so that they would exploit the earth. Actual justice lay in the hereafter. In his Bridgewater treatise of 1833 Thomas Chalmers also saw immortality alone as allowing for the continuation and consummation of the unfinished questions of life the resolution of which social and political justice demanded. In a passage of remarkable forthrightness Chalmers declared,

If there be no future state, the great moral question between heaven and earth, broken off at the middle, is frittered into a degrading mockery. There is violence done to the continuity of things. The moral constitution of man is stript of its significancy and the Author of that constitution is stript of His wisdom and authority and honour. That consistent march which we behold in all the cycles, and progressive movements of the natural economy, is, in the moral economy, brought to sudden arrest and disruption – if death annihilate the man, instead of only transforming him. And it is only the doctrine of his immortality by which all can be adjusted and harmonized.[16]

---

[15] Waterman, *Revolution, economics and religion*, pp. 114–36. Despite the current reading of Paley as a very conservative writer, which he most certainly was, there were numerous doubts during his lifetime about the full adequacy of his conservatism.

[16] Thomas Chalmers, *On the power, wisdom, and goodness of God as manifested in the adaptation of external nature to the moral and intellectual constitution of man*, new edn (Philadelphia: Lee and Blanchard, 1836), pp. 194–5. The issue of immortality haunted not only natural theologians and science; it also became a major issue of late Victorian ethical theory. See Frank Miller Turner, *Between science and religion: the reaction to scientific naturalism in late Victorian England* (New Haven: Yale University Press, 1974), pp. 44–60.

Chalmers and the other natural theologians clearly understood that
their social philosophy which scientific knowledge of nature was to
undergird demanded the doctrine of immortality. Only with the
balancing of moral accounts in the hereafter of eternity did their
ethical teaching become bearable for the overwhelming majority of
their countrymen. The natural theologians clearly understood the
potentially turbulent consequences of their vision of social justice
implied by the absence of immortality.

The importance and significance of the doctrine of immortality,
drawn from revealed religion, to the social agenda of natural
theology cannot be overestimated. If it were denied or taken away,
the entire moral vision became the very nightmare that its authors so
clearly delineated. Later Victorian scientists who chose to remove
science from the snares of natural theology found themselves directly
confronted with the very moral dilemma set forth by the natural
theologians. If those scientists rejected immortality and at the same
time wished not to cast morality and society into potential chaos,
they had to find a substitute. As science became more nearly
separated from religion during the next century, scientists and
scientific writers tended to make one of three choices. Some, like
Huxley, rejected the likelihood of achieving complete human justice
but presented science as providing tools for reform and the improvement of the human material situation. Others, like Spencer, turned
to spiritually tempered progressive secular theodicies that envisioned
progressive human improvement or justice over time on earth. For
Spencer the presence of the Unknowable, which established a kind of
distant eternal backdrop to his natural universe and evolving human
society, 'guaranteed that beneath the seeming waste of the evolutionary process lay an economy, order, purpose, and harmony'.[17] A
few, like Alfred Russel Wallace, appealed to occult religions, such as
spiritualism, which claimed to combine science with assurance of
immortality grounded on allegedly empirical data.[18] Except for those
embracing the last alternative, scientists drew the issues of society
and social justice away from direct reference to eternal things found
in natural theology and placed it in the sphere of human history.

[17] Bernard Lightman, *The origins of agnosticism: Victorian unbelief and the limits of knowledge*
(Baltimore: Johns Hopkins University Press, 1987), p. 89.
[18] See Turner, *Between science and religion*, pp. 68–133; Janet Oppenheim, *The other world:
spiritualism and psychical research in England, 1850–1914* (Cambridge: Cambridge University
Press, 1985); Malcolm J. Kottler, 'Alfred Russel Wallace, the origin of man, and
spiritualism', *Isis*, 65 (1974), 145–92.

After Paley's *Natural theology* the most famous examples of natural religion were to be found in the Bridgewater treatises of the 1830s.[19] Although the various authors – Thomas Chalmers, William Whewell, William Buckland, William Prout, Peter Mark Roget, Charles Bell, John Kidd, and William Kirby – addressed different subjects and held somewhat differing religious views, they shared the goal of demonstrating the presence of a wise, beneficent creator or first cause. For all intents and purposes, with the exceptions of Kirby and Prout, the Bridgewater authors firmly separated scientific knowledge and scripture. Buckland and Whewell in particular asserted that scripture is an inadequate guide to the study and under-standing of nature.[20]

Various recent studies that have their roots in Walter (Susan) Cannon's work have emphasized the manner in which natural theology actually provided the underpinnings of much of Darwin's thought and provided an image of nature from which the activity of God could be removed without much difficulty. There is now widespread acceptance of this general argument though there is a lively debate as to exactly when and to what extent Darwin himself removed God or the shadow of God from his own thought. The Bridgewater treatises individually and as a group, like Paley's volume, however, also prepared the way for a second secularization of thought. They laid the foundation for an image of humankind and

[19] John M. Robson, 'The fiat and finger of God: the Bridgewater treatises', in Richard J. Helmstadter and Bernard Lightman, eds., *Victorian faith in crisis: essays on continuity and change in nineteenth-century religious belief* (London: Macmillan, 1990), pp. 71–5; W. H. Brock, 'The selection of the authors of the Bridgewater treatises', *Notes and Records of the Royal Society of London*, 21 (1966), 162–79; Richard Yeo, 'William Whewell, natural theology and the philosophy of science in mid-nineteenth century Britain', *Annals of Science*, 36 (1979), 493–516; Richard Yeo, 'The principle of plenitude and natural theology in nineteenth-century Britain', *British Journal for the History of Science*, 19 (1986), 263–82; Young, *Darwin's metaphor*, pp. 126–63.

[20] Mary Buckland wrote William Whewell on 12 May 1833, 'You ask how the Bridgewater treatise goes on; I wish I could say that it had gone off with eclat as yours has done. The geology is finished but the mineralogy has advanced but little . . . By way of encouragement to my husband's labours, we have had the Bampton Lecturer holding forth in St Mary's against all modern science, (of which it need scarcely be said he is profoundly ignorant) but more particularly enlarging on the heresies and infidelities of geologists, denouncing all who assert that the world was not made in 6 days as obstinate unbelievers, etc etc . . . Alas! My poor husband. Could he be carried back a century, fire and faggot would have been his fate, and I daresay our Bampton Lecturer would have thought it his duty to assist at such an "Auto da Fé"'. Jack Morrell and Arnold Thackray, eds., *Gentlemen of science: early correspondence of the British Association for the Advancement of Science*, Camden Fourth Series, Vol. 30 (London: Royal Historical Society, 1984), p. 168. See also pp. 181–2.

commercial industrial society that did not necessarily require the presence of God or a religious setting for human life. That is to say, they presented an image of humankind and human society for which alternative naturalistic explanations and rationalizations could readily be substituted for the religious ones upon which they drew. Within the pages of the Bridgewater treatises there lay an image of commercial, industrial society which later writers would withdraw from the setting of the eternal purposes of God and then set into the saeculum of historical development.

Like previous natural theologians, all of the Bridgewater authors in differing ways and to differing extents accepted or rationalized suffering that occurred from competition in nature. Roget suggested that nature had been lavish in her productiveness in order to demonstrate to humankind 'the inexhaustible fund from which she has so prodigally drawn forth the means requisite for the maintenance of all these diversified combinations, for their repetition in endless perpetuity, and for their subordination to one harmonious scheme of general good'. Roget found himself somewhat taken aback by the spectacle of animals living off the killing of each other, a situation he termed 'this system of hostilities'. Yet even here the future author of the famous thesaurus eventually discerned evidence of harmony for good, as he explained,

We must take into account the vast accession that accrues to the mass of animal enjoyment from the exercise of those powers and faculties which are called forth by this state of constant activity; and when this consideration is combined, as it ought to be, with that of the immense multiplication of life which is admissible upon this system alone, we shall find ample reason for acknowledging the wisdom and the benevolent intentions of the Creator, who, for the sake of a vastly superior good, has permitted the existence of a minor evil.[21]

Prout for his part believed the Creator had carefully designed the predators in each climatic zone to balance the super fecundity of other animals: 'While in temperate climates we have cats and spiders, designed as checks on over-productiveness; amidst the grandeur and the luxurious development of the Tropics, the same

---

[21] Peter Mark Roget, *Animal and vegetable physiology, considered with reference to natural theology*, 2nd American, from the last London, edn (Philadelphia: Lea and Blanchard, 1839), I, 25, 47.

wise purpose is executed by the Tiger and by the Rattlesnake.'[22] Wherever there was incongruity or brutality or suffering, the Bridgewater authors usually pointed to a utilitarian purpose based on larger divine goals. Or as Whewell, who eschewed utilitarianism, suggested, since where we can have clear knowledge, God's purpose is beneficent and certain, the same wisdom must no doubt apply in those areas that 'are the darkest and most tangled recesses of our knowledge' and into which 'science has as yet cast no ray of light'.[23] From the deadly competitiveness in nature the authors had little trouble moving toward the acceptance and rationalization of similar competitiveness in contemporary civilized society or economic developments that presupposed such a competitive ethos.

Not surprisingly the Bridgewater authors presented natural theology as confirming the general superiority of humankind over the rest of the creation and as pointing toward modern European civilization as the end and natural state of humankind. John Kidd stated that both the savage and civilized were natural states but argued that humankind's end must be civilization because humankind's moral character 'is hardly attainable in an uncivilized state of society'. In emphasizing the civilized state as the providentially determined goal of humankind, all of the treatises set forth to greater and lesser degrees of specificity the proposition that the earth had been providentially prepared for human development and exploitation. Charles Bell declared,

If a man contemplate the common objects around him – if he observe the connexion between the qualities of things external and the exercise of his senses, between the senses so excited and the condition of his mind, he will perceive that he is in the centre of a magnificent system, prepared for his reception by a succession of revolutions which have affected the whole globe; and that the strictest relation is established between his intellectual capacities and the material world.

---

[22] William Prout, *Chemistry, meteorology, and the function of digestion, considered with reference to natural theology*, new edn (Philadelphia: Lea and Blanchard, 1836), p. 194. It was this very kind of argument that Charles Darwin eventually found he could not accept. Writing to Asa Gray in May 1860 about *On the origin of species*, Darwin declared, 'I had no intention to write atheistically. But I own that I cannot see as plainly as others do, and as I should wish to do, evidence of design and beneficence on all sides of us. There seems to me too much misery in the world. I cannot persuade myself that a beneficent and omnipotent God would have designedly created the Ichneumonidae with the express intention of their feeding within the living bodies of Caterpillars, or that a cat should play with mice.' Francis Darwin, *The life and letters of Charles Darwin* (New York: D. Appleton and Co., 1899), II, 105.

[23] William Whewell, *Astronomy and general physics, considered with reference to natural theology*, new edn (Philadelphia: Lea and Blanchard, 1836), p. 194. See also p. 66.

The conviction that humankind had been God's final creation further persuaded Bell that the earth had been specially and providentially created for humankind. Bell argued that God had directly created the earth and all of its landscape. He then added, as had John Ray over a century earlier,

> But cities, temples, and the memorials of past ages, bridges, aqueducts, statues, pictures, and all the elegancies and comforts of the town, are equally the work of God, through the propensities of His creatures, and, we must presume, for the fulfilment of His design. The condition of the earth has by successive revolutions been made to conform to these works of man, and afford the means for them.

All of geological history provided 'proof that it was designed that the earth should be subdued to man's use' for the establishment of society in which his higher faculties might be exercised.[24]

William Buckland's discussion of coal provided one of the most extensive examples of the argument for the providential preparation of the earth for advanced human civilization and more explicitly for the economic culture that was coming to characterize north-western Europe. Buckland analysed in considerable detail the primeval formation of coal and iron ore and emphasized their contemporary beneficial uses in the products of daily life and the processes of manufacturing. Buckland argued that however ancient may have been the time when 'these materials of beneficial dispensation were laid up in store', it could be fairly assumed that an 'ulterior prospective view to the future uses of Man, formed part of the design, with which they were, ages ago, disposed in a manner so admirably adapted to the benefit of the Human Race'. Continuing this argument in relation to coal, Buckland wrote,

> It is impossible to contemplate a disposition of things, so well adapted to afford the materials essential to supply the first wants, and to keep alive the industry of the inhabitants of our earth; and entirely to attribute such a disposition to the blind operation of *Fortuitous* causes . . . We may surely . . . feel ourselves authorized to view, in the Geological arrangements above described, a system of wise and benevolent Contrivances, prospectively subsidiary to the wants and comforts of the future inhabitants of the globe;

---

[24] John Kidd, *On the adaptation of external nature to the physical condition of man, principally with reference to the supply of his wants, and the exercise of his intellectual faculties*, new edn (Philadelphia: Lea and Blanchard, 1836), p. 14; Charles Bell, *The hand; its mechanism and vital endowments, as evincing design*, 6th edn, revised (London: John Murray, 1860), pp. 24–5, 80. See also Prout, *Chemistry, meteorology, and the function of digestion*, pp. 201–3.

and extending onwards, from its first Formation, through the subsequent
Revolutions and Convulsions that have affected the surface of our Planet.[25]

In that respect, geology demonstrated the providential manner in
which God had prepared the earth through time for the appearance
of humankind and for its exploitation of the earth and for the
improvement of its standard of living.

Buckland's discussion of coal as an example of divine providence
and benevolence involved far more than an illustration of the
argument from design. The illustration of the providential presence
of coal implied a thoroughly promethean image of the character and
destiny of humankind. Coal constituted the basis of the growing
industrial and economic power of Britain and of the comforts of
everyday life. The search for coal deposits in Britain and abroad also
represented one of the most important practical applications of
geology. It was coal that allowed human beings in the nineteenth
century to remain warm and to penetrate, inhabit, and develop
productively areas of the earth that would otherwise be hostile. By
implication Buckland clearly suggested that God had intended the
earth to be developed through the use of coal in the manner then
being carried out by Europeans.

The Bridgewater writers viewed humankind's capacity for living
in society in general and commercial society in particular as an
indication of the presence and purposes of God. The entire point of
Chalmers's treatise was the demonstration of the manner in which
humankind's collective social instincts were adapted to its physical
setting and the development of that setting. Chalmers commented,

Both in the reciprocities of domestic life, and in those wider relations, which
bind large assemblages of men into political and economic systems, we shall
discern the incontestable marks of a divine wisdom and care; principles or
laws of human nature in virtue of which the social economy moves rightly
and prosperously onward, and apart from which all would go into
derangement; affinities between man and his fellows, that harmonize the
individual with the general interests, and are obviously designed as
provisions for the well-being both of families and nations.

God had wisely adapted human moral instincts to the social realm
through 'the urgent voice of conscience within' and the possibility

---

[25] William Buckland, *Geology and mineralogy considered with reference to natural theology* (Philadelphia: Carey, Lea and Blanchard, 1837), I, 403, 409. See also, I, 59 –60.

of experiencing the 'sweets and satisfactions of virtue' and 'the essential and inherent bitterness of all that is morally evil'. God had provided the human moral constitution with an appreciation of truth over falsehood without which, 'the world of trade would ... break up into a state of anarchy, or rather be paralysed into a state of cessation and stillness'.[26]

Whewell contended that the interconnection of the physical and the moral throughout nature demonstrated their having the same Author. The atmosphere surrounding the earth and the human organs of speech and hearing permitted communication which was essential for moral development. Light and vision permitted human-kind to develop a sense of beauty and to expand their minds. Most important, the economic development of physical nature stimulated the emergence of moral instincts associated with advanced commercial civilization. Whewell asked, 'Must we not suppose that He who created the soil also inspired man with those social desires and feelings which produce cities and states, laws and institutions, arts and civilizations; and that thus the apparently inert mass of earth is a part of the same scheme as those faculties and powers with which man's moral and intellectual progress is most connected?' Whewell further observed that

> a person must be strangely constituted, who, living amid the respect for law, the admiration for what is good, the order and virtues and graces of civilized nations (all of which have their origin in some degree in the feeling of responsibility) can maintain that all these are casual and extraneous circumstances, no way contemplated in the formation of man; and that a condition in which there should be no obligation in law, no merit in self-restraint, no beauty in virtue, is equally suited to the powers and the nature of man, and was equally contemplated when those powers were given him.[27]

Similar sentiments are to be found in virtually all of the Bridgewater treatises. In the broadest sense the writers found themselves living in a competitive, commercial society. The presence of human social characteristics which allowed them to live in that society and to develop the earth through commercial means first demonstrated the wisdom of God's meshing human capacity with social setting and second indicated that God intended human beings to live in just such a society.

---

[26] Chalmers, *The power, wisdom, and goodness of God*, pp. 14, 57, 58, 163.
[27] Whewell, *Astronomy and general physics*, pp. 137, 139.

In recent years the work of Steven Shapin, James Secord, Pietro Corsi, Richard Cooter, Adrian Desmond, and Richard Yeo, among others, has demonstrated the presence of radical scientific communities among London medical men and within several provincial cities who rejected both the defence of commercial society and the contemporary social status quo found among the traditional natural theologians and much of the scientific theory of the Anglican scientific elite. From their studies these historians have attempted to conclude that there existed a significant body of scientific workers and supporters ready to accept and advocate advanced naturalistic ideas. James Secord has gone so far as to suggest, 'One might say that when Darwin finally published, he engineered not a popular revolt but a palace coup within the scientific elite.'[28] These historians have not yet fully worked through the relationship of their radical scientific thinkers usually on the fringes of socially and politically respectable science and the advocates of scientific naturalism during the third quarter of the century. If the publications of Darwin and others associated with naturalistic thought amounted only to a coup, one wonders what the fuss after 1859 was all about. The spokesmen for scientific naturalism felt they really were fighting a major battle against the adherents of traditional natural theology. They did not regard the struggle as won because naturalistic ideas had been embraced in radical London and provincial scientific and medical circles. Like their clerical Anglican forebears they sought to dissociate themselves from such people. Furthermore, as Peter Bowler has so extensively argued, a thoroughly naturalistic understanding of evolution encountered difficulty for more than half a

---

[28] James A. Secord, 'Behind the veil: Robert Chambers and *Vestiges*', in James R. Moore, ed., *History, humanity and evolution: essays for John C. Greene* (Cambridge: Cambridge University Press, 1989), p. 166. See also Stephen Shapin, 'Phrenological knowledge and the social structure of early nineteenth-century Edinburgh', *Annals of Science*, 32 (1975), 219–43, and 'The politics of observation: cerebral anatomy and social interests in Edinburgh phrenology disputes', in Roy Wallis, ed., *On the margins of science: the social construction of rejected knowledge*, Sociological Review Monographs 27 (Keele: University of Keele, 1979), pp. 139–78; Roger Cooter, *The cultural meaning of popular science: phrenology and the organization of consent in nineteenth-century Britain* (Cambridge: Cambridge University Press, 1984); Pietro Corsi, *Science and religion: Baden Powell and the Anglican debate, 1800–1860* (Cambridge: Cambridge University Press, 1988); Adrian Desmond, *The politics of evolution: morphology, medicine, and reform in radical London* (Chicago: University of Chicago Press, 1989); and Richard Yeo, 'Science and intellectual authority in mid-nineteenth-century Britain: Robert Chambers and *Vestiges of the Natural History of Creation*', in Patrick Brantlinger, ed., *Energy & entropy: science and culture in Victorian Britain* (Bloomington: Indiana University Press, 1989), pp. 1–27.

century after Darwin's publication.[29] In both the scientific and the
social venues, the spokesmen for scientific naturalism felt they had to
meet head-on the issues previously addressed by natural theologians.
Scientific publicists, including Darwin, Spencer, and Huxley, felt
not only that they must replace the scientific ideas associated with
natural theology with more nearly naturalistic ones but also that
they must draw the social vision of traditional natural theology into
the congeries of naturalistic ideas. They removed that social vision
from the cocoon of eternity and dragged it into the saeculum of
history.

As so many Darwin scholars now argue, the inheritance of both
Paleyan and Bridgewater natural theology loomed large in the mind
and intellectual development of Charles Darwin. The categories of
natural theology clearly entered into Darwin's thought throughout
the various editions of *On the origin of species*. It was, however, less in
the *Origin* than in the post-*Origin* works that Darwin explicitly
voiced criticisms regarding natural theology such as had studded his
private notebooks in the late 1830s. In 1862 he told John Murray,
his publisher, that he intended his book on the fertilization of orchids
'like a Bridgewater treatise . . . to show the perfection of the many
contrivances in Orchids' as achieved through natural selection
rather than divine providence.[30] He concluded *The variation of
animals and plants under domestication* (1868) with an extensive, sophisti-
cated, and hostile discussion of natural theology. In *The expression of
the emotions in man and animals* (1872) he presented a long naturalistic
analysis of the subject directed against Sir Charles Bell's *Expression:
its anatomy and philosophy* (3rd edn., 1844) which had assumed the
concepts of special creation and accommodation inherent in natural
theology.

But Darwin's most extensive attack on natural theology occurred
in *The descent of man* (1871). There he carried out a vendetta not
against the science of natural theology in either its traditional form
or that of Alfred Wallace's spiritualism but rather against the
philosophical anthropology of natural theology that had served to

[29] Josef L. Altholz, 'The mind of Victorian orthodoxy: Anglican responses to "Essays and
Reviews", 1860–1864', *Church History*, 51 (1982), 186–97; Peter J. Bowler, *The eclipse of
Darwinism: anti-Darwinian evolution theories in the decades around 1900* (Baltimore: Johns Hopkins
University Press, 1983), and *The non-Darwinian revolution: reinterpreting a historical myth*
(Baltimore: Johns Hopkins University Press, 1988); Lightman, *The origins of agnosticism*, pp.
146–76.
[30] Darwin, *The life and letters of Charles Darwin*, II, 441.

undergird its social vision.[31] All traditional natural theologians had assumed with very little conscious articulation certain allegedly unique moral and intellectual features of human nature which they then used to explain the purposes of divine creation. Darwin stripped away all these allegedly unique qualities of humankind and portrayed a brutish human past and a materialistic interpretation of human historical development. In effect he removed from human nature virtually all of those characteristics that natural theologians and other philosophers had assumed to be unique to human beings and to distinguish them from the rest of the animal world. In the process, however, of pursuing this religiously destructive polemic, Darwin simultaneously provided a new justification for contemporary commercial society that paralleled the social argument of the traditional natural theologians. That is to say, in *The descent of man* Darwin removed the need for a religious framework to the social vision of natural theology as in *On the origin of species* he had removed the necessity of the religious framework for explaining the contrivances of nature.

One fundamental goal of natural religion had been to avoid social turmoil by repudiating the claims of atheism and materialism. In *The descent of man* Darwin attempted to demonstrate that a naturalistic and indeed virtually materialistic concept of human nature was compatible with social stability and, as Robert Richards has recently argued, with a not wholly selfish view of social life.[32] Natural forces and human history rather than God and eternity became the backdrop for humankind and its social development. Throughout the work Darwin presented the existing social order and social values as being compatible with conceiving humankind as having been descended from brutish and primitive ancestors unrecognizable as human. Even if science might undermine religion, it would not foster social turmoil because social stability did not actually depend upon religion or a religious interpretation of human development.

Just as earlier Darwin had believed he needed to prove that natural selection could produce perfect Paleyan adaptations in nature, so in *The descent of man* Darwin felt that he must provide naturalistic explanations for those allegedly unique features of human nature on which natural theologians had built so much of

[31] Robert J. Richards, *Darwin and the emergence of evolutionary theories of mind and behavior* (Chicago: University of Chicago Press, 1987), pp. 185–90.

[32] Ibid., pp. 234–41.

their case.[33] Darwin argued that what his predecessors and contemporary critics regarded as the unique and divinely established dignity of human nature was itself the natural product of evolution, history, and culture rather than of special creation or divine providence. Darwin looked for human origins in 'an extremely remote epoch, before man had arrived at the dignity of manhood' when 'he would have been guided more by instinct and less by reason than are the lowest savages at the present time'. During that period important changes had occurred naturalistically that led eventually to the human domination of the earth. Darwin explained,

Man in the rudest state in which he now exists is the most dominant animal that has ever appeared on this earth . . . He manifestly owes this immense superiority to his intellectual faculties, to his social habits, which lead him to aid and defend his fellows, and to his corporeal structure. The supreme importance of these characters has been proved by the final arbitrament of the battle for life. Through his powers of intellect, articulate language has been evolved; and on this his wonderful advancement has mainly depended.[34]

But Darwin insisted this physical, intellectual, and social advancement had occurred without evidence or necessity of supernatural providence. Nor was there any evidence that the earth had been prepared specially to receive this creature. The human domination of the world had come through struggle with the elements and with other animals and through the natural development of humankind's inherent intellectual and social capacities.

In *The descent of man* Darwin devoted three chapters to human mental powers which natural theologians and other philosophical writers had used to demonstrate human uniqueness and divine purpose. To each of the characteristics Darwin assigned naturalistic causes. He presented a largely instrumental and pragmatic image of the human intellect, bluntly contending that 'there is no fundamental difference between man and the higher mammals in their mental faculties'.[35] Darwin found in lower animals evidence of pleasure, pain, happiness, misery, terror, suspicion, love, and jealousy. Among

[33] See ibid., pp. 185–243, and John R. Durant, 'The ascent of nature in Darwin's *Descent of Man*', in David Kohn, ed., *The Darwinian heritage* (Princeton: Princeton University Press, 1985), pp. 183–307.
[34] Charles Darwin, *The origin of species and The descent of man and selection in relation to sex* (New York: The Modern Library, n.d.), pp. 430, 431. This edition reprints the second edition of *The descent of man*.
[35] Ibid., p. 446.

higher animals he discerned excitement, ennui, wonder, curiosity, imitation, attention, memory, imagination, and the power of reasoning.[36] Darwin also denied that human beings possessed any unique capacity to improve progressively, make use of tools and fire, domesticate animals, possess property, form general concepts, have self-consciousness, employ language, or possess a sense of beauty, feelings of gratitude, belief in God, or conscience. Natural theologians had pointed to each of these characteristics to demonstrate the uniqueness of human nature and to argue that the earth had been prepared to allow these particular unique human qualities to flourish in commercial society.

Darwin's most important and extensive critiques related to the mental and moral capacities of humankind. He thought it not impossible that animals possessed some modes of self-consciousness and that human beings in some very primitive cultures might possess very little. He presented examples of animals that employed language which appeared to be at least on the level of human infants. Darwin gave numerous examples of the manner in which animals responded to beauty especially the beauty of the female of the species. Although animals could not appreciate many other varieties of beauty, the human capacity to do so was not innate to the species or displayed by all human beings. Darwin observed, 'Obviously no animal would be capable of admiring such scenes as the heavens at night, a beautiful landscape, or refined music; but such high tastes are acquired through culture, and depend on complex associations; they are not enjoyed by barbarians or by uneducated persons.'[37] In other words, arguments for the uniqueness of humankind could not be derived from the relatively few human beings who inhabited the world of the aristocracy and educated middle class.

Darwin acknowledged that animals lacked capacity for religion or belief in God. Yet he could find 'no evidence that man was aboriginally endowed with the ennobling belief in the existence of an Omnipotent God'. Rather what he found to be 'universal with less civilized races' was a capacity to believe in 'unseen or spiritual agencies'. The early modes of savage religion arose from misguided use of intellectual faculties and eventually led to gross superstitions. Darwin contended, 'These miserable and indirect consequences of our highest faculties may be compared with the incidental and

[36] Ibid., pp. 456–7.   [37] Ibid., p. 468.

occasional mistakes of the instincts of the lower animals.'[38] He compared the relationship of such misguided human beings to those between a dog and its master. Only the development of intellect, not any form of divine revelation, could deliver human beings from these early religious confusions.

Darwin also addressed himself to the moral sense. Here again, approaching the subject, as he said, from the standpoint of natural history, he declared, 'Any animal whatever, endowed with well-marked social instincts, the parental and filial affections being here included, would inevitably acquire a moral sense or conscience, as soon as its intellectual powers had become as well, or nearly as well developed, as in man.'[39] He then catalogued a vast array of examples of sociability in animals that might suggest the possible development of a moral instinct. Darwin provided a long naturalistic interpretation of the emergence of various degrees of a moral instinct in human beings. Throughout he also emphasized how the substance of morality changed from culture to culture and from historical era to historical era.

Each of these critiques stripped away the divine origin or providential purpose of one or more of the characteristics of human beings to which natural theologians had pointed to demonstrate the unique status of human nature and had then used to defend contemporary commercial society. Darwin accounted naturalistically for each of these human social characteristics and demonstrated that his outlook no less than that of the natural theologians supported human life in a competitive commercial setting. Indeed, Darwin no less than John Ray, Thomas Malthus, William Paley, and the Bridgewater authors prescriptively defended the social status quo.

The conclusions that Darwin drew, like those of the anthropologists upon whose work he frequently depended, portrayed human social progress as being achieved through competition and natural selection. For example, Darwin thought it proper that civilized nations should supplant barbarous ones. The civilized nations carried out this process of conquest 'mainly, though not exclusively, through their arts, which are the products of intellect' the latter itself having been perfected through natural selection. Within civilized societies Darwin, echoing Paley and other natural theologians, praised private property and the inheritance of wealth, observing that

[38] Ibid., pp. 468, 469, 468, 470.   [39] Ibid., p. 471–2.

the inheritance of property by itself is very far from an evil; for without the accumulation of capital the arts could not progress; and it is chiefly through their power that the civilized races have extended, and are now everywhere extending their range so as to take the place of the lower races. Nor does the moderate accumulation of wealth interfere with the process of selection. When a poor man becomes moderately rich, his children enter trades or professions in which there is struggle enough, so that the able in body and mind succeed best. The presence of a body of well-instructed men, who have not to labour for their daily bread, is important to a degree which cannot be over-estimated; as all high intellectual work is carried on by them, and on such work, material progress of all kinds mainly depends, not to mention other and higher advantages. No doubt wealth when very great tends to convert men into useless drones, but their number is never large; and some degree of elimination here occurs, for we daily see rich men, who happen to be fools or profligate, squandering away their wealth.[40]

Here and elsewhere Darwin portrayed a naturalistic analysis of the social order as supporting in most respects contemporary English social practices though he directed various barbed remarks toward the lifestyle of the aristocracy. His social views and his concept of progress in large measure appear derived from the late eighteenth-century Scottish school of social thought. Interestingly, as in the passage above, Darwin emphasized the need for persons of intellect and intellectual professions thus defending the new Victorian educated professional classes in a manner not unlike that which the early natural theologians had defended landed wealth and commercial professions.[41] Like the natural theologians before him, he accepted and rationalized a world filled with suffering, social inequality, and unfairness.

The sociology and more general synthetic philosophy of Herbert Spencer as well as anthropologists such as E. B. Tylor similarly supported the fundamental character of contemporary British and European society. That these writers as well as Darwin by differing methods and to differing degrees defended their contemporary social structure is, of course, familiar. Various historians have seen such

---

[40] Ibid., pp. 497, 502.
[41] Darwin's writing also very clearly supported a generally traditional role for women in Victorian society. See Evelleen Richards, 'Darwin and the descent of women', in David Oldroyd and Ian Langham, eds., *The wider domain of evolutionary thought* (Dordrecht: D. Reidel Publishing Co., 1983), pp. 57–112, and 'Huxley and woman's place in science: the "woman question" and the control of Victorian anthropology', in Moore, ed., *History, humanity and evolution*, pp. 253–84; Cynthia Eagle Russett, *Sexual science: the Victorian construction of womanhood* (Harvard: Harvard University Press, 1989), *passim*.

social complacency as evidence of the scientists' participation in an ideology that supported industrial society.[42] Such a view pays too little attention to the full intellectual and scientific context in which these scientists and supporters of scientific naturalism laboured. The articulation of their social views in very large measure represented a secularization of an important part of the traditional agenda of the natural theologians. As Darwin and numerous of his contemporaries used scientific analysis to defend and rationalize contemporary social relationships that went well beyond those associated with industrialism, they made unnecessary the appeal to the religious and the eternal to assure social and political stability. Science both removed the religious categories and provided substitute modes of interpretation. The process was thus doubly secular.

Yet scientific theory alone did not undermine natural religion and provide a secular world view for either science or society. Another factor that brought to a close the career of the interrelationship of science and natural religion was what might be termed the *Baconianism of everyday life*. Although Francis Bacon had pointed to the double revelation of divine knowledge through both nature and the scriptures, he had also urged natural philosophers to resist the temptation to pose unanswerable questions and questions that had no practical import on the human condition. Natural theologians had embraced the idea of the two revelations but had rejected Bacon's second contention. They had repeatedly declared that both nature and the character of the human mind demanded the posing of questions and speculations that went beyond direct observation of nature. For example, the Bridgewater writers asserted that human beings were inherently dissatisfied with secondary causes as explanations of nature and demanded recourse to final causes. Roget had commented, 'The study of these final causes is, in some measure, forced upon our attention by even the most superficial survey of nature.'[43]

Roget's assumption of the need for exploration of final causes

---

[42] J. W. Burrow, *Evolution and society: a study in Victorian social theory* (Cambridge: Cambridge University Press, 1968); J. D. Y. Peel, *Herbert Spencer: the evolution of a sociologist* (London: Heinemann, 1971); David Wiltshire, *The social and political thought of Herbert Spencer* (Oxford: Oxford University Press, 1978); George W. Stocking, Jr, *Victorian anthropology* (New York: The Free Press, 1987), pp. 144–237; James Moore, 'Theodicy and society: the crisis of the intelligentsia', in Helmstadter and Lightman, eds., *Victorian faith in crisis*, pp. 153–86, and Young, *Darwin's metaphor*, pp. 1–55, 79–163.

[43] Roget, *Animal and vegetable physiology*, I, 31.

stood rooted in the entire tradition of British natural theology. In 1668 the English poet John Dryden wrote, 'Is it not evident in these last hundred years (when the study of philosophy has been the business of all the Virtuosi in Christendom), that almost *a new Nature* has been revealed to us?'[44] Dryden's 'new nature', undergirded by Copernican astronomy and soon to receive fuller articulation in Newton's synthesis, encompassed an increasingly rational, mechanical, and predictable image of physical nature exploitable by human reason and ingenuity and existing within the confines of divine providence and eternal things. That new nature had provided the original backdrop for British natural theology and for the appeal to final causes.

In 1887, the year of Queen Victoria's Golden Jubilee, T. H. Huxley announced the emergence of a 'new Nature created by science' that had become manifested in 'every mechanical artifice, every chemically pure substance employed in manufacture, every abnormally fertile race of plants, or rapidly growing and fattening breed of animals'. Huxley's 'new Nature begotten by science upon fact' that assured the foundation of British wealth, linked vast regions, prevented disease, and conduced 'to physical and moral well-being' represented a new frame of human social and intellectual orientation no less powerful than that found in Dryden's new nature resulting from the scientific revolution.[45] The movement of thought and sensibility from awe and wonder over Dryden's 'new nature' to awe and wonder over what Huxley had termed a 'new nature' in a very real sense accomplished Bacon's goal of abandoning the pursuit of literally useless questions. Huxley's 'new nature' pointed toward a rational, mechanical, and predictable technological infrastructure that had arisen through the application of human reason and ingenuity, that involved no final causes, and that flourished within the confines of human history without reference to God. To the extent that human attention directed itself toward the rising standard of living and the wonders of modern technology rather than to the wonders of physical and organic nature, humankind itself emerged as the new creator.

As Asa Briggs argued in *Victorian things*, the most ordinary objects

44 John Dryden, 'An essay of dramatic poesy', in *Essays*, ed. W. P. Ker (Oxford: Clarendon Press, 1926), pp. 36–7 as quoted in Franklin LeVan Baumer, *Religion and the rise of scepticism* (New York: Harcourt, Brace, and Co., 1960), p. 79 (italics added).
45 T. H. Huxley, *Collected essays* (New York: D. Appleton and Co., 1894), 1, 51.

during the late nineteenth century could be discussed in a manner to arouse wonder. The title of Annie Carey's *The wonders of common things* (1873) captured the tenor of such interest. Significant numbers of books and articles appeared for popular audiences explaining how various items of everyday life were made and how they worked. The world produced by science, technology, and human invention was as splendid as physical nature explained by science. In a sense by the close of the century fascination with the human maker of matches, typewriters, fountain pens, and the like had replaced fascination with the Divine Watchmaker. The 'new nature created by science' did not require any larger metaphysical or theological framework. It was genuinely *secular* in that it existed in history with no pretensions to being surrounded by things or purposes eternal. The end of the new nature was human comfort not human speculation. To the extent that it fostered speculation, and it did, the speculation centred upon human achievements and human contrivances within time and history. Interest in the eternal vanished with the fascination of the immediate present. Late century discussions of coal in contrast to Buckland's concerned not the providential provision of its deposits but the fears of the exhaustion of its supply and the social conflict involved in its mining.[46]

Huxley's thought demonstrates another manner in which the new technology and consequent improved standard of living undermined the assumptions of natural religion. In the Romanes Lecture of 1893 Huxley rejected the suffering in nature that all of the classical natural theologians, as well as many evolutionary scientists and philosophers, had accepted. In place of the suffering of the cosmic process that stood justified by some kind of religious or secular theodicy, he espoused the pursuit of an ethical order that would directly oppose the cosmic. He declared,

Social progress means a checking of the cosmic process at every step and the substitution for it of another, which may be called the ethical process; the end of which is not the survival of those who may happen to be the fittest, in respect of the whole of the conditions which obtain, but of those who are ethically the best.

Huxley argued that in human society cooperation and help for one's fellow creatures should replace competition. He did not believe the

⁴⁶ Asa Briggs, *Victorian things* (London: Batsford, 1988), pp. 179–212, 289–386.

human race would escape all pain and sorrow, but there was no need to embrace what he termed 'the gladiatorial theory of existence'.[47]

A major aspect of the secularization of science in the modern world has involved just such a rejection of nature itself as a moral or social norm. In that regard, Huxley moved further away from the theodicies of natural theology than had Darwin or Spencer. Huxley's ethical process existed within history and within the saeculum. Huxley rejected the optimism inherent in natural theology. He could not see the smiling face of nature that Paley had portrayed, nor did he embrace Darwin's confidence that natural selection worked ultimately toward perfection of the various species. Huxley, in contrast to the natural theologians as well as to Darwin and Spencer, did not wholly accept the late Victorian social order. Although no radical, he was a clear reformer. The ethical order, unlike the cosmic order, was to be forged by human beings who would inhabit and benefit from the powers of the new nature created by science. Once the knowledge of science stood conceived as a tool to make the face of the earth more smiling and happy rather than justifying as morally right whatever existed, science was well on its way toward a secular career changing society here and now rather than in some distant future. Science had not only entered the saeculum, it had become a major factor in forging it.

[47] T. H. Huxley, *Collected works* (New York: D. Appleton and Co., 1894), IX, 81, 82.

II

Science and the wider culture

CHAPTER 5

Victorian scientific naturalism and Thomas Carlyle

During the second half of the nineteenth century the spokesmen for scientific naturalism constituted one of the most vocal and visible groups on the Victorian intellectual landscape. Combining research, polemic wit, and literary eloquence, they defended and propagated a scientific world view based on atomism, conservation of energy, and evolution. They raised the banner of the functional expertise of the scientifically educated against the resistance of religious orthodoxy, received opinion, and intellectual obscurantism. They sought to create a largely secular climate of opinion no longer dominated by religion that would permit the theories and practitioners of modern science to penetrate the institutions of education, industry, and government for the material progress and social amelioration of the nation.

Their immense energy and the multiplicity of their interests and contacts permitted them to carry their message of the benefits of scientific endeavour to audiences ranging from skilled mechanics to members of the aristocracy.[1] Thomas Henry Huxley, whose vast panoply of activities made him the most famous of the group, illustrates the multi-faceted activities of these writers. In addition to his polemical efforts on behalf of evolution, Huxley conducted private research, trained teachers at the Royal School of Mines, served as a member of the London School Board and the Devonshire

From *Victorian Studies*, 18 (1975), 325–43. With permission of the journal.
[1] Noel Annan, *Leslie Stephen: the godless Victorian* (New York: Random House, 1984); Cyril Bibby, *T. H. Huxley: scientist, humanist, and educator* (London: Watts, 1959); J. W. Burrow, *Evolution and society: a study of Victorian social theory* (Cambridge: Cambridge University Press, 1970); Frank Miller Turner, *Between science and religion: the reaction to scientific naturalism in late Victorian England* (New Haven: Yale University Press, 1974), pp. 8–37; James Paradis, *T. H. Huxley: man's place in nature* (Lincoln: University of Nebraska Press, 1978); David Wiltshire, *The social and political thought of Herbert Spencer* (New York: Oxford University Press, 1978); Bernard Lightman, *The origins of agnosticism: Victorian unbelief and the limits of knowledge* (Baltimore: Johns Hopkins University Press, 1987).

commission on scientific education, advised the government on fisheries, helped to restructure the University of London, presided for a time as president of the Royal Society, wrote textbooks, and composed essays on biology, geology, epistemology, theology, and social reform. Other members of the naturalistic coterie engaged in a similarly wide variety of intellectual and educational enterprises. John Tyndall was the successor to Faraday as superintendent of the Royal Institution. He was an active physicist, a government consultant on lighthouses, a highly gifted lecturer, and an avid mountain climber, as well as a member, with Huxley, of the scientific contingent in the Metaphysical Society. Likewise, Francis Galton could never find sufficient outlet in a single field for his considerable intellectual energies. He wrote books on travel, military encampment, eugenics, and criminology. Herbert Spencer embraced the entire realm of knowledge as he forged the evolutionary scheme of the synthetic philosophy. Leslie Stephen left Cambridge and holy orders to become a major literary critic, an historian of eighteenth-century thought, founding editor of the *Dictionary of national biography*, and a leading apologist for agnosticism and free-thought. John Morley edited the *Fortnightly Review* and later the *Pall Mall Gazette*, campaigned against religiously dominated education, wrote numerous biographies, served on two occasions as Chief Secretary for Ireland, later was Secretary of State for India, and ultimately as Lord Privy Seal resigned from the Liberal cabinet in opposition to British entry into World War I. All of these figures seemed to thrive on controversy and hard work.

Although a considerable literature has accumulated about the scientific publicists and their polemical careers, historians have too rarely sought to understand from what previous intellectual tradition or traditions they emerged. Fundamentally, the advocates of Victorian scientific naturalism stand as successors to the eighteenth-century philosophes about whom several, including Huxley, Stephen, and Morley, wrote. They shared the general epistemological outlook of the Enlightenment as refined by John Stuart Mill in his *System of logic*. Like these rationalistic forebears, they helped to sow and reap a vast harvest of knowledge from advancing research in geology, biology, physics, psychology, and physiology. They did not, however, exhibit the reserve of the philosophes about bringing harsh criticisms of religion and advanced ideas about nature to a broad public. Rather they combined the critical mentality of the eighteenth century with the fervour for popular instruction that originated in the Mechanics' Institutes, the Owenite Halls of Science, and the publications of Knight and Chambers. Their desire to penetrate a religiously dominated system of education also led the scientific publicists to embrace the enlightenment spirit of anticlericalism. But since they hoped to recruit support from the upper and middle classes, they eschewed the tactics of contemporary secularists, such as G. J. Holyoake and Charles Bradlaugh. Instead, the advocates of naturalism displayed eminent respectability, repeatedly disclaimed atheistic intentions, and refused to view their efforts as a mode of class conflict. In fact, they regarded the application of modern science to the problems of sanitation and public health as presenting one solution to that social conflict.

Nevertheless, caution must be exercised when pointing to the preeminence of the Enlightenment or positivist heritage of the naturalistic authors. The facts suggest a more complicated picture. Indeed, when considering that intellectual heritage, it is necessary to take into account their educational, social, and professional goals as well as their specific scientific ideas. Rationalistic and scientific outlooks were sometimes vehicles for pursuing social and even intellectual ends that had originated in non-rational and non-scientific sources.

Without exception the scientific publicists had *become* naturalistic or positivistic. Christian rearings, clerically dominated universities, or scientific educations liberally laced with metaphysics, idealism, and natural religion had characterized their initial encounters with the life of the mind. Huxley as a boy would go off to the woods to deliver sermons from tree stumps. Tyndall had grown up amid the rigours of Irish Orange Protestantism. Leslie Stephen was the son of a strict evangelical household and had also taken holy orders. Herbert Spencer's childhood had been passed among liberal Nonconformists in the provinces among whom he learned to detest the institutions of the state as epitomized by the Church of England. Often slowly and only with intense straining of both reason and imagination had these men moved toward a more fully naturalistic frame of mind. Even when naturalism came to dominate their scientific and religious thought, other areas of their intellect retained impressions of non-naturalistic thinking in the same manner that anthropomorphic metaphors of nature frequently crept into Darwin's language in the *On the origin of species*. It is through the recognition of the transitional nature of their intellectual development and their concern for effective social and educational policy that one encounters the rather unexpected influence on the naturalistic coterie of Thomas Carlyle.

Carlyle has not usually been numbered among the friends of rationalism and science. Participating in what his friend J. S. Mill termed 'the revolt of the human mind against the philosophy of the eighteenth century', he introduced German romanticism and idealism to the British reading public through translations, interpretive essays, and his best known work *Sartor resartus*. For more than half a century in one passage after another, Carlyle pointed to the heartlessness, social futility, and intellectual sterility of the 'European Mechanisers'. He portrayed Voltaire and Diderot as significant but essentially shallow intellects. Utilitarians with their talk of gauging social policy from measurements of human pleasure and pain were anathema to him. Among his heroes appeared not a single scientist unless one so classifies Goethe. Instead, the exploits of Odin, Mohammed, Dante, and Cromwell won his acclaim. Carlyle wanted nothing to do with Darwin's natural selection. On one occasion when Huxley crossed the street to walk with him, the older man grumbled, 'You're Huxley, aren't you; the man that says we are all descended from monkeys.'[2]

Yet Carlyle's relationship to rationalism, science, and naturalistic writers was considerably more ambiguous than it might initially appear. He was anything but ignorant of physical science. His own clouded loss of faith may in part have stemmed from study of natural philosophy at Edinburgh. He had translated encyclopaedia articles on scientific topics and had reviewed scientific books.[3] His use of scientific metaphors was frequent and exact. John Tyndall, a warm admirer of Carlyle, thought the old Scot exhibited a remarkably quick grasp of scientific matters during visits to Tyndall's laboratory. This scientist once even suggested that passages in *Sartor resartus* anticipated the formation of the law of the conservation of

[2] J. S. Mill, 'Coleridge', in *The six great humanistic essays of John Stuart Mill*, ed. Albert William Levi (New York: Washington Square Press, Inc., 1963), p. 80; Thomas Carlyle, *Sartor resartus: the life and opinions of Herr Teufelsdrockh*, ed. Charles Frederick Harrold (New York: The Odyssey Press, 1937), p. 234; Leonard Huxley, *The life and letters of Thomas Henry Huxley* (New York: D. Appleton and Co., 1900), I, 297.

[3] G. B. Tennyson, *Sartor called resartus: the genesis, structure, and style of Thomas Carlyle's first major work* (Princeton: Princeton University Press, 1965), pp. 18–24. See also the relevant sections of Fred Kaplan, *Thomas Carlyle: a biography* (Ithaca: Cornell University Press, 1983).

energy.[4] Moreover, just after the turn of the century A. W. Benn set Carlyle squarely in the English rationalist tradition, arguing that 'neither the vociferous romanticism of his youth nor the aristocratic Toryism of his old age should blind us to the undercurrent of sympathy with reforming rationalism never long unfelt beneath the roar and foam and spray of his superficial idolatrous absolutism'.[5]

A similar ambiguity surrounds the relationship of the scientific publicists to Carlyle. His books captured the imagination and channelled much of the enthusiasm of young men who came of age in the forties and fifties and who saw their own experiences mirrored in Teufelsdrockh's journey from loss of faith, purpose, and identity to an affirmation of self through work in this world. Huxley, Tyndall, Morley, Galton, and even Spencer drew upon Carlyle's wisdom in their early manhood. Several outgrew their overt veneration (especially after the Governor Eyre controversy), but still they had been moulded by the figure who, in Morley's judgement, 'in these days has done more than anybody else to fire men's hearts with a feeling for right and an eager desire for social activity'. Even when he had come to criticize rather than to admire Carlyle, Huxley still recalled, 'the bracing wholesome influence of his writings when, as a very young man, I was essaying without rudder or compass to strike out a course for myself'. Herbert Spencer grudgingly admitted both that *Sartor resartus* 'made an impression, though it did not exercise any appreciable influence' and that 'the freshness of its presentations of things, and its wonderful vigour of style, attracted me'.[6] As usual Spencer underestimated the impact though clearly Carlyle's style exercised little sway over the synthetic philosophy.

Paradoxically, highest praise of all for the greatest of popular Victorian idealists came from John Tyndall, the one Victorian scientist who had no hestitation in referring to himself as a 'materialist'. He wrote,

I must ever gratefully remember that through three long cold German winters Carlyle placed me in my tub, even when ice was on its surface, at

4 John Tyndall, *New fragments* (New York: D. Appleton and Co.), 1892, p. 386. See also the *Times*, 4 May 1881, p. 13.
5 A. W. Benn, *A history of English rationalism in the nineteenth century* (London: Longmans, Green & Co., 1906) 1, 418.
6 John Morley, 'Carlyle', in *Nineteenth-century essays*, ed. Peter Stansky (Chicago: University of Chicago Press, 1970), p. 39; Huxley, *The life and letters of Thomas Henry Huxley*, 11, 37; Herbert Spencer, *An autobiography* (London: Williams and Norgate, 1904), 1, 242. See also 'Herbert Spencer: a portrait', *Blackwood's Edinburgh Magazine*, 175 (1904), 105–10.

five o'clock every morning – not slavishly, but cheerfully, meeting each day's studies with a resolute will, determined whether victor or vanquished not to shrink from difficulty.

Carlyle along with Emerson and Fichte, Tyndall continued, 'told me what I ought to do in a way that caused me to do it, and all my consequent intellectual action is to be traced to this purely moral source ... These three unscientific men made me a practical scientific worker.'[7] Tyndall's discipleship begun during his years of study in Germany ended only when he had escorted Carlyle's body to Ecclefechan for burial.

That young men moving towards a vocation in science read Carlyle is not surprising; that they found him so intriguing and personally relevant well into adulthood and even old age requires further elucidation. Over forty years ago in an essay exploring the relationship of Huxley to Carlyle, William Irvine suggested,

What Carlyle chiefly contributed was not ideas but temperament. He developed the Victorian in Huxley ... He strengthened the moral fervor and the sense of discipline which gave to Huxley's strenuous advocacy of science an invaluable respectability at a time when science was confronted with the serried ranks of righteousness. Carlyle did not greatly change Huxley's mind, but he probably made it more influential.[8]

In point of fact Carlyle did all this and much more not only for Huxley but also for most of the leading advocates of scientific naturalism. Carlyle's message was often confused and sometimes inconsistent. But within that heady mixture contemporaries of a rationalistic and naturalistic bent of mind discovered the foundation for a view of nature, religion, and society that allowed them to regard themselves as thoroughly scientific and naturalistic without becoming either materialistic or atheistic and to accept secular society with good conscience and a finite universe without spiritual regret. In this respect Carlyle's idealist concepts and moral doctrines eased the transition from a religious apprehension of the universe to a scientific and secular one.

[7] John Tyndall, *Fragments of science*, 6th edn (New York: D. Appleton and Co., 1892), II, 96. See also James R. Moore, '1859 and all that: remaking the story of evolution-and-religion', in Robert G. Chapman and Cleveland T. Duval, eds., *Charles Darwin, 1809–1882: a centennial commemorative* (Wellington, New Zealand: Nova Pacifica, 1982), pp. 167–94.

[8] William Irvine, 'Carlyle and T. H. Huxley', in *Booker memorial studies*, ed. Hill Shine (Chapel Hill: University of North Carolina Press, 1950), p. 121.

The fundamental link between the younger naturalistic generation and Carlyle was the latter's social criticism and his call for a new social and intellectual elite. Carlyle defined broad areas of social and moral concern including health and sanitation which the naturalistic writers considered susceptible to scientific treatment. Rejecting the solutions of political liberalism and of existing ecclesiasticism, Carlyle believed the problems of Britain's social and physical well-being should be addressed by leaders whose authority and legitimacy stemmed from talent, veracity, and knowledge of facts. These ideas helped the budding scientists and scientific publicists define their own cultural function in contemporary society. They could see themselves, even if Carlyle might not, as furnishing the very mode of effective cultural leadership that his books espoused.

Both Carlyle and the naturalistic coterie were what may be termed functional liberal elitists in social policy. Both wished the older aristocracy to give way functionally, if not necessarily socially, to a new aristocracy of talent. Like Carlyle, the scientific writers desired 'to promote men of talent, to search and sift the whole society in every class for men of talent, and joyfully promote them'. The ambitious young men of the forties and fifties sought to remove aristocratic influence from the scientific societies, and especially from the Royal Society, by allowing researchers of small means but significant accomplishments to become members and officers. They favoured national endowment of science and abolition of religious tests as a means of displacing aristocratic and ecclesiastical patronage of scientific research and education. They wanted trained scientists to enter the civil service by merit. Yet they were by no means egalitarian. Once a framework for liberal advancement by merit had been achieved, the scientific publicists, like Carlyle, believed the new elite itself should formulate and direct policy. Perhaps echoing Carlyle's remark that no ship could round the Horn directed by the vote of the crew, Huxley once declared, 'I should be very sorry to find myself on board a ship in which the voices of the cook and loblolly boys counted for as much as those of the officers, upon questions of steering, or reefing topsails.'[9]

9 Thomas Carlyle, *Latter-day pamphlets* (London: Chapman and Hall, 1870), p. 159; T. H. Huxley, *Collected essays* (New York: D. Appleton and Co., 1894), I, 313. See also, Carlyle, *Latter-day pamphlets*, p. 20, and Henry Lyon, *The Royal Society, 1660–1940* (Cambridge: Cambridge University Press, 1944), pp. 260–83.

The thought and career of Francis Galton most clearly illustrates the elitist side of the naturalistic movement and its affinity with Carlyle's doctrines. As a young man Galton had read Carlyle and had been disturbed by the condition of England question. Moreover, the administrative ineptitude of the English aristocracy during the Crimean War had disillusioned Galton with the existing capacity and structure of national leadership. He did all in his power to see that in the future British soldiers would possess necessary knowledge for survival in a hostile climate.[10] Yet Galton, like Carlyle, combined social concern and fury at a decadent, dysfunctional aristocracy with contempt for democracy and equality. Galton declared,

I have no patience with the hypothesis occasionally expressed, and often implied, especially in tales written to teach children to be good, that babies are born pretty much alike, and that the sole agencies in creating differences between boy and boy, and man and man, are steady application and moral effort. It is in the most unqualified manner that I object to pretensions of natural equality.[11]

In place of the democratic ideal Galton devoted his life to the study of inheritance and particularly the inheritance of genius. By the latter part of the century he was calling for what amounted to selective breeding of human beings to assure the survival of superior men and women who could lead society and solve its problems.

A direct line of intellectual descent connects Carlyle's demand for heroes and his devotion to great men with Galton's eugenics and Karl Pearson's eulogy of the superiority of the British race.[12] Each of them regarded society as more important than the individual. Social and national greatness required men and women possessing extraordinary qualities of leadership and intellectual genius. This viewpoint largely cast aside the environmentalism of Enlightenment writers. Genius or heroism were the products of innate, inborn qualities – matters of nature rather than nurture. Carlyle, Galton, and Pearson believed environmentalism might improve the material lot of citizens, but only a line of superior leaders could set a nation on the track to greatness.

To return, however, to the 1850s and the attraction of Carlyle to

[10] Karl Pearson, *The life, letters and labours of Francis Galton* (Cambridge: Cambridge University Press, 1924), I, 13–16.
[11] Ibid., I, 61.
[12] See Karl Pearson, *National life from the standpoint of science* (London: Adam and Charles Black, 1901).

the young men of science, it should be seen that Carlyle's rejection of political solutions and his call for an aristocracy of talent capable of positive action could be interpreted as an injunction for scientists to employ their expertise in the enterprise of social reform and reconstruction. At this point what Lecky termed Carlyle's 'standard of truthfulness' and his contempt for the 'half-beliefs and insincere professions' of the age intermeshed with the positivistic and rationalistic proclivities of the younger writers.[13] Obviously he was not the only author of the day who advocated truthfulness and attacked cant and sham. But Carlyle directly related such courage of intellect to addressing contemporary social questions. Both Carlyle and the naturalistic spokesmen regarded loyalty to fact and veracity in thought, speech, and action not only as good in themselves but as constituting the legitimate foundation to claims of social and intellectual leadership and moral superiority. These shared convictions provided both with a point of departure for a critique of the existing class of intellectual leaders – the Anglican clergy.

In *Past and present, Heroes and hero worship*, and *Latter-day pamphlets* Carlyle had fulminated against a priesthood or teaching class that helped to perpetuate Morrison's Pill solutions to the condition of England. In contrast to the sham priesthood Carlyle called for men of effective and active intellect, such as Abbot Sampson, who could compose an industrious, honest, and courageous teaching class that would educate and direct their society. Too few such individuals now inhabited the Church on all levels. As he pointed out in *Latter-day pamphlets*, the times and the human condition required men of real and noble intellect. He wrote that

it must be repeated, and ever again repeated till poor mortals get to discern it, and awake from their baleful paralysis, and degradation under foul enchantments, That a man of Intellect, of real and not sham Intellect, is by the nature of him likewise inevitably a man of nobleness, a man of courage, rectitude, pious strength; who, even *because* he is and has been loyal to the Laws of the Universe, is initiated into *discernment* of the same; to this hour a Missioned of Heaven; whom if men follow, it will be well with them; whom if men do not follow, it will not be well.[14]

Formerly, the clergy, and particularly the clergymen-scientists, in the parish, on the bench of bishops, and in the universities had

[13] W. H. Lecky, 'Carlyle's message to his age', *Contemporary Review*, 60 (1891), 526.
[14] Carlyle, *Latter-day pamphlets*, p. 129.

claimed to be the men of real intellect. However, from the mid-century onward scientists and the scientifically educated regarded themselves as more loyal to the truth and as better informed about the laws of the universe than were the intellects of the Church who, so believed the scientists, employed their positions of power and prestige to block the path of scientific education and investigation.

Carlyle's model of active, practical, truth-seeking intellectuals very closely resembled the cultural self-image of the advocates of naturalism and their successors, the social and technical experts, who sought to dislodge the clergy from their position as the educators and intellectual elite of the nation. As Huxley once told broad churchman Charles Kingsley (in a letter that also discussed Carlyle's religious influence), the established caste of priests must give way to a new order of prophets:

Understand that this new school of prophets is the only one that can work miracles, the only one that can constantly appeal to nature for evidence that it is right, and you will comprehend that it is no use to try to barricade us with shovel hats and aprons, or to talk about our doctrines being 'shocking'.

The scientists regarded themselves as teachers of truth who possessed the courage to divorce themselves from what Carlyle termed 'chimeras, luxuries, and falsities' and to attempt the 'all but "impossible" return to Nature, and her veracities, and her integrities'.[15] Theirs alone was the intellectual leadership that could address the problems of physical health and well-being with more success than that of the sham ecclesiastical intellects who maintained priestly control of education, defended false or obsolete science, preached prayer as a solution to practical problems of disease, and pointed to spurious laws of the universe that could not aid men and women in this life.

Recognition of the Carlylean influence upon the definition of the scientific publicists' role in the larger society also points towards a solution to a certain paradox that surrounds their polemical careers. It has become a commonplace to assert that Huxley, Tyndall, Stephen, Spencer, and company while sharply critical of religion were not atheistic bulls in the ecclesiastical china shop. Although publicly chiding the clergy, disputing Christian doctrines, and denying the scientific validity of the Bible, privately they remained

---

[15] Huxley, *The life and letters of Thomas Henry Huxley*, I, 238; Thomas Carlyle, *Past and present*, ed. Richard D. Altick (Boston: Houghton Mifflin Co., 1965), p. 28.

men of deep moral and no little religious sensitivity. This paradox has been stated more often than it has been explained. The solution would seem to lie, at least in part, with the Carlylean heritage of their thought. In a very real sense the concept of natural supernaturalism represented a new mode of natural theology. The wonder rather than the mechanical character of nature was to arouse the awareness of a divine presence behind the material appearances. Throughout the work of many of the writers associated with scientific naturalism and agnosticism there existed along with their desire to advance the cause of contemporary science a very real desire also to provide a substitute for traditional natural religion in a manner that recalls Carlyle's own pursuit of the transcendent.[16]

More than any other popular writer during the first half of the century, Carlyle had conceptually separated religion and spirituality from their contemporary institutional and dogmatic incarnations. Religion for Carlyle was wonder, humility, and work amidst the eternities and silences. The true realm of religion and the spirit was the inner man; all else was unessential externality. Through this stance Huxley claimed Carlyle had taught him 'that a deep sense of religion was compatible with the entire absence of theology'. At the close of his controversial and openly materialistic Belfast Address of 1874 Tyndall incorporated similar sentiments on the compatibility of man's emotional character with a scientific perception of nature.[17] In this manner the younger generation came to believe they could strike at contemporary religion with no fear of attacking the divine.

Moreover, Carlyle's was one of the chief voices that persuaded mid-Victorians and many twentieth-century historians that the religious institutions of Britain were no longer in touch with the divine, but rather constituted forms of idolatry that should be criticized. In a passage illustrating this probing criticism, Carlyle exclaimed,

Condemnable Idolatry is *insincere* Idolatry, Doubt has eaten out the heart of it: a human soul is seen clinging spasmodically to an Ark of the Covenant, which it half-feels now to have become a Phantasm. This is one of the balefullest sights. Souls are no longer *filled* with their Fetish; but only

16 This point has been argued most recently and persuasively by Bernard Lightman in *The origins of agnosticism*, pp. 146–76.
17 Huxley, *The life and letters of Thomas Henry Huxley*, I, 237; Tyndall, *Fragments*, II, 200–1.

pretend to be filled ... It is the final scene in all kinds of Worship and Symbolism the sure symptom that death is nigh. It is equivalent to what we call Formalism and Worship of Formulas, in these days of ours.

Though Carlyle was not specifically addressing himself to Anglicanism in this passage, he was writing for those who had eyes to see and ears to hear. Near the close of his life Huxley described the impact of the Carlylean solvent on earlier religious loyalties:

Half a century ago, the evangelical reaction which, for a time, had braced English society was dying out, and a scum of rotten and hypocritical conventionalism clogged art, literature, science, and politics. I might quarrel with something every few paragraphs, but passing from the current platitudes to Carlyle's vigorous pages was like being transported from the stucco, pavement, and fog of a London Street to one of his own breezy moors. The country was full of boulders and bogs, to be sure, and by no means calculated for building leases; but oh the freshness and freedom of it![18]

Victorians who might not accept the clothes of idealism that Carlyle offered still learned from him the courage and rectitude of discarding the old garments of conventional opinion that stifled the exercise and maturation of the intellect. He brought cultural and moral self-confidence to men at odds with their society and established the model of the vociferous social and religious critic who disdained neither society nor the divine. He exemplified a writer who could be sharply and unmercifully critical without becoming revolutionary.

Along with the value of outspoken criticism, Carlyle had also taught the occasionally higher value of silence. He had remained particularly reticent about his own attitude toward Christianity. Until the publication in 1851 of his biography of John Sterling, few readers knew where Carlyle stood on the subject. Privately he had been more forthright. In 1835 to Sterling's charge that Teufelsdrockh and by implication his literary creator did not believe in a personal God, Carlyle had retorted:

Assure yourself, I am neither Pagan nor Turk, not circumcised Jew, but an unfortunate Christian individual resident at Chelsea in *this* year of Grace; neither Pantheist nor Pottheist, nor any *Theist* or *ist* whatsoever, having the most decided contempt for all manner of System-builders and Sectfounders – so far as contempt may be compatible with so mild a nature; feeling well beforehand (taught by experience) that all such are and even must be

[18] Thomas Carlyle, *Heroes and hero worship*, edited by P. C. Parr (Oxford: Clarendon Press, 1920), p. 111; T. H. Huxley, 'Professor Tyndall', *The Nineteenth Century* 35 (1894), 3.

wrong. By God's blessing, one has got two eyes to look with; and also a mind capable of knowing, of believing: that is all the creed I will at this time insist on.[19]

Forty years later these lines, sanitized of residual Christian rhetoric, might well have stood as a statement of Huxley's, Tyndall's, Spencer's, or Stephen's religious and metaphysical position. They, like Carlyle, preferred to search out the truth rather than to defend labels.

Philosophically and religiously, Carlyle had been an agnostic long before Huxley embraced the term for his own polemical convenience. In fact few later scientific writers stood more convinced than Carlyle of mankind's inability to discover or to articulate the answers to ultimate questions. In *Sartor resartus* he had asked, 'Which of your Philosophical Systems is other than a dream-theorem; a new quotient, confidently given out, where divisor and dividend are both unknown?' And in *Heroes and hero worship* he declared, 'Science has done much for us; but it is a poor science that would hide from us the great deep sacred infinitude of Nescience, whither we can never penetrate, on which all science swims as a mere superficial film.'[20] It was but a short step from Carlyle's Nescience to Herbert Spencer's Unknowable.

Yet the crucial philosophical element of Carlyle's impact on the scientific writers was his coupling of the doctrine of ignorance about ultimate issues with a refusal to counsel despair in this life. For John Morley, 'The prolonged and thousand-times repeated glorification of Unconsciousness, Silence, Renunciation, all come to this: We are to leave the region of things unknowable, and hold fast to the duty that lies nearest. Here, and nowhere else, is the Everlasting Yea. In action only can we have certainty.' Both explicitly and implicitly the naturalistic coterie embraced Carlyle's work ethic. Outside the realm of unanswerable questions lay sufficient queries yet unanswered but susceptible of solution to provide work for meaningful, productive living. The scientific publicists laboured tirelessly in that sphere of endeavour affirming Carlyle's contention that 'it is *in* the world that a man, devout or other, has his life to lead, his work waiting to be done'.[21]

[19] Alexander Carlyle, ed., *Letters of Thomas Carlyle to John Stuart Mill, John Sterling, and Robert Browning* (London: T. F. Unwin, Ltd, 1923), pp. 193–4.
[20] Carlyle, *Sartor resartus*, p. 54; Carlyle, *Heroes*, p. 7.
[21] Morley, 'Carlyle', p. 48; Carlyle, *Past and present*, p. 118.

Unlike writers such as Samuel Smiles who regarded work as a means to respectibility and personal self-sufficiency, Carlyle had ascribed to labour in this world a moral sanction and significance that embodied a religious or transcendental connotation. While regarding the world and man's place therein as essentially finite, he still eschewed reductionism and materialism and continued to view the earth as a sphere for hope and moral aspiration. In 1844 Carlyle told his dying friend Sterling:

We are journeying towards the Grand Silence; what lies beyond it earthly man has never known, nor will know; but all brave men have known that it was Godlike, that it was GOOD, – that the name of it was God. *Wir heisen euch hoffen.* What is right and best for us will full surely be. Tho' He slay me, yet will I trust in Him. 'ETERNO AMORE'; that is the ultimate significance of this wild clashing whirlwind which is named Life, where the Sons of Adam flicker painfully for an hour.

Even the more aggressive scientific writers occasionally espoused similar views of man's finite situation vis-à-vis a possibly larger meaning to the universe. About a quarter century after Carlyle's words to Sterling, Francis Galton in *Hereditary genius* voiced a strikingly similar speculation on the possible spiritual meaning of the finitude of individual human experience as he observed,

We are exceedingly ignorant of the reasons why we exist, confident only that individual life is a portion of some vaster system that struggles arduously onwards towards ends that are dimly seen or wholly unknown to us, by means of the various affinities – the sentiments, the intelligences, the tastes, the appetites – of innumerable personalities who ceaselessly succeed one another on the stage of existence.[22]

What permitted Carlyle and Galton, as well as Spencer, Tyndall, Huxley and others to accept finitude in a spirit of affirmation was their conviction that humankind could morally transcend both the finitude and the materials of earthly existence – a conviction undergirded by the Carlylean doctrine of natural supernaturalism.

Natural supernaturalism (set forth in *Sartor resartus* but permeating all of Carlyle's work), by asserting the grandeur and marvel of nature in the face of the absence of miracles, the limitations of human knowledge, and the ultimate mystery of things, provided the secular equivalent of a spiritual sanction to activity in this world. In

[22] Carlyle, ed., *Letters of Thomas Carlyle*, p. 275; Francis Galton, *Hereditary genius: an inquiry into its laws and consequences* (Cleveland and New York: The World Publishing Co., 1962), p. 405.

essence it attributed to the material world and experience therein the characteristics previously associated with spiritual realms of aspiration. Although natural supernaturalism epitomized a romantic, idealistic view of nature, it could be and was embraced by naturalistic authors. Morley wrote,

Natural supernaturalism . . . teaches us to behold with cheerful serenity the great gulf which is fixed round our faculty and existence on every side, while it fills us with that supreme sense of countless unseen possibilities and of the hidden, undefined movements of shadows and light over the spirit, without which the soul of man falls into hard and desolate sterility . . . It is the Supernaturalism which stirs men first, until larger fulness of years and wider experience of life draw them to a wise and not inglorious acquiescence in Naturalism.

Transmitted through Carlyle the romantic heritage of seeking the meaning of life through a particularistic or empirical apprehension and examination of nature allowed the scientific publicists to confront the naturalistic universe without regret for past supernaturalism. Natural supernaturalism supplied the finite world with the splendour previously associated with a supposedly infinite or supernatural realm. For example, Huxley could write that the doctrine of immortality 'is not half so wonderful as the conservation of force, or the indestructability of matter'. Tyndall in an almost Wordsworthian vein told an audience, 'It is the function of science, not as some think to divest this universe of its wonder and mystery, but . . . to point out the wonder and the mystery of common things.'[23]

When reading such statements, it is necessary to remember that at mid-century, and immediately after, the scientific world view of even the most advanced scientists still retained certain residual metaphysical elements. Though the trend of naturalistic scientific thought and endeavour was to limit the scope of traditional metaphysics, much of the task remains to be accomplished. Idealism still permeated British scientific thinking. For Huxley, Tyndall, Spencer, Galton, and others the natural universe might indeed be composed of nothing but matter and force, but that matter and force pertained more nearly to Comte's metaphysical stage than to the positive stage of intellectual development.

The presence of these residual metaphysical elements within the

---

[23] Morley, 'Carlyle', pp. 49–50; Huxley, *The life and letters of Thomas Henry Huxley*, I, 234; Tyndall, *Fragments*, II, 66.

scientific picture of the mid-century rendered an intellectual transition from natural supernaturalism to scientific naturalism or vice versa relatively simple. Such was especially the case with the concept of force which was a highly unrefined idea even in the hands of the most accomplished scientists dealing with it.[24] Carlyle, drawing from German writers of the 1820s, frequently spoke of force. For example, in *Heroes and hero worship* he declared,

This Universe, ah me! – what could the wild man know of it? what can we yet know? That it is a Force, and thousandfold Complexity of Forces; a Force which is *not we*. That is all; not we, it is altogether different from *us*. Force, Force, everywhere Force; we ourselves a mysterious force in the centre of that.

Force could be regarded as the basis of all physical existence and as such something akin to the divine. W. R. Grove, an important British commentator on the law of conservation of energy, closed his book on the subject by stating, 'In all phenomena the more closely they are investigated the more we are convinced that, humanly speaking, neither matter nor force can be created or annihilated, and that an essential cause is unattainable. – Causation is the will, Creation the act of God.' Many years later W. B. Carpenter, the physiological psychologist, used force as a means of asserting the presence of some form of deity in or behind physical nature.[25]

Several of the spokesmen for scientific naturalism employed force or related concepts to fend off charges of reductionist materialism. In doing so the Carlylean heritage of their thinking again appeared. Spencer's 'transfigured realism' was strongly reminiscent of the Carlylean view that the perceived world is the garment or symbol of an unperceived divinity or what Spencer called the Unknowable. Spencer wrote, 'Behind all manifestations, inner and outer, there is a Power manifested. Here, as before, it has become clear that while the nature of that Power cannot be known, yet its universal presence is the absolute fact about which there can be no relative facts.' In another passage Spencer spoke of 'the continued existence of an Unknowable as the necessary correlative of the Knowable'. Think-

---

[24] See T. S. Kuhn, 'Energy conservation as an example of simultaneous discovery', in Bernard Barber and Walter Hirsch, eds., *The sociology of science* (Glencoe, Ill.: The Free Press, 1962), pp. 486–515, and Edward L. Youmans, ed., *The correlation and conservation of forces: a series of expositions* (New York: D. Appleton and Co., 1869).

[25] Carlyle, *Heroes*, p. 8; W. R. Grove, 'The correlation of forces', in Youmans, ed., *The correlation and conservation of forces*, p. 199; W. B. Carpenter, 'On mind and will in nature', *Contemporary Review*, 20 (1872), 738–62.

ing analogous to natural supernaturalism permeated such statements as it did even more so a passage in which Galton described the physical universe in near pantheistic terms:

There is decidedly a solidarity as well as a separateness in all human, and probably in all lives whatsoever; and this consideration goes far, as I think, to establish an opinion that the constitution of the living Universe is a pure theism, and that its form of activity is what may be described as co-operative. It points to the conclusion that all life is single in its essence, but various, ever varying, and interactive in its manifestations, and that men and all other living animals are active workers and sharers in a vastly more extended system of cosmic action than any of ourselves, much less of them, can possibly comprehend. It also suggests that they may contribute, more or less unconsciously, to the manifestation of a far higher life than our own, somewhat as ... the individual cells of one of the more complex animals contribute to the manifestation of its higher order of personality.[26]

Galton was clearly suggesting the possibility of an *anima mundi* behind the appearances or what Carlyle would have termed the 'clothes' of the physical universe. Galton's musings challenged a clockwork, mechanical universe every bit as much as anything that Carlyle ever wrote. For both, the physical world may be more than it appears to the senses and the discursive reason.

As seen from the statements of Spencer and Galton, the residual metaphysical elements of science could mesh with a natural supernaturalistic outlook to give the scientific writer's idea of matter a rather different caste from that associated with Harriet Martineau or Lucretius. Often within the same lecture or essay the scientific publicists dealt with matter in two ways – in terms of scientific theory and metaphysical philosophy. In the latter regard, they usually backed away from full materialism. Clifford's mind-stuff was essentially an idealistic monism. Huxley always said that if forced to answer the unanswerable question, he would choose idealism over materialism. Tyndall, who called himself a 'materialist' and who lectured for several years on a materialistic theory of psychology, still contended that matter had been 'defined and maligned by philosophers and theologians, who are equally unaware that it is, at bottom, essentially mystical and transcendental'.[27]

[26] H. E. Steward, 'Carlyle's place in philosophy', *Monist*, 29 (1919), 179; E. Howard Collins, *An epitome of the synthetic philosophy* (New York: D. Appleton and Co., 1889), p. 314; Herbert Spencer, *First principles*, 4th edn (New York: D. Appleton and Co., 1896), p. 192d; Galton, *Hereditary Genius*, p. 428.
[27] Tyndall, *Fragments*, II, 51.

Contemporary opponents generally ignored these statements or thought them disingenuous because the anti-ecclesiastical bias of the naturalistic coterie often blinded their readers (and perhaps themselves) to the Carlylean heritage of their thought. The publicists were not only scientific educators but also popular moralists seeking to provide a new moral foundation for life in what they considered a finite universe. To come to grips with the material world was for them to wrestle with the very sources of the possibility of a moral existence. Carlyle's social critique and his natural supernaturalism were the essential foundation for the moral vision of scientific naturalism. As Tyndall explained,

As the years roll by, the term 'materialist' will lose more and more of its evil connotation; for it will be more and more seen and acknowledged that the true spiritual nature of man is bound up with his material condition. Wholesome food, pure air, cleanliness – hard work if you will, but also fair rest and recreation – these are necessary not only to physical but to spiritual wellbeing. A clogged and disordered body implies a more or less disordered mind. The seed of the spirit is cast in vain amid stones and thorns, and thus your best utterances become idle words when addressed to the acclimatised inhabitants of our slums and alleys.[28]

Since matter and material conditions were manifestations of a force retaining some characteristics associated with the divine, Tyndall had no difficulty conceiving material changes as a key to moral reformation. The Carlylean heritage permitted him to refurbish matter through a purely secular natural supernaturalism that itself implied Carlyle's imperative to work in this world.

The mid-nineteenth-century concepts of laws of science or of nature provided a second point of intersection between Carlyle's thought and residual metaphysical elements of contemporary science. Numerous scientists regarded scientific or natural laws as governing nature or as being imperatives in nature. This view of law represented a transitional stage between a juridically oriented concept of law and the early twentieth-century descriptive concept. Laws seen as juridical decrees in conjunction with the doctrines of natural religion encouraged the identification of the natural order and the moral order.

Both Carlyle and scientific writers, the latter particularly in the fifties and sixties, appealed to this rather confused concept of natural

---

[28] Tyndall, *New fragments*, p. 44.

law. At one point Carlyle argued, 'The Maker's Laws, whether they are promulgated in Sinai Thunder, to the ear or imagination, or quite otherwise promulgated, are the Laws of God; transcendent, everlasting, imperatively demanding obedience from all men ... The Universe, I say, is made by Law; the great Soul of the World is just and not unjust.' In 1860 at the time of his son's death, Huxley voiced a similar faith, when he assured Kingsley, 'I am no optimist, but I have the firmest belief that the Divine Government (if we may use such a phrase to express the sum of the "custom of matter") is wholly just.' Perhaps more significantly he had affirmed a similar view of the relationship of material and moral law in 1855 when he set out to teach science to the working class. There Huxley told his students,

I want the working classes to understand that Science and her way are great facts for them – that physical virtue is the base of all other, and that they are to be clean and temperate and all the rest – not because fellows in black and white ties tell them so, but because these are plain and patent laws of nature which they must obey 'under penalties'.[29]

This last phrase is Carlyle's. The entire statement illustrates how the scientific concept of law and a secularized natural supernaturalism allowed Huxley and others to raise matter to the realm of morality and to portray informed men of science as the successors to the clergy as expositors of the laws of both nature and morality.

The Carlylean identification of the laws of nature with moral imperatives may also have undergirded certain approaches to evolutionary ethics. For example, Lecky observed of Carlyle,

It was one of his favourite sayings 'that the soul of the Universe is just', and he believed therefore that the ultimate fate of nations, whether it be good or bad, was very much what they deserved. It is curious to observe the analogy between this teaching and the doctrine of the survival of the fittest, which a very different teacher – Charles Darwin – has made so conspicuous.[30]

It could prove all too easy for admirers of Carlyle's history and later essays in which power and strong men figure so conspicuously to link that mode of thought with the concept of struggle appearing in discussions of organic evolution.

Nevertheless, the confusion and richness of Carlyle's thought also contained the seeds for the most important nineteenth-century refutation of might-makes-right social thinking. In the Romanes

[29] Carlyle, *Past and present*, p. 227; Huxley, *The life and letters of Thomas Henry Huxley*, I, 236, 149.
[30] Lecky, 'Carlyle's message to his age', 527.

Lecture of 1893 Huxley utterly disassociated himself from evolutionary ethics and a social policy of individualistic competition justified by appeals to laws of nature which many scientific writers had substituted for the similar competitive social imperative that traditional British natural theology had also supported. The Carlylean features of this lecture are striking but have not been previously noted. Huxley was attacking the same specious use of scientific theory to justify competition that Carlyle had castigated in *Past and present*. As noted in the previous chapter, Huxley argued, 'Social progress means a checking of the cosmic process at every step and the substitution for it of another, which may be called the ethical process.' He portrayed the ethical process as the construction of a well-tilled and cultivated garden which must be made to flourish amidst the unethical cosmic process. The garden metaphor recalls a similar image that Carlyle had drawn upon fifty years earlier when he declared in *Past and present*,

What is immethodic, waste, thou shalt make methodic, regulated, arable; obedient and productive to thee. Wheresoever thou findest Disorder, there is thy eternal enemy; attack him swiftly, subdue him; make Order of him, the subject not of Chaos, but of Intelligence, Divinity, and Thee! The thistle that grows in thy path, dig it out, that a blade of useful grass, a drop of nourishing milk, may grow there instead.[31]

Like Carlyle, Huxley set forth what amounted to an intuitive work ethic evoking a Promethean vision of man who in the midst of hostile nature must create a physical and social environment that would foster virtue and a quality of life.

The emphasis on the quality of life was one of Carlyle's major contributions to scientific naturalism. From contemporary science, the spokesmen for naturalism derived their tools and their methods of reasoning and analysis. From Carlyle they derived a sense of direction and urgency for the use of their scientific knowledge. Carlyle's impetus provided the foundation for their moral commitment, and by his own example, the model of the man of letters as hero. For the scientific publicists approached their age in the guise of the man of letters confident with Carlyle that 'What he teaches, the whole world will do and make.'[32]

31 Huxley, T. H., *Collected works*, IX, 81; Carlyle, *Past and present*, p. 201.
32 Carlyle, *Heroes*, p. 141.

CHAPTER 6

Rainfall, plagues, and the Prince of Wales

In July 1872, one of the most curious articles in the history of British journalism appeared in the much respected *Contemporary Review*. The anonymous essay, entitled 'The "Prayer for the Sick" – hints towards a serious attempt to estimate its value', challenged the Christians of the nation to conduct an experiment to determine the physical efficacy of prayer. A letter from physicist John Tyndall of the Royal Institution introduced the proposal, the author of which was later identified as Henry Thompson, an eminent London surgeon.[1]

Thompson admitted that few prayers were actually open to scientific or quantitative investigation. The prayers for the sick in the Book of Common Prayer were, however, an exception and appeared to constitute a set of petitions 'from a study of which the absolute calculable value of prayer ... can almost certainly be ascertained'. These fell into two categories – general prayers said every Sunday and specific prayers offered for particular individuals. Although Thompson desired no one to be deprived of the benefits afforded by general prayers, he did propose that

one single ward or hospital, under the care of first-rate physicians and surgeons, containing certain numbers of patients afflicted with those diseases which have been best studied, and of which the mortality rates are best known, whether the diseases are those which are treated by medical or surgical remedies, should be, during a period of not less, say, than three or five years, made the object of special prayer by the whole body of the faithful, and that, at the end of that time, the mortality rates should be

From *Journal of British Studies*, 13 (1974), 46–65. With permission of the journal.

[1] Henry Thompson (anon.), 'The "Prayer for the Sick" – hints towards a serious attempt to estimate its value', *Contemporary Review*, 20 (1872), 205–10. Authorship is attributed to Henry Thompson in the British Museum Catalogue and in Zachary Cope, *The versatile Victorian, being the life of Sir Henry Thompson* (London: Harvey and Blythe, 1951), p. 108.

compared with the past rates, and also with that of other leading hospitals, similarly well managed, during the same period.

Sincerity, simplicity, and clarity marked the proposed experiment which Thompson with quiet irony observed might furnish believers with 'an occasion of demonstrating to the faithless an imperishable record of the real power of prayer'.[2]

Thus was sparked what quickly became dubbed the Prayer Gauge Debate. For more than eighteen months it enlivened the columns of the *Contemporary Review*, the *Spectator*, the *Fortnightly Review*, and the religious journals. In 1873 it supplied the topic for the Burney Prize essay competition at Cambridge. Sermons and tracts echoed the arguments of the debate for almost a decade. More than forty years later religious encyclopaedias still discussed the proposal even though it had never been carried out.[3]

Thompson's proposed experiment evoked this lively and wide-ranging response because it fell into an arena of intellectual controversy where defenders of religious orthodoxy already confronted a host of challengers. These ranged from religious liberals represented by Matthew Arnold and Robert Seeley, to respectable middle-class agnostics, such as T. H. Huxley, Leslie Stephen, and John Morley, to secular atheists led by George Holyoake and Charles Bradlaugh. Moreover, by the 1870s scientists pursuing the naturalistic impulse in geology, biology, psychology, and physiology had cast into doubt

---

[2] Thompson (anon.), 'The "Prayer for the Sick" ', 207, 210.
[3] The major documents of the debate in addition to the initial proposal and those cited elsewhere in this essay are the following: *Spectator*, 45 (1872), 846–7, 879–80, 974–5, 1011–13, 1038–9, 1042–4, 1073, 1104–7, 1139; *Guardian*, 27 (1872), 1145, 1173, 1201–2; Richard Frederick Littledale, 'The rationale of prayer', *Contemporary Review*, 20 (1872), 430–54; H. Thompson (anon.), John Tyndall, James McCosh, 'On prayer', *Contemporary Review*, 20 (1872), 763–82; Duke of Argyll, 'Prayer: the two spheres – are they two?' *Contemporary Review*, 21 (1873), 464–73; William A. Knight, 'Prayer: "The Two Spheres": they *are* two', *Contemporary Review*, 22 (1873), 20–4. See also, George John Romanes, *Christian prayer and general laws being the Burney prize essay for the year 1873, with an appendix, the physical efficacy of prayer* (London: Macmillan and Co., 1874); Phipps Onslow, *The reasonableness of prayer* (London: Christian Evidence Committee of the Society for Promoting Christian Knowledge, n.d.); F. W. Newman, *The controversy about prayer* (London: Thomas Scott, 1873); John H. Jellett, *The efficacy of prayer* (London: Macmillan and Co., 1878); C. A. Bickwith, 'The prayer-gauge debate', in *The Schaff-Herzog encyclopedia of religious knowledge*, ed. Samuel Macauley Jackson (New York and London: Funk and Wagnalls Company, 1911), IX, 157–8; Charles Frederick D'Arcy, 'Prayer (Christian, theological)', in *Encyclopedia of religion and ethics*, ed. James Hastings (Edinburgh: T. and T. Clark, 1918), X, 175. The debate also roused interest in the United States where John Tyndall toured in late 1872 with the infamy of the proposal he had introduced preceding him. See John O. Means, ed., *The prayer gauge debate* (Boston, Mass.: Congregational Publishing Society, 1876).

the facts of scripture and the foundations of traditional natural theology. Consequently, the once friendly and complementary relationship between scientists and clergy had given way to the disputes over Lyell's geology and Darwin's evolution, the barbed exchange of Huxley and Wilberforce, the controversial evenings of the Metaphysical Society, and eventually Tyndall's challenge to all religiously oriented cosmology in his Belfast Address of 1874.

Thompson's proposal also found a ready audience because it represented the culmination of a controversy over the nature of prayer that dated from at least the 1850s. The continuing occasion for this sustained debate – the longest of all in the conflict between religious and scientific spokesmen – was the practice on the part of Anglican bishops and Scottish presbyteries of appointing special days for prayer, humiliation, and thanksgiving to address the otherwise unrelated practical matters of cholera, rainfall, cattle plague, and the health of the Prince of Wales.

As a private, personal practice, prayer was not problematical to a Victorian scientist or physician. It became so only when, as in the case of prayers on special occasions, it was 'forced upon his attention as a form of physical energy, or as the equivalent of such energy'. Under those circumstances Tyndall announced the physicist claimed 'the right of subjecting it to those methods of examination from which all our present knowledge of the physical universe is derived'.[4] Yet for Thompson, Tyndall, and other crusading scientists, the underlying issue was neither the physics nor the theology of prayer, but rather the nature and direction of cultural leadership in a modernized English society. Prayers on special occasions represented a concrete form of superstition whereby clergy with the approval of the state could hinder the dispersion of scientific explanations of natural phenomena or attempt to claim credit for the eradication of natural problems that were solved by the methods of science or that passed away in the course of nature. In this manner these prayers raised the question of whether scientists, physicians, and technical experts or the clergy should set the tone for public consideration of the health and physical well-being of the nation.

These public prayers were a survival not only of an age of faith but also of a church-directed culture in which the only broadly recognized intellectual elite was the clergy who performed functions later

---

[4] John Tyndall, 'On prayer', *Contemporary Review*, 20 (1872), 764.

assumed by separate professional groups.[5] Both before and after the Reformation, the English Church had taught that practical benefits were available through prayer. Yet the Church had eschewed acquiescent fatalism or dependence on divine intervention by regarding prayer as supplementary to the activity of the natural order and human endeavour. For example, during the plagues of the 1590s and the great plague of 1603, ecclesiastical and lay authorities cooperated to forbid preaching that infection was a personal judgement against a particular person or that the time of a person's death was preordained and that preventive measures were futile. Besides raising expectations of divine action, special prayers had also provided occasions when a congregation might create or experience a sense of communal unity during a period of grave crisis. Surely this must have been the effect of the Wednesday prayer services in London during the plague of 1603, the prayers during the plague of 1625, and of similar days of humiliation proclaimed in 1645, 1657, 1658, and 1666.

Although the more rationalistic Anglican Church of the eighteenth century issued no special prayers during natural disasters, the practice reemerged on two levels during the nineteenth century.[6] In the countryside where the parson exercised considerable sway and where the custom may never have ceased, the harvest home was celebrated and prayer services were held during times of community danger. More significantly and no doubt reflecting the more general religious awakening, the Privy Council once again approved the issuance of special prayers by the Church and proclaimed special days of prayer. In 1846, 1847, and 1854 special prayers of thanksgiving were issued for abundant harvests. In 1831, 1832, 1833, and 1849 prayers were approved for relief from cholera.

In 1853 Lord Palmerston, believing the natural causes of cholera to be understood, set limits to the official use of prayer unaccompa-

5 Charles F. Mullett, *The bubonic plague and England: an essay in the history of preventive medicine* (Lexington, Ky.: University of Kentucky Press, 1956), pp. 109, 117, 162–3, 183, 187, 201; Keith Thomas, *Religion and the decline of magic* (New York: Scribner, 1971), pp. 113–24; F. P. Wilson, *The plague in Shakespeare's London* (Oxford: Clarendon Press, 1927), pp. 52–3, 70–1, 99–100, 154.

6 The nineteenth-century religious pamphlet collection at Pusey House, Oxford, includes a number of sermons and tracts on prayer, pestilence, and harvests. One that most clearly illustrates the roles of the Church and prayer in time of crisis is *Louisa Gulliford or recollections of the cholera in 1849 by a clergyman* (Luton: W. Stalker, 1863). See also *Handlist of proclamations issued by royal and other constitutional authorities 1714–1910* in *Bibliotheca Lindesiana*, VIII (Wigan: Roger and Rennick, 1913), pp. 307–8, 310, 314, 414, 462, 490, 492, 555.

nied by practical activity when he refused a request from the Presbytery of Edinburgh for the appointment of a fast day to stay the cholera. He explained to the Scottish clergy,

The Maker of the Universe has established certain laws of nature for the planet in which we live, and the weal or woe of mankind depends upon the observance or the neglect of those laws ... and it is the duty of man to attend those laws of nature and to exert the faculties which Providence has thus given to man for his own welfare.

The Home Secretary, who was then also attempting to protect the position of the utilitarian sanitary pioneer Edwin Chadwick on the Public Health Board, blamed the recent visitation of cholera on disregard of those laws. Grime and filth, Palmerston continued, would 'infallibly breed pestilence and be fruitful in death, in spite of all the prayers and fastings of a united but inactive nation'.[7] *Laborare et orare* became the policy of the government in regard to practical problems about which the law of God was known.

Palmerston's dispatch, rejected in Edinburgh and criticized elsewhere by orthodox clergy and laymen, reflected a policy that sanitary reformer and liberal clergyman Charles Kingsley characterized as that of 'the broad churchman, science, and common-sense'. Kingsley contended that by separating the government from the illicit sacerdotal influence of those who would blame the cholera on

Maynooth, the Crystal Palace, the Jerusalem bishopric, the neglect of the Church fasts, the neglect of the worship of the Virgin, the increase of the worship of the Virgin, Free-trade, Protection, any and every case but that palpable one of which the poor unwashed gas-poisoned hearers were but too well aware.[8]

Kingsley believed God had answered previous prayers for relief from cholera by revealing through the labours of scientists the origin of the disease. For this reason new prayers were inappropriate and unappreciative of divine knowledge so revealed. Yet Palmerston's letter and Kingsley's defence of it left uncertain the course of public

---

[7] Henry Fitzroy for Lord Palmerston to the Moderator of the Presbytery of Edinburgh, 19 October 1852, in Evelyn Ashley, *The life and correspondence of Henry John Temple, Viscount Palmerston* (London: Richard Bentley and His Son, 1879), II, 265–6. For a useful bibliographic guide to the history of the mid-century theories of disease that informed Palmerston's letter, see Christopher Hamlin, *A science of impurity: water analysis in nineteenth century Britain* (Berkeley: University of California Press, 1990), pp. 322–5.

[8] Charles Kingsley, 'Lord Palmerston and the Presbytery of Edinburgh', *Fraser's Magazine*, 49 (1854), 47, 51.

and ecclesiastical policy if a crisis arose for which there as yet existed no scientific solution or explanation.

That situation occurred seven years later during the very wet summer of 1860 when the harvest seemed threatened. On 24 August Bishop Samuel Wilberforce of Oxford instructed his archdeacon 'to inform the clergy of your Archdeanery that it is my desire that they will say in the service of the Church the appointed prayer for fine weather'. The Bishops of London and Rochester issued similar orders as did the Bishop of Down and Conner in Ireland. Though some of these churchmen may have expected the prayers to reflect collective community concern, Wilberforce had other intentions. He prefaced his order by observing, 'The time appears to me to have come when the continuance of wet weather, by preventing the gathering of the fruits of the earth in this season may be considered as one of the judgements of Almighty God, to be averted by our humble prayers and intercessions'. This appeal to a God who interfered with the natural order to judge and chastise allowed clergy to reassert social, political, and sacerdotal authority as witnessed by the sermon of Rev. Charles Gutch on *The gloomy summer; or God's threatened chastisement deserved for national and individual sins*. He blamed the excessive rainfall on the national sins of the Divorce Act of 1857, recent riots at St George's church in London's East End, and the war with China.[9]

During the same month of 1860, Charles Kingsley once again refused to employ prayer to exert sacerdotal influence. He told his parishioners that praying for fair weather was an act of unwarranted presumption. Rains harmful to the rural areas might aid the nation as a whole. 'How do we know', he asked, 'that they are not washing away, day by day, the seeds of pestilence in man and beast, and vegetable, and sowing instead the seeds of health and fertility, for us and for our children after us.' As a broad churchman and informed sanitary reformer, Kingsley was unwilling to utter prayers that he knew could have no remedial effect. He explained that prayers for fair weather meant asking God 'to alter the tides of the oceans, the form of the continents, the pace at which the earth spins round, the force, and light, and speed of sun and moon'.[10] Though much about

9 Wilberforce quoted in Charles Gutch, *The gloomy summer; or God's threatened chastisement deserved for national and individual sins* (London: John Masters, 1860), p. 4; see also pp. 11–15.
10 Charles Kingsley, *Why should we pray for fair weather?* (London: John W. Parker and Son, 1860), pp. 8, 9.

weather remained a mystery, men did know that it displayed the regularity of law and manifested God's rational and loving wisdom rather than His capriciousness. In this regard, Kingsley moved beyond his position of 1854 by asserting not only that scientific laws were to be observed when disclosed but also that their discovery was to be patiently awaited.

The rector of Eversley received several congratulatory letters for his sermon including one from geologist Charles Lyell. Further commendation for others who had also refused to pray for fair weather came from John Tyndall in *Mountaineering in 1861*. The sound physics of these clergymen attracted Tyndall less than their zeal for genuine solutions for the problems facing society. He explained,

Such men do service to public character, by encouraging a manly and intelligent conflict with the real causes of disease and scarcity, instead of a delusive reliance on supernatural aid. But they have also a value beyond this local and temporary one. They prepare the public mind for changes, which though inevitable could hardly, without such preparation, be wrought without violence.[11]

By their refusal to relate comprehensible natural phenomena to the judgement of Providence, these men were directing their congregations to a new view of nature and toward a more favourable understanding of the scientists who were interpreting natural problems without recourse to the supernatural. Tyndall perceived, and believed these liberal clergymen understood, that scientific and expert treatment of public health and physical well-being would require the public recognition of a new, functional intellectual elite which would in many respects displace the clergy. Therein lay the core of the debate over prayer and, as is argued in the next essay in this volume, of the more general conflict of science and religion.

The clergy through the pulpit, the educational system, the universities, and the bench of bishops constituted the wealthiest, the most favoured, the most prestigious, and most socially powerful group of intellectuals in the nation. Scientists, physicians, sanitary

[11] Frances E. Kingsley, ed., *Charles Kingsley, his letters and memories of his life* (London: Macmillan and Co., 1891), II, 112–17; Katherine M. Lyell, ed., *Life, letters, and journals of Sir Charles Lyell, Bart.* (London: John Murray, 1881), II, 336–7; John Tyndall, 'Reflections on prayer and natural law – 1861', in John Tyndall, *Fragments of Science*, 6th edn (New York: D. Appleton and Co., 1892), II, 6. Tyndall originally published these comments in *Mountaineering in 1861* (London: Longman, Green, Longman, and Roberts, 1862), but removed it from later editions of the volume.

engineers, medical officers, and the like represented an emerging
intellectual conglomerate enjoying relatively little wealth or prestige
but capable of addressing the practical problems of a modern
industrial nation. They were what Eric Hobsbawm, in a different
context, once described as 'the "new men", rising through the
interstices of the traditional social and economic structure of Victorian Britain, or anticipating a new structure'. More exactly they were
professional intellectuals whose social ideal was in Harold Perkin's
terms 'a functional one based on expertise and selection by merit'.[12]

A generation later this second group would be associated with
social imperialism and would campaign for national efficiency. By
the 1860s there was a sufficient number of professional scientifically
oriented men with considerable social ambition holding positions of
influence in the bureaucracy and the new institutions of technical
education to challenge what they considered the illicit and anachronistic interference in practical matters by the clergy and ecclesiastical hierarchy. As Tyndall argued in 1863,

Surely the men whose noble vocation it is to systematize the culture of
England, can never allow this giant power [of science] to grow up in their
midst without endeavoring to turn it to practical account. Science does not
need their protection, but it desires their friendship on honourable terms; it
wishes to work with them towards the great end of all education – the
bettering of man's estate. By continuing to decline the offered hand, they
invoke a contest which can have but one result. Science must grow . . . It is
a phase of the energy of Nature, and as such is sure, in due time, to compel
recognition, if not to win the alliance, of those who now decry its influence
and discourage its advance.[13]

In 1863 the clergy were the systematizers of culture. Tyndall sought
to undermine the role they continued to claim in regard to matters
that by right of knowledge pertained to the scientific layman. This
view of the relationship of scientists and clergy informed all of his
comments on prayer and religion. Liberal churchmen supported his
position because they believed in the unity of truth and felt that the
national Church must for its own survival accommodate the advanced mind of the nation.

The next clash over prayer, which more clearly illustrated the

[12] E. J. Hobsbawm, *Labouring men: studies in the history of labour* (London: Weidenfeld and
Nicholson, 1971), p. 257; Harold Perkin, *The origins of modern English society, 1780–1880*
(London: Routledge and Kegan Paul, 1969), p. 258.
[13] John Tyndall, *Heat considered as a mode of motion* (New York: D. Appleton and Co., 1863), p.
vi.

tension between the two intellectual elites, occurred in 1865 when the cattle plague suddenly blighted the golden age of English farming. With no cure available, financial disaster hung over the agricultural interest. A Royal Commission under Lyon Playfair invoked strict regulations for the cattle trade and ordered the slaughter of animals as a preventive measure. The activity of the commission was a significant step in the emergence of the central administrative state and of government policy based on expert scientific opinion.

Yet while the commission heard witnesses and gave advice, the clergy turned to prayer. Prayers by individual clergymen would probably not have aroused comment. On 5 October 1865, however, the Archbishop of Canterbury issued the following special prayer for use in schools, households, and families:

Oh Lord God Almighty, whose are the cattle on a thousand hills, and in whose hand is the breath of every living thing, look down, we pray Thee, in compassion upon us Thy servants, whom Thou has visited with a grievous murrain among our herds and flocks. We acknowledge our transgressions, which worthily deserve Thy chastisement, and our sin is ever before us; and in humble penitence we come to see Thy aid. In the midst of judgement do Thou, O Lord, remember mercy; stay, we pray Thee, this plague by Thy word of power, and save that provision which Thou hadst in Thy goodness granted for our sustenance. Defend us also, gracious Lord, from the pestilence with which many foreign lands have been smitten; keep it, we beseech Thee far away from our borders, and shield our homes from its ravages; so shall we ever offer unto Thee the sacrifice of praise and thanksgiving, for these Thy acts of providence over us, through Jesus Christ our Lord. Amen.

Approved by the Privy Council, this prayer invoking the concepts of sin, providence, and judgement fell within the bounds of Palmerston's policy of 1853 since the cause of the cattle plague was unknown. Nevertheless, it represented retrogression in rational church policy for during cattle plagues of the eighteenth century no similar prayers had been issued.[14]

This anomalous attempt to pursue the policy of an earlier church-directed culture roused editorial criticism. On 9 October, the *Pall Mall Gazette* noted that many laymen did not favour the prayer for

---

[14] *Guardian*, 20 (1865), 1003; *Handlist of proclamations*, p. 716; Charles F. Mullett, 'The cattle distemper in mid-eighteenth-century England', *Agricultural History*, 20 (1946), 144–65. The *Handlist of proclamations* includes no prayers for cattle or for the landed interest during the eighteenth century.

removal of the cattle plague. Their attitude did not display godlessness but rather 'an ever increasing conviction of the uniformity of the
operations of all physical law, not as a self-existent necessity, but as a
result of the fiat of the Eternal Mind'.[15] Yet prayer and general law
were not necessarily incompatible. God by His own free will might
redirect His laws in the same manner that men used knowledge of
natural laws for the good of the race.

The initial defence of the possible efficacy of prayer covered the
paper's editorial flank for three further comments harshly critical of
the sense and morality of the Primate's prayer. On 10 October the
Gazette observed that the archbishop had confused the ownership of
the stricken cattle which actually belonged to the farmers rather
than to God. The petition approached 'sublime' selfishness in
requesting the disease to be kept only from British borders. The
editorial concluded,

Of course the Primate did not mean what in this prayer he has so plainly
said; ... but ... if a form of prayer is deliberately drawn up at Lambeth for
use throughout England, we have some right to expect that our common
sense will not be outraged, and that we shall not have words offered us
which, if we interpret them, carry blasphemous and unworthy meanings.

Four days later the paper reported an editorial from the *Spectator*
which had noted, 'No one would dream of asking the Archbishop to
write a prayer in a commercial crisis, attributing a crash in the City
to God's judgement for our sins'. The archbishop's appeal to sin as
an explanation for the cattle plague, the journal argued, simply
provided a facade for the selfish fear of property loss within the
landed interest. In a final article on 17 October, the *Pall Mall Gazette*
remarked that 'just as Sabbatarian rigorism tends to promote week-
day godlessness, so these panic-stricken supplications have a tendency to foster that epicureanism in theology to which we are all of us
sufficiently disposed'.[16] The contents of the prayer thus stood in

[15] *Pall Mall Gazette*, 9 Oct. 1865, p. 1.
[16] *Pall Mall Gazette*, 10 Oct. 1865, p. 9; 14 Oct. 1865, p. 3 (See also *Spectator*, 38 14 Oct. 1865,
1140.); 17 Oct. 1865, p. 10. The *Times* on 12 Oct. 1865, p. 9, briefly entered the fray by
devoting one-and-a-half columns to a castigation of Cardinal Cullen's pastoral letter that
had blamed the cattle plague on the sceptical spirit of the age. The *Times* accused the Irish
cardinal of equating the march of intellect, the demise of war, the growth of liberal states,
and the independence of the working class with 'the anti-Christian phenomena of the latter
days'. In a blatantly anti-sacerdotal and anti-Catholic spirit the paper spoke of 'something
pathetic in the unswerving faith which can look abroad in a world like our own and believe
that modern society can ever again be reduced to a state of religious pupilage'. The paper
made no comment on the prayer from Lambeth Palace.

stark contrast to the common sense and ameliorative morality so congenial to both scientists and broad churchmen.

The *Pall Mall Gazette* editorials afforded John Tyndall a new opportunity to raise the question of the physical efficacy of prayer. In a letter published on 12 October, he admitted the initial editorial had taken a strong position by arguing that prayer stirred men to practical action and by contending that God could redirect His own laws. Yet this argument supported ancient and heathen prayers, as well as Christian, and 'justified equally the mildest and the most extravagant belief in spontaneous interference' in the natural order. The crucial issue remained, 'Who, indeed, in such a case, is to draw the line between mildness and extravagance?' Here and in a second letter appearing on 19 October, Tyndall noted that no one prayed for divine interference when the antecedents of a particular problem were clear. He continued,

Now, as a matter of fact, in cases of national supplication the antecedents are often very clear to one class of the community, though very dark to another and a larger class. This explains the fact, that while the latter are ready to resort to prayer, the former decline doing so. The difference between the classes is one of knowledge, not of religious feeling.[17]

From this perspective, the special prayer served to consolidate ignorance and clerical dominance and to further practical super-stition when the methods of practical science should be pursued.

In December 1865, the controversy moved into the columns of the journals and quarterlies. Lyon Playfair in the *North British Review* explained the policy of the government commission. At the close he addressed himself to the archbishop's prayer by suggesting that if one viewed the plague as a judgement, it was chastisement for violation of the laws of God 'which govern the animal economy'. Those violations 'inflict upon us the penalties attached to their transgression, and it is our duty to discover, understand, and obey them'.[18] That so few religious spokesmen availed themselves of the possibility for reconciliation with the scientists afforded by the latter's frequent hypostatizing natural laws as commands of God suggests the real issue in dispute was who would instruct the public in divine law rather than the character of the law itself.

[17] *Pall Mall Gazette*, 12 Oct. 1865, p. 4; 19 Oct. 1865, p. 3. See also the *Guardian*, 20 (1865), 1192, for more Tyndall correspondence.
[18] Lyon Playfair, 'The cattle plague', *North British Review*, 43 (1865), 518.

The most significant article to appear in December 1865, was that of J. Llewelyn Davies in *Macmillan's Magazine*. A liberal clergyman foreshadowing Matthew Arnold's later critique of contemporary religion, Davies termed prayers on special occasions 'a kind of mechanical prophylactic'. He saw two paths out of the present imbroglio. First, he argued that prayer should be directed only towards spiritual ends thus avoiding the issues of physics and worldly selfishness. E. B. Pusey and Canon H. P. Liddon, among others, later developed this idea more fully.[19] Without ever denying the possible or even probable physical efficacy of prayer, all of these writers regarded its greatest miracle as the action of grace on the spirit and life of the person praying. This solution permitted a reconciliation of clergy and scientists at the price of removing prayer from the more practical or everyday areas of life.

Sensitive to the failure of his first suggestion to meet the question of the physical efficacy of prayer, Davies then asked, 'Are we ready to bring this question to the practical test of experiment?' He for one was not so prepared because any such experiment would transform prayer from a spiritual petition into a 'prayer of calculation'.[20] Davies left it to his readers to draw the clear inference that the prayer for alleviation of financial loss to cattle farmers had already made prayer a matter of calculation.

These criticisms failed to still the bishops and may have steeled their resolve to pray without ceasing. On 12 January, 1866, Samuel Waldegrave, Bishop of Carlisle, preached on *The cattle plague: a warning voice to Britain from the king of nations*. Later that month the Archbishop of Canterbury unsuccessfully petitioned the cabinet to appoint a day of national humiliation. After the cabinet refused the request, the Bishops of Oxford, York, Ely, Bristol, and London appointed local days of humiliation as did the Free Church of Scotland and the Chief Rabbi of Britain.[21]

For Arthur Stanley, Dean of Westminster Abbey and leading

---

[19] J. Llewelyn Davies, 'Nature and prayer', *Macmillan's Magazine*, 13 (1865–6), 233; E. B. Pusey, *The miracles of prayer* (London: Rivington's, 1866); H. P. Liddon, *Some elements of prayer* (London: Rivington's, 1872). In the second edition of his book (London: Rivington's, 1873), p. xix, Liddon argued for the physical efficacy of prayer. He did so because he felt that without faith in the physical fruits of prayer, men would also give up faith in its spiritual benefits.

[20] Davies, 'Nature and prayer', 239.

[21] Samuel Waldegrave, *The cattle plague: a warning voice to Britain from the king of nations* (London: William Hunt and Company, 1866); *Times*, 14 Feb. 1866, p. 9; 21 Feb. 1866, p. 10; 9 March 1866, p. 5; 14 March 1866, p. 10.

spokesman for the broad Church, this day of humiliation posed a considerable difficulty. He believed that the national Church should encompass the leading intellects of the nation and must not employ its dignity and power to block or discourage intellectual discourse and discovery. What should he do on the special day of prayer? In the best broad church manner, Stanley consulted his good friend John Tyndall. The latter replied, 'With regard to humbling ourselves in the expectation that a single beast the less will die I would say in all frankness that I consider it a mere pagonism [*sic*]'. Tyndall directed his troubled friend to Davies's article, and concluded, 'I hope and think – and pardon me for thus hoping and thinking – that you will *not* pray as others will for the staying of this plague, but will ask on the contrary for strength of heart and clearness of mind to meet it manfully and fight against it intelligently'.[22]

Taking this counsel to heart, on the appointed day Stanley preached on the text, 'Thy will be done', which he contended provided the only intelligent prayer for Christians. He told the Abbey worshippers to read the plague not as a judgement but rather as 'God's own stimulus to the activity of those scientific researchers by which His supreme will in the works and laws of nature was made known to us'. Those who were not scientists should encourage the latter and should

abstain from those taunts and scoffs at science and scientific men in which the ignorant were too often disposed to indulge – ... [and] abstain from throwing those stumbling-blocks in their way which in former times made the path of science almost a path of martyrdom, and which even now make it in many cases a path of thorns and briars, a path in which the few who could walk uprightly deserved not our reproaches but our own best thanks, not our scorn but our highest honour.[23]

It is of no small significance that Stanley provided grounds for cooperation between the professions of scientist and clergyman rather than for reconciliation of their ideas.

Stanley's ecclesiastical isolation becomes apparent from reading the sermon Archibald Tait, Bishop of London and later Arch-

[22] J. Tyndall to A. Stanley, 13 March 1866, in Typescript of the Journal of John Tyndall, 1855–1872, III, p. 1318. John Tyndall Papers, Archives of the Royal Institution, London.

[23] *Times*, 21 March 1866, p. 5. Stanley may also have been guided by the suggestion of the propriety of the Lord's Prayer in Marmion Savage, 'Religion and philosophy reconciled', *Fortnightly Review*, 3 (1866), 474–6. For a response to the question of prayer similar to Stanley's but from a leading Nonconformist minister, see George Dawson, *On humiliation and fast days* (Birmingham: W. Willey, 1866).

bishop of Canterbury, preached the same day. Tait attacked the 'shallow speculations' of those who questioned the physical efficacy of prayer. He sought to impress his congregation with the idea that

they alone are wise who look upon all events of life, sad or joyful, which befall themselves or which they see befalling others, as part of God's continual judgement, as bearing many messages direct from Him to their consciences; and who thus all through the discipline of life jealously preserve a reverential sense of His nearness, and whatever happens turn continually in thought and prayer to Him.

Tait would not open the Church to the newly emerging intellectual elite of professional scientific and medical experts who by treating disease as a preventable problem could undermine his providential view of nature and could encourage citizens to turn to the technical expert rather than to God in times of natural difficulty. Perusal of printed tracts and sermons of the early months of 1866 suggests that most churchmen stood with Tait. Indeed the clergy's only appreciable response to their critics was the issuance on 9 August of a new prayer for relief from both cattle plague and impending cholera.[24]

Eventually the cattle plague abated and the cholera arrived with less than full force. On 14 November 1866, the *Times* reported that as of 10 November, the prayer against the plague had been suspended and in its place 'a form of prayer and thanksgiving for relief from the plague among cattle and for protection against cholera' had been substituted.[25] Five years passed before the question of prayer again imposed itself on the public mind, and as before it more nearly reflected a clash of elites than of ideas.

In December 1871, the British monarchy was in deep trouble. The Queen, still mourning the loss of the Prince Consort, lived in seclusion. Republican sentiments were not uncommon among radical groups. Of more immediate danger the Prince of Wales had

---

[24] *Times*, 21 March 1866, p. 5; Anon., *Prayer and the cattle plague* (London: Christian Evidence Society, 1866); R. M. Benson, *The free action of God's love amidst the fixed operations of his power: a sermon on the efficacy of prayer* (London: Rivington's, 1866); T. L. Claughton, *God's providences and judgements* (London: Rivington's, 1866); Joseph B. McCaul, *Darkness that may be felt: a warning to England at the present crisis* (London: John F. Shaw and Co., 1866); Daniel Moore, *Prayer and providence: two sermons designated to vindicate the use of prayer in relation to plague and pestilence* (London: Rivington's, 1866); C. Pritchard, *The continuity of the schemes of nature and of revelation* (London: Bell and Daldy, 1866); B. F. Smith, *Prayer and the cattle plague: two sermons* (London and Cambridge: Macmillan and Co., 1866); Robert G. Swayne, *The secret of the cattle plague* (London: Rivington's, 1866). For the new prayer, see the *Guardian*, 21 (1866), 842.

[25] *Times*, 14 Nov. 1866, p. 6; see also 7 Nov. 1866, p. 10.

contracted typhoid. On Friday, 8 December, the heir to the throne took a sudden, unexpected turn for the worse. His physicians feared he might die. Late in the evening of Saturday, 9 December, a small committee drawn from the cabinet and Privy Council, including Gladstone, the Bishop of London, and the Archbishop of Canterbury, issued orders by telegraph to the clergy that prayers taken from the visitation of the sick be read the next day for the recovery of Prince Edward. On Sunday, 10 December, throughout the kingdom the special prayers were duly offered up for the restoration of health to the heir. Then on Thursday, 14 December – the tenth anniversary of the death of Prince Albert from the same disease – the condition of the Prince of Wales decisively improved and the crisis had passed.[26]

No sooner had Edward commenced to recover than certain clergymen began to claim that his restoration to health had vindicated the much abused power of prayer. Archbishop Tait did so in the privacy of his diary. Others did so publicly. On 17 December 1871, Rev. W. H. Karslake, who would henceforth write several sermons and tracts on prayer, preached on *God's answer to a nation's prayer*. The next day Rev. Richard West wrote to the *Guardian*, 'The wonderful change in the condition of the Prince of Wales will surely impress many hitherto doubtful minds with the efficacy of prayer.' On 18 January 1872, the Privy Council issued a special prayer of thanksgiving for the deliverance of the Prince.[27]

The vindication of the efficacy of prayer received further official endorsement when the government, in a move to revive support for the monarchy, proclaimed 27 February 1872, a day of national thanksgiving for the recovery of the heir. Services were held throughout the country with the most splendid occurring at St Paul's where the Queen, accompanied by the Prince of Wales, attended thus emerging from her long years of seclusion. Later a plaque commemorating the Queen's visit and the Prince's recovery was erected in the cathedral. The power of prayer appeared to have

---

[26] *Times*, 11 Dec. 1871, p. 9; *British Medical Journal*, 9 Dec. 1871, pp. 671, 699–700.
[27] Randall T. Davidson and William Benham, *Life of Archibald Tait, Archbishop of Canterbury* (London: Macmillan and Co., 1891), II, 106; W. H. Karslake, *God's answer to a nation's prayer* (Oxford and London: J. Parker and Co., 1871); *Guardian*, 26 (1871), 1512; *Handlist of proclamations*, p. 809. Karslake's other writings in regard to prayer include *The efficacy of prayer* (London: Society for Promoting Christian Knowledge, n.d.), *England's thanksgiving for God's answer to her prayer* (Oxford and London: J. Parker and Co., 1872), *The theory of prayer with special reference to modern thought* (London: Christian Evidence Committee of the Society for Promoting Christian Knowledge, 1873), and *Modern thought in reference to the subject of prayer* (London: J. Parker and Son, 1873).

cured the heir to the throne and to have restored the Queen to the public life of her people. Thereafter, the euphoria of the religious nation reached new heights. The *Guardian* joyfully saw the service as 'a solemn recognition of the direct and personal working of the Hand of God in things of this life' and as 'a distinct National Proclamation of Faith in the reality of special and personal Providence'.[28]

In the same article the *Guardian* made a special effort to demean the medical and scientific professions. It declared that those who had seen the Prince of Wales in the cathedral 'really felt that he had been brought back to them from the very threshold of death, not by some abstract "Law of Health", not merely by human skill and tenderness, but by the mercy of the God who hears and answers prayers'. Moreover, the journal claimed that this illustration of the power of prayer 'ought to deepen in our minds the conviction that after all what we really want is not so much material civilization, or even intellectual culture, but that moral regenerating power which, as a matter of fact, has never been found except in the knowledge of God'.[29] Here was a clear challenge to those who believed 'moral regeneration might lie with improvement of the physical health of the nation.

Throughout the royal illness the professional medical periodicals had cast a chary eye on the role ascribed to Providence and prayer. They hoped to employ the Prince's case of typhoid to publicize the necessity for further sanitary reform and legislation. The *Lancet* did not criticize the special prayers of 9 December. However, on 23 December, it published a letter from Dr A. B. Munro who explained the fatal danger of ascribing preventable diseases, such as that from which the Prince of Wales suffered, to Providence or to the results of original sin:

Many good and honest people say there must always be disease, though we live in a state of sanitary perfection, it being the punishment 'of man's first disobedience'. Death is, but disease is not ... Disease is the punishment springing not from the fall of Adam, but necessarily from violation of laws of health either by ourselves personally or by our progenitors.[30]

Munro called for government action to educate the masses how to prevent disease. What he and other members of his profession saw

[28] *Handlist of proclamations*, p. 809; *Guardian*, 27 (1872), 276.
[29] *Guardian*, 27 (1872), 276.
[30] *Lancet*, 2 (1871), 907.

instead was governmental activity preparatory to the elaborate day of thanksgiving.

The medical profession became vocally resentful as the clergy explicitly and the government implicitly credited prayer rather than medical treatment for the recovery of the heir to the throne. By 27 January the harping of the clergy and the special prayer of thanksgiving led the *Lancet* to declare, 'While we recognize the hand of Providence, we still claim for modern medical science that she has signally won fresh laurels in the recovery of the Prince of Wales.' Similar professional pique emerged throughout January and early February as the journal called for new public honours for physicians, such as membership in the Privy Council. When Sir William Jenner was created a Knight of Bath and William Gull a baronet for their treatment of the royal patient, the *Lancet* considered the honours inadequate. After all the mayor of the City of London had also been created a baronet simply because the cathedral in which the major thanksgiving service had occurred lay in his city.[31]

The service itself occasioned still another blow to the ambitions of the physicians. Approximately fifteen hundred clergy attended St Paul's with several hundred soldiers and lawyers. Yet only twelve invitations had been sent to medical men. Two invitaions had been delivered to the University of London, one to the College of Physicians, and one to the College of Surgeons. In contrast, the London Board of Works received 104 invitations. The *British Medical Journal* ruefully observed, 'In the official statement of the Lord Chamberlain of the professions represented that of Medicine is not even mentioned.'[32] The physicians and their allies in other scientific professions saw their hopes for new public recognition and social prestige dashed and the triumph of their skills and methods turned into a fete for the monarchy, the Church, the politicians, and the physical efficacy of the prayers for the sick in the Book of Common Prayer.

Five months later when surgeon Henry Thompson proposed to test conclusively the effectiveness of those prayers, his critics chose to forget the earlier, heady boasting of the religious press and pulpit. For example, R. H. Hutton, editor of the *Spectator* and a devout Unitarian, reverting to Davies's theory of spiritual prayer, claimed that for Christians prayer was strictly a matter of internal moral

---

[31] *Lancet*, 1 (1872), 123, 55, 120, 160, 339.
[32] *British Medical Journal*, 2 March 1872, p. 245.

influence. He expressed surprise that anyone could ever regard prayer as 'a sort of petty dictation to God, the effect of which might be measured, like a constituent's pressure on his representative in Parliament, by the influence it exerted on the issue'.[33] But in rejecting the sincerity of the proposal, as Davies had rejected a hypothetical test of prayer, Hutton, his correspondents, and authors of other critical articles failed to observe that the specific points of Thompson's proposal constituted an abstract description of prayer as directed toward the illness of the Prince of Wales. They also chose to ignore that when the ward of the royal patient had been made the object of special national prayers and the patient had recovered, the clergy had not pointed to the moral influence of prayer, but rather had exalted in its physical efficacy.

At least two contributors to the ensuing debate understood that Thompson's scheme was intended as a challenge to the votaries of clerical culture who had demeaned the medical profession. In an article for the *Fortnightly Review*, eugenicist Francis Galton set out to prove that statistical analysis failed to support the contention that 'sick persons who pray, or are prayed for, recover, on the average more rapidly than others'. He employed his statistical presentation to make a general condemnation of the efficacy of religious practices and the ability of religious men to solve practical problems of the society. Groups involved in the difficulties of everyday life, such as physicians, businessmen, and insurance companies, paid no heed to the alleged benefits of prayer. The clergy who prescribed the use of prayer had a notorious reputation of incapacity for efficient or businesslike procedures even in Convocation. Galton concluded, 'It is common week-day opinion of the world that praying people are not practical.'[34] Yet through prayers on special occasions the clergy claimed ability to solve practical problems properly belonging in the hands of scientific experts.

This theme also appeared in a letter to the *Spectator* of 10 August. A correspondent signing himself 'Protagoras' argued that scientists

---

[33] *Spectator*, 45 (1872), 846–7.
[34] Francis Galton, 'Statistical inquiries into the efficacy of prayer', *Fortnightly Review*, 18 (1872), 127, 132. Galton had earlier offered the article to the *Contemporary Review*. James Knowles, the editor, turned it down explaining, 'I am afraid that after all my courage is not greater than Grove's. You will think that editors are a "feeble folk", and so perhaps they are, but it is certain that our constituents (who are largely clergymen) must not be tried much further just now by proposals following Tyndall's friend's on prayer – and of similar bold – or as you yourself say, "audacious character".' Karl Pearson, *The life, letters and labours of Francis Galton* (Cambridge: Cambridge University Press, 1924), II, 131.

had no intention of abolishing belief in the supernatural or reverence for God. Rather they sought to lead men to an understanding of the results of science and of their application to daily life. That end was impossible 'so long as superstitions inflict human practice, though perhaps unconsciously, in the ordinary ways of living'. Presently, popular belief in prayer and providential judgement blocked the path of sanitary reform, and 'medical men find themselves checkmated by their efforts towards the care and prevention of disease by superstitions more worthy of Central Africa than of Great Britain in the nineteenth century'.[35]

Naturalistic writers believed the removal of church-fostered superstitions from what Protagoras termed 'the ordinary ways of living' required the recognition of a new intellectual elite who would displace the clergy on all levels of society as the interpreters of natural phenomena. Liberal religious thinkers contributed to this process by personally abandoning and criticizing practices, such as prayers on special occasions, wherein the clergy appeared in a mediatory or sacerdotal role. Some, such as William A. Knight of the Free Church of Scotland, carried the spiritualization of prayer to the logical conclusion of insisting, 'The exercise of the religious function of prayer cannot directly effect any material change.' In this manner religious feeling was liberated from traditional social institutions and became a matter of spiritual exercises for consenting adults in the privacy of their homes and hearts. External and social religiosity became a matter of good sense and prudence. This trend went so far in some liberal minds that by the late 1870s James Anthony Froude argued that those who 'observe the rules of health as ascertained and laid down by science ... better deserve the name of religious men than those who neglect the means of protecting themselves which God has provided, and try to induce Him by prayers to suspend His ordinances in their favour'.[36]

Many scientists were only too ready to see themselves as the new formulators of external religious observance. Indeed they regarded themselves as the logical and natural successors to the priest. Spencer, Tyndall, Thompson, and others contended that the priestly

---

[35] *Spectator*, 45 (1872), 1012.
[36] William A. Knight, 'The function of prayer in the economy of the universe', *Contemporary Review*, 21 (1872), 185; J. A. Froude to S. G. Potter, 7 Sept. 1879, in S. G. Potter, *Prayer, as it affects the immutability of nature's God and nature's laws* (Sheffield: Pawson and Brailsford, 1879), p. 5.

caste had originated as a mediator between primitive man and a natural environment that seemed to threaten his well-being. With that image of nature banished through the triumph of science and technology, the scientist now stood as the mediator between modern man and a nature that could almost be commanded to serve his material needs. The spokesmen for the scientific professions desired the social and cultural prestige and recognition that had been and to a large degree still was accorded the clergy. Something other than self-humour led T. H. Huxley to refer to himself frequently as a bishop and to entitle his essays *Lay sermons*. Even Alfred Wallace, the least aggressive of all Victorian scientists, once suggested that clergymen be replaced by a parish officer who would instruct the people in the laws of health and sanitation. In 1874 Francis Galton closed his *English men of science* by expressing hope that scientific occupations in the universities, industry, sanitation, and statistical inquiry would give rise to 'a sort of scientific priesthood' that might address itself to practical problems of the nation and receive in turn social respect and economic support.[37]

If the movement from religion to science in Western culture represented, as some would contend, the exchange of one form of faith for another, it also meant the transfer of cultural and intellectual leadership and prestige from the exponents of one faith to those of another. In this regard the long debate over the nature of prayer suggests that the Victorian conflict between religion and science was something more than a dispute over ideas. It manifested the tension arising as the intellectual nation became more highly differentiated in functions, professions, and institutions. It was a clash between established and emerging intellectual and social elites for popular preeminence in a modern industrial and professionalized society.

[37] Herbert Spencer, *The principles of sociology* (New York: D. Appleton and Co., 1897), II-3, 247–60; Tyndall, *Fragments*, II, 135; Thompson (anon.), Tyndall, McCosh, 'On Prayer', 775; Leonard Huxley, *The life and letters of Thomas Henry Huxley* (New York: D. Appleton and Co., 1900), I, 136; II, 34, 345; Alfred Russel Wallace, *Studies scientific and social* (London: Macmillan and Co., Ltd, 1900), II, 235–53; Francis Galton, *English men of science: their nature and nurture*, 2nd edn (London: Frank Cass, 1970; 1st publ. 1874), pp. 193–4.

CHAPTER 7

The Victorian conflict between science and religion: a professional dimension

Was there a conflict between science and religion in late Victorian England? T. H. Huxley, Bishop Wilberforce, John Tyndall, Francis Galton, W. K. Clifford, and William Gladstone certainly thought so. Other contemporaries, such as Lord Tennyson, E. B. Pusey, Frederick Temple, Frederic Harrison, and Herbert Spencer feared so but hoped not. Sermons criticizing the arrogance of scientists and articles decrying the ignorance of clergy, as well as books such as John Draper's *History of the conflict between religion and science* (1874) and that of his fellow American Andrew White, *The warfare of science* (1876), with a preface by British physicist John Tyndall, suggested a bitter controversy between spokesmen for religion and science. Early twentieth-century writers including J. M. Robertson, J. B. Bury, Bertrand Russell, and Arthur Balfour assumed that a conflict had raged over the subject a generation or so earlier.[1]

Later commentators were less certain about the existence of the struggle, its dimensions, and even its issues. Robert Ensor regarded it parenthetically as '(real enough at the time)'. Charles Raven contended the debate over science and religion amounted to little

From *Isis*, 69 (1978), 356–76. With permission of the journal.
[1] T. H. Huxley, *Collected essays* (London: D. Appleton and Co., 1894), IV and V; E. B. Pusey, *Un-science, not science, adverse to faith* (London: J. Parker, 1878); Frederick Temple, *The relations between religion and science* (New York: Macmillan, 1884); Herbert Spencer, *First principles*, 4th edn (New York: D. Appleton and Co., 1896), pp. 3–136; J. W. Draper, *History of the conflict between religion and science* (New York: D. Appleton and Co., 1874); Andrew Dickson White, *The warfare of science* (London: Henry King, 1876) (White's book kept growing until it eventually became two volumes entitled *A history of the warfare of science with theology in Christendom*); Standish Meacham, *My lord bishop: the life of Samuel Wilberforce, 1805–1873* (Cambridge, Mass.: Harvard University Press, 1970), pp. 207–34; J. M. Robertson, *History of free thought in the nineteenth century* (London: Watts, 1929), I, 313–42; J. B. Bury, *History of freedom of thought* (London: Oxford University Press, 1957; originally published 1913), pp. 141–85; Bertrand Russell, *Religion and science* (New York: Holt, 1935); Lord Balfour, 'Introduction', in Joseph Needham, ed., *Science, religion, and reality* (New York: Macmillan, 1928), pp. 1–18.

more than 'a storm in a Victorian tea-cup'. R. K. Webb explained
that the number of people whose religious faith was shaken by
scientific discoveries was 'probably fairly small' but consisted of
'people whose opinions counted for much'. Owen Chadwick drew
the important distinction 'between science when it was against
religion and the scientists when they were against religion'. The
discoveries and theories of science might cast doubt on the accuracy
of the Bible, but a scientist could also use a scientific theory to attack
the Bible or to discredit the clergy for reasons that had little or no
intrinsic relationship to theory. Considerable validity attaches to
each of these assessments, particularly that of Chadwick. Furthermore, James Moore has made the immensely important observation
that the military metaphor employed by participants in the debate
determined much of its temper.[2] Yet to reduce the proportions of
the dispute and to explore its rhetorical parameters, while useful for
achieving better perspective, still fails to account for its character,
causes, or significance. Those problems – the brew in Canon Raven's
teacup – remain.

The most common approach to the substantial issues of the debate
has assumed the existence of an enduring and probably necessary
conflict between scientific and religious modes of interpreting the
world. Antagonism may arise because the naturalistic explanations
of science dispense with the metaphysical presuppositions of theology, or because particular scientific theories contradict the literal
reading of passages in the Bible, or because religious dogma and
authority interfere with scientific research. George Gaylord Simpson
succinctly outlined the major features of this interpretation:

> The conflict between science and religion has a single and simple cause. It is
> the designation as religiously canonical of any conception of the material
> world open to scientific investigation ... The religious canon ... demands
> absolute acceptance not subject to test or revision. Science necessarily

[2] Robert K. Ensor, *England, 1870–1914* (Oxford: Clarendon Press, 1936), p. 162; Charles E. Raven, *Science, religion, and the future* (Cambridge: Cambridge University Press, 1943; reprinted 1968), p. 33; R. K. Webb, *Modern England from the 18th century to the present* (New York: Dodd, Mead, 1970), p. 413; Owen Chadwick, *The Victorian Church* (New York: Oxford University Press, 1970), II, 3; James R. Moore, *The post-Darwinian controversies: a study of the Protestant struggle to come to terms with Darwin in Great Britain and America, 1870–1900* (Cambridge: Cambridge University Press, 1979), pp. 19–100. See also David C. Lindberg and Ronald L. Numbers, eds., *God and nature: historical essays on the encounter between Christianity and Science* (Berkeley: University of California Press, 1986), and John Hedley Brooke, *Science and religion: some historical perspectives* (Cambridge: Cambridge University Press, 1991), both of which include excellent bibliographies.

rejects certainty and predicates acceptance on objective testing and the possibility of continual revision. As a matter of fact, most of the dogmatic religions have exhibited a perverse talent for taking the wrong side on the most important concepts of the material universe, from the structure of the solar system to the origin of man. The result has been constant turmoil for many centuries, and the turmoil will continue as long as religious canons prejudice scientific questions.[3]

There can be no doubt that such disputes arising from epistemological differences over the role of theology as an intellectual authority were major issues at the centre of the Victorian conflict of science and religion. By the second quarter of the nineteenth century substantial developments in geology, physics, biology, physiological psychology, and the philosophy of science challenged or cast into doubt theological assumptions and portions of the Bible. During those years both Charles Lyell and Charles Darwin complained about the hindrance to scientific advance raised by metaphysics and theology. After mid-century Huxley, Tyndall, Joseph Dalton Hooker, Henry Maudsley, and others continued to press against the influence on scientific work of metaphysical and religious categories of thought and to urge the authority of critical reason and empirical verification against the authority of the Bible and natural theology.[4]

However, without questioning the presence, validity, or significance of the epistemological disagreements, it is possible to question the adequacy of the enduring-conflict approach as a wholly satisfactory historical interpretation of the Victorian conflict between science and religion. This interpretation, if not further supplemented, takes too much at face value the statements of polemical

---

3 George Gaylord Simpson, *This view of life: the world of an evolutionist* (New York: Harcourt, Brace and World, 1964), p. 214. See also Chadwick, *The Victorian Church*, II, 1–9; William H. Brock and Roy M. MacLeod, 'The "Scientists' Declaration": reflections on science and belief in the wake of *Essays and reviews*, 1864–5', *British Journal for the History of Science*, 9 (1976), 60.

4 Charles Lyell, *Principles of geology* (London: John Murray, 1830), I, 1–91; Katherine M. Lyell, ed., *Life, letters and journals of Sir Charles Lyell, Bart.* (London: John Murray, 1881), I, 263, 316–17, 445–6; Charles Darwin, *The origin of species and the descent of man* (New York: The Modern Library, n.d.), pp. 122, 135, 319–24; 367–74; Huxley, *Collected essays*, I, 18–41; Joseph Dalton Hooker, 'Presidential address', *Report of the thirty-eighth meeting of the British Association for the Advancement of Science* (London, 1869), pp. lxxiii–lxxv; Henry Maudsley, *Body and mind* (New York: D. Appleton and Co., 1875), p. 275; Charles Coulston Gillispie, *Genesis and geology: a study in the relations of scientific thought, natural theology and social opinion in Great Britain, 1790–1850* (New York: Harper Torchbook, 1959), pp. 217–28; Frank Miller Turner, *Between science and religion: the reaction to scientific naturalism in late Victorian England* (New Haven: Yale University Press, 1974), pp. 8–37.

interchange. The epistemological dichotomy, proclaimed at the time in such phrases as G. H. Lewes's 'Religion and Science, – the two mightiest antagonists', was an integral part of the debate and has come by default to provide an explanation for it. While defending Darwin's *On the origin of species*, Huxley might declare, 'Extinguished theologians lie about the cradle of every science as the strangled snakes beside that of Hercules.'[5] But the history of science has been more complex and problematical.

Statements such as Huxley's emerge from an ideology of science as well as from an attempt to account for disagreements between religious and scientific spokesmen. To pursue this track is to posit historically concrete forms for the theological and positive stages of Comte or for the mytho–poetic and critical–rational epistemological dichotomy so brilliantly delineated by Ernst Cassirer. So far as the internal development of modern science is concerned, this juxtaposition of good progressive science against evil retrogressive metaphysics and theology fails to account for false starts on the part of scientists, their adherence to incorrect theory, the overlooking of evidence that might have led to further discovery, and the enduring influence of metaphysics and religion on scientific work that continued well into the nineteenth century. Moreover, the progressionist ideology also ignores the frequent hostility of scientific authorities and the scientific community, as well as that of theologians and clergymen, to new theories that challenge existing paradigms and reputations.

To penetrate other levels of the Victorian conflict of religion and science, it is necessary to recognize that the epistemological redefinition of science to mean critical research based on empirical verification constituted only one element in a broader redefinition of the entire scientific enterprise in Great Britain. The debates over particular theories and methods were part of an extensive ongoing discussion about the character of the Victorian scientific community, its functions in society, and the values by which it judged the work of its members. These latter issues largely determined why spokesmen for religion and science clashed when they did and as they did.

In 1873 physicist James Clerk Maxwell inquired rhetorically about the condition of British science and replied,

5 G. H. Lewes, *Problems of life and mind, first series* (Boston: Osgood, 1874), I, 2; Huxley, *Collected essays*, II, 52.

It is simply this, that while the numbers of our professors and their emoluments are increasing, while the number of students is increasing, while practical instruction is being introduced and text-books multiplied, while the number and calibre of popular lecturers and popular writers in Science is increasing, original research, the fountain-head of a nation's wealth, is decreasing.

Maxwell's concern about the paucity of research was widely shared at the time. But for the purposes of this essay the activity he did observe was more significant. The expansion in the numbers of professional scientists and the widespread dispersion of scientific ideas on the popular level and within institutions of education meant science was forging ahead in British society if not necessarily in British laboratories. The result of this process, according to A. W. Benn, who witnessed it, was 'a transfer of authority from religious to naturalistic belief'. In turn, as naturalistic belief grew, 'a great part of the reverence once given to priests and to their stories of an unseen universe has been transferred to the astronomer, the geologist, the physician, and the engineer'. It was this shift of authority and prestige, noted by numerous other contemporaries, from one part of the intellectual nation to another that caused the Victorian conflict between religious and scientific spokesmen. Recognition of this development may explain why the Cambridge philosopher Henry Sidgwick termed the debate 'a great and prominent *social* fact of the present age'.[6]

The primary motivating force behind this shift in social and intellectual authority, which deeply involved the epistemological controversy, was activity within the scientific community that displayed most of the major features associated with nascent professionalism. As once characterized by Bernard Barber, these include

a high degree of generalized and systematic knowledge; primary orientation to the community interest rather than to individual self-interest; a high degree of self-control of behaviour through codes of ethics internalized in the process of work socialization and through voluntary associations organized and operated by the work specialists themselves; and a system of rewards (monetary and honorary) that is primarily a set of symbols of work

6 W. D. Niven, ed., *The scientific papers of James Clerk Maxwell* (New York: Dover, 1965), II, 356; A. W. Benn, *A history of English rationalism in the nineteenth century* (London: Longmans, Green & Co., 1906), I, 198; Henry Sidgwick, 'Presidential address to the Society for Psychical Research, July 16, 1888', in *Presidential addresses to the Society for Psychical Research* (Glasgow: Society for Psychical Research, 1912), p. 35 (italics added).

achievement and thus ends in themselves, not means to some end of individual self-interest.[7]

During the early stages of professionalism an elite from the emerging professional group attempts to project a new public image by formulating codes of ethics, strengthening professional organizations, establishing professional schools, penetrating existing educational institutions, and dispersing information to the general public. These leaders may simply be seeking to improve their social or economic position rather than self-consciously attempting to organize a profession. But to the extent that they are successful in improving their condition through these kinds of activities, their occupational group will assume to a greater or lesser degree the features of a profession.

Normally, pursuit of these ends requires the professionalizing elite to engage in conflict with persons inside and outside the existing occupational or amateur group. Within the group they must raise standards of competence, foster a common bond of purpose, and subject practitioners to the judgement of peers rather than of external social or intellectual authorities. Outside they must establish the independence of the would-be professional group, its right of self-definition, and its self-generating role in the social order. Consequently, there are usually disputes between professionals and amateurs and between professionals and outsiders who wish to impose their own definition on the group or who presently carry out the social functions that the professionalizing group wishes to share or to claim as its own exclusive domain. The mid-Victorian scientific community experienced such pangs of professionalization, and the conflict of science and religion was one of the by-products.

During the early years of the nineteenth century the major characteristics of British science were amateurism, aristocratic patronage, minuscule government support, limited employment opportunities, and peripheral inclusion within the clerically dominated universities and secondary schools. The Royal Society was little more than a fashionable club as befitted a normally amateur

---

7 Bernard Barber, 'Some problems in the sociology of the professions', *Daedalus*, 92 (1963), 672. See also J. A. Jackson, ed., *Professions and professionalization* (Cambridge: Cambridge University Press, 1970); E. Mendelsohn, 'The emergence of science as a profession in nineteenth century Europe', in K. Hill, ed., *The management of scientists* (Boston, Mass.: Beacon Press, 1964), pp. 3–48; Harold J. Perkin, *The rise of professional society: England since 1880* (London: Routledge, 1989).

occupation of gentlemen. In 1851 the ever critical Charles Babbage complained, 'Science in England is not a profession: its cultivators are scarcely recognized even as a class. Our language itself contains no *single* term by which their occupation can be expressed.'[8] Reverend William Whewell, the Cambridge mathematician, philosopher of science, and early leader of the British Association, had invented the word *scientist* in 1834 and reasserted its usefulness in 1840, but the term enjoyed little currency until very late in the century. Even the Devonshire Commission in the seventies found it necessary to define *science* to mean physical rather than moral science. During the first half of the century, all too few people within or without the scientific world related the advancement of physical science to national health, physical well-being, military security, or economic strength.[9]

Although before mid-century the utility of science for manufacturing, agriculture, and improvement of the working class received attention in the Mechanics' Institutes, the Society for the Diffusion of Useful Knowledge, the British Association for the Advancement of Science, and University College London, the function of scientific knowledge as a buttress for natural theology still continued to figure prominently among the public justifications for its pursuit. Early presidents of the British Association anxious to separate science from any connection with irreligious or politically radical thought repeatedly urged the interdependent relationship of science and theology. For example, in 1849 Reverend Thomas Romney Robinson, an astronomer, reminded the Association that

science is not necessarily wisdom. To know, is not the sole nor even the highest office of the intellect; and it loses all its glory unless it acts in furtherance of the great end of man's life. That end is, as both reason and revelation unite in telling us, to acquire the feelings and habits that will lead us to love and seek what is good in all its forms, and guide us by following its traces to the first Great Cause of all, where only we find it pure and unclouded. If science be cultivated in congruity with this, it is the most precious possession we can have – the most divine endowment. But if it be perverted to minister to any wicked or ignoble purpose – if it even be

8 Charles Babbage, *The exposition of 1851, or views of the industry, the science, and the government of England* (London: John Murray, 1851), p. 189. See also Sydney Ross, ' "Scientist": the story of a word', *Annals of science*, 18 (1962), 65–86.

9 *Third report of the Royal Commission on Scientific Instruction and the Advancement of Science* (1873), in *British parliamentary papers, education: science and technology* (Shannon: Irish University Press, 1970), IV, 15.

permitted to take too absolute a hold of the mind, or overshadow that
which should be paramount over all, the perception of right, the sense of
Duty – if it does not increase in us the consciousness of an Almighty and All-
beneficent presence, – it lowers instead of raising us in the great scale of
existence.[10]

Such convictions were not mere rhetorical window dressing. Many
scientists considered the moral and metaphysical imperatives of
natural theology as a proper and integral part of their vocation and
not as an intrusion of extraneous categories imposed by outside
institutions. Those religious convictions and the more general framework of natural theology influenced the behaviour of men of science
in their capacity as practising scientists, defined the scope and
intellectual context of much scientific work, and frequently determined the kinds of questions and conclusions deemed appropriate or
inappropriate for research. In this respect, natural theology,
whether derivative of the mechanical reasoning of William Paley
and the Bridgewater treatises or the idealist metaphysics of Richard
Owen, could pose a major intellectual barrier to a thoroughly
naturalistic approach to the investigation of the universe.[11]

Although by mid-century some scientists had come to question or
to reject the epistemological limitations established by regard for
natural theology, those influences remained present throughout
much of the scientific community. This division of opinion about the
method and scope of science displayed itself in the debates over
geology, natural selection, and the place of humankind in nature.
However, as Robinson's statement indicates, the impact of religion
extended beyond the strictly intellectual issue of epistemology.
Scientific research stood subordinate to moral values, a concept of
God, and a view of human nature that had been formulated by
clergy and religious writers. Certain questions, areas of inquiry,
methods of research, and conclusions were discouraged or proscribed
because they carried the implication of impiety, immorality, or
blasphemy. These limitations reflected the social context of early
nineteenth-century science in which clergy and laymen with strong
religious convictions controlled access to much scientific patronage

[10] *Report of the nineteenth meeting of the British Association for the Advancement of Science* (London, 1850), pp. xliii–xliv.
[11] The very real conceptual difficulties posed by natural theology to Darwin's own thought are explored in Dov Ospovat, *The development of Darwin's theory: natural history, natural theology, and natural selection, 1838–1853* (Cambridge: Cambridge University Press, 1981).

and employment. On more than one occasion practitioners of science, such as Charles Lyell and William Lawrence, had curbed or modified expression of their opinions for fear of offending both clerical and scientific colleagues.[12] The pervasive influence of natural theology and the derivative influence of the clergy meant the early Victorian scientific community was not yet self-defining in regard to its own function.

From the 1840s onward the size, character, structure, ideology, and leadership of the Victorian scientific world underwent considerable transformation and eventually emerged possessing most of the characteristics associated with a modern scientific community.[13] Between 1850 and 1880 the memberships of all the major scientific societies markedly increased, with many of them doubling their numbers. Total memberships during that period grew from 4,597 to 12,314. Even allowing for multiple memberships, there can be little doubt that the number of scientists rose considerably during the third quarter of the century. This increase in the size of the scientific community finds further confirmation in the expansion of the physics and chemistry faculties. In 1850 there were seventeen physics professors and two other faculty members teaching physics in the United Kingdom. By 1880 the figures had risen to twenty-eight and twenty-two respectively. The number of chemistry professors in 1850 was eleven, with four other chemistry faculty members. By 1880 the university chemistry faculties had expanded to twenty-five professors and thirty-four other instructors. Figures for the other sciences if calculated would probably reveal similar magnitudes of expansion.[14]

Directly tied to the growth of the scientific community was a new direction and character in its leadership. In 1847 the rules for membership in the Royal Society were reformed to favour the future

---

[12] Leonard G. Wilson, *Charles Lyell, the years to 1841: the revolution in geology* (New Haven: Yale University Press, 1972), pp. 310–15; Peter G. Mudford, 'William Lawrence and the natural history of man', *Journal of the History of Ideas*, 29 (1968), 430–6.

[13] '... the "scientist" is himself a social construct of the last hundred years or so. And, as usually understood, so are "science", "the scientific community", and "the scientific career"'. Steven Shapin and Arnold Thackray, 'Prosopography as a research tool in the history of science: the British scientific community, 1700–1900', *History of Science*, 12 (1974), 3.

[14] Dr Roy M. McLeod very generously furnished these figures to the author. The membership figures include the Chemical, the Geological, the Royal Anthropological, the Royal Astronomical, the Royal Entomological, the Royal Microscopical, the Royal Statistical, and the Zoological Societies.

inclusion of practitioners whose achievements were scientific rather than social. That reform also included provisions for reducing the size of the society by limiting new memberships to fifteen annually. The long-term result would be a smaller society composed of practising men of science. The year of the Royal Society reforms also saw the formation of the Philosophical Club, whose membership was limited to forty-seven persons each of whom had to be a researching and publishing scientist.[15] From the 1850s onward a group of newly arrived scientists whom Leonard Huxley later called 'the young guard of science' took up the public championship of professionalized science.[16] The 'young guard' included as its chief spokesmen T. H. Huxley, John Tyndall, Joseph Dalton Hooker, George Busk, Edward Frankland, Thomas Archer Hirst, John Lubbock, William Spottiswoode, and Herbert Spencer, all of whom composed the X-Club, and Henry Cole, Norman Lockyer, Francis Galton, and Lyon Playfair.[17]

By the 1870s, in terms of editorships, professorships, and offices in the major societies, these men had established themselves as a major segment of the elite of the Victorian scientific world. Lockyer was the chief editor of *Nature* from its founding in 1869 until 1919. Hooker, Spottiswoode, and Huxley occupied the presidency of the Royal Society from 1873 until 1885. At one time or another between 1850 and 1900 one or more of this coterie served as president of the British Association for the Advancement of Science, the Anthropological Society, the Chemical Society, the Royal College of Surgeons, the Institute of Chemistry, the Ethnological Society, the Geological Society, and the Mathematical Society. They also held key positions in the Royal School of Mines, the Royal Institution, University College London, the Royal Botanical Gardens at Kew, the Royal Naval College, and the Solar Physics Observatory. They were also

---

[15] Henry Lyon, *The Royal Society, 1660–1940* (Cambridge: Cambridge University Press, 1944), pp. 260–3, 282–3; T. G. Bonney, *Annals of the Philosophical Club* (London: Macmillan, 1919), pp. 1–3.

[16] Leonard Huxley, *Life and letters of Sir Joseph Dalton Hooker* (London: John Murray, 1918), I, 541.

[17] Other names, such as John S. Burdon-Sanderson, might obviously be added to this group. Three of the persons included may seem problematical. Galton held no professional offices, but worked consistently for the practical application of science and for its professional organization. Neither Henry Cole nor Herbert Spencer was a scientist, but the former as Secretary of the Department of Science and Art was one of the persons most vocal in calling for links between science and industry and the latter was treated by his contemporaries as a scientific figure.

frequently consulted by the government on issues of scientific research, industry, and education.[18]

Such achievements had not been easy. These scientists had generally grown up on the peripheries of the English intellectual establishment. With a few exceptions they had not been educated in the English universities but in their Scottish counterparts or in London medical schools, the civil service, the military, or in provincial dissenting communities. Although gifted and often brilliant, they had possessed no ready access to the higher echelons of Victorian society. There were all too few jobs that depended on merit rather than patronage. Neither public opinion nor government policy at mid-century generally recognized their social utility as scientists. The key to their own future social and financial security was the establishment of a great public appreciation for science and its contribution to the welfare of the nation.

As expressed in 1868 in the prospectus of a short-lived journal called *Scientific Opinion*, such ambitious young scientists needed to advocate 'the cause of Science and the interests of scientific men in England, to enforce . . . the claims of science upon the general public, to secure her followers their proper need of recompense and social distinction and to help them in their daily pursuits'. To those professionalizing ends, 'the young protagonists in science'[19] both individually and on occasion collectively participated in the Royal Society, the Philosophical Club, the British Association, and more specialized societies, delivered popular lectures to a variety of audiences, wrote textbooks, were active in the establishment of the unsuccessful *Reader* and the spectacularly successful *Nature*, served on and testified before government commissions for furthering scientific

---

[18] Consult the relevant articles in the *Dictionary of national biography* and the *Dictionary of scientific biography*. See also D. S. L. Cardwell, *The organization of science in England*, revised edn (London: Heinemann, 1972), pp. 84–98; Martin Fichman, 'Ideological factors in the dissemination of Darwinism in England, 1860–1890', in Everett Mendelsohn, ed., *Transformation and tradition in the sciences* (Cambridge: Cambridge University Press, 1984), pp. 471–85; and the following series of important articles by Roy M. MacLeod: 'The alkali acts administration, 1863–1884: the emergence of the civil scientist', *Victorian Studies*, 9 (1965), 85–112; 'Science and government in Victorian England: lighthouse illumination and the Board of Trade, 1866–1886', *Isis*, 60 (1969), 4–38; 'The X-Club: a social network of science in late-Victorian England', *Notes and Records of the Royal Society of London*, 24 (1970), 305–22; 'Of medals and men: a reward system in Victorian science', *Notes and Records of the Royal Society of London*, 26 (1971), 81–105; 'The support of Victorian science: the endowment of research movement in Great Britain, 1868–1900', *Minerva*, 9 (1971), 197–230.

[19] Quoted in *Nature*, 224 (1969), 435; Huxley, *Life and letters of Sir Joseph Dalton Hooker*, II, 54.

education, campaigned for the national endowment of research, and attempted to protect future physiological and medical research by doing battle with antivivisectionists.[20] They repeatedly sought to relate the advance of science and of its practitioners to the physical, economic, and military security of the nation, to the alleviation of social injustice, to the Carlylean injunction for a new aristocracy of merit, and to the cult of the expert inherited from their utilitarian forerunners.

Championship of the 'vigilant verification' of the empirical method and of a thoroughly naturalistic approach to science was integrally related to these professionalizing efforts.[21] The positivist epistemology constituted both a cause and a weapon. The 'young guard' agreed among themselves that science should be pursued without regard for religious dogma, natural theology, or the opinions of religious authorities. But neither such critical science nor its practitioners could flourish where the religious beliefs of clergy and other scientists could and did directly influence evaluation of work, patronage of research, and appointments in scientific institutions, the universities, and the public schools. By claiming their own epistemology as the exclusive foundation for legitimate science and as the correct model for knowledge generally, the professionalizing scientists sought to undermine the intellectual legitimacy of alternative modes of scientific thought and practice. Positivist epistemology provided an intellectual solvent to cleanse contemporary science of metaphysical and theological survivals. By excluding the kinds of questions as well as the answers that might arise from theological concerns, such positivistic methods also served to discredit the wider cultural influence of organized religion. Intellectual and social advance went hand in hand. For as the advocates of professional and critical science came to enjoy greater social prestige, their view of the purpose and character of science became more widely accepted, though not necessarily for philosophical or scientific reasons.

[20] John Francis Byrne, *The Reader: a review of literature, science, and the arts, 1863–1867* (Ann Arbor: University Microfilms, 1965); Arthur Jack Meadows, *Science and controversy: a biography of Sir Norman Lockyer* (Cambridge, Mass.: MIT Press, 1972), pp. 1–38; Richard D. French, *Antivivisection and medical science in Victorian society* (Princeton: Princeton University Press, 1975), pp. 60–111.

[21] G. H. Lewes, *History of philosophy from Thales to Comte*, 4th edn (London: Longmans, Green, 1871), I, xxxix. For further discussion of the character and function of this empirical epistemology, see David L. Hull, *Darwin and his critics: the reception of Darwin's theory of evolution by the scientific community* (Cambridge, Mass.: Harvard University Press, 1973), pp. 37–67, and Turner, *Between science and religion*, pp. 17–23.

The drive to organize a more professionally oriented scientific community and to define science in a more critical fashion brought the crusading scientists into conflict with two groups of people. The first were supporters of organized religion who wished to maintain a large measure of control over education and to retain religion as the source of moral and social values. The second group was the religiously minded sector of the pre-professional scientific community, which included both clergymen and laymen. The debate within the scientific world deserves prior consideration because much of the harshest rhetoric stemmed from the determination of the aggressive, professionally minded scientists to exorcise from their ranks clergymen-scientists and lay scientists who regarded the study of physical nature as serving natural theology or as standing subordinate to theology and religious authority.

Since the seventeenth century the parson-naturalist and the academic clergyman-scientist had played a major and by no means inglorious role in British science, as the names of John Ray, Joseph Priestley, John Stevens Henslow, Adam Sedgwick, and William Whewell attest. Such scientists were often contributing members of the Royal Society and in some cases recipients of high awards for their work. During the 1830s the clerical scientists had joined the effort to found the British Association for the Advancement of Science and had served as its officers. For them natural science and natural theology, the clerical and the scientific callings, were not simply compatible, but complementary. From at least the 1840s onward, however, their position had become increasingly difficult. The naturalistic bent of theories in geology, biology, and physiological psychology drove deep wedges into existing reconciliations of scientific theory with revelation or theology. The faith that the truth of revelation and the truth of science must be the same had become severely strained. The place of humankind in nature particularly raised difficulties. Fewer lay scientists remained concerned with meshing science and religion.

Besides urging a completely naturalistic view of nature and banishment of religious purposes and categories from scientific work, the drive by young lay scientists toward professionalization struck the clerical scientists on two other levels. The first was that of the degree of expertise that might qualify a person and his work for professional recognition and monetary support. In 1859 Huxley told Hooker in regard to a proposed research fund,

If there is to be any fund raised at all, I am quite of your mind that it should be a scientific fund and not a mere naturalists' fund ... For the word 'Naturalist' unfortunately includes a far lower order of men than chemist, physicist, or mathematician. You don't call a man a mathematician because he has spent his life in getting as far as quadratics; but every fool who can make bad species and worse genera is a 'Naturalist'.[22]

Here was the cutting edge of the professionalizing spirit before which, as much as before the edge of objectivity, the amateur parson-naturalist fell. With or without the impact of Darwin and other new theories, the amateur's day as a 'man of science' was drawing to a close. As persons of Huxley's opinion and ambitions came to control the meagre research funds administered by the Royal Society, the British Association, and other professional scientific societies, amateur scientists with marginal training and expertise could expect both less support and less recognition.

Second, the clerical scientists stood accused of dual loyalties that were incompatible with pursuit of thoroughly naturalistic science according to which theological, teleological, and metaphysical concerns stood banned both as matters for investigation and as principles of explanation. The emerging professional coteries considered 'scientifical-geological-theologians', such as Hugh Miller and Adam Sedgwick, who continued to attempt to reconcile science and revelation, as public embarrassments who resembled 'asses between bundles of hay, distorting their consciences to meet the double-call of their public profession'.[23] In the professional scientific community there would be little or no room for the person of two callings. Science and the scientist must service the profession or community at large but not some particular religious doctrine, sect, or church to which scientific activity was subordinate. In this respect Philip Gosse and the Victoria Institute were as much a conclave of amateurs surviving into the dawn of the professional era as they were a group of orthodox theologians.

The professionalizers were not content merely to note or to ridicule the intellectual problems of the clerical scientist. In some cases they set out to prove that no clergyman could be a genuine man of science. Such an argument provided a secondary theme for Francis Galton's *English men of science: their nature and nurture* (1874).

[22] Leonard Huxley, *The life and letters of Thomas Henry Huxley* (New York: D. Appleton and Co., 1900), I, 177.
[23] Huxley, *Life and letters of Sir Joseph Dalton Hooker*, I, 520.

This book was both a pioneering work of statistical inquiry and a professional manifesto that contended, 'The pursuit of science is uncongenial to the priestly character.' To support this contention Galton noted that very few men whom he defined as scientists came from clerical homes. His own experience on scientific councils, he believed, confirmed his view of the incapacity of clergymen for serious scientific work. Galton explained that between 1850 and 1870 clergymen had occupied only 16 out of 660 positions on the councils of the major scientific societies, and he insisted that 'they have in nearly every case been attached to those subdivisions of science which have the fewest salient points to scratch or jar against dogma'. He quickly added, 'There is not a single biológist among them.'[24]

Galton's tactic was a commonplace one within emerging professional groups: edging out marginal members on the grounds of alleged indifference or incompetence. His real charge against the clergymen-scientists was that they were clergymen first, scientists second, and thus could not be good professionals as he and others had begun to define the term. Galton hoped to persuade his readers that since clergymen by virtue of their theological vocation could not be genuine scientists and could not honestly teach science, professional men of science seeking to serve the material needs of the entire community should occupy these positions of research and teaching in the universities and public schools at present occupied by clergy or persons appointed and controlled by clergy. The message was also relevant to the managers of the new school-board schools. Galton hoped those teaching positions as well as employment in government agencies would eventually 'give rise to the establishment of a sort of scientific priesthood throughout the kingdom, whose high duties would have reference to the health and well-being of the nation in its broadest sense, and whose emoluments and social position would be made commensurate with the importance and variety of their functions'.[25] Banishment of clergymen

[24] Francis Galton, *English men of science: their nature and nurture*, 2nd edn (London: Frank Cass, 1970; 1st publ. 1874), pp. 24, 26. For this polemical passage Galton was compelled to fall back on his own experience with clergymen and scientists because the respondents to his questionnaire had overwhelmingly insisted that the religious training of their youth and even their present religious convictions did not interfere with their scientific work. See ibid., pp. 126–201, and Victor L. Hilts, *A guide to Francis Galton's* English men of science (Philadelphia: Transactions of the American Philosophical Society, 1975), N.S. 65, pp. 5, 29–31.

[25] Galton, *English men of science*, p. 260.

from positions of influence in the scientific world and the abolishment of clerically dominated education were essential to that goal.

For purposes of inclusion in his data Galton had defined a 'man of science' with professionalizing aims in mind. To qualify, a person had to have been elected to the Royal Society after 1850, that is, three years after the important membership reforms. Second, the scientist must have earned a medal for his work, presided over a learned society or section of the British Association, have been elected to the Council of the Royal Society, or occupied a professorship in an important college or university. These distinctly professional criteria effectively excluded both amateur aristocratic practitioners of science and the more notable of the clerical scientists, most of whom had been elected to the Royal Society prior to the reforms of 1847. Consequently no matter what the quality of the work of the clerical scientists or the number of scientific honours and offices achieved, those people had almost no impact on Galton's data. Had he not so skewed his numbers by choosing the date of 1850, more clergymen would have been included. Moreover, some of those investigators would have been deeply involved with geology during a period when that science did indeed jar against dogma.[26]

Galton's handling of his evidence in effect made prescriptive a steady decrease in the number of clergymen-scientists occupying significant positions in the scientific community. This process of clerical withdrawal from the world of science commenced in the third quarter of the century and is quite apparent in the figures recording the number of Anglican clergymen who were members of the Royal Society at various intervals during the last half of the century (see Table 1).[27] During the entire lifetime of the Philosophical Club (1847–1901), the professionally oriented offshoot of the Royal Society, only two clergymen-scientists, Adam Sedgwick and Baden Powell, ever graced the membership roll.[28]

The figures for major participation by Anglican clergy in the

---

[26] Ibid., p. 4. In one case, that of Rev. John Stevens Henslow, Galton actually solicited information on a clergyman-scientist. Henslow was dead, but his son provided information. (The reasons for Galton's decision in this case are not known.) Hilts, *Guide*, pp. 13–14.

[27] The figures for this table have been calculated from the Royal Society membership lists published annually during the nineteenth century under the title of *The Royal Society*.

[28] See the membership lists and biographical sketches in Bonney, *Annals of the Philosophical Club*.

Table 1. *Anglican clergymen members of the Royal Society, 1849–99*

Year	Total membership	Anglican clergy	Clerical percentage of total membership
1849	741	72	9.7
1859	636	57	8.96
1869	544	44	8.1
1879	488	27	5.5
1889	466	17	3.6
1899	449	14	3.1

Table 2. *Anglican clergymen presiding over sections of the British Association for the Advancement of Science, 1831–1900*

	1831–65	1866–1900
Mathematics	15	2
Chemistry	4	0
Geology	6	0
Biology	8	1
Mechanical	8	0

British Association are equally striking. They are also perhaps even more indicative because the standards of the Association were less rigorous than those of the Royal Society (see Table 2).[29] From 1831 to 1865, the first thirty-five years of the Association's history, nine clergymen held the office of president, the last one in 1862. During the second thirty-five years of the Association's existence no clergyman was president. Prior to 1865 a total of fifty-two Anglican clergymen served in the rather honorary post of one of the Association's several vice presidents. From 1866 to 1900 the number fell to nineteen. A similar pattern occurred among the local secretaries of the Association who helped with the local arrangements for the annual meetings. During the first forty years (1831–70) twenty-one clergymen attended to this task; between 1871 and 1900 only five clergymen did so. The number of Anglican clergymen presiding over the individual sections of the Association repeated the picture

[29] These figures have been calculated from the officer lists published in the *Report of the seventy-first meeting of the British Association for the Advancement of Science* (London, 1901), pp. xl–lxxxiii.

of clerical departure. In each case, clergymen gave way to lay professionals.

This gradual severance of Anglican clergy from the world of British science reflected changes in the religious community as well as the harassment of the professionalizing scientists and the dispersion of theories incompatible with the Bible and natural theology. When early Victorian clerical scientists of stature, such as Sedgwick, Powell, and Whewell, died, there were few replacements from the ranks of the clergy. Many young clergymen not unnaturally had come to regard science as the enemy rather than the helpmate of religion. But reasons unrelated to developments in the scientific community also shaped this new attitude. A considerable body of clergy influenced by the Oxford Movement wanted the Anglican Church itself to become more autonomous from extra-ecclesiastical and extra-theological influences and to define its mission and character in terms of its own peculiar institutional and theological values. Most prominently they sought to liberate the Church of England from domination by the secular state. This movement also contained an intellectual component. Church tradition in addition to the Bible was to define doctrine and to serve as the foundation for religious truth and practice. Adjustment of theology for compatibility with science, such as had occurred in England since the age of Newton, implied a surrender of part of the intellectual and theological autonomy of the Church and more particularly the clergy to non-religious authority. Science, especially as defined by the professional man of science and as accepted by the contemporary liberal or broad church theologian, was part and parcel of the liberalism rejected by the Tractarians and their followers.

As these clergymen – probably the most dynamic element in the mid-century Church – defined the priesthood in distinctly clerical, theological, and devotional terms, it became increasingly difficult for men who might wish to combine the priesthood and the scientific calling to do so. For professional scientists that double vocation seemed retrogressive, but for the high church clergy it seemed too progressive and potentially rationalizing. Consequently, within the Church of England a clergyman-scientist confronted the choice of perpetuating traditional natural theology and risking ridicule by scientists or attempting further rationalization of theology in accord with science and encountering persecution by fellow clergymen.[30] The new rising clericalism in the Church gave further credibility to the stereotyped clergyman who disliked science and progressive thought generally.[31] The growing absence of clerical scientists seemed to prove that clergymen could not be scientists. Reform of the universities, removal of religious tests, and new opportunities for employment of scientifically trained persons in the government, in school-board schools, in the civic universities, and sometimes in industry meant that the Church and ecclesiastical patronage were no longer paths to the scientific career. By the third quarter of the century it had become increasingly clear that to be a scientist was one vocation and to be a clergyman was another. The professionalizing scientists seized upon these developments, not wholly of their own making, to effect an intellectual and social reorientation of the scientific community.

Yet fewer clergy in the ranks of the scientific world solved only part of the professional problem. Lay scientists, such as the powerful and much disliked Richard Owen, still retained active religious convictions, curried favour with the ecclesiastical hierarchy, and subordinated their intellectual enterprise to theological values. This traditional and pre-professional outlook manifested itself in several British Association presidential addresses during the sixties and early seventies and in the famous 'Scientists' Declaration' of 1865. So long as this reverent spirit did not measurably interfere with a person's teaching, research, or peer evaluation, there was minimal pro-

[30] See n. 23 above and Chadwick, *The Victorian Church*, I, 309–24, 455–68, 476–80, 487–91; Kenneth A. Thompson, *Bureaucracy and church reform: the organizational response of the Church of England to social change, 1800–1965* (Oxford: Clarendon Press, 1970), pp. 26–55, 117–21; M. A. Crowther, *Church embattled: religious controversy in mid-Victorian England* (Hamden, Conn.: Archon Books, 1970), pp. 13–39, 138–240; Meacham, *My lord bishop*, pp. 207–34; F. W. Farrar, 'The Church and her younger members', in *Authorized report of the Church Congress held at Dublin* (Dublin: Hodges, Smith, and Foster, 1868), pp. 143–7. In regard to the changing character of the Anglican clergy during the third quarter of the century, the author wishes to acknowledge the aid of conversations with Prof. Josef Altholz of the University of Minnesota.

[31] 'The clergy have their ideal conception of men of science, and men of science have an equally ideal notion of the clergy. The ordinary parson creates an imaginary being bent on destroying the fact of a revelation, the truths of religion, and the difference between a man and a brute. This imaginary being he christens Professor Huxley. On the other hand, the man of science constructs an equally imaginary being who resists every step of physical research, who is blind to the most obvious facts, who has no sense of truth, and who is labouring to make others as blind and as untruthful as himself. This imaginary being he styles the English Parson.' J. R. Green, 'Professor Huxley on science and the clergy', *The Saturday Review*, 24 (1867), 692. Such mutually distorting appeals to stereotypes are a common occurrence during struggles over professionalization.

fessional difficulty. For example, despite his compromising with ecclesiastical authorities, his regular church attendance, and his reluctance to accept the antiquity of man and natural selection, no one really doubted Charles Lyell's professional loyalty. Nor did James Clerk Maxwell's theistic speculations based on the nature of molecules raise questions. The same was true of W. B. Carpenter, a distinguished Unitarian physiologist, who hoped that science might still provide some grounds for a personal theism. His faith was not professionally pernicious, and he stood more than ready to do battle with spiritualists and the antivivisectionists. All of these men generally succeeded in separating their personal religious faith from a critical, professional approach to scientific research.[32]

There were, however, other more harmful cases of scientific allegiance to traditional religion. In 1875 P. G. Tait and Balfour Stewart published *The unseen universe*, in which they attempted to prove the validity of the Christian doctrine of immortality. These writers were answered and their speculations thoroughly criticized.[33] But the more significant target was any lay scientist who actually employed his scientific expertise to reconcile science with the doctrines of an ecclesiastical organization. Such a person had to be attacked frontally, for he was a remnant of those earlier scientific men who were, in Huxley's words, 'citizens of two states, in which mutually unintelligible languages were spoken and mutually incompatible laws were enforced'.[34] Professionally minded scientists would not tolerate persons who employed or seemed to employ science for ecclesiastical ends or in hope of ecclesiastical commendation.

St George Jackson Mivart, a Roman Catholic biologist, was just such a professional apostate who proved an irresistible and necessary

---

[32] Roy M. MacLeod, 'Evolutionism and Richard Owen, 1830–1868: an episode in Darwin's century', *Isis*, 56 (1965), 259–80; Brock and MacLeod, 'The "Scientists' Declaration" '; Wilson, *Charles Lyell*, pp. 310–315; W. B. Carpenter, 'On mind and will in nature', *Contemporary Review*, 20 (1872), 738–62, and *Mesmerism, spiritualism, etc., historically & scientifically considered* (New York: D. Appleton and Co., 1877); James Clerk Maxwell, 'Molecule', *Encyclopaedia Britannica*, 9th edn (Edinburgh: A. and C. Black, 1875); Lewis Campbell and William Garnett, *The life of James Clerk Maxwell* (London: Macmillan, 1882), pp. 321–2, 338–40, 393, 404.

[33] P. G. Tait and Balfour Stewart, *The unseen universe; or physical speculations on a future state* (London: Macmillan, 1875); W. K. Clifford, *Lectures and essays*, ed. Leslie Stephen and Frederick Pollock (London: Macmillan, 1901), I, 283–300; P. M. Heimann, '*The unseen universe*: physics and the philosophy of nature in Victorian Britain', *British Journal for the History of Science*, 6 (1972), 73–9.

[34] T. H. Huxley, 'Past and present', *Nature*, 51 (1894), 1.

target for professionalizing wrath. He had been a Huxley student, an adherent to natural selection, and a peripheral member of the Darwin circle. But in the late 1860s, Mivart came to entertain doubts (as did others at the time) about the sufficiency of natural selection alone to determine species. In the *Genesis of species* (1871) he expressed his newly found scepticism and set forth supplementary explanations. The same year he also criticized an article on marriage and divorce written by George Darwin and did so in such a manner as to cast aspersions on the younger Darwin's moral character. Each of these factors invited attack, but what particularly aroused Huxley and required detailed refutation was Mivart's contention that evolution was perfectly compatible with the church fathers and later Roman Catholic theologians. After numerous references to Augustine and Suarez, Mivart declared, 'It is then evident that ancient and most venerable theological authorities distinctly assert *derivative* creation and thus harmonize with all that modern science can possibly require ... The various extracts given show clearly how far "evolution" is from any necessary opposition to the most orthodox theology.'[35] In this fashion Mivart hoped to reconcile the Roman Catholic Church of Pius IX to the general doctrines of modern science.

Mivart's immediate reward was perhaps the most scathing review essay ever to come from Huxley's pen. The proposed reconciliation might have saved evolution for the Church, but it would have directly undercut arguments for the pursuit of science oriented toward the profession and the community rather than toward the approval of ecclesiastical authorities. Mivart was also in effect suggesting that little difference separated religious and scientific epistemology. If sustained, Mivart's analysis would have perpetuated the dual citizenship in scientific work that Huxley and others of his opinion abhorred. To those of Huxley's professional persuasion, it was essential that evolution not be embraced by the Roman Catholic Church.

Consequently, Huxley spent several hours in an Edinburgh library reading Augustine and Suarez to assure himself, and later readers of 'Mr. Darwin's critics' (1871), that the teaching of the Roman Catholic Church was absolutely irreconcilable with evolu-

---

[35] St George Jackson Mivart, *The genesis of species* (New York: D. Appleton and Co., 1871), p. 283. See also Jacob W. Gruber, *A conscience in conflict: the life of St. George Jackson Mivart* (New York: Columbia University Press, 1960), pp. 52–114.

tion. Huxley also warned that no one should imagine that 'he is, or can be, both a true son of the Church and a loyal soldier of science'. That opinion came as a severe shock to the beleaguered Mivart, who replied that 'it is not ... without surprise that I learned my one unpardonable sin ... the one great offence disqualifying me from being "a loyal soldier of science" – was my attempt to show that there is no real antagonism between the Christian religion and evolution'.[36] Mivart, like most of the historians after him, assumed that the antagonism between science and religion related primarily to ideas, when in fact it was also profoundly involved with men and institutions. Still regarding physical science as intimately related to natural theology, in good Baconian fashion, he had quite understand-ably failed to perceive that the issue at stake was not only the substance of theory but also the character of the scientific com-munity and the right of its members to set the parameters of their thought, education, epistemology, employment, and social utility independent of considerations for religious doctrine or ecclesiastical organization.

Outside the boundaries of the scientific community the profession-ally minded scientists confronted further obstacles to their redefini-tion of the direction and role of science. As Peter Marsh has observed, 'Above Victorian England's nagging doubts there was a thick layer of organized activity among all Christian denominations, thicker than at any time since the Civil War.' This activity consti-tuted the religious counterpart to the popular diffusion of science previously described by Clerk Maxwell. Between 1850 and 1880 ten new Anglican theological colleges were founded, and the number of priests rose from 17,320 in 1851 to 21,663 in 1881. From 1868 to 1880, approximately seventy new urban parishes were organized annually. In 1888 a spokesman at the Anglican Church Congress reported that between 1860 and 1885 over £80.5 million had been expended on building and restoring churches, missions, charities, and education. The ritualist movement and the restoration of Anglican conventual life continued to revitalize Anglo-Catholi-cism. In 1878 the Lambeth Conference approved reinstitution of auricular confession on a voluntary basis. Beginning in the late fifties and culminating in the seventies with the visit of the American evangelists Dwight Moody and Ira Sankey, revivals took place

---

[36] Huxley, *Collected essays*, II, 149; St George Jackson Mivart, *Essays and criticisms* (London: James R. Osgood, McIlvaine, 1892), II, 60.

throughout the nation. Nonconformists and their preachers, such as Charles Spurgeon, were reaching the height of their influence. Under the leadership of Cardinal Manning, English Roman Catholicism made considerable headway among the poor. The third quarter of the century also witnessed a broad Roman Catholic religious revival in Ireland. These developments, as well as the launching of the Salvation Army, the intrusion of Spiritualism from America, and the spectacle of the miracle of Lourdes in France, proved fundamental to the scientists' perception of their situation in the general society and intellectual nation. John Morley was not alone in his conviction that 'our age of science is also the age of deepening superstition and reviving sacerdotalism'.[37]

This climate of aggressive corporate and devotional religious revival, as much as their own naturalistic theories, brought the scientists into conflict with the clergy. Because of their friendships with liberal churchmen and their mutual resistance to theological excess, unorthodox men of science have sometimes been portrayed as holding a position 'in which theological dogma was being attacked not for the sake of undercutting religious faith, but as a means of freeing that faith for what were regarded as nobler and more adequate forms in which it could find expression'.[38] This interpretation is largely, if not wholly, incorrect. It ignores the frequent disagreements between liberal theologians and advocates of science and obscures the social and professional goals of the professionalizing scientists.[39] The latter sought to reform religion for the sake not of

[37] P. T. Marsh, *The Victorian Church in decline* (London: Routledge and Kegan Paul, 1969), p. 66; John Morley, *The struggle for national education*, 2nd edn (London: Chapman and Hall, 1873), p. 63.

[38] Maurice Mandelbaum, *History, man & reason: a study in nineteenth century thought* (Baltimore: Johns Hopkins University Press, 1971), p. 30. For variations of this theme, see Walter Houghton, *The Victorian frame of mind, 1830–1870* (New Haven: Yale University Press, 1957), pp. 48–53, 70–1; William Irvine, *Apes, angels, and Victorians: the story of Darwin, Huxley, and evolution* (New York: McGraw Hill, 1955), pp. 127–34, 339–41; Robert Young, 'The impact of Darwin on conventional thought', in Anthony Symondson, ed., *The Victorian crisis of faith* (London: Society for Promoting Christian Knowledge, 1970), pp. 13–36.

[39] During the 1830s and 1840s many scientists had seen their work as leading to a higher, more rational conception of the deity. However, by the 1860s and later this impulse had become much more rare. Unorthodox scientists, such as Huxley, Tyndall, Galton, and Spencer, repeatedly protested that they opposed ecclesiasticism and particular theological doctrines rather than religion itself; and they also allowed a limited role in personal life for inner emotional experiences which they, like contemporary religious liberals, classified as 'religious'. Such adherence to vague modes of liberal religion proved existentially useful to some of these scientists and also separated them from less respectable working-class atheists and secularists. But the critical scientists adamantly opposed religion as it was generally defined by liberal Anglicans such as Benjamin Jowett. Furthermore, both James Martineau

purifying religious life but of improving the lot of science in Victorian society. The intellectual authority frequently ascribed to the clergy, the Bible, and theological concepts such as divine providence exerted a pernicious influence on the practical affairs of everyday life. Traditional religious authority provided the justification for Sabbatarianism, restrictive marriage laws, prayers to change the weather and to prevent disease, religiously dominated education, and other social practices that inhibited the discovery, diffusion, and application of scientific truth. So long as that authority and those practices continued, the scientists could not achieve the cultural and social influence necessary for the establishment and improvement of their professional position.

Education provided the major arena for confrontation and conflict. In the mid-1860s liberal Bishop Connop Thirlwall, who was also a major historian of Greece, shrewdly observed that much of the hostility between scientists and clergymen arose because 'Science is debarred its rightful share of influence in the education of the national mind.'[40] Penetration of the educational system at both the secondary and university levels would ensure the dispersion of scientific knowledge and eventually lead to broader applications throughout the society. Achievement of a larger share of educational

and R. H. Hutton understood that scientific naturalism was basically antithetical to both traditional and liberal Christianity. As the broad church impulse came to have less and less influence within the Church, the scientists made fewer and fewer accommodations. Lightman persuasively contends they intended to establish a new version of natural theology which would have been based on new scientific theory. These new versions of natural theology, however, were in no manner set forth as accommodations to either traditional or liberal versions of Christianity. See Huxley, *The life and letters of Thomas Henry Huxley*, I, 233–9, II, 9; Huxley, *Life and letters of Sir Joseph Dalton Hooker*, II, 198–201; John Tyndall, *Fragments of Science*, 6th edn (New York: D. Appleton and Co., 1892), II, 198–201; Karl Pearson, *The life, letters and labours of Francis Galton* (Cambridge: Cambridge University Press, 1930), IIIB, 471–2; Herbert Spencer, *First principles* (New York: P. F. Collier, n.d.), pp. 1–38; Evelyn Abbott and Lewis Campbell, eds., *Letters of Benjamin Jowett* (New York: E. P. Dutton, 1899), p. 190; James Martineau, *Essays, reviews, and addresses* (London: Longmans, Green, and Co., 1891), III, 185–218; IV, 165–268; Richard Holt Hutton, *Aspects of religious and scientific thought*, ed. Elizabeth M. Roscoe (London: Macmillan, 1899); Bernard Lightman, *The origins of agnosticism: Victorian unbelief and the limits of knowledge* (Baltimore: Johns Hopkins University Press, 1987); and Ruth Barton, 'Evolution: the Whitworth gun in Huxley's war for the liberation of science from theology', in David Oldroyd and Ian Langham, eds., *The wider domain of evolutionary thought* (Dordrecht: D. Reidel Publishing Co., 1983), pp. 261–87.

40 Connop Thirlwall, *Essays, speeches, and sermons*, ed. J. J. Stewart Perowne (London: Richard Bentley, 1880), p. 287. Thirlwall drew his distinction between literary men and scientists rather than clergy and scientists, but from the essay it is clear that by literary men he meant clergy educated for their calling in the classics. For a direct challenge by a scientist to clerical educators, see John Tyndall, *Heat considered as a mode of motion* (New York: D. Appleton and Co., 1863), p. vi.

influence also meant to the professional scientific elite attainment of social legitimacy and prestige and of new areas of employment for students of science. The scientists' assault on the education system necessarily required confrontation with the religious groups who controlled it and guided its curriculum. Acquiring professional inclusion in the major educational institutions involved attacking the sufficiency of strictly literary training, calling for removal of theological tests in the universities and informal requirements in the public schools, opposing denominational control of the school boards after the Education Act of 1870, and demanding that the science taught be science as defined by professional scientists. This process involved more frequent clashes with Roman Catholics and Anglicans than with Protestant Nonconformists who in the seventies were themselves frequently calling for non-sectarian education.

A large measure of the scientists' complaint against religious influence over education and culture generally was reserved for Roman Catholicism, which Huxley described as 'our great antagonist' and 'that damnable perverter of mankind'.[41] Linking the advance of science to anti-Catholicism allowed the cause of the professional scientists to benefit from the widespread popular anti-papist sentiment in Britain. But much more was involved than anti-Catholicism. Under the pontificate of Pius IX the Roman Catholic Church epitomized the most extreme mode of religious authority

[41] T. H. Huxley, *Science and education* (New York: D. Appleton and Co., 1898), p. 120; Huxley, *The life and letters of Thomas Henry Huxley*, II, 242. During one session of the London School Board Huxley seems clearly to have used an appeal to anti-Catholicism to consolidate his position among other members who were otherwise somewhat unsympathetic to his general point of view. See *Times*, 28 Oct. 1871, p. 11. Anti-Catholicism permeated the writings of the scientists and their allies. For examples of this sentiment, consult Edward B. Tylor, *Anahuac: or Mexico and the Mexicans, ancient and modern* (London: Longman, Green, Longman and Roberts, 1861), pp. 20, 126, 289; and Clifford, *Lectures and essays*, II, 233–4. In Draper's *History of the conflict between religion and science*, as well as in the various editions of White's *Warfare of science with theology in Christendom*, the religion and theology in question were primarily Roman Catholicism. Apparently outside Catholic journals few commentators noticed the anti-Catholic bias of the scientists. Three exceptions were Robert Buchanan, 'Lucretius and modern materialism', *New Quarterly Magazine*, 6 (1876), 18; J. R. Seeley, *Natural religion* (Boston, Mass.: Roberts Brothers, 1882), *passim*; T. W. Marshall, *My clerical friends and their relations to modern thought* (London: Burnes, Oakes, and Company, 1873), pp. 263–70. Owen Chadwick in passing noted the problem of Catholicism for the scientists but did not emphasize it. However, a newspaper article which he cites as an example of interest in the conflict refers only to the problems of science with Roman Catholicism. Chadwick, *The Victorian Church*, II, 2–3; *Times*, 25 May 1864, pp. 8–9. Jeffrey Von Arx has explored other aspects of anti-Catholicism among advanced thinkers in *Preventive progress: a study of the relationships of religion, politics and the historiography of progress in the work of some nineteenth-century British historians* (Cambridge, Mass.: Harvard University Press, 1985).

and clerical pretension for control of intellectual life. The Church had specifically condemned the theory, methods, conclusions, and practice of modern science. However, as much as the general condemnation of the *Syllabus of errors* (1864), the role of the Roman Catholic Church in Ireland accounted for the intense antipathy of the scientists. So long as Catholicism permeated Ireland and its hierarchy dominated the Catholic University, science and its practitioners could play no effective role in that nation. Ireland stood as an object lesson in the potential ecclesiastical blight of a nation; and the scientists, who were generally unionists, regarded Ireland as an integral part of Britain.[42]

It was against Irish Catholicism and more particularly against its impact on education that John Tyndall directed his notorious Belfast Address of 1874. In the course of that presidential address to the British Association Tyndall declared that men of science 'claim, and ... shall wrest from theology, the entire domain of cosmological theory. All schemes and systems which infringe upon the domain of science must, in so far as they do this, submit to its control, and relinquish all thought of controlling it.'[43] Probably no single incident in the conflict of religion and science raised so much furore. Most contemporaries interpreted Tyndall's remarks as applying to all churches. However, a careful reading of the address and of Tyndall's later 'Apology for the Belfast Address' (1874) reveals that by theology he meant Roman Catholicism in particular. A few months earlier the Irish Catholic hierarchy had refused the request of the laity for inclusion of physical science in the curriculum of the Catholic University. To a scientist with eyes to see, ecclesiasticism was alive, well, and prospering across the Irish Sea. Tyndall, who was an Anglo-Irishman, used his presidential address to chastise the Irish Catholic religious authorities.[44] But the widespread hostile criticism of the address throughout the British religious community suggested that Irish Catholic bishops were not the only religious

[42] Gladstone's policy of Irish Home Rule and resentment over the fate of General Gordon were among the reasons for Huxley's debating Gladstone over Genesis. Huxley later explained, 'It was most important at that moment to shake him in the minds of sensible men'. Huxley, *The life and letters of Thomas Henry Huxley*, II, 450; see also II, 124, 130. Tyndall also attacked Gladstone on the Home Rule issue; see John Tyndall, *Mr. Gladstone and home rule*, 2nd edn (Edinburgh and London: William Blackwood, 1887).
[43] Tyndall, *Fragments*, II, 197.
[44] *Ibid.*, II, 196–7, 210–18. On the petition of the Irish Catholic laity, see *Times*, 2 Dec. 1873, p. 7. Tyndall renewed his advice to Roman Catholics in the 'Prefatory Note' (1876) to White, *The warfare of science* (1876 edn), pp. iii–iv.

authorities who aspired to limit the cosmological speculations of their flocks.

Within England the scientists were fighting a similar battle, although against a weaker mode of ecclesiasticism. Since the late thirties, provision of education for the nation had constituted the chief claim of the Church of England to social utility. Although the Education Act of 1870 destroyed the Anglican pretension to monopoly in that area, the Church continued to exercise widespread educational influence. Indeed the provisions of the Education Act served to stir new Anglican activity to avoid imposition of school-board schools. However, probably at no time in modern history did the Anglican Church appear to be less of a *national* establishment. The ritualist controversy persuaded many people that the Church harboured potential or secret Roman Catholic clergy. The hostile reaction to *Essays and reviews* discouraged hopes that the Church might become more liberal and inclusive from within. The judicial actions initiated against both the liberal reviewers and the high church ritualists cast the Church of England in the role of a persecutor. In 1867 J. R. Green, the historian, complained, 'At the present the breadth of the Church is brought sharply out against the narrowness of the clergy. They do not even represent the Church. What then do they represent? Not the educated laity – not the intelligence of England – but its unintelligence.'[45] Throughout the third quarter of the century the Anglican clergy appeared to the general public to be pursuing party goals within the Church and denominational ascendancy within the nation.

Such an institution in the eyes of many citizens seemed unfit to be the schoolmaster of the nation. Later the Church had to oppose raising standards of scientific education because the added cost would harm already tight budgets.[46] All of these conditions permitted the professional scientists not only to compare their rationalism with the faith of the clergy but also to contrast both implicitly and explicitly their own enlightened, practical, and unselfish goals with the apparently narrow, vested, dysfunctional, and denominational interests of the clergy. In opposition to Irish Catholic and Anglican

[45] Leslie Stephen, ed., *The letters of J. R. Green* (New York: Macmillan, 1901), p. 142. About the same time Joseph Dalton Hooker told a correspondent, 'The worst of it is that the present condition of things prevents the rising talent and candid thinkers from entering the Church at all, and we shall be bepastored with fools, knaves, or imbeciles.' Huxley, *Life and letters of Sir Joseph Dalton Hooker*, II, 57.

[46] Marsh, *The Victorian Church in decline*, pp. 79–81.

ecclesiastical authorities who spurned the inclusion of science and
other practical subjects favoured by middle-class parents, the scientists emerged as the educational party of national efficiency and
imperial vision whose concerns and self-interest were at one with the
medical, economic, military, and industrial requirements of the
nation.

The internal ideology of much, though certainly not all, early
Victorian science had been related to tracing the presence of the
Creator in the creation. But that of the more nearly professionalized
science in the second half of the century became the glorification and
strengthening of the nation and its wealth. In 1870, during the
Franco-Prussian War, Norman Lockyer argued,

As there is little doubt that a scientific training for the young officer means
large capabilities for combination and administration when that officer
comes to command, we must not be surprised if the organization of our
army, if it is to do its work with the minimum of science, will, at some future
time, again break down as effectually as it did in the Crimea, or that our
troops will find themselves over-matched should the time ever come when
they will be matched with a foe who knows how to profit to the utmost from
scientific aids.

During the same period Henry Cole repeatedly pointed to the
necessity for better scientific education as the key to Britain's
continued economic supremacy. Edition after edition of *Nature*
carried the same message. In 1875 the Devonshire Commission on
which Huxley served and for which Lockyer was secretary declared
that 'considering the increasing importance of Science to the Material Interests of the Country, we cannot but regard its almost total
exclusion from the training of the upper and middle classes as little
less than a national misfortune'.[47] The linking of the fortunes of
science with the fate of the nation climaxed at the turn of the century
when the elderly Lockyer lectured the British Association on 'The
influence of brain power in history' (1903) and when Karl Pearson
in a whole series of books and articles proclaimed the necessity for
scientists to advise the government and for politicians to pursue
scientific policies and procedures in all areas of national life. These

---

[47] Norman Lockyer, *Education and national progress: essays and addresses, 1870–1905* (London:
Macmillan, 1906), p. 4; *Sixth report of the Royal Commission on scientific instruction and the
advancement of science* (1875), in *British parliamentary papers, education: science and technical*, IV,
24.

were the arguments of concerned, patriotic Englishmen. But they were also the arguments of persons who understood that only by connecting in the public mind the future of their emerging profession with the welfare of the nation could they attain the financial support, employment, prestige, and public influence they desired.

Commenting in the mid-1920s on Draper's *History of the conflict between religion and science*, Arthur Balfour observed, 'It is not perhaps surprising that the most interesting characteristic of Dr. Draper's volume of 1873 is its total want of interest for readers in 1925.' That development had not, however, come about because of any genuine intellectual reconciliation of science and religion. As David Lack contended, 'The basic conflict is unresolved.'[48] Rather the social and professional context of science in Britain had changed. By World War I most Christian theologians had abandoned natural theology, and the clergy no longer seriously sought either to rival or to complement scientists as interpreters of physical nature. From the standpoint of the scientists, their efforts to carve out for themselves an independent social and intellectual sphere had largely succeeded. The scientific community had become self-defining. Scientists had established themselves firmly throughout the educational system and could pursue research and teaching free from ecclesiastical interference. Science, as defined by the profession rather than for the profession, had become a part of national life. Politicians, such as Balfour and Haldane, though theists and authors of books on religious philosophy, no longer defended the Bible as had Gladstone. Rather they joined the chorus of spokesmen urging the national and imperial significance of science in light of the German economic and military threat.

Asa Briggs once wrote, 'The conflict between science and religion petered out, giving way to new debates about the nature not of the Universe but of society.'[49] However, at its centre much of the debate, including consideration of epistemological and scientific theory, had involved controversy about the social structure of the intellectual nation as well as about the structure of knowledge and of the universe. When the former set of issues had been resolved, many

[48] Lord Balfour, 'Introduction', in Needham, ed., *Science, religion and reality*, p. 4 (Balfour alludes to Draper's preface of 1873; the book appeared in 1874); David Lack, *Evolutionary theory and Christian belief* (London: Methuen, 1957), p. 9.
[49] Asa Briggs, *The age of improvement, 1783–1867* (New York: David McKay, 1964), p. 488.

of the latter no longer furnished grounds for continued dispute. In this regard the Victorian conflict of science and religion represents one chapter in the still-to-be-written intellectual and social history of the emergence of the professionalized society in the West.

CHAPTER 8

Public science in Britain: 1880–1919

'The aim of physical science is to observe and interpret natural phenomena', declared British physicist James Clerk Maxwell in the South Kensington Museum handbook.[1] Although most of his contemporaries would readily have agreed with Maxwell, present-day intellectual historians and historians of science believe that the analysis and understanding of the Victorian scientific enterprise, as well as of science generally, must extend far beyond the parameters suggested by Maxwell's definition. Numerous recent studies have firmly established that much of the intellectual content, methodological orientation, and professional organization of science cannot be separated from its social and cultural environments even if those environments are not wholly determinant of scientific activity.[2] Scientists in their capacity as observers and interpreters of physical nature still remain part of the larger social order, and between them and it there exists a dialectical relationship of mutual influence and interaction. As one element of this complex situation, scientists find that they must justify their activities to the political powers and other social institutions upon whose good will, patronage, funding, and cooperation they depend. Indeed in the past century and a half no single group of Western intellectuals has more successfully persuaded both governments and private foundations and corporations of their worthiness for receiving financing as have those persons engaged in scientific activity. The body of rhetoric, argument, and polemic produced in this particular process may be

From *Isis*, 71 (1980), 598–608. With permission of the journal.
[1] W. D. Niven, ed., *The scientific papers of James Clerk Maxwell* (New York: Dover, 1965), II, 505.
[2] For recent considerations of this much debated issue see Stephen Shapin, 'History of science and its sociological reconstruction', *History of science*, 20 (1982), 157–211, and Martin J. S. Rudwick, *The great Devonian controversy: the shaping of scientific knowledge among gentlemanly specialists* (Chicago: University of Chicago Press, 1985) pp. 401–56.

termed *public science*, and those who sustain this particular enterprise may be regarded as *public scientists*.

Public scientists do not propagate scientific knowledge for its own sake, and their work may have little or nothing to do with the actual motivations or goals of scientific research. Rather they consciously attempt to persuade the public or influential sectors thereof that science both supports and nurtures broadly accepted social, political, moral, and religious goals and values, and that it is therefore worthy of receiving public attention, encouragement, and financing. The pursuit of public science has involved lobbying various non-scientific elites, persuading the public or government that science can perform desired social and economic functions, defining as important those public issues that scientists can address through their particular knowledge or expertise, stressing professional standards among scientists, and defining the position of scientists vis-à-vis other rival intellectual or social elites, such as the clergy, literary scholars, social scientists, or businessmen. At the same time the public scientist remains both scientist and citizen, and his statements may and usually do reflect honestly held civic opinions as well as views that aid the position of science in the community.

The present essay constitutes a limited, speculative probe into the character of British public science from approximately 1880 to the conclusion of World War I. The analysis must remain speculative because this period in the history of British science has received relatively little attention, and the conclusions must also be tentative, directed toward raising questions and stimulating responses rather than toward suggesting final answers. The discussion assumes the character of a probe because its sources have been restricted to the most readily available statements on the public function of science. These include the presidential addresses of the British Association, the columns of *Nature*, and the major public utterances of men of science as they appeared in the leading journals and newspapers of the day. More conclusive opinions about this era of British public science must await examination of the journals of each of the major scientific societies, testimony of scientists before major parliamentary commissions from the 1870s through World War I, the specific interactions of scientists with various government departments, and the literature and publications of the medical profession.

I THE THREE PERIODS OF NINETEENTH-CENTURY BRITISH
PUBLIC SCIENCE

Although from the time of Bacon there have appeared within the
world of British science a number of spokesmen who have interpreted and championed the scientific endeavour to the larger
intellectual and political community, the nineteenth and early
twentieth centuries constituted the premier age of British public
science. Seminal scientific discoveries and theoretical achievements
coincided with the application of new technology to transportation
and manufacture and with the appearance of an improved quality of
everyday material life. During these years the career of British public
science divided into three more or less distinct periods. The first,
extending from the opening of the century to approximately the
Great Exhibition of 1851, saw such public scientists as Humphry
Davy, Charles Babbage, and the leaders of the early British Association for the Advancement of Science urge the importance of science
as a mode of useful knowledge, an instrument of self-improvement,
an aid to profitable, rational, and usually individualistic economic
activity, and a pillar of natural religion.[3] These decades witnessed
what Morris Berman has termed the transformation 'from science-
as-avocation to science-as-enterprise'. And the scientific enterprise,
like economic enterprise, was to be private. At the British Association meeting in 1851 the astronomer George Airy remarked, 'In
Science, as well as in almost everything else, our national genius
inclines us to prefer voluntary associations of private persons to
organizations of any kind dependent on the State.'[4] This widely, if
not universally, shared opinion flourished in the climate of Britain's
early industrial advance and the gospel of free trade. Furthermore,
in the first half of the century both the utilitarianism and the natural
religion that informed the social attitudes of scientists emphasized
the self-adjustment of the social mechanism or portrayed social
problems as matters for technical solution.

The second era of Victorian public science extended from the

---

[3] Jack Morell and Arnold Thackray, *Gentlemen of science: early years of the British Association for
the Advancement of Science* (Oxford: Clarendon Press, 1981). The bibliography of this work
covers the relevant literature.

[4] Morris Berman, *Social change and scientific organization: the Royal Institution, 1799–1844* (Ithaca,
N.Y.: Cornell University Press, 1978), p. 93; *Report of the twentieth meeting of the British
Association for the Advancement of Science* (London, 1851), p. li. (Hereafter these reports will be
cited as *British Association report* and the year.)

early 1850s through the late 1870s. During this period the great
Victorian scientific publicists – Thomas Huxley, John Tyndall,
William K. Clifford, and others – employed the theories of evolution, atomism, and the conservation of energy as instruments to
challenge the cultural dominance of the clergy, to attack religion
and metaphysics in scientific thought, and to forge a genuinely self-
conscious professional scientific community based on science pursued according to strictly naturalistic premises.[5] They repeatedly
equated the progress of science with the progress of civilization.
According to them science promised to establish new material
comfort, better health and physical well-being, intellectual liberty
from the clergy and other traditional authorities, and, when incorporated into the educational system, social mobility. They in effect
appealed to the intellectual equivalent of free trade with the heady
confidence that if scientists could only set their ideas, values, and
prowess before the public, the requisite support and recognition
would be forthcoming.

The early 1870s were years of real expectation for the scientific
community. British scientists had begun in considerable measure to
transform themselves into an independent, professionally self-defined
community and one recognized as such by other intellectuals and
professional groups. The state had for some time consulted scientific
experts on an *ad hoc* basis and was beginning to employ a few scientists
in the civil service and on administrative advisory boards. Reform of
the education system after 1870 seemed to promise potential new
influence and employment for scientists. The appointment of the
Devonshire Commission in 1872 by a Liberal government raised
further expectations that the state would recognize and encourage
science. The same year Francis Galton envisioned 'a sort of scientific
priesthood' that would furnish the teachers, researchers, and government administrators of the not distant future.[6]

Yet all of this intense activity proved to be a false political dawn.
As so ably delineated in the articles of Roy MacLeod, scientists soon
confronted frustration on all sides.[7] Despite a vigorous campaign,

[5] Frank Miller Turner, *Between science and religion: the reaction to scientific naturalism in late
   Victorian England* (New Haven: Yale University Press, 1974), pp. 8–37.
[6] Francis Galton, *English men of science: their nature and nurture*, 2nd edn (London: Frank Cass,
   1970; 1st publ. 1874), p. 260.
[7] Roy M. MacLeod, 'The alkali acts administration, 1863–1884: the emergence of the civil
   scientist', *Victorian Studies*, 9 (1965), 85–112; Roy M. MacLeod, 'The support of Victorian

national endowment for research was not forthcoming. The proposals of the Devonshire Commission fell on deaf ears. Those scientists whom the government did employ or did consult found their advice frequently not taken or their influence circumvented by civil servants operating according to the imperatives of treasury control. Scientists, like other groups of intellectuals who during the 1860s had hoped to participate broadly in public life, found themselves able to exert relatively little direct power or influence in the civic arena. The state refused to patronize them in a regular fashion; industry ignored them; and the education system only marginally incorporated them.

The disappointments and frustrations of the mid-1870s were the occasion for the opening of a new era in Victorian public science, during which it became more civic-minded and state-oriented. After approximately 1875 the spokesmen for British science shifted their rhetoric and the emphasis of their policy from the values of peace, cosmopolitanism, self-improvement, material comfort, social mobility, and intellectual progress toward the values of collectivism, nationalism, military preparedness, patriotism, political elitism, and social imperialism. Instead of being promoted as an instrument for improving the student morally and bringing greater physical security or personal profit to humankind, science came to be portrayed as a means to create and educate better citizens for state service and stable politics, and to ensure the military security and economic efficiency of the nation. Most indicative of the change in the attitude and rhetoric of public science between 1860 and 1900 was the replacement of priests and obscurantist clergy by politicians and complacent manufacturers as the primary perceived enemies of the progress and application of scientific knowledge.

II THE 1870S: THE SHIFT IN THE THEMES OF PUBLIC SCIENCE

Three factors account for this relatively sudden and quite striking shift in the themes of late nineteenth-century public science. First, as is well known, the Paris Exhibition of 1867, followed by the warnings

science: the endowment of research movement in Great Britain, 1868–1900', *Minerva*, 9 (1971), 197–230. See Christopher Hamlin, *A science of impurity: water analysis in nineteenth century Britain* (Berkeley: University of California Press, 1990), for an account of the relationship of scientists dealing with a single long-term problem to both the government and private enterprise.

206 Science and the wider culture

of Colonel Alexander Strange to the British Association in 1868, led many British scientists, as well as other citizens, to perceive German competition first as an industrial and later as a military threat. To the public scientists Germany both posed a problem to British commercial and military superiority and provided an opportunity for linking science to the national interest. The British scientific community, many of whose members had been trained in Germany, envied the organization, public recognition, and financial support enjoyed by German science. British scientific writers began to claim that only similar structures and endowment could save the British economic and military position. In 1887 T.H. Huxley demanded in the *Times* that the nation organize for victory in the industrial war that it had entered upon.[8] Although there is little question that British research lagged behind that of Germany, the claims of the scientists require a more sceptical evaluation than they have received in the past. The danger from Germany may have been genuine, but the scientists defined it in such a manner as to portray their own particular expertise and the kinds of technical education they could provide as the best solution for the problem. They were in effect suggesting that the economic and military welfare of the nation might best be secured by a new group of the professional middle class rather than by one of the traditional social or political elites. Scientists would continue to sound these themes well past World War I.

As public scientists began to exploit the German menace, many of them also recognized that they must begin to nurture a friendly constituency within the political nation, including both members of Parliament and the voting public at large. That lesson had been driven home to them by the success of the antivivisectionist movement, the second major cause for the shift of strategy in late Victorian public science. In 1876 the antivivisectionists had achieved passage of the Cruelty to Animals Act, which limited the scope of physiological experimentation. For about a decade thereafter the administration of the statute narrowed the character and extent of such investigation. Moreover, for many years after 1876 the

---

[8] *Times*, 20 Jan. 1887, p. 8. Although others had previously noted Britain's precarious economic position, Huxley's letter became a point of reference for scientific writers for well over a decade. Considering how often it was later cited by scientists, the letter must be regarded as one of his most important and influential public statements. See also D. Cardwell, *The organization of science in England*, revised edn (London: Heinemann, 1972), pp. 111–20, and George Haines IV, *Essays on German influence upon English education and science, 1850–1919* (Hamden, Conn.: Archon Books, 1969), pp. 3–20.

antivivisectionists agitated for an even more restrictive measure. The antivivisectionists demonstrated for the first time that sustained political agitation modelled after other moral reform movements could achieve legal restrictions on professional scientific research. Henceforth public scientists understood that they would need to persuade an often hostile public opinion of the social and national utility of experimental science. As the antivivisectionists largely captured the humanitarian position in the public forum, the scientists began to appeal to the national utility of science. For example, in 1879 E. Ray Lankester, a vocal opponent of the antivivisectionists, declared, 'The full and earnest cultivation of Science – the Knowledge of Causes – is that to which we have to look for the protection of our race – even of this English branch of it – from relapse and degeneration.'[9] In claiming national usefulness for science, scientists attempted to counterbalance the limitations placed on scientific work by a particularistic political movement.

Finally, the unresponsiveness of the political system to the self-perceived needs of scientists during the 1870s undermined their faith in that system. The reports of the Devonshire Commission closed the era of voluntarism and individualism in public science by declaring that henceforth only the resources of the nation-state would be sufficient to support modern science. The reports also asserted that adequate financing of science was a national duty.[10] The refusal of both Conservative and Liberal governments to carry out the recommendation of the Devonshire Commission for a ministry of science and a science advisory council stood as a reminder to the scientific community that it had failed to secure government endowment of research or to participate successfully in government decisions, while the antivivisectionist statute and its administration demonstrated the political success of those who would confine scientific inquiry. Moreover, as early as the first Gladstone ministry, following the dispute

9　E. Ray Lankester, *The advancement of science: occasional essays and addresses* (London: Macmillan, 1890), p. 50. See also Richard D. French, *Antivivisection and medical science in Victorian society* (Princeton: Princeton University Press, 1975).
10　In its eighth report (1875) the Devonshire Commission argued, 'But whatever may be the disposition of individuals to conduct researches at their own cost, the Advancement of Modern Science requires Investigations and Observations extending over areas so large and periods so long that the means and lives of nations are alone commensurate with them.' The same report asserted that government was 'bound to assume that large portion of the National Duty which individuals do not attempt to perform, or cannot satisfactorily accomplish'. *Eighth report of the Royal Commission on scientific instruction and the advancement of science* (1875), Cd 1298, p. 24.

over the management of Kew Gardens between Joseph Dalton Hooker and Acton Smee Ayrton, First Commissioner of Public Works, many scientists had begun to distrust politicians and civil servants. John Tyndall as scientific adviser to Trinity House and the Board of Trade had come to grief over the question of the illumination of lighthouses. Testimony before the Devonshire Commission even by sympathetic political figures revealed the difficulties that men of science could expect to encounter when trying to influence public policy.[11] Clearly the attitude of the politicians and of the political classes could no longer be ignored by the scientific community.

III THE ATTACK ON PARTY AND DEMOCRATIC POLITICS

In the late 1870s various scientific writers began to question the competence and good intentions of political leaders, who they thought paid little note to the national duty of fostering science, and to criticize the adequacy of the political system that permitted such deplorable inaction. These initial criticisms echoed attacks on the liberal state voiced during the Crimean War, but more important they foreshadowed a much more vehement future condemnation. Scientists soon argued that the contemporary British political structure failed to address genuine, self-evident national problems because it lacked scientific procedures itself. They contended that science and scientists in their role as citizens possessed special civic or political worth and the capacity to exercise a highly salutary influence over the political system. In turn, they pictured science itself as not only the victim of pluralistic, partisan, democratic politics, but also as the potential instrument for salvaging the beleaguered national interest from the dangers posed by partisan politics. Scientists came to define good government, sound politics, and true patriotism as efficient administration based on the principles of science and carried out by persons with scientific education.

One of the earliest examples of this polemical tactic of the public scientists appeared during January 1880 in an article in *Nature* most probably written by the editor, Norman Lockyer. The essay criticized

[11] Roy M. MacLeod, 'The Ayrton incident: a commentary on the relations of science and government in England, 1870–1873', in Arnold Thackray and Everett Mendelsohn, eds., *Science and values: patterns of tradition and change* (New York: Humanities Press, 1974), pp. 45–80; Roy M. MacLeod, 'Science and government in Victorian England: lighthouse illumination and the Board of Trade, 1866–1886', *Isis*, 60 (1969), 4–38; *Royal Commission on scientific instruction and the advancement of science, Minutes of evidence*, (1874), Cd 958, pp. 338–54.

the absence of the scientific spirit in British political campaigns. If science or the scientific attitude were to infuse the political process, Gladstone and Disraeli would honestly outline all sides of controversial questions, draw reasoned conclusions, and then offer solutions. The writer advised public men who wished to learn 'the science of statesmanship' and who intended 'to guide their conduct by its principles' to abandon public agitation and 'to take to calm but rigid scientific research in their own department'. Once such scientific statesmanship rather than 'mere party prejudice' became 'the guiding principle in the conduct of public affairs, this nation would be more fitted than ever to survive and play the leading part in the affairs of the world'. Advancement of scientific education in the schools and universities would best ensure the future attainment of scientific statesmanship. In October of the same year, at the opening of Mason College in Birmingham, Huxley sounded a similar theme though in less strident language. Noting how broad the British electorate had become, he contended that to avoid despotism and to attain 'self-restraining freedom' citizens would gradually be required 'to bring themselves to deal with political as they now deal with scientific questions; to be as ashamed of undue haste and partisan prejudice in the one case as in the other'.[12] For Huxley social and political issues had to be addressed by those who grasped their underlying principles. Both he and the writer for *Nature* were redefining politics so that it would be understood no longer as a contest for power and policy but as a mode of administration for which scientists or the scientifically educated were particularly suited.

Similar criticism of partisan politics was not uncommon within the general British intellectual community at this time. During the 1860s many young men in the universities and the learned professions had supported political liberalism and the extension of the franchise in the expectation that a reformed political system would permit them to play a large role in public life. By the 1880s those expectations had largely failed to be realized.[13] The scientists, with

---

[12] *Nature*, 21 (1880), 296; T. H. Huxley, *Science and culture and other essays* (New York: D. Appleton and Co., 1882), p. 29.

[13] John Roach, 'Liberalism and the Victorian intelligentsia', *Cambridge Historical Journal*, 12 (1957), 58–81; Christopher Harvie, *The lights of liberalism: university liberals and the challenge of democracy* (London: Allen Lane, 1976); Christopher Kent, *Brains and numbers: elitism, Comtism, and democracy in mid-Victorian England* (Toronto: University of Toronto Press, 1978). See also E. J. Hobsbawm, *Labouring men: studies in the history of labour* (London: Weidenfeld and Nicolson, 1971), pp. 250–71, for a discussion of the Fabians that relates them to a similar intellectual pattern.

their drive for public support and recognition stymied by the mid-1870s, were part of this larger picture. Like other intellectuals they began to attack the political system itself. Eventually they questioned the principle of democracy, which in their view inhibited the application of trained intelligence to public affairs and blocked the advance of intelligent persons.

Public scientists voiced these sentiments for over a quarter century. In 1885 Lyon Playfair, who for years had criticized the absence of adequate numbers of medical men in the administrative apparatus of the health and sanitary laws, told the British Association that the government was not responding to the 'duty of statecraft' that required the promotion of science. The same year *Nature* editorialized against the 'endless party squabbles' that prevented undertaking the 'useful national work' of an education programme nurturing science. In 1894 the young H.G. Wells warned the readers of *Nature* that the scientific community must recognize that henceforth it depended on a democratic political system for its support. Two years later *Nature* again criticized 'the political system which does not consider it necessary that the educational and scientific welfare of the country should be the business of those who are able to appreciate the work done, to see the necessity of reforms, and to know the direction in which developments should take place'. All of these complaints were voiced well before the trauma of the Boer War raised the issue of national efficiency. After the war the criticisms of the scientists over the unresponsiveness of the political structures became even more strident. In 1901 Ray Lankester told the scientific community that it was 'useless to address the democracy'. In 1909 the zoologist Adam Sedgwick explained to the students of the Imperial College, London, that democratic governments could not be expected to support research because that policy brought them 'no popularity and no votes'.[14]

IV SCIENCE AND CITIZENSHIP

While some scientists criticized or despaired of partisan politics, others argued that the scientific frame of mind could exercise salutary

---

[14] *British Association report* (1885), p. 5; *Nature*, 31 (1885), 549; 50 (1894), 300; 54 (1896), 386; 63 (1901) Suppl., p. iii; 77 (1909), 154. See also the addresses of Henry E. Roscoe, J. B. Sanderson, Douglas Galton, William Turner, and William Ramsay, *British Association report* (1887), p. 28; (1893), pp. 3–4; (1895), p. 35; (1900), p. 5, (1911), pp. 5, 22.

influence over the political scene and save democracy from certain of its pitfalls. In 1892 Karl Pearson, who had long been interested in political and social questions, claimed in the first edition of *The Grammar of Science* that 'the scientific habit of mind' was nothing less than 'an essential for good citizenship'. Citizens trained in scientific theory would be 'less likely to be led by mere appeal to the passions or by blind emotional excitement to sanction acts which in the end may lead to social disaster'. More important, Pearson suggested, the application of scientific method to public questions could contribute to the same kind of 'practical unanimity of judgement' that resulted from the scientific investigation of physical nature. Pearson also portrayed scientific education of citizens as a strong engine that might overcome the individual selfish interests of the voters. Science, with its procedures for classifying facts and then making judgements from them – 'judgements independent of the idiosyncrasies of the individual mind' – could aid citizens in working their way through the political morass of conflicting particular interests toward a consideration of the general social good.[15] Pearson, ignoring the past thirty years of heated debate over the issue of evolution, promoted an ideal of scientific procedure that when transferred to politics required the subordination of the individual to some concept of the general interest, one that would in all likelihood be determined by an administrative bureaucracy staffed from the professional classes.

Other public scientists, less philosophical than Pearson, argued that science could inculcate in the citizenry social and moral habits that would benefit the nation politically and militarily. In 1898 Henry Armstrong, Professor of Chemistry at the City and Guilds Institute, suggested that the experience of learning some laboratory science might develop the habit of weighing and measuring judgements, giving attention to detail, pursuing logical thought, and achieving reasoned personal decisions. In other words, training in science would foster the habits of respectable self-restraint among those citizens, largely from the lower classes, assumed to lack those qualities. In the wake of the Boer War both Armstrong and John Perry, who taught electrical engineering at the Royal College of Science in London, specifically linked the virtues of scientific education to the values that Baden-Powell had championed in his

[15] Karl Pearson, *The grammar of science* (London: J. M. Dent, 1951: 1st publ. 1892), pp. 12, 13, 22, 11.

military manual *Aids to Scouting* (1899). In 1901 Armstrong declared, 'It is clear that to win our battles in the future preparations must be made in the school workshops rather than in the playing-fields. In fact, scientific method *must* be introduced into schools in order that some preparation may be given for successful scouting in the world'.[16] Scientific education would nurture the capacity for national preparedness and efficiency that party politicians who merely curried the favour of the voters must necessarily neglect. The scientific writers were promising that training in even elementary science, by increasing the sense of discipline among the lower social orders, would contribute to the kind of social control that the late Victorian and Edwardian middle classes thought necessary.

Some public scientists went beyond arguing that scientific education and thought would improve political and civic behaviour. Those who supported the eugenics movement promised that the proper application of scientific knowledge could quite literally produce a population with a larger proportion of efficient, productive citizens and a smaller proportion of civically less desirable citizens. Edwardian public science and the eugenics movement were not synonymous. The latter was narrower in its scope but wider in its social base than public science. Many scientists who were outspoken in their demands for state aid to scientific research or in their calls for national efficiency did not support eugenics or openly criticized it. Nonetheless the eugenics movement did represent one important factor in the larger picture of public science.

Eugenics was the single theoretical development actively exploited by turn-of-the-century public science.[17] This situation contrasted sharply with the mid-Victorian championship of atomism, conservation of energy, and evolution. The contrast is of no small

[16] Henry E. Armstrong, *The teaching of scientific method and other papers on education*, 2nd edn (London: Macmillan, 1910), pp. 257, 14; John Perry, *England's neglect of science* (London: T. Fisher Unwin, 1900), p. 8; Armstrong, *The teaching of scientific method*, p. 15.
[17] G. R. Searle, *Eugenics and politics in Britain, 1900–1914* (Leyden: Noordhoff International, 1976); Donald MacKenzie, 'Eugenics in Britain', *Social studies of science*, 6 (1976), 499–532; Donald MacKenzie, 'Karl Pearson and the professional middle class', *Annals of science*, 36 (1979), 125–144; Donald MacKenzie, *Statistics in Britain 1865–1930: the social construction of scientific knowledge* (Edinburgh: Edinburgh University Press, 1981); *Nature*, 63 (1901), Suppl. pp. iii-vi. See also Brian Wynne, 'Physics and psychics: science, symbolic action, and social control in late Victorian England', in Barry Barnes and Stephen Shapin, eds., *Natural order: historical studies of scientific culture* (Beverly Hills, Calif.: Sage Publications, 1979), pp. 167–90. Wynne sees a conservative political bias in Cambridge physics near the turn of the century. Although there may have been conservative implications in such theory, the concepts of physics played little or no role in the broad discussion of public science at the time.

significance. The major voices of late nineteenth-century public science tended to be chemists, physicists, and engineers. Unlike earlier public scientists they confronted, not intellectual obscurantism or religious superstition, but rather public and political indifference to their claims of technical expertise. Eugenics fit into this larger pattern because of its claim to be a mode of scientific knowledge and social engineering that would provide direct civic benefits to the nation-state. Donald MacKenzie has persuasively argued that the eugenics movement should be regarded as an attempt to provide 'a legitimation of the social position of the professional middle class, and an argument for its enhancement'.[18] In that regard the eugenicists, who included social workers, lawyers, physicians, and statisticians, as well as scientists, were asserting for the broad professional middle class the same kind of claim to social utility and the rewards thereof that public scientists had been setting forth since the 1880s. Indeed some scientific advocates of eugenics had been attracted to those theories as much for their political and social implications as for their scientific adequacy.

In the hands of its chief scientific adherents, including Francis Galton and Karl Pearson, eugenics became the civic science par excellence. As Galton explained in 1904, 'The aim of Eugenics is ... to cause the useful classes in the community to contribute *more* than their proportion to the next generation.' The beneficial result would be an improvement in the tone of political life and an expanded national ability 'to fulfil our vast imperial opportunities'. Four years later Galton even more explicitly delineated the civic character of eugenics. He predicted that the work of local eugenics societies would include tabulation of information on the qualities of individuals and families in particular regions of the country. The people whose various personal qualities had been so tabulated would then be evaluated according to their 'civic worthiness', by which Galton meant 'the value to the State, of a person, as it would probably be assessed by experts, or say, by such of his fellow-workers as have earned the respect of the community in the midst of which they live'. Galton felt that such public opinion could be moulded 'to arouse in citizens a just pride in their own civic worthiness' and that in such a manner the present generation would become more willing to make the personal sacrifices required to fulfil 'the more virile desire of

[18] MacKenzie, 'Eugenics in Britain', p. 501.

promoting the natural gifts and the national efficiency of future generations'.[19] Rather than ascertaining the place of humankind in nature – the great question of mid-Victorian public science – the eugenicists sought to determine the proper place of human beings in society and to foster a society in which scientists and other members of the professional middle class would receive due respect and exercise proper influence.

The eugenicists were not alone in asserting that scientists might upgrade the quality of society and politics. Without necessarily adhering to a eugenicist position, other public scientists contended that men of science were themselves particularly good citizens who, by virtue of their being scientists, carried into national life habits, skills, and moral qualities especially useful to the nation and particularly admired by the society at large. In 1899 Michael Foster, the Cambridge physiologist and later Member of Parliament, associated the qualities of truthfulness, alertness of mind, and 'the courage of steadfast endurance' with the scientist. Foster claimed that although scientists were 'no stronger, no better than other men, they possess a strength which . . . is not their own but is that of the science whose servants they are'. He felt their constant contact and relationship with the truthfulness and rigour of nature meant that scientists must also particularly cultivate those worthy qualities in themselves. In 1908 Dr Henry Bovey, Rector of the recently chartered Imperial College of Science and Technology, praised the scientific profession in similar terms, giving a decidedly civic twist to his remarks:

The constant effort to eliminate error tends toward the development of truth and accuracy. The cultivation of the will in overcoming obstacles should produce the sturdier manly virtues; the patient waiting on nature's working encourages the gaining of a wise self-restraint, which we may hope to see employed in the directing of life; and the emphasis laid on the pursuit of truth for its own sake should help to overcome the spirit of commercialism . . . which is an ever present danger of the application of science to life.

By providing such training, Bovey contended, the Imperial College produced 'at once good scientific men and good citzens' who would serve the nation by putting 'the true service of man above their

[19] Francis Galton, 'Eugenics: its definition, scope and aims', *Sociological Papers*, 1 (1904), 47; *Nature*, 78 (1908), 646, 647.

personal success' and who would also search for truth, follow the laws of economy, and avoid waste.[20]

The moral and civic qualities that Foster and Bovey associated with the scientist and portrayed as being nurtured through scientific training were the same qualities that public scientists had for many years accused non-scientifically educated politicians of lacking or even spurning in pursuit of particularistic partisan goals. From the 1880s onward public scientists had criticized the ignorance of politicians and civil servants on scientific matters and had suggested that such lack of knowledge made them unfit to address great national issues. Huxley certainly in part intended his foray of 1885 and 1886 against Gladstone over the Bible simply to discredit the Liberal minister on the grounds of his sheer ignorance. Lyon Playfair frequently attacked the literary spirit that informed the minds and education of men in political life. In 1900 John Perry, one of the most outspoken critics of England's neglect of science, quite correctly observed that 'almost all the most important, the most brilliant, the most expensively educated people in England' remained uninformed about both the principles and methods of science. He further argued that 'this ignorance of our great men tends to create ignorance in our future leaders; is hurtful to the strength of the nation now, and retards our development in all ways'. In 1902 Henry Armstrong, writing in the conservative *National Review*, claimed that politicians educated strictly in literary studies prevented the introduction of more science into the educational system. The next year *Nature* bemoaned the neglect of sufficient science in the new entrance requirements for Woolwich and Sandhurst.[21]

To emphasize the danger posed to the nation by this lack of scientific knowledge on the part of the governing elite, public scientists stressed the necessity of scientific solutions for political and social problems. In 1914 at its last prewar meeting the British Association heard William Bateson, who though not a member of the Eugenics Society was still an advocate of the application of the principles of heredity to social issues, declare: 'At every turn the

[20] *British Association report* (1899), pp. 16–17; *Nature*, 78 (1908), 616. See also Armstrong, *The teaching of scientific method*, p. x.

[21] Leonard Huxley, *The life and letters of Thomas Henry Huxley* (New York: D. Appleton and Co., 1900), II, 124, 130, 450; Lyon Playfair, *Subjects of social welfare* (London: Cassell, 1889), p. 37; *Nature*, 62 (1900), 221; Henry Armstrong, 'The need of general culture at Oxford and Cambridge', *National Review*, 40 (1902–3), 57–71 (see also E. Ray Lankester's address, *British Association report* (1906), pp. 38–9); *Nature*, 69 (1903–4), 85–6, 321–3.

student of political science is confronted with problems that demand biological knowledge for their solution.'[22] At the same meeting Armstrong thoroughly discounted the likelihood of politicians or civil servants voluntarily seeking such knowledge or consulting those who possessed it when he observed,

Our Admiralty, and to a far less extent our War Office, have called science into their service, but our public departments generally will have none of it. Even the elements of an understanding of the methods of science are not thought to be essential to the education of a Civil Servant; such knowledge is not required even in the highest branches of the Indian Service – no politician is for one moment supposed to need it; we are governed almost entirely by the literary spirit.[23]

Writers in the columns of *Nature* and other major scientific and non-scientific public journals repeated this argument throughout the opening decade of the century. The attacks on the political system and the civil service were not a matter of tilting at polemical windmills. As MacLeod's important essay on science and the Treasury demonstrated, these complaints grew out of the actual experience of scientists dealing with political figures or bureaucrats who had been trained in the classics and who, even if sympathetic to science, understood too little about scientific research to deal systematically or consistently with the subject.[24]

The concern for the scientific education of the political and administrative elite was directly related to the contemporary attack on compulsory Greek at Oxford and Cambridge. Many, though not all, public scientists deplored the requirements of Greek for matriculation at the ancient universities.[25] As will be seen in the last essay in

[22] *British Association report* (1914), p. 38. Bateson though quite sympathetic with the eugenics movement did not join the Eugenics Society. See Beatrice Bateson, ed., *William Bateson, F.R.S., naturalist: his essays and addresses* (Cambridge: Cambridge University Press, 1928), pp. 334–55, 371–2, 456; and William Coleman, 'Bateson and chromosomes: conservative thought in science', *Centaurus*, 15 (1970), 292–305.

[23] *Nature*, 94 (1914), 215. Such remarks revived one of the major themes of the Devonshire Commission, which in its sixth report had stated, '[C]onsidering the increasing importance of science to the Material Interests of the Country, we cannot but regard its almost total exclusion from the training of the upper and middle classes as little less than a national misfortune.' *Sixth report of the Royal Commission on scientific instruction and the advancement of science* (1875), Cd 1279, p. 10.

[24] Roy M. MacLeod, 'Science and the Treasury: principles, personalities, and policies, 1870–1885', in G. L'E. Turner, ed., *The patronage of science in the nineteenth century* (Leyden: Noordhoff International, 1976), pp. 115–72.

[25] *Nature*, 60 (1900), 221–6; Armstrong, 'The need of general culture at Oxford and Cambridge'; E. Ray Lankester, 'Compulsory science versus compulsory Greek', *Nineteenth Century*, 69 (1911), 499–514.

this volume, the idealist character of late Victorian and Edwardian classical education was particularly unfriendly to rationalism and scientific outlooks. Furthermore, classical education retained far more prestige than did scientific. Viewed in the larger context of turn-of-the-century public science, the criticism of Greek and of literary education did not originate simply from a general desire to expand scientific education or to maintain adequate scientific research. Science was being taught at the civic universities, and brilliant research was being carried out at Oxford and Cambridge. Rather scientific critics intended their demands for revision of the university curriculum to redirect the education of the future national political elite as much as to enlarge the numbers of research scientists and science teachers. Having generally despaired of receiving sufficient support from the processes of democratic politics, the public scientists sought to nurture a new awareness of science and its worth among future political leaders and state administrators. A political elite educated in science might be expected to draw scientists into positions of influence through appointments and advisory roles in the bureaucracy. Once the universities and the military academies, where more scientific education was also being demanded, placed as much emphasis on science as on classical studies, the secondary feeder schools would likewise change their programmes and employ more persons educated in science as teachers.

V THE BRITISH SCIENCE GUILD

Certain political and military spokesmen shared the critical view of partisan politics and the desire for efficient government voiced by the public scientists. Most prominent among them were Arthur Balfour, Lord Rosebery, R. B. Haldane, and Alfred Milner.[26] They and other social imperialists received favourable press in *Nature*, where their speeches were frequently reported and their books reviewed. Balfour, like the Conservative Prime Minister Lord Salisbury, served as president of the British Association. Salisbury had

---

[26] Bernard Semmel, *Imperialism and social reform: English social-imperial thought, 1895–1914* (London: George Allen and Unwin, 1960); G. R. Searle, *The quest for national efficiency: a study in British politics and political thought, 1899–1914* (Oxford: Basil Blackwell, 1971); Robert J. Scally, *The origins of the Lloyd George coalition: the politics of social imperialism, 1900–1918* (Princeton: Princeton University Press, 1975); L. S. Jacyna, 'Science and social order in the thought of A. J. Balfour', *Isis*, 71 (1980), 11–34. It should, of course, be noted that none of these political figures was himself above the sharpest partisan activities.

aided in the founding of the National Physical Laboratory in 1899, and Haldane was instrumental in the reorganization of London science that resulted in the Imperial College of Science and Industry. These politicians regarded the issues of a strong defence and industrial efficiency as questions of the national interest and a means of winning elections. The scientists also understood the matters to be of national concern, but they realized that the more fully the political and military leadership stressed those issues the more likely it would be that benefits of government support and patronage would flow to the scientific community. Indeed one of the important unexplored problems in this era is the relationship of scientists to the military and to political figures who were sympathetic to the military. As W. H. Brock has shown, the army and navy had throughout the nineteenth century been the major channels of state funding to scientists.[27] Norman Lockyer had early in his career served as a clerk in the War Office. Military officers were themselves familiar with and generally supportive of science. Furthermore, the military represented one mode of technical expertise recognized and admired by the society and incorporated within the system of government.

In 1905 public scientists and sympathetic politicians joined forces at the first meeting of the British Science Guild, founded the previous year. The leading political figure was R. B. Haldane, who served as president until 1913. The most active scientist was Lockyer, the editor of *Nature*, who had in 1903 lectured the British Association on 'The influence of brain power in history'.[28] The announcement in *Nature* of the formation of the Guild specifically contrasted its purpose with that of the other existing scientific societies and in so doing demonstrated the difference between this era of public science and the one that had preceded:

The Science Guild . . . is not identical in aim with any existing society. *The promotion of natural knowledge is outside its sphere.* Its purpose is to stimulate, not so much the acquisition of scientific knowledge, as the appreciation of its value, and the advantage of employing the methods of scientific inquiry,

[27] W. H. Brock, 'The spectrum of scientific patronage', in Turner, ed., *Patronage of science*, pp. 173–206. See also Frederick Augustus Abel's address, *British Association report* (1890), pp. 25–37.

[28] For a reprint of that address as well as other important essays by Lockyer, consult Norman Lockyer, *Education and national progress: essays and addresses, 1870–1905* (London: Macmillan, 1906). See also Arthur Jack Meadows, *Science and controversy: a biography of Sir Norman Lockyer* (Cambridge, Mass.: MIT Press, 1972), pp. 258–79.

the study of cause and effect, in affairs of every kind. Such methods are not less applicable to the problems which confront the statesman, the official, the merchant, the manufacturer, the soldier, and the schoolmaster, than to those of the chemist or the biologist; and the value of a scientific education lies in the cultivation which it gives of the power to grasp and apply the principles of investigation employed in the laboratory to the problems which modern life presents in peace or war.

The Guild saw its purpose as employing science 'to further the progress and increase the welfare of the Empire', to lobby the government on scientific questions, to promote the use of science in manufacturing, and to further scientific education. The imperial connection was quite prominent. For example, in 1907 the Guild joined with the British Empire League to host a dinner for the visiting colonial Prime Ministers, and its officers also sought to establish colonial branches.[29]

In the Romanes Lecture of 1905 Ray Lankester called for 'the formation of a political union which would make due respect to efficiency, that is to say, to a knowledge of Nature, a test question in all political contests'. He urged that only politicians educated in science or pledged to consult scientific advisers should receive the support of the proposed union. The domestic political policy of the British Science Guild did not go quite that far, but it did certainly display hostility toward contemporary liberal democratic politics. In 1910, with the questions of the Lloyd George Budget, the House of Lords, and new battleships on the public mind, the Guild set as its prize essay topic: 'The best way of carrying on the struggle for existence and securing the survival of the fittest in national affairs'. Among questions suggested as pertinent to the paper was 'whether a system of party government is sufficient to secure all the best interests of the State in those directions in which brain power and a special knowledge are needed, or whether a body free from the influence of party politics and on which the most important national activities are represented by the most distinguished persons is desirable'.[30] The Devonshire Commission had suggested a council on science as wise public policy; the British Science Guild sought to make government by distinguished experts a matter of patriotism. By 1912 the Guild had a membership of 900 and was clearly a conservative,

---

[29] *Nature*, 72 (1904), 586 (italics added), 585; 76 (1907), 37, 79; 79 (1909), 379–82.
[30] E. Ray Lankester, *Nature and man* (Oxford: Clarendon Press, 1905), p. 61; *Nature*, 83 (1910), 100.

social imperialist pressure group seeking to combine the intellectual prestige of science with the political attraction of efficiency and empire.

The British Science Guild promoted the same values of efficiency, eugenic social reconstruction, and collectivist intervention that various professional middle-class groups, including civil servants, were urging upon the nation in place of the Gladstonean liberal inheritance. The public scientists, the eugenicists, and the Fabians all fit this broader pattern. Their social and political asset was their brain power or technical expertise, which Lockyer had praised in 1903. They lacked sufficient financial capital to make significant impact on the economy and had too small a political constituency to affect the political scene. Consequently they found both the political and economic systems slow to recognize or reward them for the contribution they hoped to make and from which they expected to profit. Their plight was well described in 1902 by H. G. Wells. In *Anticipations of the reaction of mechanical and scientific progress upon human life and thought* Wells portrayed the frustration experienced by 'the emergent class of capable men' who found themselves unable to make meaningful contributions to contemporary public life. They were educated useful persons who possessed little inclination and possibly few of the talents required to work their way up through the political party structures. Furthermore, the normal workaday politician responding to the pressure of his constituency and party was unlikely to perceive the talents of such capable people or to draw them into civic life. Wells predicted that ultimately this new class would make its impact on contemporary public affairs only 'through the concussions of war'. Lockyer's address the next year on brain power represented a restatement of the same theme. Other scientific writers joined the chorus of praise for the value of science and technical expertise in modern warfare. A writer in *Nature* declared in 1907, 'The future struggles for supremacy among nations of the world will be contests between minds, and muscles will be at a discount.'[31] In no small degree the wish was father to the thought. The scientists were attempting to define the character of modern warfare and the manner of its preparation so as to enhance their own possible contribution to it and subsequent recognition through it.

[31] H. G. Wells, *Anticipations of the reaction of mechanical and scientific progress upon human life and thought* (New York and London: Harper, 1902), pp. 179, 189; *Nature*, 76 (1907), 37.

VI PUBLIC SCIENCE IN WORLD WAR I

Early in the summer of 1914, despite their talk about science and modern warfare, the public scientists had little reason to expect the situation of their profession in the near future to differ substantially from that of the past three decades. The war both changed the frame of political reference and permitted the scientists to bring their case to the fore in a new manner. Their tactics were largely opportunistic but essentially continued a political strategy well established prior to the conflict. In its first wartime editorial *Nature* moved rapidly to urge circumvention of the political system and full utilization of scientists in the war effort. In early September 1914 the editorial column declared,

The terrible war which is now raging, not only near our shores, but also much further afield, is teaching us many lessons, among them that the things which make most for a nation's life are apt not to be considered by the partisans of party politics. But it also shows that the British nation is sound enough at heart to throw off the trammels of party politics when a supreme moment arrives.

The editorial, which also commended the work of the British Science Guild, was not voicing early wartime patriotic exuberance but rather was repeating the political rhetoric that had characterized British public science for no less than forty years. In late October 1914 *Nature* again reminded readers, 'This war, in contradistinction to all previous wars, is a war in which pure and applied science plays a conspicuous part'. Later wartime editorials and articles by scientists such as William Ramsay and R. A. Gregory continued the same line of argument and frequently pointed out how much more scientists contributed to the national defence than did politicians.[32] Just as in peacetime the public scientists had scorned democracy, in wartime they suggested that victory lay neither with the vast democratic army in the trenches nor with partisan politicians, but rather with a small number of scientific experts exercising their brain power.

Not confined to *Nature* alone, these attitudes also appeared in other scientific journals. In its own first wartime editorial *Chemical*

---

[32] *Nature*, 94 (1914–15), 29, 221, 276, 512; 95 (1915), 309–11, 509–10, 562–4; 96 (1915–16), 195–7, 335–6, 643–4, 671–3. See also the wartime volumes of the *Journal of the British Science Guild* the first of which appeared in September 1915.

News pointed out the role of chemists in the war effort and in the future postwar commercial competition with Germany. In *Science Progress* Ronald Ross, formerly of the Indian Medical Service and at the outbreak of the war deeply involved in questions of public health, stressed the danger to the national interest posed by partisan politics. His terms were perhaps the most bitter and exaggerated of any contemporary scientific writer:

Aggressive militarism is a disease of aristocratic government and party-politics is a disease of democracy. Neither is essential to the form of government concerned. Democracy is government by free discussion but free discussion does not necessarily imply party discussion – on the contrary it excludes it. As every man of science knows, in order to reach the truth free discussion must first consider all the related facts and then form an unbiased judgement. But the very nature of party-politics is that the final judgement should be tramelled by the exigencies of the party. Thus party-politicians seldom judge honestly and therefore seldom reach the truth ... and the utterance of a party-politician is utterly worthless on any question which is touched by his politics.

Ross's article came in the wake of a public campaign led by *Science Progress* during the early months of 1914 to raise salaries and the general public appreciation of scientists.[33] Ross and others not only wanted science to play a part in the war but also clearly intended that participation to lead to new political influence for scientists in the period of peace that would follow the conflict.

The accusation by scientists of incompetence and lack of scientific procedures in government became even more vitriolic and opportunistic as the errors and failures of the first months of the war came to light. For example, on 7 December 1915 E. B. Poulton delivered the Romanes Lecture for that year, entitled *Science and the great war*. The Oxford biologist, who was sympathetic to eugenics, explicitly set out 'to show that the failures which have occurred are nearly all due to the national neglect of science and the excessive predominance in Parliament, and especially in the Government, of the spirit that is most antagonistic to science – the spirit of the advocate'. The overrepresentation of lawyers and the rare membership of scientists in Parliament meant that the institution could not consider vital national questions in a truly deliberative manner. The lawyer or advocate attempted to make a good case and to present the appearance of truth, whereas 'the scientific man labours to strip off appearance and discover whether the true or the false is hidden beneath'. For Poulton 'the great danger of the lawyer-politician was the tendency to compromise'. That political habit was out of place during wartime when genuine knowledge had to be attained. The munitions problem demonstrated that those directing the war effort had not sought such knowledge. The British Science Guild, which began publishing a journal in 1915, sponsored the reprinting of Poulton's lecture. The general tenor of his remarks reflected the eugenicist position that a larger proportion of competent people was required in the general population and government. Poulton's attack on lawyers also manifests the tension between an established and an emerging professional group that MacKenzie and Norton have associated with the eugenics movement.[34]

Throughout the war public scientists also continued to reassert the long standing charge that politicians were ignorant of scientific matters. In early January 1916 Oliver Lodge addressed the Educational Association and deplored 'the widespread ignorance of natural facts even among our leaders, and consequent contempt for investigation and expert knowledge'. Shortly thereafter the aged Ray Lankester wrote to the *Times* in support of Lodge and criticized the absence of significant science requirements for the civil service exams. On 2 February 1916 the *Times* published a memorandum of the newly formed Committee on the Neglect of Science signed by over thirty prominent scientists, many of whom belonged to the British Science Guild or had long been critical of the liberal state and partisan politics. The memorandum asserted,

It is admitted on all sides that we have suffered checks since the war began, due directly as well as indirectly to a lack of knowledge on the part of our legislators and administrative officials of what is called 'science', or 'physical science'... Not only are our highest Ministers of State ignorant of science, but the same defect runs throughout almost all the public departments of the Civil Service. It is nearly universal in the House of Commons.

The group specifically pointed to the initial failure to embargo lard headed for Germany although the product might be used in the manufacture of munitions. The committee urged reform in the

---

34 E. B. Poulton, *Science and the great war* (Oxford: Clarendon Press, 1915), pp. 4, 10, 13; MacKenzie, 'Karl Pearson and the professional middle class', pp. 125–44; Bernard Norton, 'Karl Pearson and statistics: the social origins of scientific innovation', *Social Studies of Science*, 8 (1978), 3–34.

educational system and in the requirements for the civil service. Their memorandum concluded, 'Our success now, and in the difficult time of reorganization after the war, depends largely on the possession by our leaders and administrators of scientific method and the scientific habit of mind.'[35] This sentiment constituted an article of public faith within the scientific community, but its adherents rarely demonstrated why or how it must be true.

Two very important government committees formed during the war duplicated in their reports the attitudes of the private Committee on the Neglect of Science. In 1916 the Committee of the Privy Council for Scientific and Industrial Research issued a report that urged the harnessing of the brain power of the nation for the future peace and for vast new cooperation in research. In 1918 the Prime Minister's Committee to Inquire into the Position of Physical Science in National Education, chaired by J. J. Thompson, pressed for more science and less emphasis on the classics in the universities and for science requirements in the civil service and Indian service. Both reports represented the enunciation of the long standing goals of British public science rather than a recognition of significant lessons learned from the war experience.[36]

Public scientists had for a generation urged the use of experts in government and abandonment of partisanship. The establishment of the Lloyd George coalition in late 1916 seemed to open the way for such government in the national interest. *Nature* immediately welcomed the new opportunity announcing that

the Government formed by Mr. Lloyd George consists mostly of men who know instead of men who have been given appointments because of their political claims. The whole nation welcomes this first endeavour to reconstruct on a scientific basis its politics, its statesmanship, its commerce, its education, and its civil and industrial administration. It has been

[35] *Times*, 4 Jan. 1916, p. 4; 14 Jan. 1916, p. 9; 26 Jan. 1916, p. 9; 2 Feb. 1916, p. 10. The following scientists attached their names to the Neglect of Science Memorandum: Sir T. Clifford Allbutt, Dr Henry E. Armstrong, Lord Berkeley, Prof. Rowland Biffen, Prof. Gilbert C. Bourne, Louis Brennan, Dr J. D. Ewart, Prof. J. S. Fleming, Prof. A. G. Green, Prof. J. W. Gregory, Prof. E. H. Griffiths, Prof. S. J. Hickson, Prof. L. E. Hill, Prof. J. P. Hill, Sir E. Ray Lankester, Dr P. Chalmers Mitchell, Sir Henry Morris, Sir William Osier, Hon. Sir Charles A. Parsons, Prof. Karl Pearson, Prof. W. H. Perkin, Dr John Perry, Dr J. C. Phillip, Prof. E. B. Poulton, Sir William Ramsay, Lord Rayleigh, Major Sir Ronald Ross, Dr A. E. Shipley, Prof. E. H. Starling, Prof. J. Arthur Thomson, Sir Edward Thorpe, Sir William Augustus Tilden, Prof. H. H. Turner, Sir John Williams, Prof. T. B. Wood.
[36] *Report of the committee of the Privy Council for scientific and industrial research for the year 1915–16* (1916), Cd 8336, p. 9; *Report of the Prime Minister's committee to inquire into the position of physical science in national education* (1918), Cd 9011.

fashionable in political circles to distrust the man who has made it his business to know, and to assume that he must be kept under control by official administrators; but we hope the appointments to offices in the new government signify that this view has now gone for ever, and has been superseded by the one in which national use is made of the most capable men.[37]

The language echoes that of Wells's *Anticipations*. The concussions of war had opened the path to political influence and counsel for the capable men of science who stood ready both to assist the nation and to advance their own prestige and standing.

Yet the war only temporarily modified the position of science. The conflict had not changed the political system. It had, if anything, rendered politics more responsive to democratic pressures. Labour rather than the scientific community won the political victory of the war experience. By the close of the hostilities spokesmen for science quickly perceived their predicament. The issue was how to secure a place for science and scientists in the effort toward postwar reconstruction. At the time of the armistice *Nature* clearly seemed more overwhelmed by the dangers of peace than it had been four years earlier by the prospect of war. Calling for the continued employment of scientists in high places, it asserted,

Democracy has hitherto permitted itself to be swayed by eloquence, and has elected to be governed by men of words rather than by men of knowledge and action. The consequence is that men are entrusted with power, not because of any fitness they have shown for the offices they occupy, but because of their political influence or friendships. Scientific and technical experts have been used, but only as hewers of wood and drawers of water, while the administrative control has usually been in the hands of officials with no special qualifications for their directors.

The Coupon Election of 1918 maintained the wartime coalition of Lloyd George, but the election did not aid the cause of science in the House of Commons. The *Times* criticized the absence of men of science in the new Parliament. Shortly thereafter, on 30 January 1919, *Nature* called for the raising of a political fund and the formation of a 'group of prospective scientific candidates got together under a leader of enthusiasm familiar with the inner labyrinth of the political world'.[38] The scientific community still found itself crying for entry to the political arena.

37 *Nature*, 98 (1916), 285.
38 *Nature*, 102 (1918), 202; *Times*, 21 Jan. 1919, p. 6; *Nature*, 102 (1919), 422.

VII CONCLUSION

Although in 1919 and thereafter scientists did not significantly participate in parliamentary politics, they had achieved other modes of recognition belied by the pessimistic postwar rhetoric of *Nature*. By the close of the war the scientific community had securely established itself as a major intellectual interest group with direct channels to the government and with improved opportunities for receiving state funds. Out of the wartime advisory committee on science and research there emerged the Department of Scientific and Industrial Research, where as in the National Physical Laboratory a struggle ensued between the scientists and the civil service.[39] Shortly after the war Oxford and Cambridge dropped the requirement for compulsory Greek, and scientific education began to flourish more freely. Not, however, until 1979 and the election of Margaret Thatcher did a person trained in science head a British government. Ironically, her first budget reduced expenditures for science.

The delineation of the character of later Victorian and early twentieth-century public science casts some light on two other developments in the British scientific community. The rhetoric and ideology of public science not only favoured the position of science generally but also especially aided the position of the most elite group of scientists within the profession. That elite received the most esteemed professorships and the key positions in the government and civil service. They used those positions to improve their own lot and that of scientists like themselves. Since the qualification for honour and recognition was brain power, those who allegedly possessed the most brain power received the most prestige. Consequently it is not surprising that by 1917 the professional elite that had so closely associated itself with the espoused goals of public science found itself confronted by the National Union of Scientific Workers.[40] Public scientists had been primarily concerned with establishing an

[39] Russell Moseley, 'The origins and early years of the National Physical Laboratory: a chapter in the pre-history of British science policy', *Minerva*, 16 (1978), 222–50; Eric Hutchinson, 'The struggle over the National Physical Laboratory in 1918', *Minerva*, 7 (1969), 373–98; Ian Varcoe, 'Scientists, government and organized research in Great Britain, 1914–1916: the early history of the DSIR', *Minerva*, 8 (1970), 192–216; Eric Hutchinson, 'Scientists as an inferior class: the early years of the DSIR', *Minerva*, 8 (1970), 396–411.

[40] Russell Moseley, 'Tadpoles and frogs: some aspects of the professionalization of British physics, 1870–1939', *Social Studies of Science*, 7 (1977), 423–46; Roy and Kay MacLeod, 'The contradictions of professionalism: scientists, trade unionism and the First World War', *Social Studies of Science*, 9 (1979), 1–32.

improved position for science in the society and had paid little attention to establishing equity, justice, and civility among the workers in their own professional household.

Second, public science from the late Victorian period onward (and in many respects from a much earlier period) had closely associated itself in its rhetoric and announced aims with the existing capitalist economic system and the military, even as it attacked the political structures and prescribed reformist cures for many social problems. Spokesmen for public science sought to improve the position of science so that its workers might enjoy more economic prosperity and security and social prestige within the existing society. The national interest that science was to serve was the same national interest that would benefit from a strong defence and more efficient manufacturing. Serving the public interest would not require any professional sacrifice on the part of scientists nor bring them into any significant opposition with other dominant political and social elites. In the 1930s the socialist scientists of the sort examined by Gary Werskey began to demand instead that science address itself to the social needs and welfare of the population as a whole. Consequently they necessarily ran headlong into the opposition of the scientific establishment, whose ideology derived from the turn-of-the-century drive to secure for science a place of honour among professional middle-class groups.[41] The socialistic scientists' critique of both the military connections of British science and its failure to care for the social welfare of the lower classes was in direct conflict with the late Victorian and Edwardian public science. However, the ideology of socialist scientists like J. D. Bernal also derived largely from late Victorian public science. Bernal wanted major state support of science for what he percieved to be the general welfare and good of the nation. What he and others of his generation transformed was the definition of what constituted the public good or national interest that science should serve.

This speculative probe of late Victorian and early twentieth-century public science may suggest one avenue whereby historians can begin to ascertain the place of the scientific community in the

[41] Gary Werskey, *The visible college: the collective biography of British scientific socialists of the 1930's* (New York: Holt, Rinehart and Winston, 1978). See also Gary Werskey, '*Nature* and politics between the wars', *Nature*, 224 (1969), 462–72, and William McGucken, *Scientists, society, and state: the social relations of science movement in Great Britain, 1931–1947* (Columbus: Ohio State University Press, 1984).

modern British political and intellectual nations. The major requirement is to recognize public science as such, that is, to recognize that
scientific writers were often formulating a polemic for science as a
social and intellectual institution within British society and were
devising a public ideology for workers in science. Historians of late
nineteenth-century British science – and there are too few such
historians – have generally accepted the scientific community's own
evaluation of their predicament and their own characterization of
Britain's scientific backwardness. Most commentators have not
asked whether the public statements by scientists about science
related to the activity of the scientific community as investigators of
nature or to their professional political and social goals. Nor have
they asked how the constant complaint about the neglect of science
may have aided the growth of the influence of science. This
uncritical reading of the documents of public science has led
historians to take at face value speeches, reports, and essays by
scientists about the condition of science when in fact those writings
simply repeated self-serving arguments and polemics that had long
flourished in the public domain. To this revised understanding of the
British situation will need to be added a comparative dimension
through examinations of the role of scientists in public life in other
major nations.[42] Only then will historians be able to provide a full
account of the astonishing success of scientists as intellectuals in the
political arena, the ideological roots of government funding for
scientific enterprise, and the relationship of scientific activity and the
social order from the late nineteenth century onwards.

[42] Several important recent studies have appeared. These include Daniel Pick, *Faces of
degeneration: a European disorder, c. 1848–c. 1918* (Cambridge: Cambridge University Press,
1989); Paul Weindling, *Health, race and German politics between national unification and Nazism,
1870–1945* (Cambridge: Cambridge University Press, 1989); Jeffrey Allan Johnson, *The
Kaiser's chemists: science and modernization in imperial Germany* (Chapel Hill: University of North
Carolina Press, 1990); Jack D. Ellis, *The physician-legislators of France: medicine and politics in the
early Third Republic, 1870–1914* (Cambridge: Cambridge University Press, 1990); William H.
Schneider, *Quality and quantity: the quest for biological regeneration in twentieth-century France*
(Cambridge: Cambridge University Press, 1990).

III

Moderns and ancients

CHAPTER 9

British politics and the demise of the Roman republic: 1700–1939

During the past quarter century scholars from several disciplines have established the central metaphorical function of the demise of the ancient Roman republic for both literary and political discourse in eighteenth-century Britain.[1] But the reverse side of that inquiry – the impact of the analogy between Britain and Rome on the modern historical interpretation of the ancient republic – has received virtually no attention.[2] This oversight has concealed a remarkable modern British historiographical phenomenon that did not end at the close of the eighteenth century. Rather, for over two hundred years modern British political ideologies and preoccupations determined not only how the collapse of the Roman republic would be interpreted but also in large measure even whether it would receive historical examination. The various shifts of historical interpretation from the age of Queen Anne through that of

From *The Historical Journal*, 29 (1986), 577–99. With permission of Cambridge University Press.

[1] Caroline Robbins, *The eighteenth-century Commonwealthman: studies in the transmission, development and circumstance of English liberal thought from the restoration of Charles II until the War with the Thirteen Colonies* (Cambridge, Mass.: Harvard University Press, 1959); Caroline Robbins, ed., *Two English republican tracts* (Cambridge: Cambridge University Press, 1969); Isaac Kramnick, *Bolingbroke and his circle: the politics of nostalgia in the age of Walpole* (Cambridge, Mass.: Harvard University Press, 1968); Gordon Wood, *The creation of the American Republic, 1776–1787* (Chapel Hill: University of North Carolina Press, 1969); Bernard Bailyn, *The ideological origins of the American Revolution* (Cambridge, Mass.: Harvard University Press, 1967); J. G. A. Pocock, *The Machiavellian moment: Florentine political thought and the Atlantic republican tradition* (Princeton: Princeton University Press, 1975); Reed Browning, *Political and constitutional ideas of the court Whigs* (Baton Rouge and London: Louisiana State University Press, 1982), pp. 1–34, 210–56; J. A. W. Gunn, *Beyond liberty and property: the process of self-recognition in eighteenth-century political thought* (Kingston and Montreal: McGill-Queens University Press, 1983), pp. 1–42.

[2] Notable exceptions are Addison Ward, 'The Tory view of Roman history', *Studies in English Literature, 1500–1900*, 4 (1964), 413–56; J. W. Johnson, *The formation of English neoclassical thought* (Princeton: Princeton University Press, 1967); Howard D. Weinbrot, *Augustus Caesar in 'Augustan' England* (Princeton: Princeton University Press, 1978); and Zwi Yavetz, *Julius Caesar and his public image* (Ithaca: Cornell University Press, 1983).

Chamberlain illustrate with stunning and disturbing clarity the relentless manner in which contemporary political concerns can shape, revise, and eventually overwhelm modes of historical understanding without the discovery of significant new evidence or the application of new methodology. By the twentieth century methodology itself, in the form of prosopography, in part served the ends of political commentary.

I

An essayist in the *Monthly Review* of 1764 succinctly stated the assumptions that informed eighteenth-century discussion of the Roman republic:

It is certain, that a thorough acquaintance with the Roman government must afford the most useful information to the subjects of a free State, and more especially to our own: for there is undoubtedly a very strong resemblance between the general forms of each; both being of a mixed nature, compounded of royalty, aristocracy, and democracy, though the respective powers of these three orders were, in each constitution, blended together in very different proportions. The fundamental principles in each, however, being so nearly similar, many profitable conclusions may be drawn from a comparison between the Roman State and our own; and from the fatal effects of party zeal, public corruption, and popular licentiousness in the one, we may form probable conjectures with regard to the consequences which the same circumstances must produce in the other.[3]

As indicated in this passage, the congruence between Britain and the Roman republic lay in the allegedly mixed constitution of each state. Ancient political philosophers had written extensively about mixed polities consisting of elements of monarchy, oligarchy, and democracy. Polybius had specifically analysed the strength of the constitution of the Roman Republic in those terms. Renaissance civic humanists, particularly Machiavelli, had drawn the ancient concept into modern political thought. From at least the middle of the seventeenth century English political thinkers and active politicians often indebted to Machiavelli had discussed their own political structures in terms of a mixed polity. By the early eighteenth century, the metaphors of the mixed and the balanced constitutions had become central to British political discourse.

---

[3] *Monthly Review*, 30 (1764), 107–8.

Because the Roman example had been cited throughout the centuries of debate over mixed polities, it was natural for British commentators to discuss Rome and also to pass rather facilely between consideration of the British and the Roman scenes. Extensive polemical use of the analogy initially appeared in political pamphlets including *An essay upon the constitution of the Roman government* (written *c.* 1699; published 1726) by Walter Moyle; *A discourse upon the public revenues and on the trade of England* (1698) by Charles Davanant; *A discourse on the contests and dissentions between the nobles and the commons in Athens and Rome with the consequences they had upon both those states* (1701) by Jonathan Swift; *Cato's letters* (1720–24) by John Trenchard and Thomas Gordon; *Remarks on the history of England* (1730) and *Dissertation on parties* (1733–4) by Lord Bolingbroke; and later in the century *Reflections on the rise and fall of the ancient republics adapted to the present state of Great Britain* (1759) by Edward Wortley Montagu. The interpretation of Roman history adopted by these writers was essentially that of Machiavelli's *Discourses* with its moral explanation of the collapse of ancient republican liberty. Machiavelli, like his ancient sources, had ascribed the loss of Roman freedom to the impact of luxury following the defeat of Carthage. Luxury had fostered individual selfishness and thereby displaced patriotic virtue. Those moral developments in turn fostered the establishment of personally ambitious independent military commanders no longer obedient to the Senate. As a result of this corruption the later Roman republic lacked the political balance that Polybius had perceived as functioning so wisely and efficaciously in an earlier age.

The specific British context for establishing the analogy between the fate of the Roman republic and modern Britain was the country-party critique of the court-Whig political supremacy. Writing from the Commonwealth political tradition, now rendered so familiar by the work of Professors Robbins, Bailyn, Pocock, Kramnick, and others, these pamphleteers urged that the proper balance of the British constitution and thus the essential guarantee of liberty had been undermined since the settlement of 1688, first by William III and his ministers, then by the Whigs of the court of Queen Anne, and finally, and most despicably, by Robert Walpole under the first two Hanoverians.[4] The indications of this ongoing betrayal of

---

[4] See works cited in n. 1 and also H. T. Dickinson, *Liberty and property: political ideology in eighteenth-century Britain* (London: Weidenfeld and Nicholson, 1977), pp. 102–18, 162–92.

liberty were excessive commercialism, a large national debt, a standing army, placemen in Parliament, and an overly strong central executive authority sustained by patronage and novel financial structures. The new forms of commercial wealth and crown monetary resources were overwhelming the political influence in Parliament of the genuinely independent men of landed wealth and thereby the balance of the British polity. The country-party use of the Roman example to sustain its indictment of modern politics operated in a circular and self-confirming manner. The particular, economic, and moral factors identified by the country-party ideologists as pernicious to liberty were those that Machiavelli had extrapolated from his own interpretation of the Roman republic and then applied to free states generally. The country-party writers commenced their thinking with that well-established Machiavellian canon of political evils, discovered them present in the British scene, and then enforced the argument for their corrosive influence by appealing to the case of Rome.

The proscribed Tories and disaffected Whigs who contributed to this critique of court ministers and their policies had no real chance of attaining power, but they and their pamphlets were a fundamental part of the world of eighteenth-century politics. The court-Whigs could not and did not ignore these writers. Court-party writers attempted to nullify the utility of the analogy between Britain and the Roman republic by offering a different interpretation of the demise of the republic and by denying the validity of the analogy. Yet, throughout the polemical exchanges, it was the country-party pamphleteers and commentators who established the parameters for the debate.

The first book of considerable length sponsored by court-Whigs in response to the Roman polemic of the opposition pamphlets was *The history of the life of Marcus Tullius Cicero* published in 1741 by Conyers Middleton, an Anglican clergyman of questionable orthodoxy who served as the principal library keeper at Cambridge. His chief patron was Lord Hervey, the prominent Whig courtier, and the list of subscribers to the biography included Walpole himself. Not unexpectedly for a writer with such friends, Middleton reminded Hervey, 'In old Rome, the public honours were laid open to the virtue of the Citizen; which, by raising them in their turns to the command of that mighty Empire, produced a race of Nobles, superior even to kings.'[5] No reader would have missed the implied parallel between the ancient Roman and modern British nobility. Moreover, Middleton's statement was compatible with the rather extreme view of Hervey and certain other court-Whigs that modern English liberty dated only from the expulsion of the Stuarts just as Roman liberty dated from the overthrow of the monarchy and the emergence of senatorial government.

In direct contradiction of both the Machiavellian and country-party views of the situation, Middleton asserted that even in its closing decades the Roman republic had been a free state. He thus specifically denied that the existence of a narrow political oligarchy, standing armies, public debt, and politically active commercial classes, in and of themselves, endangered liberty. Although Middleton deplored the violence and bloodshed of Sulla's proscriptions, he regarded the latter's aristocratic restoration as the only plausible structural safeguard against the rise of independent military commanders. It had been the collapse of that aristocratic order – the overwhelming of virtuous senators such as Cicero by evil, unpatriotic persons – and not economic prosperity that had resulted in the loss of liberty. Middleton in effect argued that what had been good for Roman senators had been good for republican institutions. By implication the same was true for the narrow Whig political oligarchy and modern British freedom. Middleton, furthermore, praised Cicero's vision of a union of the 'good' men of the state, the *Concordia omnium Bonorum*, which bore no small resemblance to the Walpolean coalition between the Whig nobility and the expanding urban commercial interests. The country-party opposition never tired of Catonic berating of the political corruption allegedly fostered by the intrusion of commercial wealth into political life. Cicero in his effort to unite the ancient senatorial and equestrian orders had known better and so, Middleton implied, did wise modern Whig ministers, who embodied Ciceronian public virtue.[6]

Outright conspiracy rather than commercial prosperity or domestic political consolidation posed in Middleton's view the fundamental danger to both ancient and modern liberty. The virtuous, patriotic Cicero had struggled with one conspirator after another

5 Conyers Middleton, *The history of the life of Marcus Tullius Cicero* (London: printed by James Bettenham, 1741), I, iii.
6 Ibid., I, 32–4, 48–50, 152–3.

from Catiline to Pompey to Caesar to Octavian.[7] These were the genuinely evil political figures who had conspired against liberty, launched armies against republican institutions, appealed to crowd tumult, and loosed the likes of Clodius and his gangs against the people and Senate of Rome. In similar fashion Walpole and other virtuous court-Whigs loyal to the Hanoverian dynasty and the revolution settlement had daily to confront the reality of Jacobite conspiracy, the possibility of invasion by the Pretender, and crowd violence such as had occurred during the Excise crisis of 1733. Furthermore, while Cicero in the past and Walpole in the present laboured to preserve a free political order, they heard themselves and their works denigrated by Cato and the country-party writers for contributing to the loss of virtue. Just as Cato had been mistaken in his analysis of the last years of the republic, his modern counterparts were by implication wrong about the dangers truly confronting British liberty and order.

A later Hanoverian propagandist Thomas Blackwell in *Memoirs of the court of Augustus* (1753–63) reversed Middleton's tactic. He embraced the country-party interpretation of Roman history in order to refute its relevance to the British scene. The fundamental causes of the demise of ancient republican liberty had been the undue influence gained by the Tribunes and 'the irreparable loss' of Roman morality fostered by luxury. The villain who seized on this deteriorating moral and political situation was Julius Caesar, whom Blackwell described as possessed by 'a strange Depravity of Inclination and Hatred of Order' that led him to side 'with the low licentious Populace'. As consul he had 'perverted' the office and 'turned its Power to oppress the Men, and bear down the Measures he ought to have defended'. As 'the most ambitious Profligate that ever was born', he had used the vice and corruption of the day 'as handles to get into Power, to debauch the Army, overturn the Laws, and set up a Tyranny under the name of *Perpetual Dictator*'. Although once in power Caesar had manifested some humaneness, ultimately this 'grand Usurper' through 'his Treason and Rebellions' had caused 'more Murder, Devastation and Misery than ever Tyrant

---

[7] Ibid., I, 225. See Browning, *Political and constitutional ideas of the court Whigs*, pp. 210–56, for the explicit Ciceronianism of Walpole's supporters. Browning's views and those of the present essay in regard to Middleton dissent from Robbins, *The eighteenth-century Commonwealthman*, pp. 291–3.

committed'.[8] Blackwell even went so far as to defend the action of Caesar's assassins.

Blackwell, who also wrote a pioneering study of Homer, was a strong Scottish supporter of the Hanoverians. He received his appointment as principal of Marischal College in the University of Aberdeen from George II in 1748. He dedicated the first two volumes of his *Memoirs of the court of Augustus* in turn to Henry Pelham and to the Duke of Newcastle. His editor dedicated the posthumous third volume to the Earl of Bute. It would seem almost certain that Blackwell equated the character and ambition of Caesar with those of the Stuart pretender. Blackwell, however, rejected the implicit fatalism and pessimism of the country-party attack on luxury and the concomitant view that human beings could improve politics only by restoration of an earlier mode of virtue. The luxury afforded by modern prosperity need not inevitably lead to the results that ancient luxury had fostered in Rome. Britain enjoyed important humanly devised political safeguards that Rome had not possessed. These included a representative system of government inhibiting a Caesarean appeal to the people, an orderly succession to political office, a tripartite division of political power, and an army controlled by civilian authorities. Such institutional bulwarks of liberty, secure under an aristocratically dominated Parliament and the Hanoverian monarchs, could save Britain from the fate of the Roman republic.[9] In effect Blackwell, like Hume, contended for the supremacy of political structures over moral influences in public life. Since the country-party critique ignored the structural differences between Britain and Rome, their much vaunted analogy was invalid and inappropriate.

The vehemence of Blackwell's attack on Caesar reflected the political anxieties of a Scottish Whig. His confidence in modern political structures bespoke the outlook of that mid-century generation of Scottish intellectuals committed to the transformation of their land into a politically stable and economically prosperous country by dint of human industry and ingenuity. At the same time, portions of Blackwell's *Memoirs of the court of Augustus* would also

[8] Thomas Blackwell, *Memoirs of the court of Augustus*, 3 vols. (Edinburgh: A. Millar, 1753–63), I, 194, 166, 178, 376, 8; II, 183. For reviews of Blackwell, see *Critical Review*, I (1756), 66–74; *Monthly Review*, 8 (1753), 420–38; 14 (1756), 223–37; *Literary Magazine*, I (1756), 41–2, 239–40. See also Weinbrot, *Augustus Caesar in 'Augustan' England, passim*.
[9] Blackwell, *Memoirs of the court of Augustus*, I, 133, 144–7, 194, 376–8; II, 272–3, 373–9.

appear to have been a direct response to the early volumes of *The Roman history from the building of Rome to the ruin of the Commonwealth* (4 vols., 1738–71) by Nathaniel Hooke. These volumes were the most extensive mid-century English commentary on the republic. They challenged every major feature of the court-Whig interpretation of Roman history and carried the traditional country-party version of the story to new levels of radicalism by the appropriation of a Harringtonian concept of politics.

Hooke, who was a Roman Catholic friend of Alexander Pope with Jacobite connections, commenced his analysis of the later republic in the second volume of *The Roman history*, published in 1745, the year of the last Jacobite uprising. Hooke immediately distinguished himself from virtually all other contemporary commentators by championing the Gracchi and thereby laying the groundwork for a favourable portrait of Julius Caesar. Whereas previous historians had regarded the Gracchi as illegal challengers of proper consti-tutionalism, Hooke contended that by attacking the problem of maldistribution of land, Tiberius Gracchus had attempted to cure the source of 'a disorder directly tending to the ruin of public liberty'.[10] By establishing a large group of independent landowners from previously dependent propertyless citizens, Tiberius would have created the Harringtonian prerequisite for a genuinely free state. Thus reformed, the republic might have forestalled the later turmoil arising from the vast number of landless citizens who became prey to and dependent on the ambitious machinations of the wealthier citizens.

The senators, not the Gracchi, had been 'the oppressors of their country, men determined to enslave Rome'. Hooke was unrelent-ing in his attack on the ancient senatorial order that had illicitly used the word *liberty* to describe a state in which 'the bulk of a people have neither property, nor the privilege of living by their labour'. In his third volume, published posthumously in 1764, Hooke, using terms directly applicable to mid-eighteenth-century Britain, denied that the late republic had been a free state. He declared that

---

[10] Nathaniel Hooke, *The Roman history from the building of Rome to the ruin of the Commonwealth*, 4 vols. (London, printed by James Bettenham, 1738–71), II, 532. The only extensive discussion of Hooke occurs in Ward, 'The Tory view of Roman history'. This little-known, excellent article is somewhat dated because it appeared before the major work on the ideological character of eighteenth-century politics.

nothing can be more absurd than to imagine *Liberty* and *Equality*, and Aequilibrium of power, to endure in a State, where the majority of those, who make the laws, and determine the most important affairs of the Public, have no land, no stable Property; and who for a subsistence, depend chiefly on what they can get by selling their votes to the rich and the ambitious.

All of the evils of the Harringtonian nightmare of landless, dependent men unable to protect or experience liberty had been realized in the closing decades of the republic. Corruption was rampant as from the moment of Sulla's aristocratic restoration onward 'the *Freedom of the Roman People* ... was surely, at best, no better than the freedom of outlaws and banditti' and the much lauded Roman Senate became 'notoriously a Spelunca Latronum'. The equestrian order who Cicero hoped might cooperate with the senators were a 'knavish', moneyed interest who 'had a great part of the inferior People dependent upon them'.[11]

By the final decade of the republic the citizenry confronted not the choice of slavery or liberty, but rather that of anarchy or government by the Triumvirate. After the initial partnership between Pompey and Caesar floundered, each stepped forward to lead respectively 'the two permanent and distinct parties in the republic, *the Aristocracy and the People*'. Once triumphant in the civil wars, Caesar ruled wisely and benevolently and without monarchical ambition. As dictator he continued the previous policy of his consulate and attempted to redress the politically pernicious maldistribution of land. In Hooke's narrative, Caesar stood as one of those heroic figures of the civic humanist tradition who possess the capacity, if permitted to exercise it, of restoring a state to its original principles. Hooke denied any patriotic motives on the part of Caesar's assassins, and reminded his readers that what followed Caesar's death was a civil war resulting in a 'despotic monarchy established by law'.[12]

Hooke's polemic against the ancient Roman senatorial order meshed with certain mid-century shifts in the British critique of the Whig ascendance.[13] During the first four decades of the century,

---

[11] Hooke, *Roman history*, II, 534; III, 5, 223 fn, 286.
[12] Ibid., IV, 4, 447. Many of Hooke's views received further diffusion in Oliver Goldsmith's *The Roman history from the foundation of the city of Rome, to the destruction of the Western Empire*, 2 vols. (London: S. Baker, 1769).
[13] See J. G. A. Pocock, '1776: the revolution against parliament', Alison Gilbert Olson, 'Parliament, empire and parliamentary law, 1776', and John Brewer, 'English radicalism in the age of George III', in J. G. A. Pocock, ed., *Three British revolutions: 1641, 1688, 1776* (Princeton: Princeton University Press, 1980), pp. 265–367.

opposition critics had portrayed the monarch or his ministers as potential tyrants. By mid-century, such criticism came to be directed toward the Whig-dominated Parliament as parliamentary statutes were employed to restructure Scottish society after the Jacobite rebellion, to enclose land to create larger estates, to expand the government revenue beyond the base of the land tax, to fight wars all over the world, and to repudiate the results of parliamentary elections. By the mid-1760s Wilkesite radicals at home and American colonists abroad were protesting the aggrandizement of Parliament. Hooke's repudiation of the equation of political liberty with the supremacy of Parliament, or the Roman Senate, in public life thus found numerous echoes from the mid-century onward. Hooke had sounded many of the themes that would dominate the age of the democratic revolution, so it is not surprising that his volumes remained in print until 1830, as one popular movement after another challenged modern aristocracies and in some cases championed modern Caesars.

Hooke's *Roman history* was at once both radical and nostalgic in its demand for political liberty based on wider landownership. The political goal was forward-looking, while the economic vision belonged to an earlier day. The accusation of political corruption combined Machiavellian morality with Harringtonian structural analysis. As noted, Blackwell had addressed himself to some of these matters in the *Memoirs of the court of Augustus*, but the chief critique of Hooke's work appeared in Adam Ferguson's *History of the progress and termination of the Roman Republic* (4 vols., 1783; revised, 5 vols., 1799). Ferguson was Professor of Moral Philosophy at Edinburgh and author of the renowned *Essay on the history of civil society* (1767). He stood firmly in the camp of court-oriented political opinion, having served as secretary to the British commissioners seeking reconciliation with the rebellious American colonies. He dedicated the volumes on the Roman republic to George III.

Ferguson was a natural conservative who was also deeply imbued with the advanced social thought of late eighteenth-century Scotland.[14] Ferguson believed a wise and successful polity that secured

---

[14] There exists no substantial discussion of Ferguson as an historian. See David Kettler, *The social and political thought of Adam Ferguson* (Columbus, Ohio: Ohio State University Press, 1965); Duncan Forbes, 'Introduction', to Adam Ferguson, *An essay on the history of civil society* (Edinburgh: Edinburgh University Press, 1966), pp. xiii–xli; and David Spadafora, *The idea of progress in eighteenth-century Britain* (New Haven: Yale University Press, 1990), pp. 253–320.

liberty of persons and property required both appropriate structures and patriotic citizens. As a highlander and one-time army chaplain, Ferguson admired the patriotism and civic virtue of small, relatively undeveloped states. For that reason he had no hesitation in attacking the political corruption and the personal immorality of leaders in the Roman republic. But unlike country-party writers who voiced such sentiments, Ferguson did not believe sound morality or restored virtue could have saved ancient republican liberty. Like other of the Scottish social thinkers Ferguson contended that human society developed through various economic stages and that the particular modes of government appropriate for one stage of development were inappropriate for others. Any attempt to impose a political structure on a country without taking into account its size, the nature of its economy, the degrees of social distinction, and the intensity of patriotism at that moment was both fruitless and misguided. This developmental outlook led Ferguson in effect to historicize into irrelevance the country-party programme of political regeneration and to attack as mischievous all efforts at radical reconstruction of the political and economic fabric.

This political eclecticism also led Ferguson to criticize the Gracchi directly and, by implication, all Harringtonian calls for political reform through economic equality. Democracy and equality were possible in geographically small republics but not in states, such as the late Roman republic, that ruled an empire. The Gracchi had not grasped this political truth, nor had they understood the fundamental utility of the various social distinctions within such imperial states. According to Ferguson,

The distinction of poor and rich, in States of any considerable extent, are as necessary as labour and good government itself. The poor being destined to labour, the rich, by the advantages of education, independence, and leisure, are qualified for public affairs. And the empire being now greatly extended, owed its safety and the order of its government to a respectable aristocracy, founded on the distinctions of fortune, as well as personal qualities, or the merit of national service. The rich were not, without some violent convulsion, to be stript of estates which they themselves had acquired by industry, or which, so originally acquired, they had inherited from their ancestors. The poor were not qualified at once to mix with persons of a better education, and inured to a better condition. The project [of the Gracchi] seemed to be as ruinous to government as it was to the security of property, and tended to place the members of the commonwealth, by one rash and precipitate step, in situations in which they were not qualified to act.

The policy of the Gracchi to foster greater equality in landholding was doomed to failure. Their ill-advised substitution of 'popular tumults for sober councils and a regular magistracy' contributed to further turmoil by raising the prospect of anarchy and violent usurpation.[15] Ferguson thus implicitly accused the Gracchi of misunderstanding the historical appropriateness and inappropriateness of particular kinds of political structures, and of ignoring the most fundamental aspects of the Lockean concept of property appropriated through industry, transmitted through inheritance, and secured through good government. By implication Hooke and other Harringtonians were guilty of the same errors.

Ferguson criticized all later popular Roman leaders and praised the supporters of the Senate. He commended Sulla for rescuing Rome from the 'scene of wild devastation, attended with murders, rapes, and every species of outrage' that had prevailed under Marius. Sulla's confiscations and proscriptions had been necessary sacrifices 'offered at the shrine of public order, to provide for the future peace of his country'. Despite their harshness those measures had prolonged 'the struggles of virtuous men for the preservation of their country'. Their efforts might well have succeeded 'if the spirit of legal monarchy could at once have been infused into every part of the commonwealth; or if, without further pangs or convulsions, the authority of a Prince, tempered with that of a Senate, had been firmly established'.[16] In other words, the liberty of the republic and its good order might have been preserved had its ancient aristocracy been wise enough to have established the kind of political structures Britain had enjoyed since the departure of the Stuarts.

But, instead, what the Roman republic experienced was a contest among various aristocratic leaders seeking to aggrandize themselves through a tumultuous appeal to the populace and assaults on the Senate. Whereas previous commentators had portrayed those figures, and most particularly Caesar, as prototypes for the Pretender, Ferguson's descriptions bore a close resemblance to the modern members of the aristocracy, gentry, or respectable commer-

---

[15] Adam Ferguson, *The history of the progress and termination of the Roman Republic*, new edn, 5 vols. (Edinburgh: Bell and Bradfute, 1799), I, 390–1, 401.
[16] Ibid., II, 170, 208, 209; IV, 140.

cial classes who had made common cause with the lower orders to challenge the authority of the Hanoverian monarchy and the British Parliament during the Wilkesite protests, the American Revolution, the Yorkshire Association Movement, the Irish troubles, and the Gordon riots. This shift in polemical emphasis and target was not accidental. From the 1760s through the 1780s the country-party ideology identified earlier in the century with Tory, radical Whig, and Jacobite opposition to the Hanoverian regime and Whig dominance had been appropriated by more radical political groups. These radicals in both Britain and America pointed to the alleged corruption of the British government and particularly of Parliament as a basis for direct appeals to the people and recognition of popular leaders.

Ferguson intended his discussion of Caesar to question the morality and good intentions of ancient and modern political radicals, to reject the notion that alleged decay in a state justifies disruptive political behaviour, and to point to the ultimate loss of liberty sustained through an appeal to popular politics. Ferguson described Caesar as a person with abilities 'worthy of a great prince' who had sought power only 'to gratify his personal vanity, not to correct the political errors of the times'. Caesar, like radical critics of the British government in Ferguson's day, had rejected alliances with his own social class and had instead 'courted the populace in preference to the Senate or better sort of the People'. He chose to make himself 'the chief among those who, being abandoned to every vice, saw the remains of virtue in their country with distaste and aversion'. Capable of receiving public honour equivalent to that of Cato, Cicero, or the Scipios, he had rather 'preferred being a superior among profligate men, the leader of soldiers of fortune'. Without actually defending the assassination, Ferguson nonetheless regarded the event as 'a striking example of what the arrogant have to fear in trifling with the feelings of men whom they ought to respect'.[17]

Turmoil and eventually tyranny came in the wake of the actions of Caesar and other ancient Romans who had prevented 'the spirit of legal monarchy' from prevailing. By implication, similar results could be anticipated from the behaviour of modern selfish political leaders radically discontent with the rule of Parliament and the Hanoverian monarchy. Too radical an attack or too unscrupulous

[17] Ibid., IV, 111, 140; II, 369; IV, 101, 160.

methods of behaviour could destroy the very structure that popular leaders claimed they wished to reform. That the Roman republic required extensive political reconstruction and a more centralized executive did not justify 'the pretensions of every profligate person who may affect to place himself in the estate of sovereign'. Nor did the general turmoil and crisis of the late republic exonerate those who turned the situation to their own ends: 'Caesar and Pompey are blamed, not because the republic had an end, but because they themselves were the evils by which it perished.' Furthermore, destruction of the republic, by definition, destroyed the relevance of the standards of republican political morality. For this reason, Ferguson refrained from personal criticism of Octavian, even though he found the Principate odious. The values by which he had criticized Caesar no longer applied to Octavian who had emerged as 'leader of a party, born at a time when the competition for superiority was general, and when sovereignty or death were the alternatives to be chosen by persons of such rank and pretensions as his own'.[18] The triumph of Octavian and consequent establishment of the Principate stood as dire warnings to those who would preserve modern liberty and virtue by overturning or threatening to overturn the existing political order. Those who supported popular leaders in the name of liberty might well find themselves ultimately living under a despotic government against which appeal to previous political values would be meaningless.

Ferguson's was the last significant eighteenth-century history of the Roman republic. As domestic political radicals became more nearly democratic in their demands, Greek history with its narrative of turbulent democracies became a more useful polemical device for defending the status quo.[19] With the outbreak of a revolution in France, the establishment of a French republic of virtue, and the emergence of the Caesarism of Napoleon, it became difficult for British landowners and merchants of any political outlook to receive solace or polemical advantage from the events of the last decades of the Roman republic. But two other factors were also at work. Virtually all eighteenth-century British commentary on the republic was overwhelmingly secular in character. Human history itself rather than revelation, theology, or national traditions had consti-

[18] Ibid., v, 82–3, 83, 85.
[19] Frank M. Turner, *The Greek heritage in Victorian Britain* (New Haven: Yale University Press, 1981), pp. 189–204.

tuted the major source of wisdom about human nature in the political setting. The general ideological reaction to the French Revolution, especially the writings of Edmund Burke, embraced a traditionalist view of the ancient British constitution and a distinctly religious view of political life. British history and traditions rather than Roman became the appropriate source of knowledge about the political structures of the nation. The intense religiosity of Burke's polemic and other reactions to the dechristianization policies in France similarly crushed for a time the concept of politics as a realm of secular human activity that could be profitably illustrated through the model of the pagan republic.

II

Not a single genuinely significant or distinguished British history of the Roman republic appeared during the first half of the nineteenth century.[20] That situation might have been different had not Thomas Arnold, the headmaster of Rugby, died prematurely in 1842. In 1838 he had commenced publication of *A history of Rome* which, by his death, had reached only the Second Punic War. Confronted with a truncated history, Arnold's literary executors 'completed' the narrative by republishing a long series of articles that Arnold had written between 1823 and 1827 for the *Encyclopaedia Metropolitana*. These youthful essays reappeared in 1845 as the *History of the later Roman commonwealth*, and constituted the most extensive British discussion of the subject to appear in the first half of the century. Though in and of themselves unimportant, these volumes clearly illustrate the manner in which the ideological reaction to the French Revolution and to the movement for parliamentary reform had redirected in a Christian manner the presuppositions of political thought and concomitantly the interpretation of the late Roman republic.

Despite his youthful flirtation with Jacobin ideals and his later moderate political liberalism, Arnold was a more or less traditional Tory in the 1820s so far as issues of political authority were concerned. Within his treatment of the Roman republic the familiar

[20] The sole claimant might be George Long's *The decline of the Roman Republic*, 5 vols. (London: Bell and Daldy, 1864–74), but these volumes amounted to little more than a paraphrase of the ancient sources.

eighteenth-century secular political framework was virtually absent. Roman history displayed the virtues of neither human political ingenuity nor ancient political liberty. Rather, it manifested the follies of fallen human nature. In direct contrast to the previously unchallenged admiration for Roman patriotism and political capacity, Arnold castigated the Romans for 'the fatal habit of making their country the supreme object of their duty'. The Christian dispensation alone had permitted Europeans to be 'guided by purer principles' of political and social behaviour. The value of a knowledge of Roman history resided in the contrast thus revealed between pagan and Christian times. The Roman republic presented human nature at 'the highest point in intellectual and moral discoveries which it has ever reached without the assistance of revelation'. That distinctly human sight from which writers of the civic humanist tradition had long sought guidance was, for Arnold, less than edifying and indicated the turmoil and immorality that might occur in modern times as a result of 'the destruction of Christianity, which some avowedly, and many indirectly, consider as desirable'.[21] Republican Rome thus stood as a warning to all those who, like the enlightened writers of the previous century, urged consideration of politics without resort to revelation.

Arnold's Christian and generally Burkean political perspective allowed the exercise of his not inconsiderable gift for moral diatribe. Tiberius Gracchus was the well-intentioned author of a mistaken policy; his brother was simply a rebel whose 'death was the deserved punishment of rebellion'. Marius rose to power by persecuting 'everything most noble, most exalted, and most sacred'. Julius Caesar ingratiated himself into the political system through 'numerous adulteries committed with women of the noblest families', and by other 'profligacies' that drew scorn upon him 'even amidst the lax morality of his contemporaries'. Cato was a genuine patriot, but 'the pride and coarseness of [his] mind ... led him to indulge his selfish feelings by suicide, rather than live for the happiness of his family and friends'. Octavian's victory manifested 'successful wickedness' at work in the world. Rays of moral hope appeared on this dreary landscape of fallen humanity only after the birth of Jesus when 'amidst all the evil which is most prominent in the records of history,

---

[21] Thomas Arnold, *History of the later Roman Commonwealth, from the end of the Second Punic War to the death of Caesar; and the reign of Augustus with a life of Trajan*, 2nd edn, 2 vols. (London: B. Fellowes, 1849), I, 20, 59, 60.

a power of good was silently at work, with an influence continually increasing'.[22] For Arnold the turmoil of the republic was the result of sin, and the power required to rectify the situation had necessarily to originate outside the human political arena.

Arnold's comments and presuppositions are indicative of the immense intellectual distance that lay between the political thought of the eighteenth and the first quarter of the nineteenth centuries. Concern with order had replaced prescriptive admiration for ancient liberty and balanced polity, and that concern would inform virtually all later Victorian interpretations of the Roman republic. Furthermore, although the distinctly religious outlook present in Arnold's early Roman essays would subside, it would never completely disappear from the analysis of later nineteenth-century writers. Most important in this respect, virtually all subsequent Roman historians shared to one degree or another Arnold's view of the Principate as a providential vehicle for the diffusion of early Christianity throughout the Mediterranean world. By mid-century these two factors combined with certain disillusionment over liberal democracy in practice to establish a general Victorian approval of the demise of the republic and to provide the foundation for the Victorian apotheosis of Julius Caesar.

III

Extravagant praise for Julius Caesar was the keynote to virtually all Victorian histories of the later Roman republic, whether written in Britain or elsewhere. Theodor Mommsen's *History of Rome* (1854; tr. 1862) was the most famous work of its kind, but it achieved influence in no small measure because so many other historians and other writers had prepared the way.[23] In 1832 Thomas DeQuincey had contributed a series on 'The Caesars' to *Blackwood's Magazine*. The entire analysis was favourable to the collapse of the republic and the establishment of the Principate. In a remarkable passage that approvingly compared Julius Caesar's conquest of Rome to rape, DeQuincey wholly supported the destruction of republican liberties. He declared,

---

[22] Ibid., I, 109, 119, 263; II, 37, 291, 400.
[23] Theodor Mommsen, *The history of Rome*, tr. William P. Dickson, 4 vols. (London: R. Bentley, 1862–7; German publication 1854–6). Book v deals with Julius Caesar.

It is false to say that with Caesar came the destruction of Roman greatness. Peace, hollow rhetoricians! Until Caesar came, Rome was a minor; by him, she attained her majority, and fulfilled her destiny. Caius Julius, you say, deflowered the virgin purity of her civil liberties. Doubtless, then, Rome had risen immaculate from the arms of Sylla and Marius. But, if it were Caius Julius who deflowered Rome, if under him she forfeited her dowery of civic purity, if to him she first unloosed her maiden zone, then be it affirmed boldly – that she reserved her greatest favours for the noblest of her wooers . . . Did Julius deflower Rome? Then, by that consummation, he caused her to fulfil the functions of her nature; he compelled her to exchange the imperfect and inchoate condition of a mere *foemina* for the perfections of a *mulier* . . . The rape [if such it were] of Caesar, her final Romulus, completed for Rome that which the rape under Romulus, her earliest Caesar, had prosperously begun. And thus by one godlike man was a nation-city matured; and from the everlasting and nameless city was a man produced – capable of taming her indomitable nature, and of forcing her to immolate her wild virginity to the state best fitted for the destined 'mother of empires'. Peace, then, rhetoricians, false threnodists of false liberty! hollow chanters over the ashes of a hollow republic![24]

This brutal and extravagant assertion reflected the not infrequent romantic tendency to praise strong historical figures who seemed to possess the capacity to shape their own and later times. It also reflected the general tendency of DeQuincey to discuss and consider politics in an extremely illiberal manner. Such rhetoric could not have carried the day for the mid- and late Victorian cult of Julius Caesar; yet in their fervent acquiescence to authoritarian politics DeQuincey's views foreshadowed the later more politely argued historical analysis.

It had been Napoleon's career that made such championship of the once-despised figure of Caesar both plausible and polemically useful. Napoleon's halt to the bickerings of the corrupt French Directory, his imposition of efficient laws and administration on France, his expansion of the French Empire, and his overturning of the old regime across much of the continent invited the drawing of parallels between himself and Caesar as did his conscious imitation of the Roman political order wherein he held first the office of Consul and then of Emperor. DeQuincey linked the two rulers in his articles of 1832, as did the French writer Victor Duruy in his *History*

---

[24] Thomas DeQuincey, 'The Caesars', *Blackwood's Edinburgh Magazine*, 32 (1832), 542. See also John Barrell, *The infection of Thomas DeQuincey: a psychopathology of imperialism* (New Haven: Yale University Press, 1991), pp. 159ff.

of Rome and the Roman people (1843). The analogy received virtually official sanction when Emperor Louis Napoleon published a biography of Caesar in 1865.[25]

The major British statement of the Napoleonic or Bonapartist interpretation of Caesar appeared in Charles Merivale's *A history of the Romans under the Empire* (7 vols.; 1850–64), the early volumes of which contained the most extensive mid-century commentary on the later republic. After his education at the British East India Company college at Hailybury and then at Cambridge, Merivale pursued an ecclesiastically uneventful life in the Church of England where he eventually received the deanship of Ely. Merivale, whose brother was Under-Secretary of State for the colonies, admired the Roman Empire for its peace, its sound administration, and the general security of its citizens and subjects. He also firmly, though unobtrusively, believed it had served as a providential vehicle for the spread of Christianity, a view shared by virtually all other historians for the rest of the century. These benefits afforded by the Empire directly influenced Merivale's account of its formation.

Merivale's extraordinary hatred and contempt for the landlord oligarchy of the late republic led him to justify virtually all of its enemies as well as the suffering and violence that had marked its collapse. He viewed the Gracchi as wise and well-intentioned reformers who had sought to restore 'the needier citizens to a state of honourable independence'.[26] Merivale's concept of independence extended well beyond that of Hooke's virtuous freeholder to include persons possessing commercial wealth. In that respect Merivale's analytic framework reflected the influence of late eighteenth- and early nineteenth-century social thinkers who had transferred the concept of virtue from the landowning classes to the industrious middling ranks of society. Influenced by such classical economic theory, Merivale championed the role in the late republic of the monied equestrian order whom Hooke, true to his Harringtonian

[25] Thomas DeQuincey, *The works of Thomas DeQuincey* (New York: Hurd and Houghton, 1878), VII, 9–64; Victor Duruy, *Histoire des Romains et des peuples soumis à leur domination*, 2 vols. (Paris: Hachette, 1843). See also Wilhelm Drumann, *Geschichte Roms in seinem Uebergange von der republikanischen zur monarchischen verfassung* (Koenigsberg: Gebrüder Bornträger, 1837); and George Long, tr. and ed., *The civil wars of Rome: select lives translated from Plutarch with notes* (London: C. Knight & Co., 1846), III, 259. Louis Napoleon's contribution to this literature appeared as *Histoire de Jules César*, 2 vols. (New York: D. Appleton et cie. Libraires-Éditeurs, 1865).

[26] Charles Merivale, *A history of the Romans under the Empire*, 2nd edn (London: Longman, Brown, Green, and Longmans, 1852), I, 13.

outlook, had detested as heartily as the corrupt landowners. No mid-century politician or economist attached a more favourable interpretation to the dynamism of the Victorian middle class than Merivale did to the activity of its alleged ancient Roman counterpart.

During the last years of the Republic the leaders of the equestrian order, experiencing the oppression of the landed oligarchy, had turned to Caesar – 'the greatest name in history' – to forge a political structure with a base wider than the landed classes, but excluding the general populace. The selfishness of the nobles and the incompetence of the populace had created a political vacuum into which stepped Caesar as 'the true captain and lawgiver and prophet of the age'. In contrast to 'the great evil of the Sullan revolution', Caesar assumed as his guiding principle 'the elevation of the middle class of citizens, to constitute the ultimate source of political authority'. He thereby established a new direction for Roman politics and 'laid the foundations of the empire in the will of the middle classes'. Merivale asserted that Caesar's long-range goal had been a 'popular monarchy' that would successfully combine 'the discordant elements of despotism and freedom'. Whatever unfortunate personal ambition appeared in the trappings of oriental monarchy during the latter weeks of Caesar's life, Merivale blamed on the cunning womanly wiles of Cleopatra.[27]

In the third volume of *A history of the Romans under the Empire* (1851) Merivale contended that the imperial structures founded by Augustus simply extended the principle of popular monarchy initiated by Caesar. Careful examination of the Principate demonstrated that the imperial system recognized 'in its most solemn formulas the popular will as the foundation of political power', and repudiated 'alike the fantastic principles of patriarchal autocracy and of feudal sovereignty'. Augustus's possession of the tribuneship indicated his authority rested 'on the presumed will of the nation'. Whatever autocratic power actually resided in the Princeps stood justified by the elimination of evils associated with previous aristocratic authority on the one hand and by 'the extension of rights, the protection of property, and the multiplication of enjoyments and expansion of the natural affections' among citizens of the Empire on the other.[28]

As contemporaries noted, events in France and the rhetoric of

[27] Ibid., I, 97, 146, 143; II, 406; I, ix, 407.
[28] Ibid., III, 441, 465, 555.

mid-century Bonapartism clearly influenced Merivale's analysis of the late republic and early Empire. Roman citizens, according to Merivale, had turned to the monarchy of Augustus 'to preserve society in Rome'. After the proscriptions first of Sulla and then of the Second Triumvirate, Romans stood 'ready to exalt to the skies the usurper who refrained from taking all their lives and properties'. They looked 'to certain established principles of social organization' and to 'the subordination of classes, the hierarchy of families, the customs of antiquity, and the traditions of religion' rather than to free speech, open discussion, and a liberal press to provide security and stability.[29] All these features which Merivale ascribed to the Principate had counterparts in the regime of Louis Napoleon. Like Augustus, he was the somewhat distant relative of a great reforming military-commander-predecessor who had attacked a corrupt aristocracy. Louis Napoleon was advancing the causes of safe property and capitalist expansion. His careful nurturing of the French Catholic Church resembled Augustus's perpetuation of traditional religion within a new political order. Whatever Merivale's views about British politics, and they are uncertain, he clearly thought the liberal state was no prescription for societies confronting political turmoil and social disruption.

Although Merivale's history set the stage for the generally uncritical acceptance of Mommsen's championship of Caesar, British readers did not need to await the German historian for confirmation of Merivale's authoritarian views. In 1854 Archdeacon John Williams published *The life of Julius Caesar* which was followed the next year by Henry G. Liddell's *History of Rome from the earliest times to the establishment of the Empire*.[30] While criticizing Caesar's personal morality, both clergymen praised his political achievements. In 1855 Richard Congreve, the most outspoken of the early British positivists, echoed this Anglican commendation in *The Roman Empire of the West*. He praised the peace, stability, and prosperity of the Empire as having 'justified the long period of suffering, of war, of conquest' associated with the actions of Caesar. The imperial structures founded by Augustus had wisely substituted 'an imperial despotism

[29] Ibid., III, 547; IV, 8, 56–7; I, vii–viii. For contemporary commentary on the parallels with French developments, see *Edinburgh Review*, 92 (1850), 69–70; *Eclectic Review*, 95 (1852), 433; *Fraser's Magazine*, 47 (1853), 662, 668–9.

[30] John Williams, *The life of Julius Caesar* (London: G. Routledge and Sons, 1854); Henry G. Liddell, *A history of Rome from the earliest times to the establishment of the Empire*, 2 vols. (London: J. Murray, 1855).

for the free play and conflict of parties characteristic of a free state'. Both ancient and modern times, according to Congreve, required 'a dictatorship of progress'.[31]

These mid-century authoritarian and pro-Caesar interpretations of the late Roman republic reflected impatience with a number of contemporary political matters voiced in other contexts by various writers. The sharp political and social clashes of the 1840s between the landed interest and the Anti-Corn Law League and between the Chartists and the manufacturing interest led many people, such as Carlyle and his disciples, to demand strong central political leadership. The rather directionless aristocratic ministries of the post-Corn Law Repeal decade did little to assuage doubts about the adequacy of the liberal state. The onset of the Crimean War in 1854 fostered new public questioning, as seen in Congreve's lectures, about the adequacy of parliamentary regimes to forge reform at home and peace abroad. There were numerous calls for the leadership of a strong figure.[32] The firm hand of Palmerston for a time settled those doubts though they were never far removed from the minds of numerous articulate Victorians. Such intellectual criticism of the liberal state in a somewhat different guise reappeared in the late 1870s and, as a quarter century earlier, one result was a reassertion by an historian of the positive, heroic political qualities of Julius Caesar.

The renewed appeal to Caesar as a vehicle for attacking contemporary British politics first appeared in James Anthony Froude's *Caesar: a sketch* of 1879. This volume reflected a widespread disillusionment with partisan politics that overcame numerous university intellectuals, as well as many scientists, in the decade following passage of the Second Reform Act. Popular agitation over temperance, antivivisection, denominational rivalries, and foreign policy convinced Froude and others that democratic, partisan politics could not address the real needs and problems of the nation.

---

[31] Richard Congreve, *The Roman Empire of the West* (London: J. W. Parker, 1855), pp. 7, 175. For a critique of Congreve, see Goldwin Smith, 'Review of Mr. Congreve's "Roman Empire of the West" ', in *Oxford Essays: 1856* (London: J. W. Parker and Sons, 1856), pp. 295–31. See Edward Spencer Beesly's positivist approval of Roman monarchical government in his 1865 and 1867 *Fortnightly Review* articles, republished as *Catiline, Clodius, and Tiberius* (New York: G. E. Stechert & Co., 1924). For an analysis in a similar but somewhat more restrained vein, consult J. R. Seeley, 'Roman imperialism: the great Roman revolution', *Macmillan's Magazine*, 20 (1869), 185–97.

[32] Olive Anderson, *A liberal state at war: English politics and economics during the Crimean War* (London: Macmillan, 1967).

Consequently, whereas Merivale and his lesser followers had regarded Caesar as a popular middle-class-based leader opposing a corrupt aristocracy, Froude portrayed Caesar as a genuinely democratic leader overcoming the bungling and selfish machinations of politicians.

Froude had, of course, made his reputation as a Tudor historian. His biography of Caesar surprised readers and generally embarrassed admirers. According to Froude, the late Roman republic was only a pale imitation of the once proud state whose citizens had possessed not 'freedom to do as they pleased, but freedom to do what was right' and in which 'every citizen, before he arrived at his civil privileges, had been schooled in the discipline of obedience'. That ancient state had declined into 'a plutocracy' governed by a corrupt, decadent aristocracy. During his term as Consul, Caesar had come to realize that any substantial reform would require enactment 'over the Senate's head' by his own will and by 'the sovereign power of the nation'. The years in Gaul led him to understand that the true Roman patriots resided in the legions abroad rather than in the city itself. Through a curious application of contract theory, Froude contended that the Roman Senate had rendered the constitution a dead letter by having ignored the common good of Rome for over a century. As 'a brilliant democratic general' Caesar set out to correct the situation. After crushing the oligarchy, he had intended to restore 'as much of popular liberty as was consistent with the responsibilities of such a government as the Empire required'. With his murder at the hands of defenders of the old order, the possibility of Roman liberty had ended. Throughout his career Caesar had, in Froude's view, embodied political and social forces larger than himself, and had served as 'the reluctant instrument of the power which metes out to men the inevitable penalties of their own misdeeds'. Froude went further than any major historian in linking the accomplishments of Caesar to the providential purposes of the Christian God when he wrote,

As the soil must be prepared before the wheat can be sown, so before the Kingdom of Heaven could throw up its shoots there was needed a kingdom of this world where the nations were neither torn in pieces by violence nor were rushing after false ideals and spurious ambitions. Such a kingdom was the Empire of the Caesars – a kingdom where peaceful men could work, think, and speak as they pleased, and travel freely among provinces . . . And this spirit, which confined government to its simplest duties, while it left

opinion unfettered, was especially present in Julius Caesar himself ...
Strange and startling resemblance between the fate of the founder of the
kingdom of this world and of the Founder of the kingdom not of this world,
for which the first was a preparation. Each was denounced for making
himself a king. Each was maligned as the friend of publicans and sinners;
each was betrayed by those whom he had loved and cared for; each was put
to death; and Caesar also was believed to have risen again and ascended
into heaven and become a divine being.[33]

Froude removed the latter portion of this passage from a later
edition of his biography, but his first impulse demonstrated the
extremes to which he was prepared to go in justifying what he
regarded as the wisdom of Caesar's overthrowing of republican
government.

   Towards the close of the century the concern for balancing liberty
with order, stability, and sound administration coalesced into the
ideology of social imperialism. Spokesmen for this political outlook,
who included many of the public scientists discussed in an earlier
essay as well as historians and political commentators, rejected
politics conceived as a partisan contest for power and place and
instead regarded politics as a matter of achieving rational, efficient
administration that addressed truly national rather than particularistic interests and problems. These writers and commentators
admired political figures, whom they usually termed 'Statesmen',
who were capable like Froude's Caesar of actually embodying great
national purposes. Social imperialists also usually combined a strong
interest in Britain's imperial and military security with a related
concern for addressing the social question which they regarded as
intrinsically related to strength in foreign policy.

   This ideology, which may well have been the single most important bond among politically minded intellectuals at the close of the
century, permeated W. Ward Fowler's *Julius Caesar and the foundation
of the Roman imperial system* (1891). Fowler was a fellow of Lincoln
College whose admiration for Mommsen's view of Caesar easily
meshed with sympathy for the attitudes associated with social
imperialism. For Fowler, Caesar had embodied 'the principles of
intelligent government by a single man'. He had ultimately fulfilled
the promises of social reform and extension of citizenship to con-
quered peoples originally articulated by the Gracchi whom Fowler,

---

[33] James Anthony Froude, *Caesar: a sketch* (New York: G. Scribner's Sons, 1879), pp. 10, 21,
   195, 388, 526, 525, 548–50.

using the favourite phrase of social imperialists, described as 'real statesmen'. For a century after their deaths the selfish Roman Senate had ignored the general good of the nation, had pursued only particularistic interests, and had thwarted all later statesmen who advocated 'the ideals – new then in the political world – of progress and development'.[34] The result of this senatorial obstruction was constitutional paralysis, the establishment of extraordinary military commands, and the pursuit of personal political supremacy by various individual leaders.

Of those commanders who struggled for ascendancy only Caesar possessed the vision and capacity to rise above his own and other particularistic interests. Repeatedly comparing Caesar to Cromwell, Fowler argued that circumstances rather than selfish ambition had led both to establish 'the government of a single man, resting on military force, but expressing in some degree the will and the needs of a weary and distracted people'. For his own part, Caesar had drawn exclusive power unto himself in order to work for 'the salvation of the state' and to oversee 'the re-construction of the Empire on a rational and humanitarian basis'. Fowler was neither unaware nor uncritical of the despotic tendencies of the final weeks of Caesar's rule, but the presuppositions of social imperialism allowed him to defend Caesar despite these flaws. Through his attempt to govern according to the dictates of 'facts and knowledge', Caesar had provided an example of '*scientific intelligence*' brought 'to bear on the problems of government'. His mode of personal administration, despite certain faults, implied his overall intention to substitute 'the autocracy of a single hardworking man' for 'the selfish rule of a city-aristocracy'.[35]

Fowler and other turn-of-the-century Roman historians after him, including H. F. Pelham, T. M. Taylor, and William Heitland, asserted that Caesar had undertaken autocratic government solely for the general good of the state in opposition to what Heitland termed 'worthless factions using the cry of public good as a cloak for party ends'. For all of these writers, Caesar stood forth as the wise statesman of the social imperialist vision who could, by power of

---

[34] W. Warde Fowler, *Julius Caesar and the foundation of the Roman imperial system* (London and New York: G. P. Putnam's Sons, 1894; originally published 1891), pp. 2, 22, 26. See also Raymond H. Coon, *William Warde Fowler, an Oxford humanist* (Oxford: B. Blackwell, 1934); and for Fowler's admiration of Mommsen see W. W. Fowler, *Roman essays and Interpretations* (Oxford: Clarendon Press, 1920), pp. 258–68.

[35] Fowler, *Julius Caesar and the foundation of the Roman imperial system*, pp. 86, 91, 242, 358, 383.

intellect and patriotism of character, rise above particularistic interests and govern for the common good and the real interests of the nation. In a characteristic passage Taylor wrote that Caesar's work of government

was undertaken not by a party politician for party reasons, but by the master of the Roman Empire determined to use his power for the good of the Empire as a whole. Caesar's rule was the triumph of order. For years the Government had been falling into chaos under the short-sighted rule of an incompetent Aristocracy; in 67 B.C. the people had revolted; the demand for efficiency had resulted in the Gabinian Law and the Empire was the logical outcome of this revolt. Caesar had begun his political career as a Democrat, and the democratic tendencies which had been growing for generations all found their expression in Caesar's monarchy. A change in the central government was necessary and experience had shown that such a change could only be effective if the strong rule of a single disinterested man was substituted for the sordid and incapable government of the Senate.[36]

The autocratic Caesar provided a convenient vehicle of the histori-cal imagination to voice modern frustration with administrative inefficiency, political pluralism and indecisive leadership.

This critique of the late-nineteenth-century liberal state repre-sented only one strain of contemporary political thought, but it was the outlook that dominated British Roman studies for over fifty years. A few Roman historians and commentators dissented from this position and from the admiration for Caesar associated with it. Those dissenters included Anthony Trollope, the novelist, and J. L. Strachan-Davidson, successor to Jowett as Master of Balliol, as well as the Ciceronian scholars William Forsyth and R. Y. Tyrrell.[37] These writers vigorously championed Cicero and asserted in one way or another that no analysis of the late Roman republic could

---

[36] William Heitland, *The Roman Republic* (Cambridge: Cambridge University Press, 1909), III, 69; T. M. Taylor, *A constitutional and political history of Rome from the earliest times to the reign of Domitian* (London: Methuen & Co., 1899), p. 374. See also H. F. Pelham, *Outlines of Roman history* (New York and London: G. P. Putnam's Sons, 1893).

[37] William Forsyth, *Life of Marcus Tullius Cicero*, 5th American edn (New York: Scribner, Armstrong, and Co., 1878; dedication date 1863); Anthony Trollope, *The life of Cicero*, 2 vols. (London: Chapman and Hall, 1880); Robert Yelverton Tyrrell, *The correspondence of M. Tullius Cicero*, 5 vols. (London and Dublin: Hodges, Foster & Figgis, 1879–97); J. L. Strachan-Davidson, *Cicero and the fall of the Roman Republic* (New York and London: G. P. Putnam's Sons, 1894). See also Anthony Trollope, 'Merivale's history of the Romans', *Dublin University Magazine*, 37 (1851), 611–24; 48 (1856), 30–47.

obscure 'the plain truth that liberty and absolutism cannot live together'.[38] These protests, despite the vigour and eloquence of their authors, had no effect on the British writing of Roman history. Indeed, modification of the extravagant Victorian praise for Caesar among Roman historians stemmed not from the cause of Cicero but rather from a novel appreciation for the work of Augustus. Still one more time modern British political preoccupations dictated a shift in the analysis and interpretation of the late Roman republic and early Empire.

IV

Generally speaking throughout the eighteenth and nineteenth centuries, Augustus had been portrayed as an insincere person who governed in an absolute and despotic manner through the fictitious preservation of republican institutions. Merivale had regarded the Principate as authoritarian, but rooted in the popular will; other writers favourable to Caesar alone had seen the regime as the illiberal result of the lost Caesarean opportunity. However, in 1910 H. F. Pelham, writing in the eleventh edition of the *Encyclopaedia Britannica*, noted that historians were achieving a clearer understanding of the situation in Rome following Caesar's death and the civil wars. They were consequently coming to view Augustus 'not merely as an astute and successful intriguer, or an accomplished political actor, but as one of the world's great men, a statesman who conceived and carried through a scheme of political reconstruction which kept the empire together, and secured peace and tranquility and preserved civilization for more than two centuries'.[39]

Two factors accounted for this reevaluation of Augustus, which culminated in 1934 with an entire chapter of the *Cambridge Ancient History* being devoted to 'The achievement of Augustus'. First, from 1875 onward, Mommsen set forth the concept of the *dyarchy* whereby he interpreted the Principate as a system of genuinely joint power sharing between Augustus and the Senate. British historians of Rome quickly adopted the concept and used it to exonerate Augus-

[38] J. L. Strachan-Davidson, 'Froude's Caesar', *Quarterly Review*, 148 (1879), 477.
[39] H. F. Pelham, 'Augustus', *Encyclopaedia Britannica*, 11th edn (New York: Cambridge University Press, 1911).

tus from the traditional accusations of unlimited absolutism.[40] Second, just after the turn of the century, there arose a new appreciation for the difficulties of the political reconstruction and administration that Augustus had confronted. The methods he had used to address the situation particularly appealed to Edwardian writers. By this decade, British critics of the liberal state were less enamoured with the idea of a great man who might heroically impose organization where confusion had reigned. They tended instead to pursue goals of either administrative efficiency or administrative reform within a parliamentary system. Efficient administrators, civil servants, military officers, and imperial proconsuls in a collective manner might provide the strong executive influence required for competent government and could do so in a sometimes co-operative and sometimes antagonistic relationship to a parliament dominated by mere politicians. The career and achievement of Augustus appealed to persons of this outlook whether they were conservative or radical.

In 1902 E. S. Schuckburgh and in 1903 John B. Firth published the first book-length biographies of Augustus to appear in the English language. A third biography appeared in 1914 by René Francis, and between the wars, John Buchan, the novelist and governor general of Canada, contributed still another. The message of these biographies, as well as of other scholarly commentary of the period, was the same. Although, as an historical personality, Augustus might seem less interesting and exciting than Julius Caesar, it had been Augustus who brought peace and security to the Roman world. As Shuckburgh wrote,

He found his world, as it seemed, on the verge of complete collapse. He evoked order out of chaos; got rid one after the other of every element of opposition; established what was practically a new form of government without too violent a breach with the past; breathed fresh meaning into old names and institutions, and could stand forth as a reformer rather than an innovator, while even those who lost most by the change were soothed into

---

[40] Theodor Mommsen, *Romisches Staatrecht*, 3 vols. (Leipzig: S. Hirzel, 1871–88), II, 875ff; III, 1252ff. See also, *English Historical Review*, I (1886), 350–61; Taylor, *A constitutional and political history of Rome*, p. 473; J. B. Bury, *A history of the Roman Empire from its foundations to the death of Marcus Aurelius*, third impression (London: J. Murray, 1900; originally publ. 1893), pp. 15–17, 29–32; F. D. Adcock, 'The achievement of Augustus', in S. A. Cook, F. D. Adcock, and M. P. Charles Worth, eds., *Cambridge ancient history* (Cambridge: Cambridge University Press, 1934), X, 583–606; Mason Hammond, *The Augustan Principate in theory and practice during the Julio-Claudian Period* (Cambridge, Mass.: Harvard University, 1933).

submission without glaring loss of self-respect . . . He and not Julius was the founder of the Empire, and it was to him that succeeding emperors looked back as the origin of their powers.

For his part Firth praised Augustus for having been 'no daring reformer' and for having preserved republican institutions while attempting to establish a more adequate government. The secure borders and well-supplied treasury of the Augustan Principate displayed 'the practical imagination which goes to make a successful businessman and a practical statesman'.[41] Firth thus reduced the once heroic, rational statesman of the social imperialists into a supremely competent, if personally dull, administrator. Subsequent commentators on Augustus urged much the same argument for well over thirty years – the very same years when effecting domestic social reform, winning the Great War, and governing a distant Empire seemed to much of the British political elite to be a matter of achieving sound, efficient, even colourless administration and eradicating or reducing to a level of minimal interference the hurly-burly of pluralistic parliamentary politics and nationalistic movements.

To extend this analysis beyond the Roman histories of the 1920s would expand still further an already long essay, but one brief closing observation is required. The most important British history of the late republic to be written in this century was, of course, Sir Ronald Syme's *The Roman Revolution* (1939). That seminal volume steered Roman studies in English toward prosopography and is thus regarded as marking a major historiographical turning point. Yet, in its normative narrative and commentary, Syme's work stands in a line of direct intellectual continuity with the previous debate over the Roman republic and in certain respects harkens back to the eighteenth-century analyses of Hooke and Ferguson. Indeed the prosopographical method tends to assume that only by delineating the motives and interests of individuals can one understand the manifestations of collective behaviour. That methodological outlook implicitly rejects the social imperialist or the administrative view of politics as a process of surmounting or transcending various modes of

[41] E. S. Shuckburgh, *Augustus: the life and times of the founder of the Roman Empire (B.C. 63–A.D. 14)*, second impression (London: T. F. Unwin, 1905; originally publ. 1902), p. v; John B. Firth, *Augustus Caesar and the organization of the Empire of Rome* (New York and London: G. P. Putnam's Sons, 1903), pp. 180, 364. See also René Francis, *Augustus: his life and work* (London: G. G. Harrap & Company, 1914), and John Buchan, *Augustus* (London and Boston: Houghton Mifflin Company, 1937).

particularism. The fabric and imperatives of political power emerge from the warp and woof of the strands of special or particular interest not in their elimination. Eighteenth-century historians of Rome with their strong concern about property asserted a similar concept of politics almost intuitively. The historians who from the mid-nineteenth century had lauded Caesar and Augustus rejected that view as the first step in their attack on the adequacy of the modern liberal state. Syme reasserted much of the eighteenth-century attitude as a result of his methodology, his secular view of politics, and his reaction to events of the twentieth century.

A profoundly moral imperative informed all of Syme's analysis of the demise of the republic and his intricate tracing of the intermeshing political and social relationships in Roman political life. He wrote quite unabashedly in his preface that 'it is not necessary to praise political success or to idealise the men who win wealth and honours through civil war'. That moral presupposition, which may have had its origins in his witnessing in Rome the speeches and other political activities of Mussolini, led him to distinguish himself from his immediate British predecessors and to adopt 'a deliberately critical attitude toward Augustus'. Like Ferguson over a century earlier, he called Augustus an 'adventurer', and portrayed him as a victorious leader of a rather tawdry 'faction' (another eighteenth-century term) rather than as an Olympian statesman-administrator of the social imperialistic mould. And the goal of that ancient leader, and more important of the followers who sustained him, was the overthrow of the state, not its transcendence. Syme observed,

Octavianus' following could not raise the semblance even of being a party. It was in truth what in defamation the most admirable causes had often been called – a faction; its activity lay beyond the constitution and beyond the laws ... The cause of Caesar's heir was purely revolutionary in origin, attracting all the enemies of society – old soldiers who had dissipated gratuities and farms, fraudulent financiers, unscrupulous freemen, ambitious sons of ruined families from the local gentry or towns of Italy. The hazards were palpable, and so were the rewards – land, money and power, the estates and prerogatives of the nobility for their enjoyment, and the daughters of patricians for their brides.[42]

The description of this faction which, as Syme noted, also included

---

[42] Ronald Syme, *The Roman Revolution* (Oxford: Oxford University Press, 1979; originally publ. 1939), pp. viii, vii, 130, 134. On Syme's experience living in Rome under Mussolini, see Hugh Lloyd-Jones, *Classical survivals* (London: Duckworth, 1982), pp. 74ff.

wealthy patricians bears close resemblance to the description of the same group as had been furnished by Ferguson who, from a very different historical and ideological vantage point, had also grasped the revolutionary and socially disruptive character of the triumph of Augustus.

The passage quoted above, and Syme's general analysis of Augustus's victory, were also directly applicable to the victories of contemporary authoritarian movements over modern liberal democratic constitutions. Syme wrote of the demise of the Roman republic, again echoing the eighteenth century: 'There is something more important than political liberty; and political rights are a means, not an end in themselves. That end is security of life and property; it could not be guaranteed by the constitution of Republican Rome.'[43] The failure of that guarantee in the first century BC had resulted in the onslaught of the Roman Revolution; such failures in Syme's own day had resulted in the collapse of liberal constitutional government across much of the continent. The interweaving of ancient history and modern political preoccupations that had commenced in the era of the Glorious Revolution thus continued unabated to the eve of World War II and no doubt beyond.

[43] Syme, *The Roman Revolution*, p. 513.

CHAPTER 10

Ancient materialism and modern science: Lucretius among the Victorians

The ninth edition of the *Encyclopaedia Britannica* is one of the most significant yet least explored documents of Victorian intellectual history. Like other old encyclopaedias with discarded theories, dated articles, and incomplete bibliographies, it has been relegated to the darker and mustier aisles of library stacks where scholars too rarely wander. The ninth edition, published between 1875 and 1889, deserves a better fate. Under the leadership of T. Spencer Baynes, its editors determined to present 'the influence of the modern spirit' in literature, history, philosophy, religion, and the sciences.[1] For the first time articles on biblical criticism, comparative religion, psychology, and evolution found their way into *Britannica's* finely printed columns. Contributors such as T. H. Huxley, James Clerk Maxwell, W. Robertson Smith, and James Ward guaranteed not only distinguished but also often pioneering essays many of which constituted short monographs on their subjects.

Besides illuminating the general state of late Victorian scholarship, the twenty-five volumes of the encyclopaedia provide the historian with a useful point of departure for examining the impact of advanced ideas and theories on more traditional areas of intellectual life. A striking example of a standard entry that unexpectedly reflected the larger controversies of the day was W. Y. Sellar's essay on the Roman poet Lucretius. Sellar opened the six-page article by emphasizing the new interest and relevance that had of late been accorded this ancient author. Sellar explained,

Lucretius ... more than any of the great Roman writers, has acquired a new interest in the present day. This result is due, not so much to a truer

From *Victorian Studies*, 16 (1973), 329–48. With permission of the journal.
[1] T. S. Baynes, 'Prefatory note', *Encyclopaedia Britannica*, 9th edn, (Edinburgh: A. and C. Black, 1875), I, vii; Herman Kogan, *The great E.B.: the story of the Encyclopedia Britannica* (Chicago: Chicago University Press), 1958), pp. 52–60.

perception of the force and purity of his style, of the majesty and pathos of his poetry, or of the great sincerity of his nature, as to the recognition of the relation of his subject to many of the questions on which speculative curiosity is now engaged. It would be misleading to speak of him, or of the Greek philosophers whose tenets he expounds, as anticipating the more advanced scientific hypotheses of modern times. But it is in his poem that we find the most complete account of the chief effort of the ancient mind to explain the beginning of things, and to understand the course of nature and man's relation to it. Physical philosophy in the present day is occupied with the same problems as those which are discussed in the first two books of the *De Rerum Natura*. The renewed curiosity as to the origin of life, the primitive condition of man, and his progressive advance to civilization finds an attraction in the treatment of the same subjects in the fifth book. The old war between science and theology, which has been revived in the present generation, is fought, though with different weapons, yet in the same ardent and uncompromising spirit throughout the whole poem, as it is in the writings of living thinkers.

These observations would have been practically unthinkable only a quarter century earlier. The same is true of Sellar's additional judgement, 'The supposed "atheism" of Lucretius proceeds from a more deeply reverential spirit than that of the majority of professed believers in all times.'[2]

These opinions were the product of an ironic twist in Victorian classical criticism that occurred after 1868. From that date until after the turn of the century every major and almost every minor comment, article, or book about Lucretius concentrated on his relationship to contemporary scientific theory and to the conflict between religious and scientific writers.[3] During this period classi-

---

[2] W. Y. Sellar, 'Lucretius', *Encyclopaedia Britannica*, 9th edn, xv, 50, 55.
[3] E. W. Adams, 'Lucretius and his science', *The Gentleman's Magazine*, 277 (1894), 188–99; Alfred Benn, 'Epicurus and Lucretius', *Westminster Review*, n.s., 61 (1882), 299–346; Robert Buchanan, 'Lucretius and modern materialism', *New Quarterly Magazine*, 6 (1876), 1–30; C. B. Cayley, 'Lucretius on nature', *Fortnightly Review*, 8 (1867), 590–1; R. C. Jebb, 'Lucretius', *Macmillan's*, 12, (1865), 49–59; Fleeming Jenkin, 'The atomic theory of Lucretius', *North British Review*, 48 (1868), 211–42; W. H. Mallock, *Lucretius* (Edinburgh and London: W. Blackwood and Sons, 1898; originally publ. 1878); John Masson, 'The atomic theory of Lucretius', *British Quarterly Review*, 62 (1875), 335–77; John Masson, 'Lucretius, Tyndall, Picton, Martineau: some theories of matter and its relation to life', *British Quarterly Review*, 75 (1882), 324–51; John Masson, 'Lucretius' argument for free will', *Journal of Philology*, 12 (1883), 127–36; John Masson, *The atomic theory of Lucretius* (Edinburgh and London: W. Blackwood and Sons, 1884); John Masson, *Lucretius: Epicurean and poet* (New York: E. P. Dutton and Co., 1907); W. Y. Sellar, *The Roman poets of the republic* (Oxford: Oxford University Press, 1863); J. A. Symonds, 'Lucretius', *Fortnightly Review*, 23 (1875), 44–62; John Veitch, *Lucretius and the atomic theory* (Glasgow: J. Maclehose, 1875); William Wallace, *Epicureanism* (New York: Pot Young and Co., 1880). This list does not pretend to include every article or book on Lucretius, but it does include most, if not all, major works.

cal scholars, men of letters, and philosophers discovered commentaries on Lucretius to be convenient vehicles for attacking scientific naturalism. Surprisingly, as in Sellar's discussion, Lucretius more often than not emerged on the side of the angels.

The story of Lucretius among the Victorians constitutes more than a footnote to the history of classical scholarship. It may serve to clarify a problem intrinsic to an understanding of the Victorian conflict of science and religion. Professor Mandelbaum many years ago pointed to this issue when he observed the tendency for both contemporaries and later historians to confuse materialism with positivistic naturalism:

In the light of the repeated, explicit disavowals of materialism on the part of Comte and Spencer, and on the part of Bernard, Huxley, and Mach, among others, one might wonder how any such confusion was possible. The answer lies in the fact that positivism and materialism had two elements in common: both held that the sciences represented the most reliable knowledge attainable. It was on the basis of these similarities that those who opposed what was later to be called 'scientism' felt justified in identifying positivism with materialism, helping to give currency to the myth that materialism dominated philosophy in the nineteenth century.[4]

At the very highest level of intellectual endeavour, Mandelbaum was probably correct in his suggested explanation of the confusion. Moreover, as he noted, materialism was a term defined differently by different writers, with its most common meaning being that of psychophysical parallelism rather than materialistic metaphysics. The variety itself bred confusion.

Nevertheless, two other explanations may be offered to suggest why, at least in Great Britain, the religious and philosophical opponents of naturalistic positivism or scientific naturalism considered the advocates of those positions to be materialists. In the first place, scientific publicists, such as John Tyndall, T. H. Huxley, Herbert Spencer, and W. K. Clifford, encouraged the confusion. Tyndall called himself a materialist and lectured on 'scientific materialism'. During the protoplasmic debates of the sixties and seventies, Huxley popularized the concept of the physical basis of life which to a layman or suspicious clergyman sounded very much like materialism. When insisting that he employed 'a union of materialistic terminology with a repudiation of materialistic philosophy',

---

[4] Maurice Mandelbaum, *History, man & reason: a study in nineteenth century thought* (Baltimore: Johns Hopkins University Press, 1971), p. 23.

Huxley drew a distinction often quite understandably lost on his audience. In *First Principles* Spencer wrote of interpreting 'the detailed phenomena of Life, and Mind, and Society, in terms of Matter, Motion, and Force'. Clifford's theory of 'mind-stuff' hardly removed the materialistic spectre.[5] All of these scientific authors illustrated the uniformity of nature by allusions to the atomic theory. Consequently, the rhetoric of their scientific essays and lectures permitted their readers and listeners to consider them materialists.

A second reason for the contemporary equation of naturalistic and scientific thought with philosophical materialism is more complex and brings us back to the subject of Lucretius. Some of the Victorian critics of scientific naturalism, such as John Tulloch, James Martineau, Robert Flint, Robert Buchanan, John Masson, W. H. Mallock, and John Veitch, may have hoped, and even fervently desired, that Huxley, Tyndall, Clifford, Spencer and others of their persuasion did embrace and advocate philosophical materialism. That opponents of scientific naturalism may actually have welcomed this materialistic possibility is the clear suggestion of the Lucretian commentaries of the last thirty-three years of the century – commentaries faithfully reflected in Sellar's *Britannica* essay.

Considering the apprehensions about materialism voiced by many Victorian contemporaries and emphasized by later historians, it may seem unlikely or paradoxical that opponents of naturalism wanted scientific writers to be materialists. However, for liberal Christians, free of bibliolatry and of belief in miracles, a genuine materialistic opponent could prove an inviting and opportune target. If liberal Christians could plausibly argue that the scientific publicists were the much feared materialists, they could pursue a strategy outlined in a different context by the Unitarian divine, James Martineau, when he wrote,

To get rid of a troublesome discoverer or vigorous thinker, there is no readier way – and it has the advantage of being at once cheap and stinging – than to dismiss his new ideas as stale fallacies dug up again out of the discarded rubbish of the past. This is the buffet which lazy commonplace

---

5 John Tyndall, *Fragments of science*, 6th edn (New York: D. Appleton and Co., 1892), II, 75–90; T. H. Huxley, *Collected essays* (New York: D. Appleton and Co., 1894), I, 155; Herbert Spencer, *First principles*, 4th edn (New York: P. F. Collier and Son, 1901), p. 468; W. K. Clifford, *Lectures and essays*, ed. Leslie Stephen and Frederick Pollard (London: Macmillan, 1901), II, 1–73. See also Gerald L. Geison, 'The protoplasmic theory of life and the vitalist–mechanical debate', *Isis*, 60 (1969), 272–92.

delights to inflict on every man who threatens to leave a mark upon his age.[6]

The portrayal of Huxley and company as revivers of an ancient and inadequate philosophy provided a threefold polemical advantage. The scientific publicists would lose the benefit of novelty, and their modernity would stand discredited. Liberal Christians could make themselves appear more intellectually advanced and even modern than men of science. Secondly, the defenders of religion would achieve a new, much needed self-assurance and self-confidence from knowledge that they opposed a philosophy that Christianity had overcome in the past and by implication could overcome again. Finally, by combating modern scientific thought through classicism, these traditional writers could display the intellectual relevance of the classics at a time of its growing educational rivalry with science.

Certain fortuitous developments in the late sixties and early seventies allowed religious writers to pursue this strategy through commentaries on Lucretius. The direct by-product of this polemical manoeuvre was a complete reversal in critical appreciation for the Roman poet who during the first half of the century had been judged strictly on the artistic merit of his verse.

The opinions of Thomas Babington Macaulay were perhaps typical of those early years. He carried a Latin edition of *De rerum natura* to India where he read the poem several times. Macaulay's marginalia recorded his initial reaction with comments such as 'Stuff', 'Folly', 'Nonsense', 'Wretched Reasoning', 'Exceedingly Absurd', 'This is drivelling'. Upon completing a second reading, he noted in the margin,

It is a great pity that the poem is in an unfinished state. The philosophy is for the most part utterly worthless; but in energy, perspicuity, variety of illustration, knowledge of life and manners, talent for description, sense of the beauty of the external world, and elevation and dignity of moral feeling, he had hardly ever an equal.[7]

The latter qualities stirred Macaulay to yet another reading.

The essayist's private comments reflected the general critical

[6] James Martineau, *Essays, reviews, and addresses* (London: Longmans, Green, and Co., 1891), II, 464.

[7] Hugh Sykes Davies, 'Macaulay's *Marginalia* to Lucretius', in Lucretius, *De Rerum Natura*, translated by R. C. Trevelyan (Cambridge: Cambridge University Press, 1937), p. 279; George Otto Trevelyan, *The life and letters of Lord Macaulay* (New York: Harper and Brothers Publishers, 1876), I, 410.

appraisal of Lucretius – a fine poet, a wretched philosopher. The seventh edition of the *Encyclopaedia Britannica* published in 1842 carried an entry on Lucretius of less than two columns and made no reference to the scientific bearing of his poem. The eighth edition of 1857 did likewise. In 1855, in an earlier essay on Lucretius, W. Y. Sellar declared that

notwithstanding the tribute we pay to the value of many of his scientific observations, and the admiration we accord to his great powers of understanding, it would neither be profitable nor interesting to enter into all the details of a system of physical philosophy, which the subsequent inquiries, not of one or two men in one age, but of centuries and nations, have overthrown, and which by the inadequacy of its materials, its erroneous method, and its ambitious aim, was from its origin doomed to perish, though perhaps even in its decay to animate and fructify a sounder system.

Two years later Matthew Arnold, perceiving in Lucretius a spirit akin to the modern, observed, 'Depression and *ennui*; these are the characteristics stamped on how many of the representative works of modern times! they are also the characteristics stamped on the poem of Lucretius.'[8] Yet Arnold concluded that Lucretius was too melancholy to be considered an adequate interpreter of life in the Roman republic.

Lucretius emerged in his most familiar Victorian textual guise in 1860 when H. A. J. Munro of Trinity College, Cambridge, published a critical edition of *De rerum natura* with a Latin introduction. In 1864 he supplemented the original edition with further commentary and an English translation which was favourably received and remained in print past the middle of the twentieth century.[9] The

---

[8] 'Lucretius', *Encyclopaedia Britannica*, 7th edn (Edinburgh: Adam and Charles Black, 1842), XIII, 589–90; 'Lucretius', *Encyclopaedia Britannica*, 8th edn (Edinburgh: Adam and Charles Black, 1857), XIII, 714–15; W. Y. Sellar, 'Lucretius and the poetic characteristics of his age', in *Oxford essays contributed by members of the university* (London: John W. Parker and Sons, 1855), p. 31; Matthew Arnold, *Essays in criticism: third series* (Boston: The Bull Publishing Co., 1910), p. 71.

[9] Titi Lucreti Cari, *De rerum natura libri sex*, Recognovit H. A. J. Munro (Cambridge: Deighton, Bell, and Co., 1860); Titi Lucreti Cari, *De rerum natura libri sex*, with a translation and notes by H. A. J. Munro (Cambridge: Deighton, Bell, and Co., 1864). See the following reviews: Anon., 'Munro's Lucretius', *Fraser's*, 74 (1866), 443; John Conington, 'Munro's Lucretius', *Edinburgh Review*, 72 (1865), 238–57; Jebb, 'Lucretius'. For an interesting sketch of Munro's personality, consult J. D. Duff, 'Introduction', Lucretius, *On the nature of things*, translated by H. A. J. Munro (London: George Bell & Sons, 1908), pp. v–xii. The Munro translation remained accessible in Whitney J. Oakes, ed., *The Stoic and Epicurean philosophers* (New York: The Modern Library, 1940).

English translation, however, occasioned the same essentially negative comments previously directed toward the work. For example, the young Cambridge classical scholar R. C. Jebb noted,

In modern times the De Rerum Natura is read, not as a treatise, but merely as a poem. In one point of view, indeed, it is a curiosity in the history of thought. No extant work so vigorously embodies the spirit of ancient physical research – the eager scrutiny of Nature's surface without a suspicion of anything beneath, the effort to seize the world-problem at a glance, the utter disregard of experiment. *But the particular dogmas have no interest for the nineteenth century.*[10]

Three years later in 1868 Tennyson indirectly challenged Jebb's final assertion by publishing 'Lucretius' for which he had consulted Munro about the Latin poet's thought and style. While implicitly suggesting subtle parallels between Lucretian materialism and modern atomism, the poem did not portray Lucretius as a precursor of the modern scientist. Nevertheless, for all its ambiguity Tennyson's 'Lucretius' did mark the beginning of a new appreciation for Lucretius and his philosophy.[11]

The year in which the poet laureate related the tale of Lucretius's succumbing to his wife's love potion also witnessed the appearance of the first article linking the ancient writer to contemporary scientific thought. The author was Fleeming Jenkin, a Scottish scientist best remembered for having posed one of the objections to natural selection that genuinely disturbed Darwin and for having had his life recorded in a no longer read biography by Robert Louis Stevenson. Jenkin's essay, 'The atomic theory of Lucretius', published in the *North British Review*, was a careful exploratory discourse to which Lucretian commentators would refer for the rest of the century. Outlining the received view of Lucretius, Jenkin wrote,

Lucretius is often alluded to as an atheistical writer, who held the silly opinion that the universe was the result of a fortuitous concourse of atoms; readers are asked to consider how long letters must be shaken in a bag before a completed annotated edition of Shakespeare could result from the process; and after being reminded how much more complex the universe is than the works of Shakespeare, they are expected to hold Lucretius, with his teachers and his followers, in derision.

[10] Jebb, 'Lucretius', p. 55 (italics added).
[11] Alfred Lord Tennyson, *The poems of Tennyson*, ed. Christopher Ricks (London: Longmans, 1969), 1206–17.

Jenkin countered this opinion by suggesting, 'We may profitably consider what the real tenets of Lucretius were, especially now that men of science are beginning, after a long pause in the inquiry, once more eagerly to attempt some explanation of the ultimate condition of matter.'[12] He thus set the precedent for considering the thought of Lucretius in relation to modern ideas and scientific theory and for drawing parallels between the work of an ancient poet and the endeavours of contemporary scientists.

Jenkin concentrated on Lucretius's basic propositions that nothing can come from nothing, that the universe is orderly, and that atoms alone are the constituent elements of nature. On these topics the Latin poet and modern man of science stood in close agreement. Jenkin argued,

We shall find that almost all the propositions which refer simply to the constitution of matter are worthy of the highest admiration, as either certainly true, or as foreshadowing in a remarkable way doctrines since held by most eminent naturalists. Confine the following statements to matter as we can observe it, to physical science in fact, and they form a basis which even now would require but little modification to be acceptable to a modern student of physics.

At no point, however, did Jenkin contend that modern theory and Lucretian speculation were identical. He simply maintained that the poet, along with Democritus and Epicurus, had begun speculation that had ultimately led to 'a mechanical theory by which the phenomena of inorganic matter can be mathematically deduced from the motion of materials endowed with a few simple properties'. Moreover, he cautiously observed that the readers of Thomson and Clerk Maxwell 'will also perceive the vast difference between the old hazy speculations and the endeavours of modern science'.[13]

So far as reasoned discussion of the relationship between Lucretius and modern science was concerned, Jenkin's article should have been both the beginning and the end of the matter. Instead, however, of closing the subject, this essay became the foundation for all later attempts to equate classical and modern atomism to the detriment and condemnation of the latter. That such became the

---

[12] Jenkin, 'The atomic theory of Lucretius', p. 211; see also Peter J. Vorzimmer, *Charles Darwin: the years of controversy, The Origin of Species and its critics, 1859–1882* (Philadelphia: Temple University Press, 1970), pp. 90–126, 148–57; Robert Louis Stevenson, *Memoir of Fleeming Jenkin* (New York: Charles Scribner's Sons, 1887).

[13] Jenkin, 'The atomic theory of Lucretius', pp. 227, 242.

case was the unwitting fault of another, very distinguished man of science.

Professor John Tyndall's Belfast Address of 1874 thrust Lucretius into the mainstream of contemporary polemics over science, religion, and philosophy and sent the professor's critics back to Jenkin's essay. Tyndall was a highly regarded physicist, the successor to Faraday at the Royal Institution, a member of the X-Club and of the Metaphysical Society, and a gifted expositor of scientific theory to non-professional audiences.[14] Since 1868 he had delivered a series of semi-popular papers on what he called 'scientific materialism' but what would today be termed psychological materialism. He was also a well-known critic of contemporary theology and clericalism and one of the participants in the debate over the efficacy of prayer.

In 1874 as president of the British Association for the Advancement of Science Tyndall delivered the traditional presidential address. He broke, however, with tradition by employing the address to advocate his own naturalistic view of the development of scientific thought rather than to review the developments of the past year. Whereas British Association presidents had generally presented religion and science as necessarily compatible, Tyndall spoke with particular hostility about the role of religion and religious institutions as hindrances to the development of modern science. During the previous decade as the debate over Darwinism had divided the British scientific community, some British Association presidents had mildly criticized religion as it related to scientific endeavour. Tyndall for his part declared what amounted to all out war on theology. His long, garrulous speech shook contemporaries in a manner almost incomprehensible today and set off a controversy that did not subside for several years.[15] One feature of that controversy was the paradoxical emergence of Lucretius as an ally of religion against contemporary naturalism.

In the course of the address, Tyndall traced the rise of the atomic hypothesis from the Greeks to Spencer, Thomson, and Clerk Maxwell. In the process Lucretius had become a point of special focus.

[14] W. H. Brock, N. D. McMillan, and R. C. Mollan, eds., *John Tyndall: essays on a natural philosopher* (Dublin: Royal Dublin Society, 1981).
[15] A. S. Eve and C. H. Creasy, *Life and work of John Tyndall* (London: Macmillan and Co., Ltd, 1945), pp. 179–94; Philip H. Gray, 'The problem of free will in a scientific universe: René Descartes to John Tyndall', *The Journal of General Psychology*, 80 (1969), 57–72; Tyndall, *Fragments*, II, 135–201; Ruth Barton, 'J. Tyndall, pantheist: a rereading of the Belfast address', *Osiris*, 2nd ser., 3, (1987) 111–34.

Though not the originator of classical materialism, Lucretius gave posterity the best and most eloquent explication of the theory. Tyndall declared that Lucretius had possessed 'strong scientific imagination'. He especially praised the poet's 'destruction of superstition'.[16] Moreover, in the central portion of the address Tyndall included an imaginary dialogue between Bishop Butler and a latterday disciple of Lucretius. By the conclusion of the speech, Lucretius appeared to be the upholder of true science in the ancient world, a noble enemy of superstition, and a pioneer in the struggle to liberate science from the ideals, opinions, cosmology, and institutions of religion and theology.

From the rostrum of the respected British Association John Tyndall had associated modern scientific theory with classical materialism and thus made it all too easy for his opponents to compare him and his goals with Lucretius. Munro's contention that Lucretius's 'purpose in writing is not to gratify scientific curiosity, but to free men from the two great obstacles to happiness and tranquility of mind, fear of the gods and fear of death' might also have served as an apt description of Tyndall's intention in the Belfast Address.[17] He had directly related modern science and its practitioners' desire to understand the world naturalistically and to improve the standard of living to the ancient materialist and his desire to rid the world of superstitions and apprehensions that arose from pagan religion. The voice of the former echoed the voice of the latter. Tyndall thus prepared the ground for criticism of modern naturalistic thought via critiques of classical materialism. The defenders of religion could suddenly reap all the polemical advantages of confronting materialistic opponents.

Religious and idealist writers were not slow to perceive and to seize upon Tyndall's rhetorical blunder. In 1874 James Martineau wrote of 'the *new* "book of Genesis", which resorts to Lucretius for its beginnings'. The next year John Veitch of the University of Glasgow wrote, 'What Lucretius put, on imperfect grounds certainly, in regard to the origin and the end of the sensible world, modern science, according to its present knowledge or assumptions, generally approves.' Robert Flint, another Scottish writer, declared, 'The atomic materialism of the present day is still substantially the

---

[16] Tyndall, *Fragments*, II, 144, 142.
[17] T. Lucreti Cari, *De rerum natura libri sex*, with notes and a translation by H. A. J. Munro, 4th edn, finally revised (London: G. Bell and Sons., Ltd, 1928), II, 35.

materialism which Epicurus and Lucretius propounded.' John Tulloch, the Principal of St Andrews, carried these assertions still further
when he urged,

It may surely be said that the course of materialistic thought shows little
sign of originality. With all the commotion it again makes in our day, it is
where it was, standing by the names of Democritus, Epicurus, and
Lucretius. It vaunts itself of new and higher methods of investigation, but
its theories are not a whit more valid and satisfactory than they were in
former centuries; and the powerful language of Lucretius, to which the pen
of Tyndall naturally reverts, is probably to this day their best and most
felicitous expression.[18]

Lucretius thus became a pawn in the struggle for cultural domination between the men of science and the men of religion and
idealism. The latter not only captured Lucretius from Tyndall but
also attempted to incorporate him as a bishop in their own forces.

Three authors bore the primary responsibility for the new religious acclaim afforded to Lucretius. In 1875 John Veitch published
a small volume entitled *Lucretius and the atomic theory*. W. H. Mallock,
the irrepressible gadfly of modern thought, presented his considered
opinions to the public in *Lucretius* during 1878. The most prolific and
persistent of the Lucretian commentators was John Masson, a
lecturer in classics at the Edinburgh Provincial College. Commencing in 1875 Masson wrote several articles on the poet. These as well
as some new material appeared in 1883 as *The atomic theory of Lucretius
contrasted with modern doctrines of atoms and evolution*. In 1907 Masson
carried his cause into the new century with *Lucretius: Epicurean and
poet* which long remained cited in scholarly works on Lucretius and
Epicureanism.[19] Other discussions of Lucretius were primarily
derivations from or reactions to these commentaries.

The Lucretian commentators pursued a simple but ingenious
strategy. Supported by Tyndall's address, they contended that

[18] James Martineau, *Modern materialism in its relations to religion and theology* (New York: G. P.
Putnam's Sons, 1877), p. 19; Veitch, *Lucretius and the atomic theory*, pp. 34–5; Robert Flint,
Anti-theistic theories (Edinburgh and London: W. Blackwood and Sons, 1879), pp. 57; John
Tulloch, *Modern theories in philosophy and religion* (Edinburgh and London: W. Blackwood and
Sons, 1884), pp. 143–4.
[19] The following twentieth-century works list Masson's second book in their bibliographies:
Cyril Bailey, *The Greek Atomists and Epicurus* (New York: Russell & Russell, 1964), p. 596;
R. D. Hicks, *Stoic and Epicurean* (New York: Russell & Russell, 1962), p. 401; *The Oxford
classical dictionary*, ed. H. H. Scullard and N. G. L. Hammond, 2nd edn (Oxford: Oxford
University Press, 1970), p. 624; E. E. Sikes, *Lucretius: poet and philospher* (Cambridge:
Cambridge University Press, 1936).

Lucretius had anticipated the doctrines espoused by modern scientists. They then argued that the Lucretian theories and philosophy were either inadequate or incorrect and that by direct implication so were the similar ideas set forth by Huxley, Tyndall, Spencer, and Clifford. Finally, they suggested that Lucretius's critique of religion had been appropriate and necessary for the development of pure religion. His particular arguments, however, as resurrected by Huxley, Tyndall, and others from the camp of scientific naturalism had in the course of two millennia become inapplicable and invalid. Therefore the anti-religious arguments of the scientific publicists were both irrelevant and anachronistic.

Pursuit of this strategy required a subtle but crucial sleight of hand in regard to the purposes and intellectual priorities of both Lucretius and the scientific popularizers. It was essential that Lucretius appear to be a man of science who happened to employ scientific theory against religion and that the scientific publicists appear to be primarily enemies of religion who employed archaic science against modern faith. This meant that Lucretius must be considered first and foremost as a scientific writer rather than a poet. Mallock saw little true poetry in *De rerum natura*. Rather, he explained,

We must be careful ... not to read our own sentiments into Lucretius; nor to think that, though he gives us all the pictures of storm, and cloud, and sunshine, of sea and valley, as accurately, and with as much care, as a modern poet might, that he was like a modern poet in his feeling about them. The case is quite otherwise. In his description of nature, Lucretius is a utilitarian, not a sentimentalist. His descriptions are not pictures to be looked at for themselves; they are diagrams to illustrate the text of his scientific discourses.

Attempting to reverse the opinions of the first half of the century, Mallock argued, 'Primarily, and before all things, the work is a scientific treatise – as strictly scientific (at least in the author's intention) as a modern treatise on optics, or geology, or the origin of species; and except as far as metre goes, it has in many places as little poetry as these have.' For Mallock and the others, Lucretius was a scientist first and a poet second. The scientific theory instead of the poetry in *De rerum natura* constituted the 'foundation of its special interest for ourselves'. Rather than to produce a masterpiece of creative imagination, the 'great aim' of Lucretius had been 'to explain facts, and to show convincingly that his explanations are the true ones'.[20]

Having established Lucretius as a man of science, Mallock and his fellow writers turned their attention to the relationship of this master of classical science to contemporary Victorian thought. Comparison of Lucretius and modern scientific writers provided a means for criticizing the latter. Key to the whole procedure was the assumption made plausible by their own pronouncements that the scientific publicists were philosophical materialists. As such, they could be attacked for espousing a faulty and inadequate philosophy, for illicitly claiming originality for their ideas, and for misunderstanding the nature of modern religion.

John Veitch led the attack on the faulty philosophy common to both Lucretius and his latter-day followers. Convinced that atomists old and new had confused abstraction with reality, Veitch argued, 'The atomic position as put in ancient and in modern times seems to me to be simply the result of a vulgar or irreflective realism.' He complained that the atoms of the philosopher or of the scientist speaking as philosopher were not the atoms of the chemist in the laboratory. The latter employed the concept for a practical purpose, but the atomic theory could provide no adequate foundation for a speculative philosophy. Veitch explained, 'The truth is that people have supposed that they were constructing an atomic theory of the world, when they were really dealing only with atoms in the abstract, fixing their weight, quantity, shape, as things to be considered in certain mutual relations, without raising any questions as to how they got combined.' Whether espoused in the verse of Lucretius or the prose of Tyndall, the atomic theory illicitly transferred the 'wholly relative conception of sensible reality to an absolute sphere, or one in which we cease to be and to know'.[21] Such reasoning might account for structure and order, but not for the achievement of structure and order.

John Masson eagerly compared Lucretius's atomism with W. K. Clifford's concept of mind-stuff, explaining, 'The two doctrines illuminate each other.' The mutual illumination exposed the inadequate materialism common to both authors: '"The mind cannot come into being", he [Lucretius] says, "without the body, nor can it exist far from sinews and blood". Thus Lucretius seems to anticipate

[20] Mallock, *Lucretius*, pp. 148–89, 3, 4.
[21] Veitch, *Lucretius and the atomic theory*, pp. 85, 66–7, 84.

Clifford. Because he can find no trace of a nervous system in any of the elements, he decides that it is not possible for Intelligence to dwell in any of them.'[22] Clifford, according to Masson, had merely restated Lucretius's materialistic proposition without contributing anything further to the solution of problems intrinsic to it.

The Scottish classicist derived special pleasure from the failure of both Lucretius and Clifford to account for free will. This problem clearly illustrated the affinity between the Lucretian concept of Declination and Clifford's belief in the independence of the mind-stuff atoms. Masson contended,

Professor Clifford, in order to explain the evolution of Mind from atoms, asserts that every atom of matter corresponds to an atom of Mind-Stuff – that is, of something analogous to Mind. He thus builds up Mind out of a multitude of mind-atoms – that is to say, of elementary feelings which can exist by themselves as 'individuals', *simplicitate*, as much as can the Lucretian atoms, but which are almost as small in comparison with the consciousness of any one human being as Lucretius's atoms are in comparison with a human body. Lucretius, again, who believes in Free-will, can only explain it by assigning Free-will to the atoms. The reasoning of both, starting from a similar standpoint, is substantially the same, and the two theories of 'Mind-Stuff' and of Atomic Declination deserve to be placed side by side.

Both theories illustrated, 'Materialism confessing its own weakness to account, unaided, for the origin of Mind'.[23] So long as Clifford offered no improvement to classical materialism, his thought was inadequate and incomplete and should be dismissed.

To undermine the scientific publicists' claims to novelty and originality, Veitch, Mallock, and Masson portrayed Lucretius as the precursor of major theories associated with nineteenth-century science. Obviously, he had anticipated the atomic theory. Like Jenkin in 1868, they saw the proposition that nothing comes from nothing as a succinct statement of the law of the conservation of energy. Veitch and Masson also considered Lucretius's discussion of the dissolution of all structures formed by atoms and his concept of a principle of decay as clearly foreshadowing the second law of thermodynamics.[24]

The most belaboured of their contentions was that Lucretius had anticipated Darwin. Here they were clearly muddled, but perhaps

[22] Masson, *The atomic theory*, pp. 132–3, 148.
[23] Masson, *Lucretius*, p. 234. See also John Masson, 'Lucretius' argument for free will'.
[24] Masson, *The atomic theory*, pp. 30–1; Veitch, *Lucretius and the atomic theory*, pp. 32–3.

no more so than others who equated the concept of evolution with the Darwinian mechanism of natural selection. To substantiate this claim Mallock and Masson appealed to Book v of *De rerum natura* in which Lucretius had described the life cycles of the organic world. Mallock argues that the poet both had and had not anticipated Darwin. Lucretius surely had grasped the idea of the survival of the fittest, but he had not understood that all species could descend from some original specie via natural selection. Mallock cryptically concluded, 'It will thus be seen that the Darwinian theory is an advance on, and differs from, the Lucretian mainly and essentially in this – the way in which the variety is produced which is the subject of the selecting process common to both systems.'[25] There can be little doubt that Mallock, a quite well-read and knowledgeable writer, knew he was overstating his case.

On the other hand, Masson was perhaps honestly naive in supposing that Lucretius had understood the Darwinian view of nature. He stressed Lucretius's portrayal of struggle in nature and argued,

When we review Lucretius's explanation of the origin and history of life upon the earth, we see that it is based on a clear perception of Darwin's doctrine, that in the organic world none but the fittest continue to exist because these alone have been able to perpetuate themselves. Beyond question, Lucretius had a firm grasp of this central doctrine of Darwinism.

A few lines later Masson retreated from so firm a commitment and suggested, 'It is certain that his philosophy implies Evolution; and he may fairly be taken to support it, though, of course, his conception of such a process must have been the vaguest kind, speaking from a modern stand-point.' Despite this uncertainty and confusion, H. F. Osborn, the early historian of evolution, sustained Masson and Mallock by including Lucretius within the evolutionary tradition.[26]

Mallock and Masson pointed out the theoretical similarities between Lucretius and modern scientists not only to disparage the novelty and originality of the latter, but also to illustrate their similar use of science as a weapon against religion. Mallock acknowledged that much of Lucretius's theory was 'of course completely valueless' and in many respects different from modern science. Yet there remained a 'strange likeness to our modern teaching that runs

---

[25] Mallock, *Lucretius*, p. 50.
[26] Ibid., pp. 166, 170; Henry Fairfield Osborn, *From the Greeks to Darwin*, 2nd edn (New York: Charles Scribner's Sons, 1929), pp. 95–7.

through all this difference'. The strange likeness consisted of the strong anti-religious bias arising from their common materialism. Mallock declared,

Couched under other forms, arrived at by other courses, the first principles of Lucretius, and many of his last conclusions, are the same, or all but the same, as those which are now startling the world as new revelations – revelations so new and so startling that we can as yet only half accept them. In the first place, his mission and his attitude, to view the matter broadly, are entirely analogous to those of our modern physicists. He comes forward just as they do, as the champion of natural science, claiming that by it, and by it alone, we are to understand man's life, and to explain the universe. It is his doctrine, just as it is theirs, that no event can occur either in the outer world about us, or in the inner world of our own consciousness, that is not connected with some material change, and it is not conceivably explicable in terms of matter. And he makes this claim for science, just as it is made now, against all theology and against all religion. To these he ascribes, just as is done by some modern thinkers, a large part of the ills men suffer from. To a certain extent, too, he professes the belief, so often now held out to us, that once religion, with its blighting influence, is exterminated, there are prospects of 'a better and above all, a happier state of existence', for the human race. Indeed, so like is much of his general language to what we hear continually in our day, so inspired does it seem to be with just the same animus, that we might at times almost fancy he was Professor Tyndall, or one of the two Mills, confuting the arguments of Paley or of Butler, or deriding the narratives of the book of Genesis.[27]

Here was the foundation for the most ingenious of the traps prepared by the Lucretian commentators.

That Lucretius should have believed materialism would undermine the paganism and superstition of his day was both understandable and laudable. The concept denoted a daring mind and a spirit zealous for pure religion. That modern authors should pursue the same line of argument, however, suggested they were interested in abolishing a religion that thanks to Lucretius and others had become purified. Lucretius had been honest and even noble in his endeavour; the moderns were dishonest, ignoble, and happily anachronistic in theirs.

Commencing with Jenkin's essay of 1868, the Lucretian commentators emphasized that the Roman poet had struggled against the crudities of paganism rather than against religion generally. Jenkin had been very precise on this point, observing,

[27] Mallock, *Lucretius*, pp. 4, 5, 5–6.

Let us not be too indignant at this scornful rejection of divine agency. Divinity to him meant either the old Pagan gods or the pale abstract idea of a First Cause, which explained nothing, being but one form of statement that something was left to be explained. What wonder that he rejected both? We may admire those old philosophers who could clothe divinity with noble attributes, and find in their hearts the motive for their faith, but we need not therefore despise those who, smitten with the great truth that nature's laws are constant, fancied that in this consistency they saw the proof that nature's laws are self-existent.[28]

Lucretius deserved no rebuke for rejecting the gods when the only concept of God at his disposal was incompatible with the idea of the uniformity of nature.

A writer who had combated paganism must rank as one of the religious and cultural heroes who had prepared men for the purer and higher faith of rational Christianity. Lucretius's gods were wholly different from the God of moderately liberal nineteenth-century Christians. As Mallock explained,

The crude and puerile theology with which he had to combat, it was easy enough to prove a useless factor in any theory of the conduct or existence of life. Starting with his empty space and atoms, as the raw materials of everything, he could show easily enough that no such gods as the world, he knew, believed in, could be of any assistance in explaining how the universe was manufactured. But the God which modern science encounters, and whose aid it is endeavouring to dispense with, is a very different God from these; He is a God to whom time and space are nothing, and who is beyond the atoms themselves, making them what they are, and being the one cause of their existence.[29]

Against the modern Christian God of law and immanence the modern Lucretian materialistic arguments were useless. Tyndall, Huxley, Clifford, and other scientific publicists pursued a vendetta against a capricious God in which modern Christians no longer believed. Their critique of Christianity was therefore anachronistic and irrelevant.

Mallock contended that in *De rerum natura* one could view the struggle of an infant science and an infant religion.[30] Since the time of Lucretius religion had matured and become based on the facts of subjective human consciousness. The scientific publicists in their understanding of religion, however, remained in their infantile

---

[28] Jenkin, 'The atomic theory of Lucretius', p. 228.
[29] Mallock, *Lucretius*, p. 165.
[30] Ibid., pp. 6–7.

stage. Confronted with the modern religion of feeling and subjective consciousness, modern naturalistic or materialistic writers were helpless. They could only maintain their offensive position by constructing a religious straw man that bore little or no resemblance to modern Christianity.

As might be expected, John Masson carried the argument even further. In Lucretius he discerned 'a deep sincerity of emotion and a strange directness of utterance which speaks a human spirit that is true, and at once compels our sympathy'. The poet had done 'good service to religion' by lifting men to a higher conception of the divine. He noted, 'How vividly do we realize the atmosphere of fear, the cramped and darkened lives which false religion ever engenders! And our deepest heart assents to his protest that the soul of man is not to be scared nor coerced by mere force, however vast.' Moreover, Masson discovered in *De rerum natura* teachings that had prepared the way for and that were complementary to those of Christ:

There would seem, at first, something utterly irreconcilable between Lucretius with his daring Naturalism and that other Teacher, the one exhorting us to 'consider the lilies', how in the beauty of their Divine idea they prompt humility and trust, while the other is never done with repeating, *Considerat opera atomorum.* But is the antagonism so complete as it would appear? Is there not a common note in Lucretius's deep compassion for his brothers 'wandering all astray as they seek for the path of life'? And yet again, in the earnestness with which he bids us 'each man lay aside his own affairs, and set his heart first of all to learn the nature of things'? Often and passionately as Lucretius insists that priestcraft and ritual are not religion, and fear is not reverence, do we not find the very same warnings reiterated in the Four Gospels as earnestly and as often, though the meaning is deeper?[31]

Masson thus transformed Lucretius into a pagan John the Baptist preparing the way for the true Lord and pure religion. In this respect he resembled other Victorian classical commentators who saw various aspects of Roman culture as providentially preparatory of the Christian dispensation.

The high, reverential, moral, and spiritual purposes that Masson ascribed to Lucretius naturally contrasted most unfavourably with the anti-religious zeal of the nineteenth-century scientific popularizers. He noted, 'There is nothing in Lucretius even approaching the

---

[31] Masson, *Lucretius*, p. xiii; Masson, *The atomic theory*, p. 198; Masson, *Lucretius*, pp. xxiii–xxiv, xxx–xxxi.

concentrated bitterness with which Clifford regards every kind and degree of religious belief'.[32] The later writers knowingly committed errors that Lucretius had committed from ignorance. For example, Clerk Maxwell had suggested that the uniformity of atoms bespoke a material world compatible with and perhaps even requiring the effective presence of a deity. Lucretius could not have known this theory.[33] However, John Tyndall was acquainted with it and still persisted in reading God out of the physical universe. Lucretius could be forgiven his error, but such generosity could not be extended to Tyndall.

Sellar's *Britannica* article and introductions to secondary school textbooks, such as that of J. D. Duff written in 1888, bear witness to the success of the Lucretian commentators.[34] Of more significance was the response of the scientific writers. They could not ignore the reinterpretation of Lucretius since one of their own spokesmen had allowed it to come about. Yet they faced the difficult task of proving a negative. Moreover, they had no intention of surrendering Lucretius to the defenders of religion and traditional thought.

While continuing to include Lucretius as a major figure in the naturalistic tradition, the scientific writers repudiated the idea that his theories were scientific. W. K. Clifford had immediately perceived the polemical advantage Tyndall had given his opponents in the Belfast Address. Clifford had hastened to explain that no one could expect to understand or to criticize modern atomism by reading *De rerum natura*. He argued, 'The difference between the two is mainly this: the atomic theory of Democritus was a guess, and no more than a guess . . . On the contrary the view of the constitution of matter which is held by scientific men in the present day is not a guess at all.'[35] The confusion, however, persisted, exacerbated by the professional debates over the nature and structure of the atom.[36]

In 1875, the classicist, historian, essayist, and former Christian, J. A. Symonds, also sought to set Lucretius into a better perspective. He admitted the Latin poet had opposed teleology and acknow-

[32] Masson, *The atomic theory*, p. 175.
[33] Ibid., p. 2.
[34] J. D. Duff, 'Introduction', (1888) in T. Lucreti Cari, *De rerum natura: liber quintus*, ed. J. D. Duff (Cambridge: Cambridge University Press, 1909), pp. ix–xxx.
[35] Clifford, *Lectures and essays*, 1, 224–5.
[36] W. H. Brock and D. M. Knight, 'The atomic debates: "memorable and interesting evenings in the life of the chemical society" ', *Isis*, 61 (1965), 5–25; George M. Fleck, 'Atomism in late nineteenth-century physical chemistry', *Journal of the History of Ideas*, 24 (1963), 106–14; D. M. Knight, *Atoms and elements* (London: Hutchinson and Co., Ltd, 1967).

ledged that he might even have foreshadowed the ideas of universal dissolution and evolution. Nevertheless, Symonds argued,

To press these points, and to neglect the gap which separates Lucretius from thinkers fortified by the discoveries of modern chemistry, astronomy, physiology, and so forth, would be childish. All we can do is to point to the fact that the circumambient atmosphere of human ignorance, with reference to the main matters of speculation, remains undissipated. The mass of experience acquired since the age of Lucretius is enormous, and is infinitely valuable; while our power of tabulating, methodizing, and extending the sphere of experimental knowledge seems to be unlimited. Only ontological deductions, whether negative or affirmative, remain pretty much where they were.[37]

But the matter would not rest as Masson and Mallock took up the Lucretian cudgels.

During the next few years other naturalistic writers continued to reply, if only obliquely, to the Lucretian commentators. In 1882 Alfred Benn, later the historian of nineteenth-century rationalism, observed in the *Westminster Review* that Epicurus and Lucretius had recently become as much overestimated as they had previously been underestimated. He spurned the attempts to portray Lucretius as the forerunner of nineteenth-century scientific achievement. He contended, 'What has been singled out as an anticipation of the Darwinian theory was only one application of a very comprehensive method for eliminating design from the universe.' Moreover, he continued,

When Lucretius speaks of *foedera Naturae*, he means, not what we understand by laws of Nature – that is, uniformities of causation underlying all phenomenal differences, to understand which is an exaltation of human dignity through the added power of prevision and control which it bestows – but rather the limiting possibilities of existence, the barriers against which human hopes and aspirations dash themselves in vain – an objective logic which guards us against fallacies rather than enables us to arrive at positive conclusions.

Epicurus and Lucretius had in reality never been interested in science for its own sake or for the sake of practical application. 'Epicurus, on the contrary,' Benn explained, 'declares that physics would not be worth attending to if the mind could be set free from religious terror in any other manner'.[38]

37 Symonds, 'Lucretius', 60.
38 Benn, 'Epicurus and Lucretius', pp. 321, 333, 302.

In 1887 Huxley felt called upon to reiterate the difference between the classical atomic theories and those of the nineteenth century. He wrote,

In antiquity, they meant little more than vague speculation; at the present day, they indicate definite physical conceptions, susceptible of mathematical treatment, and giving rise to innumerable deductions, the value of which can be experimentally tested. The old notions produced little more than floods of dialectics; the new are powerful aids toward the increase of solid knowledge.

Huxley's own career in a sense belied his arguments. The modern theories, while producing solid practical results, had also produced as much polemical dialectic as had those of the classical speculators. Huxley's essays and those of Clifford and Tyndall demonstrated that modern scientific writers were as eager to deduce social, philosophical, or religious conclusions from theories of matter and organic evolution as had been Lucretius. Indeed, in their most familiar guise as platform or periodical debaters, they more nearly resembled Lucretius than scientific investigators. Samuel Butler recognized the ambiguity of their position when he confided to his notebook, 'Huxley and Co. are always abusing me for being a literary man – and yet they are always trying to be literary men themselves.'[39]

The final postscripts to the Victorian commentaries on Lucretius appeared in the twentieth century. In 1910 the editors of the eleventh edition of the *Encyclopaedia Britannica* retained Sellar's article but revised it so as to omit his comments on the scientific relevance of Lucretius. Only in 1928, however, was a complete repudiation of the late Victorian view point advanced. In the fourth and finally revised edition of Munro's Lucretius, E. N. Da C. Andrade, a fellow of University College London, contributed a new introductory essay entitled 'The scientific significance of Lucretius'. For Andrade that significance was very small. He quoted a letter from Lord Kelvin in which the great Victorian physicist reported, 'I have been reading Lucretius much helped by Munro's translation, and trying hard on my own account to make something out of the clash of atoms, but with little success.' Andrade for his part cautioned the student of Lucretius,

Care must be taken to avoid the easy and sensational feat of reading into Lucretius definite opinions in matters of detail which we have reached since

---

[39] Huxley, *Collected essays*, 1, 80; Samuel Butler, *Further extracts from the notebooks of Samuel Butler*, ed. A. T. Bartholomew (London: Jonathan Cape, 1934), p. 125.

his time, but which he cannot possibly have held. His atoms, born of irreligious enthusiasm and philosophical necessity, cannot possibly have seemed to him what our children of experiment are to us.

The most telling reason cited by Andrade for the irrelevance of Lucretius to modern science was the turn of the century modifications in the atomic theory espoused by Tyndall and his contemporaries, 'We have recently had to modify the indestructibility which the nineteenth century claimed for atoms.'[40] It was the new physics of the twentieth century rather than any new critical reading of the poet himself that brought to a close the scientific career of Lucretius.

[40] W. Y. Sellar, 'Lucretius', *Encyclopaedia Britannica*, 11th edn (New York: Cambridge University Press, 1911), XVII, 107–9; E. N. Da C. Andrade, 'The scientific significance of Lucretius', in T. Lucreti Cari, *De rerum natura libri sex*, 4th edn (1928), II, viii, viii–ix, xxii.

CHAPTER 11

Virgil in Victorian classical contexts

To explore Victorian classicism in its several manifestations is in a sense to pass through a wing of a very old house which virtually all the present generation have forgotten and perhaps never even visited but where once the entire family of another era gathered, where children were reared and where they played, and where earlier members of the family grew into intellectual maturity and adulthood. It is a part of the house that has stood long abandoned though not dismantled as other wings were added and other children came of age. Yet neither the architectural lines of the new structure nor the character of the later children inhabiting it would be the same without those earlier structures or the experiences that occurred in the now-uninhabited corridors. In that regard, to study Victorian classicism is to attempt to deal with Victorian culture on its own terms. It is to consider a topic much of which is today irrelevant but which held a centrality for the intellectual experience of the Victorian educated elites that is difficult for scholars at the end of the twentieth century even to begin to comprehend.

The Victorians inherited the documents, plastic remains, and architectural ruins of antiquity. They also inherited previous interpretations and uses of those ancient materials. But Victorian writers, scholars, commentators, and artists forged the classical tradition for themselves as they came to understand it and to use it in their own cultural contexts. What A. C. Bradley wrote in 1881 about ancient myths in modern poetry applied to the whole spectrum of Victorian appropriations of antiquity: 'The problem is to reshape the material they give us, that it may express ideas, feelings, experiences interest-

Portions of this essay from *Browning Institute Studies*, 10 (1982), 1–14, and from G. Clarke, ed., *Rediscovering hellenism: the hellenic inheritance and the English imagination* (Cambridge: Cambridge University Press, 1989), pp. 61–81. With permission of the journal and of Cambridge University Press.

ing to us, in a form natural and poetically attractive to us.' Like the framers of the canon of aesthetic taste governing the appreciation of ancient sculpture, analysed by Francis Haskell and Nicholas Penny in *Taste and the antique*, the Victorians transformed the ancient world and its remains into a living tradition that spoke to themselves and through which they could speak to and argue with each other.[1] The now apparently staid and static world of Victorian classicism is one that *came into being*. It was not always there. It was constructed and reconstructed throughout the nineteenth century.

I

The Victorians were concerned with antiquity not because it was interesting in and of itself, but because their modern cultural structures rendered commentary about the ancient world useful and relevant. The Victorian debates over classical issues occurred in an institutional context in which the classics lay at the core. The undergraduate curriculum at the two ancient English universities as well as the Scottish centred on training in the classics. The cultural influence of these curricular structures worked in two directions. The language requirements in Greek and Latin for admission to Oxford and Cambridge meant that the secondary schools intending to send students to the universities concentrated their training on the ancient languages. Success in learning the languages led to admission to the universities where the student received further education in the classics. This training in turn served students after their university years because from mid-century onward the civil service examinations that led to government positions favoured persons accomplished in Greek and Latin.[2]

Not only did the curricular requirements and structures of the universities encourage pursuit of classical study, but the increasingly public orientation of the universities provided an important context for consideration of antiquity. Graduates of Oxford and Cambridge,

---

[1] Andrew Cecil Bradley, 'Old mythology in modern poetry', *Macmillan's Magazine*, 44 (1881), 30; Francis Haskell and Nicholas Penny, *Taste and the antique* (New Haven: Yale University Press, 1981).

[2] 'Memorandum of the council of the Society for the Promotion of Hellenic Studies on the place of Greek in education', *Journal of Hellenic Studies* 36 (1916), lxix–lxxii; J. R. De S. Honey, *Tom Brown's universe: the development of the English public school in the nineteenth century* (London: Millington, 1977), pp. 8–9, 128–34; James Bowen, 'Education, ideology and the ruling class: hellenism and English public schools in the nineteenth century', Clarke, ed., *Rediscovering hellenism*, pp. 161–86.

whether through the civil service or other career paths, were expected to assume significant positions in the religious, political, administrative, and intellectual life of the nation. These people and those whom they wished to address and influence within the social and political elite were through their common educational background familiar in no small degree with the classical world. As John Grote, the Cambridge philosopher, observed in 1856,

Classical study ... is a point of intellectual sympathy among men over a considerable surface of the world, for those who have forgotten their actual Greek and Latin bear still generally with them many traces of its influence, and in fact it is this which, more than anything, makes them, in common parlance, educated men. That any one subject should be thus extensively cultivated, so as to make such sympathy possible, is a most happy circumstance, supposing it simply historical and accidental. The destruction or disuse of it will destroy one bond of intellectual communion among civilized men, and will be, in this respect, a step not of improvement. And though studies more definitely useful might succeed it, there is an utility lost, and one which will hardly be considered trifling.

What Grote termed the 'bond of intellectual communion among civilized men' allowed the classics to provide a frame of common cultural reference for discussion and debate among the British elite.[3] This structure meant that examination of issues from antiquity by public figures could in a more or less socially exclusive manner explore potentially disruptive or subversive modern topics carefully concealed in the garb of the ancients. To the extent that interpretations about modern topics could be encased in the discourse of classical scholarship and then assigned in the universities, publications about topics from antiquity could influence future public leaders.

Professional Victorian classical scholars regarded their chief task as the establishment of authentic Greek and Latin texts, with the writing of interpretive studies or essays very much a secondary task in their view. Until the last quarter of the nineteenth century the vast majority of writers publishing the major interpretive classical studies and essays were amateur scholars whose personal interest in the classics was subservient to another occupation, professional calling, or self-determined social or political goal. The significance of amateurism upon Victorian classicism in the endeavour of interpre-

---

[3] John Grote, 'Old studies and new', in *Cambridge essays: 1856* (London: J. W. Parker and Sons, 1856), p. 114.

tation and commentary and the orientation of such amateur scholars toward public life can hardly be overestimated. Between 1784 and 1856 the authors of the three major English histories of Greece were William Mitford, MP and country squire, Connop Thirlwall, Cambridge clergyman scholar and later bishop and active member of the House of Lords, and George Grote, City of London banker and radical MP. Their concern with Greek history arose from what they regarded as its applicability to British political and intellectual life as they understood it from their particular political perspectives. The small amount of Roman history written during the Victorian period also frequently came from the pens of amateur scholars, such as Charles Merivale. The person who composed more Homeric commentary than any other British author of the century was William Gladstone, who wrote in the quite explicit hope of making Oxford political and religious education relevant to the modern age. Until the last quarter of the century all the major commentators on Greek art were either practising sculptors or men of letters, such as John Ruskin and Walter Pater. Virtually all the explication and criticism of Greek philosophy came from George Grote or Anglican churchmen. Matthew Arnold, the writer who enshrined the most influential concept of Hellenism in the English language was a school inspector. All of these amateur authors and scholars in one way or another wanted to influence the opinions and taste of the British educated elites, and they believed they could do so by addressing that public through books and essays on the classics.

This social and educational context of Victorian classical study meant that the remains of the ancient world did not stand as pristine monuments receiving disinterested or unengaged observation, analysis, or admiration. Victorian commentary on the ancient world rather tended to bend with and conform itself to various contemporary shifts of value and cultural concern. The ancient cultures resembled plants the contours of which responded to shifts in the particular lights of interpretation cast upon them. In that regard Victorian writers virtually never approached ancient civilizations in a naive or disinterested manner. They brought to them polemical expectations and exceedingly present-minded historical or philosophical frameworks for interpreting ancient peoples. They rarely left the ancients to speak for themselves. Modern non-classical intellectual concepts and orientations consistently provided the primary context for the Victorian consideration of the classics and in doing so ironically made the discussion of the ancient world vitally relevant, intellectually dynamic, and potentially subversive. Though a persistent presence in the intellectual life of the century, Victorian classicism was not an island of calm in the midst of a turbulent cultural sea. It more nearly resembled a whirling eddy driven by various cross currents and unexpected winds.

A topic from antiquity genuinely engaged Victorian writers and spurred public controversy only if it could be made relevant to a contemporary concern. Usually one of three reasons accounted for this perception of relevance. First, the classical subject or question might have a rather straightforward direct polemical application. What appeared to be clear-cut parallels fostered discussion and debate as commentators appropriated the ancient past to illustrate polemical points about the present. For example, the replacement in political debate and discourse of the Roman republic by the Athenian democracy during the late eighteenth and early nineteenth centuries testified to the manner in which British writers chose those elements of antiquity that seemed most immediately useful to them. Discussion of the character of Athenian democracy originated in the wake of the American Revolution and the Yorkshire Association Movement and then closely paralleled the emergence of liberal democracy in nineteenth-century British politics. The Athenian democratic experience held the relevance for Victorian commentators that the demise of the Roman republican oligarchy had held for eighteenth-century political polemicists.

Second, in a more subtle and indirect fashion disagreement or controversy within the ancient sources themselves could invite a nineteenth-century commentator to attempt to sort out the substantial differences because a particular outcome might then lend itself to modern polemical uses. Indeed for many Victorians ancient textual discrepancies were worth considering (ascertainment of correct texts aside) only if the resulting interpretation had a direct modern application. Such was the situation in regard to discrepancies about the character and mission of Socrates in the testimony of Plato, Xenophon, Aristophanes, and Aristotle. Depending upon which ancient source one most highly valued or emphasized, Socrates could be drawn into either the modern idealist or the positivist philosophical camp. Furthermore, the problems of the four accounts of the historical Socrates suggested ways for scholars to extricate themselves from the troubling issues surrounding discrepancies in the narratives of the four Gospels and the problem of the historical Jesus.

Finally, an issue drawn from antiquity could become unexpectedly relevant and polemically inviting because of the intellectual stature, philosophical orientation, or public reputation of the modern writer who first broached the subject. Such was clearly the situation created by Hegel's interpretation of Socrates, George Grote's discussion of Athens, Benjamin Jowett's rendering of Plato, and physicist John Tyndall's comments on Lucretius in his Belfast Address of 1874. In each case the eminence of the writer and the contemporary philosophical or political outlook with which he was associated evoked criticism and debate over the classical subject he had discussed.

Public debate over classical topics both furthered discussion and spurred actual scholarship. That mutually shaping influence produced a paradoxical result. Because classical knowledge had been made directly relevant to controversy in public life, there was always a strong impetus to revise classical learning and to make it shore up one contemporary opinion or undermine another. As one commentator set forth an interpretation of a classical subject that held a particular implication for some aspects of contemporary public debate, a writer from an opposing school of thought would seek to counter. New evidence would be sought or new interpretive arguments set forth. As the new knowledge and conceptual frameworks became delineated, the modern understanding of the Greek and Roman worlds became at once more certain and more circumscribed. That newly attained precision meant the ancient world eventually became less relevant to public issues. In effect over time, the classics ceased to be useful to British public life when scholars and their students came to understand that the Greeks and Romans had not resembled Englishmen and that Englishmen did not resemble Greeks or Romans. Consequently, only when the knowledge of the classics became professionalized and academically solid, did the classics become culturally irrelevant.

II

The context and character of Victorian classical studies themselves could also determine the fortunes of an ancient figure. Such was clearly the case with Virgil. In contrast to most, if not all, other major ancient figures or topics Virgil remained almost entirely the subject of *professional* scholarship. With the exceptions of William Gladstone, Charles Merivale, and Frederic Myers, the chief commentators on Virgil enjoyed university appointments usually in Latin literature. This situation was not an accident. Virgil had long been studied as a part of both Latin and more general European literature. The Victorian treatment of Virgil stemmed neither from an independent consideration of his work nor from contemporary debates aroused by his poetry. Rather the Victorian reputation of Virgil was a function of the novel, burgeoning nineteenth-century admiration for Homer on the one hand and for the Emperor Augustus on the other. Although the revisionist views of Homer and Augustus resulted from modern literary and political concerns, the latter virtually always affected the reading of Virgil in a derivative rather than a direct fashion. The Victorian evaluation of Virgil consequently arose through debates over classical subjects rather than over modern ones and from changing evaluations of the relative merits of different portions of ancient literature and different ancient political leaders.

The most powerful classical literary force in the nineteenth century was the appreciation of Homer and of Greek literature in general often championed in Britain by amateur scholars. This situation contrasted sharply with that of the previous century when Alexander Pope had commented on the novelty of reading Homer and had felt the necessity of defending the beauties and power of the more ancient poet against his Roman successor. During the Victorian era it was left to professional university scholars to defend Virgil in the wake of the Homeric and Hellenic literary onslaught. Even the most gifted and enthusiastic of his interpreters displayed a remarkable lack of scholarly excitement and an almost ponderous sense of duty about their task. As John Conington, the Corpus Professor of Latin, translator, and editor of Virgil, wrote in 1863,

Virgil interests me chiefly because he is a Latin poet: as a student of poetry, I take delight in tracing, word by word, his delicate intricacies of expression, which stimulate curiosity while they baffle analysis, as well as in endeavouring to appreciate the broader features of his work as a whole and its place in the history of literature: as a student of Latin, I am interested in comparing his language with that of his predecessors and successors, and in observing the light which his use of his native tongue throws on the various unsolved or half-solved problems in Latin grammar.[4]

In this regard, Virgil remained for the most part the object of detached professional rather than deeply passionate or engaged scholarship. Virgil tended to be studied because he was there, could not be ignored, and had enjoyed for centuries a high reputation. He and his works lay embedded in the larger world of antiquity and his image changed because of the manner in which nineteenth-century concerns shaped and reshaped the larger body of ancient literature and history. The initial demise of respect for Virgil and the later partial recovery of his reputation occurred entirely within the context of classical scholarship and commentary themselves.

Although throughout the eighteenth century Virgil's association with Augustus and the collapse of Roman republican liberty led to considerable political disparagement of his poetry, Virgil's poetry remained highly esteemed so long as the canons of neoclassical poetics held sway.[5] That is to say, so long as epic poems were criticized and evaluated in terms of established standards of taste and excellence that emphasized refinement and gave only minimal concern to questions of history and original genius, Virgil's reputation remained intact. Toward the close of the eighteenth century, however, several factors combined to displace Virgil in critical estimation and to create an 'impatience' with his work that a late Victorian critic suggested might a hundred years later 'seem as inexplicable as the contempt with which the virtuosi of the first half of the eighteenth century regarded the remains of medieval architecture'.[6] As has been often pointed out, Virgil's reputation in England suffered because in the mind of the literary public he was so closely associated with the Augustan poets against whom the Romantics rebelled.[7] But the decline of Virgil's reputation

---

[4] John Conington, *The works of Virgil with a commentary*, 3rd edn (London: Whittaker and Co., 1876), II, vi.

[5] R. D. Williams, 'Changing attitudes to Virgil: a study in the history of taste from Dryden to Tennyson', in D. R. Dudley, ed., *Virgil* (New York: Basic Books, 1969), p. 123. See also T. W. Harrison, 'English Virgil: the Aeneid in the XVIII century', *Philologica Pragensia*, 10 (1967), 1–11, 80–91: Donald Foerster, *The fortunes of epic poetry: a study in English and American criticism, 1750–1950* (Washington, D.C.: Catholic University of America Press, 1962), pp. 15–29, 76, 134–9; Howard D. Weinbrot, *Augustus Caesar in 'Augustan' England* (Princeton: Princeton University Press, 1978), *passim*.

[6] George Augustus Simcox, *A history of Latin literature from Ennius to Boethius* (New York: Harper and Brothers, 1883), p. 253.

[7] Donald M. Foerster, *Homer in English criticism: the historical approach in the eighteenth century* (New Haven: Yale University Press, 1947).

occurred less because of changing aesthetic taste per se than because
of the manner in which those changes in taste raised Homer to
unprecedented heights of appreciation. The general nineteenth-
century attack on Virgil arose from direct, unfavourable compari-
sons with Homer rather than from disparagement based on abstract
literary aesthetics.

By the end of the eighteenth century Thomas Blackwell's *An
enquiry into the life and writings of Homer* (1735) and Robert Wood's
Essay upon the original genius and writings of Homer (1775) had persuaded critics that Homer provided a vivid and historically accurate
portrait of the age in which he had lived. To read and study Homer
in contrast to Virgil was actually to enter the life of a primitive
epoch, a knowledge of which could also be used for comparative
purposes when reading the Old Testament. Second, the admiration
for the primitive and the truly ancient that swept both Scottish and
English criticism accrued to the benefit of Homer over Virgil. Poetry
of a primitive age received far greater admiration than derivative
poetry of a civilized or refined epoch. Third, the emphasis on
original genius that characterized Romantic poetic criticism led to
the estimation of Homer over Virgil who appeared simply an
imitator of the more ancient and original Greek poetic genius. Much
of this romantic poetic theory originated in Germany among critics
themselves deeply committed to Hellenism. Consequently, wherever
the impact of German criticism and thought made itself felt in
nineteenth-century Britain, there was a tendency for the Greeks to
predominate over the Romans and, in this case, Homer over Virgil.
Finally, the romantic emphasis on heroes and great men similarly
led to a higher estimation of Achilles than Aeneas. Achilles appeared
larger than life and more fully tragic. By comparison as W. S.
Landor commented, Aeneas seemed 'more fitted to invade a hen-
coop than to win a kingdom or a woman'.[8]

The early Victorian estimation of Virgil was not, however, simply
genteelly critical; it was genuinely hostile. The impetus for that
hostility had originated among German scholars. Most important
among these B. G. Niebuhr, the German historian of Rome who
enjoyed broad influence in British intellectual circles, had repeatedly
cast doubt on the character and quality of Virgil's achievement

---

[8] Quoted in Foerster, *The fate of the epic* from John Forster, *Walter Savage Landor* (Boston,
1869), p. 545.

portraying the Aeneid as a pale imitation of Homer's epics. Of the Aeneid, Niebuhr commented,

Its contents were certainly national: yet one can scarcely believe that even a Roman, if impartial, could receive any genuine enjoyment from his story. To us it is unfortunately but too plain, how little the poet has succeeded in raising the shadowy names, for which he was forced to invent characters, into living beings, like the heroes of Homer. Perhaps it is a problem which defies solution, to form an epic poem on an argument which has not lived for centuries in popular songs and tales, as the common property of a nation, so that the cycle of stories which comprises it, and the persons who act a part in it, are familiar to every one. Assuredly this problem was beyond the powers of Virgil, whose genius was barren in creating, great as was his talent for embellishing.

Niebuhr uncompromisingly stated that the Aeneid 'is a complete failure' and 'an unhappy idea from beginning to end'.[9] Accepting Wolf's view of Homeric composition based on popular poems, Niebuhr regarded Virgil writing without the benefit of such popular legends and literature as having worked at a distinct disadvantage from his Greek predecessor. Virgil had constantly needed to borrow from Homer and other poets in composing the Aeneid. The result was then necessarily derivative and without links to the real life and national associations of the Roman people. Niebuhr believed that Virgil's reputation had become so extensive during the Middle Ages because the readers of that era did not have access to Homer. Niebuhr's unbounded admiration for Homer and depreciation of Virgil are not atypical of the attitudes that seized the whole European scholarly world. For the entire century Roman literature in general and Virgil in particular remained on the defensive as a result of the heady enthusiasm for Greece and the Homeric epics.

The negative German assessments made their way into English evaluations of Virgil. These appeared in articles and in the context of general discussions of Roman literature, such as T. B. Macaulay's preface to his *Lays of ancient Rome* (1842), since there were no book length discussions of Virgil. The anonymous article in the seventh edition of the *Encyclopaedia Britannica* (1842) left little doubt as to the

9 B. G. Niebuhr, *The history of Rome*, translated by Julius Charles Hare and Connop Thirlwall, from the 3rd London edn, revised (Philadelphia: Lea and Blanchard, 1844), I, III; B. G. Niebuhr, *The history of Rome from the First Punic War to the death of Constantine*, ed. Leonhard Schmitz, Forming the Fifth Volume of the Entire History (Philadelphia: Lea and Blanchard, 1844), v, 78. On the influence of Niebuhr on studies of Virgil see W. Y. Sellar, *The Roman poets of the Augustan age: Virgil* (Oxford: Clarendon Press, 1877), pp. 68–77.

serious inferiority of Virgil to Homer. The author condemned Virgil's Eclogues as imitations amounting to little more than transla-tions of Theocritus. Virgil's admitted strength

in soundness of judgement and correctness of taste; in depth of tenderness of feeling; in chastened fancy and imagination; in vivid and picturesque description; in the power of appreciating and portraying beauty, whether in nature or art; of depicting passion and touching the chords of human sympathy; in matchless beauty of diction and in harmony and splendour of versification

did not compensate for his deficiency 'in the power of creating and bodying forth original compositions'. Without the presence of origi-nal genius and creativity, all of Virgil's other very considerable poetic virtues commanded mere acknowledgement but neither respect nor admiration. Furthermore, Virgil had been ill-advised to undertake such an epic poem because 'neither the age which produced it, nor the genius of the poet, was favourable to such an achievement'. No less important, the political goal of the poem – 'the exaltation of Augustus' – led to fatal flaws in composition. Such was especially the situation with the portrayal of Aeneas whom Virgil had necessarily 'represented as the mere passive instrument of fate' about whom 'there is consequently little . . . of heroic daring'.[10]

The single harshest English attack on Virgil and the Aeneid during the nineteenth century came from the pen of William Gladstone, better known among his contemporaries for his cham-pioning of Homer. Gladstone's polemic appeared in the *Quarterly Review* of 1857, one year before he published his three-volume *Studies in Homer and the Homeric age* (1858). Gladstone could acknowledge that 'in regard to its external form, the Aeneid is pehaps, as a whole, the most majestic poem the European mind has in any age pro-duced'. Yet, despite their stateliness, the diction, meter, and rhythm of Virgil's epic more nearly resembled 'the performance of a trained athlete, between trick and strength, than the grandeur of free and simple Nature, as it is seen in the ancient warrior, in Diomed or Achilles; or in Homer, the ancient warrior's only bard'. Behind these and other shortcomings of the poet lay Virgil's political situation which had proved 'fatal to the attainment of the very highest excellence'. Echoing Niebuhr, Gladstone reminded his readers,

[10] 'Virgil', *Encyclopaedia Britannica*, 7th edn (Edinburgh: Adam and Charles Black, 1842). See also the section on Virgil in the article on 'Poetry' in the same edition for similarly critical comments.

'While Homer sang for national glory, the poem of Virgil is toned throughout to a spirit of courtierlike adulation. No muse, however vigorous, can maintain an upright gait under so base a burden.' In contrast to Homer's grounding in Greek life, Virgil sang to the emperor not the Romans himself. In his poetic composition Virgil thus had 'to bear in mind, not the great foundations of emotion in the human heart, but his town-house on the Esquiline, and his country-house on the road from Naples to Pozzuoli'. Throughout the composition of the poem, Virgil had been 'obliged to discharge his functions as a poet subject to his higher obligations and liabilities as a courtly parasite of Augustus'.[11]

All of the deficiencies of Virgil's position and the political climate reflected themselves in the character of the hero of the epic of whom Gladstone scornfully declared, 'It is perhaps hardly possible to exhaust the topics of censure which may be justly used against the Aeneas of Virgil'. Aeneas presented to readers 'moral deficiencies' and 'intellectual mediocrity' unredeemed by other virtues. He stood forth as neither a true statesman nor a warrior, but merely as the creation of the poet. His conduct toward Dido was nothing less than 'vile', and the excuses he offered for these actions were 'wretched'. Aeneas's deficiencies of character reflected 'the feeble and deterior-ated conception of human nature at large' as formed by Virgil's thought. The poet had treated mankind as 'but a shallow being', and 'had not sounded the depths of the heart, nor measured either the strength of good or the strength of evil that may abide in it'.[12]

The deepest difficulty for Gladstone presented by the character of Virgil's hero and the poet's position of subservience to Augustus was that of insincerity. As Lionel Trilling argued persuasively some years ago, sincerity emerged as a fundamental touchstone of the character of personal experience during the late eighteenth and early nine-teenth centuries. In contrast to Homer, the Roman poet never appeared to be forthright, authentic, or personally sincere. Glad-stone contended that since Virgil had constructed his work for 'a corrupt court, and not for mankind at large', it had been impossible for him to 'take his stand upon those deep and broad foundations in human nature which gave Homer a position of universal command'. Virgil had also laboured under the disadvantage of a prevailing

[11] William Gladstone, 'Homer and his successors in epic poetry', *Quarterly Review*, 101 (1857), 82, 84, 82, 89, 87.
[12] Ibid., 84, 85.

religion that stood 'undermined at once by philosophy and by licentiousness, and subsisted only as a machinery, and that terribly discredited, for civil ends'. As a result of these shortcomings, there ran throughout the Aeneid 'a vein of untruthfulness' that was 'as strong and as remarkable as is the genuineness of thought and feeling in the Homeric poems'.[13]

The intensity of Gladstone's polemic against Virgil – perhaps the harshest directed against any figure in the ancient world by a Victorian commentator – must be read in the context of his self-proclaimed mission of infusing Homer into the life and curriculum of Oxford. Gladstone was determined to discredit Virgil and Latin literature in general as a potential rival to Homer within university circles. He believed, wrongly as it turned out, that he could lead the universities to embrace an interpretation of Homer that sustained Christianity and a moderately liberal view of politics based on the Homeric monarchies.[14] But while those private political and educational ends account for the timing of Gladstone's article, those eccentric purposes do not account for the absence of substantial protests against his condemnation of Virgil. Gladstone would seem to have touched all of the correct bases of mid-Victorian distaste for the Aeneid. It was imitative, innocuous, and insincere. Unlike the epics of Homer, the Aeneid revealed neither the mind of an original poetic genius nor the customs of an age from which the Victorians felt they could learn new insights into the human condition. It had been written in service to and adulation of a despotic emperor.

III

In 1859 H. A. J. Munro reviewing a new edition of Virgil's work predicted that 'during the next half century the reputation of the poet will stand much higher than it has done in that which has just elapsed, in the course of which it probably reached its nadir'.[15] Munro's prediction came true but through an ironic path. There were two potential directions toward a reevaluation of Virgil. Either

---

[13] Ibid., 88, 89. Gladstone repeated most of this criticism in *Studies in Homer and the Homeric age* (Oxford: Oxford University Press, 1858), III, 502–34. For a discussion of Gladstone's views of Virgil in relation to others, see 'Virgil and his modern critics', *National Review*, 8 (1859), 84–112.

[14] Frank M. Turner, *The Greek heritage in Victorian Britain* (New Haven: Yale University Press, 1981), pp. 159–77, 236–43.

[15] H. A. J. Munro, '*The Works of Virgil*, with a commentary by John Conington', *Journal of Sacred and Classical Philology*, 4 (1859), 286.

the Roman literature of which his poetry was the highest achievement or the emperor whom he served might receive new appreciation. The latter proved to be the path toward the improvement of Virgil's late Victorian reputation. The resurgence of appreciation for Augustus rather than any decline in admiration for Homer shifted the attitude toward Virgil during the second half of the century.

Roman literature in general remained on the aesthetic defensive for the entire nineteenth century. The difficulties Roman literature as literature confronted in the wake of the Greek revival and romantic aesthetics became clear in the most impressive effort to defend it. In 1855 John Conington attempted to delineate the respective virtues and values of Greek and Latin literature. Emphasizing the relative novelty of the interest in Greek literature, he first ascribed to the study of Latin certain of the values then associated almost solely with Greek. Although students of Latin did learn to render English into Latin, the most important reason for mastery of Latin was not communication among scholars, as it certainly had been for over a thousand years, but rather 'the historical value which attaches to it, both in itself, and as containing the records of the thought and feeling of a large section of the ancient world'. The most fundamental reason to study Latin, now that the importance of Greece stood recognized, was to be found 'in the historical position actually occupied by Roman literature, in relation both to that which went before and to that which has followed it'.[16] Remarkable in Conington's arguments is the manner in which they reflect an historicized evaluation of Roman literature. The value and importance of Roman literature lay for Conington in the manner in which it opened an understanding of three historical epochs: that which went before during which the Greek models were established, that during which earlier Roman literature itself flourished, and those later centuries during which Roman literature constituted models of excellence. Roman literature was thus of no less value as a vehicle toward historical understanding than was Greek.

Conington also sought to counter the argument from romantic aesthetics that Roman literature was lacking because of its derivative and imitative relationship to the earlier and more creative Greek literature. He explained,

[16] John Conington, 'The academical study of Latin' (1855), in J. A. Symonds, ed., *Miscellaneous writings of John Conington* (London: Longmans, Green, and Co., 1872), I, 205, 207.

In speaking of Roman literature as imitative, it must not be forgotten that
the reproach is not peculiar to it, but attaches to the whole of the literature
of modern Europe. Greece, in its independent, instinctive development, set
the example which subsequent nations have followed with more or less
distinct consciousness ... Rome may seem to have been more of a copyist
than any of its successors, partly as being actually more indebted to Greece,
partly from the lateness of its intellectual growth, which suggests the notion
of rational deliberation rather than of creative energy; but the difference
must not be exaggerated in either case. If modern nations have followed
Greece less closely than Rome did, it is attributable to the fact, among other
causes, that they have had Rome as well as Greece to follow.

The art of imitation had certain of its own rewards. The copyist may
reveal beauties lost to a less observant eye; the work of the imitator
may reveal more clearly than the original the character of the laws of
composition. In the latter regard, 'an imitative literature is pecu-
liarly adapted, by the determinateness of the art employed, for
showing what literature really is'. But most important the imitator
may actually become the chief educator. Such was clearly the role of
Rome and its literature. Conington insisted,

What Greece was to Rome, Rome has been to modern times – the great
educator, the humanizer of its barbarous conqueror, the mother of intellect,
art, and civilization. That part of our culture which we have not worked
out for ourselves, or received from contemporary nations, we owe almost
wholly to Rome, and to Greece only through Rome, just as our language,
saturated throughout with Latin, has assimilated but few particles of Greek.

Conington's arguments clearly reveal the defensiveness inherent in
mid- and late- Victorian considerations of Roman literature. Its
interpreters simply could not make it as exciting, original, or
historical as Greek literature. Literary taste and arguments based on
literary value could not and would not restore Virgil's reputation.
The Aeneid and Roman literature in general might be made to
resemble Greek literature in a functional manner, but similarity of
function was a far cry from the claim of Greek literature to
originality, action, character delineation, and scope of portrayal of
human nature. So far as ancient poetry was concerned, Benjamin
Hall Kennedy summed up the preponderance of Victorian opinion
when he declared, 'Whatever rank be assigned to Virgil, all are now
agreed that Homer is the greatest poet of classical antiquity.' Virgil
had studied and imitated the poetry of the past while Homer had
created it. Critics simply could not bring themselves to place 'the

poetic student of an Augustan age above the spontaneous singer of a youthful civilization, teeming with fresh and vigorous life'.[17]

Politics rather than literary taste changed Virgil's reputation in the nineteenth century as it had similarly aided his fortunes in his own lifetime. The new late Victorian appreciation for Virgil was grounded in the mid-century restoration of the importance and achievement of Augustus. The earliest foundation for this shift in opinion more favourable to Virgil had been laid just a year before the publication of Gladstone's article. In volume IV of *A history of the Romans under the empire*, published in 1856, Charles Merivale made a number of favourable comments about Virgil. They were rooted in his determination to present an even more favourable portrait of Augustus who had previously been treated as a political opportunist, an intriguer, and ultimately a tyrant. Merivale rejected all of these views. As explored more fully in a previous essay in this volume, Merivale portrayed Augustus as having carried out the very positive programme, originally begun by his uncle Julius, of reforming a corrupt society and tottering political structure. He saw both rulers as having attempted to found a popular monarchy grounded in the support of the Roman middle classes. The favourable transformation of the image of Augustus which in England commenced seriously with Merivale led directly to the reevaluation of Virgil from political rather than poetical considerations. Virgil never overcame the poetic dominance of Homer, but by the close of the century he had been largely relieved of political condemnation.

His admiring portrait of Augustus and the Principate allowed Merivale to render what had by mid-century become uncharacteristic praise to Virgil. Merivale presented Virgil as having supported Augustus from a combination of concern for political and social stability and genuine religious piety. Merivale argued that Virgil's

ardour in the cause of law, order, and tradition assumed the character of a religious sentiment, and he conceived himself devoted to a great moral mission. His purpose widened, and his enthusiasm grew deeper, as he contemplated the sins of his countrymen, and the means by which alone they might be expiated: their abandonment, on the one hand, of the first

---

[17] Ibid., 207–8, 208, 212; Benjamin Hall Kennedy, *The works of Virgil with a commentary and appendices for the use of schools and colleges*, 3rd edn, enlarged and revised (London: Longmans, Green, and Co., 1881), pp. xli. Kennedy was Regius Professor of Greek at Cambridge, but his comment reflected the opinion of a broad spectrum of commentators, Conington being the major exception.

duties of their being; on the other, the restoration of belief, and a return to the principles of the past.

In this regard Virgil's spirit belonged 'to the Ages of Faith'. In his Eclogues Virgil had attempted 'to revive some of the simple tastes and sentiments of the olden time, and perpetuated, amidst the vices and corruptions of the empire, a pure stream of sober and innocent enjoyments'.[18] In the Georgics, Virgil had set forth the praise of industry and labour and had shown them to be favoured by the gods.

It was in the Aeneid, however, that Virgil most clearly and forcefully brought to the fore the religious basis of 'the institutions of an imperial republic'. Waxing eloquent over the religious message of the Aeneid, Merivale wrote,

The grand religious idea which breathes throughout his Aeneid, is the persuasion that the Romans are the sons and successors of the Trojans, the chosen race of heaven, of divine lineage and royal pretensions, whose destinies have engaged all the care of Olympus from the beginning, till they reach at last their consummation in the blissful regeneration of the empire. It maintains the existence of Providence as the bond of the Roman commonwealth. *Yes! there are Gods*, it proclaims, and the glories of Rome demonstrate it. Yes! there are Gods above, and the Romans are their children and their ministers upon earth, exercising in their name a delegated sovereignty, sparing those who yield, but beating down the proud. This is the mission of the race of Assaracus, to vindicate the ways of God to man, to impose upon him the yoke of an eternal peace, and bring all wars to an end for ever![19]

The enormous religious task that Virgil had set before himself was to enclose the Roman experience of the past and the present into a sacred narrative that gave a divine purpose and meaning to the entire Roman experience. Furthermore, according to Merivale, Virgil intended the Romans to understand that since they were themselves descended from the Olympians whose government under Jove was monarchical, it was not a dishonour for them to submit themselves to a monarchical government.

In Merivale's analysis Aeneas emerged as the fit successor of Hector, and Aeneas's piety allowed him to recover his legitimate patrimony after many years of trials and suffering. Similarly Augus-

[18] Charles Merivale, *The history of the Romans under the Empire* (London: Longman, Brown, Green, and Longmans, 1856), IV, 574, 575.
[19] Ibid., 578, 578–9.

tus recovered his patrimony and in doing so brought peace to Rome. Merivale acknowledged the proclivity of Aeneas to weep at every crisis, his 'baseness' in deserting Dido, and 'the moral injustice of the attack on Turnus', but those deficiencies in character and in Virgil's own artistry did not really undermine the vast religious drama of the Aeneid and its message. Whatever those deficiencies may have been, they were not the result of slavish politics on Virgil's part. Merivale quite simply declared, 'The honour his writings pay to the principle of religious belief was certainly not assumed for a political purpose.' Merivale asserted that the general melancholy of the poem removed any thought of political obsequiousness. Finally, despite any defect that might be ascribed to it, the Aeneid remained 'the most complete picture of the national mind at its highest elevation, the most precious document of national history, if the history of an age is revealed in its ideas, no less than in its events and incidents'.[20]

Merivale's comments set the stage for the late Victorian revival of both Virgil and Augustus. Whereas previously Virgil's historicity had been attacked, now it stood vindicated not as a portrait of historical action but as an historical record of ideas and of national ideals epitomized in the mind of the poet himself rather than in a heritage of popular songs and legends. Augustus stood forth as the founder of an empire justified on the one hand by a kind of democratic consent and on the other by decades of peace and stability. As has been seen in other essays, such stability came to be highly prized by those numerous Victorian intellectuals and classicists who in the second half of the century became fearful of the domestic political turmoil of the liberal state and more concerned about the assumption of British imperial duty.

During the last quarter of the century various commentators accommodated Virgil to the Victorian poetic audience in light of these new political sensitivities. Their approach was to suggest the wisdom of the emperor and the political order that Virgil had supported and then to defend Virgil's poetics by making him resemble Homer or other Greek authors. In this manner late Victorian Virgilian criticism combined a revisionist version of Roman political history with an appropriation of romantic aesthetics and Arnoldian Hellenism.

Henry Nettleship, the Corpus Professor of Latin Literature at

[20] Ibid., 583, 584, 585.

Oxford, made the first contribution to the Hellenization of Virgil. In
'Suggestions introductory to a study of the Aeneid' (1875), Nettleship like virtually all late century commentators remarked on the
manner in which the revived estimation of Homer had led to the
undervaluing of Virgil. Nettleship assigned to Virgil a literary and
historical mission necessarily and distinctly different from Homer's.
According to Nettleship, the fundamental themes of the Aeneid were
'the building up of the Roman empire under ... Providence' and
hence 'the conquering and civilizing of the rude tribes of Italy'. The
adventures of Aeneas portrayed 'the subjugation of semi-barbarous
tribes under a high civilization and religion' and 'the conquering
and civilizing power of Rome directed by a divine providence' and
his early preparation for that high task. Aeneas symbolized the
civilizing qualities of human life contrasted with the qualities of
primitive religion, social organization, and warfare in Homer.
Aeneas was the providential instrument of the gods for the realization of civilized life; he was not their plaything on the battlefield.
Nettleship urged,

Aeneas is the son of a goddess, and his life the working out of the divine
decrees. The opposition to these decrees is ... the work of inferior deities
and the baser human passions. Aeneas is conceived by Virgil as embodying
in his character the qualities of a warrior, ruler, and a civilizer of men, the
legendary impersonation of all that was great in the achievements of Rome.
His mission is to carry on a contest in Italy, to crush the resistance of its
warlike tribes, to give them customs and build them cities.

In a sense Nettleship was arguing that Aeneas represented the very
forces of civilization that brought an end to the modes of human life
seen in the Homeric epics. Once the character and role of Aeneas
were thus understood, he emerged not simply as the chief protagonist of an epic poem but also as a 'lawgiver and civilizer' such as
Alcides and Theseus.[21] Nettleship directly championed the ages of
civilization over ages of primitive life. Whatever the attractiveness of
the Homeric epics, the growth of civilization was required for the
achievement of peace. That was the message of Virgil. The life of
peace, stability, and economic growth demanded the virtues of
civilization, and Virgil's Aeneas championed those values.

For Nettleship, Aeneas must be understood in the light of his

[21] Henry Nettleship, *Lectures and essays on subjects connected with Latin literature and scholarship*
(Oxford: Clarendon Press, 1885), pp. 103, 104, 108, 124, 103.

higher duty and calling such as did not exist for Homer's characters. Aeneas's quintessential piety led him to follow the lead of the gods over his own individual desires. The epithet 'pius' repeatedly applied to Aeneas suggested qualities different from those of Homeric heroes. In place of courage in battle and emphasis on personal honour, the chief qualities of Aeneas were those 'of the son who loves his father, of the king who loves his subjects, of the worshipper who reverences the gods'. Whereas Gladstone and other commentators attempted to compare the character of Aeneas to that of figures from Homer, Nettleship emphasized their fundamental incongruity. The Homeric poems centred on the private or personal qualities of their protagonists. Virgil's purpose which differed from Homer's was 'not so much to delineate "character" as to exhibit the conflict of forces'.[22] Virgil's Aeneid portrayed characters who embodied qualities and destinies essential to Rome's development and history. In all these respects the qualities of character that emerge in the Aeneid were those conservative ones that held society together. They were the qualities that Arnold had championed and had associated with culture and with fifth-century Greece.

In his effort to hellenize Virgil, Nettleship almost contemptuously rejected the imitative quality of Virgil's poetry as constituting any literary or aesthetic shortcoming. Virtually all Roman poetry was imitative. It was simply the characteristic of the age. More to the point than lack of originality was the manner in which Virgil drew upon the thought and spirit of Greece to narrate his story. Interference from lesser divinities and his own passions posed the major difficulties confronting Aeneas in carrying out his mission. To articulate that theme Virgil had wisely drawn upon Greek tragedy. Nettleship argued,

The deeper and more religious view of the conflict of individual inclination with the divine will which is presented, according to their different manners, by Aeschylus and Sophocles, and though in a less marked manner by Euripides, was impossible to the simplicity of the Homeric times. The reign of mythology was, in the age of the Attic drama, past, and that of thought had begun, or, in other words, mythology gave the form and thought the matter to the creative power of the poet. This is precisely the case with the mythology of the Aeneid in its relation to the inner ideas of the poem.

Furthermore, the spiritual and religious concepts that informed Virgil were 'very like the spirit which animates the action and play

[22] Ibid., pp. 104, 130.

of character with which Greek tragedy has made us familiar'.
Virgil's plot involved the resistance of human passion and individual
inclination to divine purposes. It was the portrayal of 'human
passion bent on its own fulfilment in contempt of the gods, and
ending, as it can only end, in infatuation and ruin'. Virgil had
explored the conflict of human passions and divine purposes 'with all
the dignity and purity of Sophocles'.[23]

Nettleship's Virgil was to be sure certainly no Homer, but that
was just exactly the point. Because of the character of the age in
which he lived, Virgil could not have been a Homer any more than
could the Greek tragedians. Yet Virgil, though using the legends of
early Rome, had composed verse in a manner that deeply resembled
the best literary forms and spiritual values of fifth-century Greek
tragedy. The highest ethical and spiritual values informed the
narrative of the Aeneid. Wrongdoing led to sadness, suffering, and
punishment. The will of the higher spiritual powers could be ignored
only at the peril of the individual who sought to escape a divinely
ordained mission. In those regards Virgil was as Greek or Hellenic as
any Roman poet might be and his great poem championed not
warring heroes out for glory but the task of civilizing empire.
Although Nettleship made no mention of Britain's imperial mission,
clearly as he presented the poem, the Aeneid was a work whose
reading might benefit the young men in English universities destined
to join the Indian civil service or other outposts of late-century
empire.

All of these themes allowed Nettleship to present an interpretation
of Aeneas and Dido directly at odds with those of Gladstone.
Nettleship contended that the Dido episode had been 'worked out
very much in the spirit of the Greek tragedy, the confused moral
conflicts of which it thoroughly recalls'. Virgil intended the incident
to represent the struggle of human passions against divine will. His
narration resembled 'the kind of struggle represented in the Ajax
and the Trachiniae of Sophocles, where the loser loses and the
winner wins without any end being served except the assertion of
superior power'. Modern readers had encountered difficulty with
the Dido story because of their failure to recognize its inherently
Greek tragic character. According to Nettleship,

---

[23] Ibid., pp. 124, 125. See Conington, *The works of Virgil*, II, 6–24, for another assessment of
Virgil's relationship to Greek literature.

The real difficulty which a modern reader finds in realizing such situations is that we are accustomed and expect to see the right prevail and the wrong beaten; but this is not the spirit of the Greek tragedy, where it seems as if the natural moral feelings were playing blindly around undiscovered centres, where the powers at work are not commensurate with our ideas of the powers of right and the reverse, and where the righteous issue, as we understand it, is only dimly discerned, if discerned at all, by the straining eye.

Virgil had not intended to arouse sympathy for Dido or for Aeneas. The fundamental sin of Aeneas was not his infatuation with Dido and his later abandonment of her but rather his relinquishing 'his mission by allying himself, against the oracles, with a foreign queen'. The incident itself represented Virgil's assimilating post-Homeric Greek stories such as those of Theseus, Jason, Heracles, and Agamemnon and the tragedies based on them in which women played similar roles. Nettleship contended, 'Virgil indeed could hardly have absorbed the spirit of the Greek drama as he wished to absorb it had the Aeneid lacked some such episode as that of Dido.'[24] In this manner Nettleship accepted the imitative character of Virgil and transformed it into an assimilative genius.

This interpretation allowed Nettleship to cast Aeneas's encounter with Dido in a more favourable light than Gladstone and earlier commentators. His wrong was not a sin against the woman but against the will of the gods. Nettleship commented,

Aeneas, the future lawgiver of Italy, is brought face to face with the great city rising under the sceptre of Dido. Admiration for the queen and her work touches his imagination, love for the woman his heart: as Caesar was half won by Cleopatra, Aeneas is half won by Dido: the king and the queen alike forget their mission, the half-built walls are left unfinished, the works of war and defence are abandoned. But the commands of Heaven are clear, the founder of Rome must not be united to an Eastern queen: in this as in all things he must represent the idea of a true Roman. He crushes his love, follows the express commands of Jupiter and of his father's spirit, and leaves the queen to her fate.[25]

For Nettleship and others the Carthaginian queen represented the dangers of the East, the demands of passion, and the ensnaring qualities of women. In fleeing Dido, Aeneas was escaping a temptress who would have led him away from duty and his divine mission.

---

[24] Nettleship, *Lectures and essays*, pp. 129, 130.
[25] Ibid., pp. 104–5.

Other commentators of the 1870s similarly defended Aeneas from criticism for having abandoned Dido. J. R. Green, better known for his popular histories of England, saw Dido as embodying extreme human passions. Commenting unsympathetically on her fury at being rejected, he wrote,

> She dashes herself against the rooted purpose of Aeneas as the storm-winds, to use Virgil's image, dash themselves from this quarter and that against the rooted oak. The madness of her failure drives her through the streets like a Maenad in the nightly orgies of Cithaeron; she flies at last to her chamber like a beast at bay, and gazes out, distracted, at the Trojan shipmen putting off busily from the shores.

For Green, Dido stood as the direct foil to the character of Aeneas. He argued, 'Impulse, passion, the mighty energies of unbridled will, are wrought up into a figure of unequalled beauty, and then set against the true manhood of the founder and type of Rome, the manhood of duty, of self-sacrifice, of self-control.'[26]

In sharp contrast to commentators in the first half of the century Nettleship and Green transformed Aeneas into a symbol of duty and Rome's providentially determined destiny. They demeaned Dido and reduced her from the status of a woman wronged into a figure of seduction, uncontrolled passion, and rejection of duty and of the gods. She was a daemon to be escaped in the pursuit of a higher destiny. In turn that higher destiny stood justified by the political success of Augustus. Green contended that Virgil intended Dido to symbolize not only the later danger that Carthage would bring to Rome but all of the forces of 'passion, greed, lawless self-seeking, personal ambition, the decay of the older Roman sense of unselfish duty, of that "pietas" which subordinated the interest of the individual man to the common interest of the State' which would henceforth 'be the real enemy of Rome'.[27] Virgil associated all of those values with the East epitomized in Dido and saw them as dangers to the peace emerging under Augustus. The alternative had been Antony who had given himself over to the East and the Egyptian Queen.

Writing in the same decade Frederic W. H. Myers also found the character of Dido troubling. He contended that previous ancient

[26] John R. Green, *Stray studies from England and Italy* (New York: Harper and Brothers, Publishers, 1876), pp. 243, 238.
[27] Ibid., p. 245.

writers in both Greek and Latin had presented the tragedies that might follow from the passion of love. But in Virgil the reader confronted the unsatisfactory situation of love involving sin and rejection of duty. Myers saw Virgil's Dido as providing 'an insight into the female heart which is seldom gained by the exercise of imagination alone'. Yet Myers found himself sharply critical of the passionate image of Dido. He explained that

when we compare the Fourth Aeneid with later poems on the same lofty level – with the *Vita Nuova*, for instance, or with *Laodamia* – we feel how far our whole conception of womanhood has advanced since Virgil's day under the influence of Christianity, chivalry, civilization. A nature like Dido's will now repel as much as it attracts us. For we have learnt that a woman may be childlike as well as impassioned, and soft as well as strong; that she may flow with all love's fire and yet be delicately obedient to the lightest whisper of honour.

Myers believed the delineation of 'the highest and truest form of love, as distinguished both from friendship and from passion' was the product of the Middle Ages and in particular of Dante. Only in that literature did love emerge as an 'instinct of a worship which should be purer and more pervading than any personal desire'.[28] In this passage one sees Myers projecting on to Dido those misogynist fears of female passion and sensuality that seem to have so very much informed late century social attitudes.[29] His comments on Dido as well as those of Nettleship and Green reflect the fear of women and the misogyny that so extensively touched late century literature and culture. That widely shared apprehension of power and potential irrationality of women allowed commentators to depreciate Dido and to rationalize Aeneas's actions. All three of them found Dido at once attractive and repulsive. She was a sexual force which must be resisted and fled lest she call forth the passion of the moment to the detriment of higher ends. Dido represented to all three a force that

---

[28] Frederic W. H. Myers, *Essays: classical* (London: Macmillan and Co., 1883), pp. 125, 130, 130–1.

[29] Nina Auerbach, *Woman and the demon: the life of a Victorian myth* (Cambridge, Mass.: Harvard University Press, 1982); Bram Dijkstra, *Idols of perversity: fantasies of feminine evil in fin-de-siècle culture* (New York: Oxford University Press, 1986); Joseph A. Kestner, *Mythology and misogyny: the social discourse of nineteenth-century British classical-subject painting* (Madison, Wis.: University of Wisconsin Press, 1989); Joy S. Kasson, *Marble queens and captives: women in nineteenth-century American sculpture* (New Haven: Yale University Press, 1990); Janet Oppenheim, *'Shattered nerves': doctors, patients, and depression in Victorian England* (New York: Oxford University Press, 1991), pp. 181–232.

would urge both men and women to do as they like and to abandon culture and social mores necessary for a settled life, community, and a strong state. In Arnold's terms she would seem for these commentators to have epitomized the moral and sexual anarchy that undermined both personal and collective culture.

Nettleship drew together his concern for the civilizing mission of Aeneas and his admiration for stability to defend Virgil's religion and politics. Nettleship argued that the piety and religion that informed the Aeneid were sincere. The Georgics gave evidence of Virgil's affection for the old gods and of his understanding that religion lay at the heart of social life and of humankind's relationship to nature. No less did Virgil appreciate the power of the state religion as 'the outward representation of the belief that a Providence governed the progress of the Roman empire'.[30] This faith no less than his admiration for Augustus permeated the Aeneid. The promulgation of this faith was essential to Virgil's purpose. It was incorrect to see Virgil as merely flattering Augustus in his encouragement of the emerging cult of the Caesars.[31] Nettleship believed the worship of the Caesars had arisen from popular sentiment as the natural development of the religious temper in the Roman world at the time. Virgil had mixed his admiration for the new state religion with incidents illustrating the transmigration and purification of souls drawn from Orphic poetry and also present in the myths of Plato. The result was a poem that unlike any other fully reflected the immense spectrum of religious elements in Roman history and society. The display of these beliefs thus presented 'the most complete and classical monument of its age'.[32]

The most extensive discussion of Virgil during the 1870s and for the rest of the century for that matter was W. Y. Sellar's *The Roman poets of the Augustan age* (1877), the first book-length treatment of Virgil in English. He also contributed the article on Virgil, as well as on Lucretius, to the ninth and eleventh editions of the *Encyclopaedia Britannica*. Sellar, who taught Latin literature as Professor of Humanity at Edinburgh, pursued independently many of the same themes Nettleship had set forth.[33] A generally defensive tone filled the

---

[30] Nettleship, *Lectures and essays*, p. 133.
[31] On this point see Henry Nettleship, *Ancient lives of Vergil with an essay on the poems of Vergil in connection with his life and times* (Oxford: Clarendon Press, 1879).
[32] Nettleship, *Lectures and essays*, p. 141.
[33] Sellar read Nettleship's essay as he was completing his own study. Sellar, *The Roman poets of the Augustan age: Virgil*, p. vii.

entire volume bearing witness to the enormous dominance exercised by Homeric poetry on the university scene. Like every other late century scholar of Virgil, Sellar admitted that Homer was the more interesting, exciting, and original poet. The emergence of Homer since the eighteenth century as a widely read poet meant that the character of the heroic age would be learned directly through his work and not as it had been presented and modified in the later verse of Virgil. Sellar openly confessed that Virgil 'never again can enter into rivalry with Homer as the inspired poet of heroic action'.[34] In that respect Virgil had been clearly displaced.

Virgil's future reputation and appreciation according to Sellar must rest upon understanding his distinct place in Latin literature. In that literary and historical venue Virgil stood forth preeminently as 'a representative writer – representative both of the general national idea and of the sentiment and culture of his own age'. It was that representative and national mission which in part accounted for the generally criticized flatness of Virgil's characters in the Aeneid. Homer's epics had their origin in 'the pure epic impulse' of relating the story of human action and character. Consequently Homer was first and foremost interested in the personalities and activities of his protagonists. The origins and fundamental concerns of Virgil's poem were distinctly different. Sellar explained,

The germ of the Aeneid ... is to be sought in the national idea and sentiment, in the imperial position of Rome, in her marvellous destiny, and in its culmination in the Augustan Age. The actions and sufferings of the characters that play their part in the poem were to be only secondary objects of interest; the primary object was to be found in the race to whose future career these actions and sufferings were the appointed means ... Actors and action did not spring out of the spontaneous movement of the imagination, but were chosen by a refined calculation to fulfil the end which Virgil had in view. What Aeneas and his followers want in personal interest, is supposed to accrue to them as instruments in the hands of destiny. A new type of epic poetry is thus realized. The Iliad and the Odyssey are essentially poems of personal, the Aeneid is the epic of national fortunes.[35]

One looked to Virgil for knowledge of life, feelings, and attitudes from the first century. In this manner the late Victorian Virgil became, like the late eighteenth-century Homer, a spokesman of his

---

[34] Ibid., p. 78.   [35] Ibid., pp. 78, 297.

own day and the provider of an important and valid historical record, though of a civilized rather than a primitive age.

Sellar also attempted to draw the Roman poet directly into Matthew Arnold's strain of cultural Hellenism. According to Sellar, 'The Augustan Age was pre-eminently an age of culture, and Virgil was pre-eminently the most cultivated man belonging to the age.' Virgil profited from the 'careful study and application of the principles of art, as well as by an elaborate culture' which character-ized the Augustan Age so that he might achieve 'the sustained perfection of a long poem'. Through his deep familiarity with the writings of both the Greeks and the Romans who had preceded him, as well as through his fascination with myths and traditions of early antiquity, Virgil's poems came to be prized by his countrymen 'as a great repertory of their secular and sacred learning'. To the extent that nineteenth-century poets had looked too exclusively to Homer, they had separated themselves from important Virgilian virtues and influences that had positively touched earlier European literature. Sellar argued,

That Virgil was once the object of the greatest reverence is a reason for not lightly putting his claims aside now ... The course of time brings with it losses as well as gains in sensibility. Though the thoughts of the Latin poet may not help us to understand the spirit of our own era, they are a bond of union with the genius and culture of Europe in other times. If poetry ever exercises a healing and reconciling influence on life, the deep and tranquil charm of Virgil may prove some antidote to the excitement, the restlessness, the unsettlement of opinion in the present day.[36]

These remarks directly echoed Matthew Arnold's Preface of 1854, and his later discussions of the role of the concepts of culture and Hellenism. In his own day the originality of Virgil had been his emphasis on the Arnoldian values of community, labour, piety, and love of national life rather than on any kind of anarchic or disorderly individualism.

Although these values were specially present in the Eclogues and the Georgics, Sellar brought these Arnoldian outlooks to bear in particular on his interpretation of the Aeneid. That epic obviously owed much to Homer and other Greek literature. Yet there were important Roman values and outlooks upon which it drew. The Romans were a people 'who had an instinctive consciousness of a long destiny; who built, acted, and wrote with a view to a distant

[36] Ibid., pp. 84, 86, 85, 91–2.

future'. They also had long displayed an admiration for great men that was similar to modern hero worship. This tendency rapidly allied itself with poetry. The Romans in all things thought of works of vast scope achieved only through perseverance and patience. It was the presence of such values in Roman epic poetry generally and the Aeneid in particular that in Sellar's view separated them from Homer:

The Roman epic and Roman history originated in the same feeling and impulse – the sentiment of national glory, the desire to perpetuate the great actions and the career of conquest, which were the constituent elements of that glory. The impulse both of poets and historians was to build up a great commemorative monument; not as among the Greeks, to present the spectacle of human life in its most animated, varied, and noble movements. To a Roman historian and to a Roman poet the character and the fate of individuals derived their chief interest from their bearing on the glory and fortune of the State. In the Greek epic, on the other hand, the interest in Achilles and Hector is much more vivid than that felt in the success of the Greek or Trojan cause . . . The idea of Rome, as the one object of supreme interest to gods and men, in the past, present, and future, imparts the unity of sentiment, tone, and purpose which is characteristic of the type of Roman epic poetry and of Roman history.

Virgil realized that Rome stood at an historical turning point unprecedented since the defeat of Hannibal. It was a moment 'calculated to re-awaken the sense of national life, of the mission to subdue and govern the world assigned to Rome, and of the divine guardianship of which she was the object'. Virgil's genius was to grasp that 'the epic poet of a cultivated age' must be more than an artist; he must be able to 'feel more strongly than others, and give expression to the deepest tendencies of his own time'.[37] His poetry must be more than a work of imagination; it must be charged with a special sense and understanding of the present. In this regard Virgil set out upon a poetic mission different from Homer's.

In the Aeneid, according to Sellar, Virgil had been inspired by the expansion of Rome. As a representative work of the age it set forth 'the pride of empire' as the most prominent mode of national sentiment. The establishment of empire illustrated the Roman capacity for conquest and administration upon which the sense of national self-esteem rested. Virgil attempted to soften and humanize 'the idea of the Imperial State, representing her as not only the

[37] Ibid., pp. 281, 284–5, 294, 296.

conqueror but the civilizer of the ancient world, and the transmitter of that civilization to the world of the future'. Furthermore, the patriotism of Virgil was as much Italian patriotism as it was Roman imperialism. But for Virgil religious sentiment was inseparable from imperial patriotism. His goal was to demonstrate that the history and development of Rome arose from divine purpose. Virgil based his religious view on the 'thought of an unseen Power, working by means of omens and miracles on the mind of the hero of the poem, with the distant aim of establishing universal empire in the hands of a people, obedient to divine will and observant of all religious ceremonies'.[38] To this Virgil added his own sense of personal faith and hope displayed in the visits to the underworld, the emphasis on family responsibility, and his recounting of numerous religious rites and rituals.

Sellar's analysis reflected the changing character of nineteenth-century concepts of nationalism and the national. When Niebuhr ascribed national qualities to Homeric verse and denied them to Virgil, nationalism tended to be associated with cultural or ethnic life. The ancient songs and ballads wherein Wolfian theory found the origins of Homer's epics fit that pattern of cultural nationalism that had roots in Herder's theories of *volkgeist*. By the 1870s in the wake of Italian and German unification the character of nationalism had sharply changed. In the theories of Mazzini, for example, it had been associated with divine purpose and destinies for nations and peoples. The conflicts that had seen Piedmont unite Italy and Prussia unite Germany brought statecraft and powerful leaders to the fore. This shifting and developing character of both nationalism and the national leader stood fully reflected in Sellar's comments and those of other critics of Virgil during the 1870s. National goals seemed less likely to be achieved through the spontaneity of popular culture than through the calculations of statesmen. In such a climate the crafted, calculated verse and narrative of Virgil praising an ancient ruler who had brought unity and peace to Rome through force and by eliminating the republic might again find interest.

Sellar accepted Merivale's favourable analysis of the rise of Augustus explaining in considerable detail why Romans generally, and Virgil in particular, had welcomed the Principate as a release from turmoil, war, and destruction. Sellar contended,

[38] Ibid., pp. 322, 324–5, 339.

His poems, better than any other witnesses, enable us to understand how weary the Roman world was of the wars, disturbances, and anarchy of the preceding century, how ardently it longed for the restoration of order and national unity, how thankfully it accepted the rule of the man who could alone effect this restoration, and how hopefully it looked forward to a new era of peace and prosperity, of glory and empire, under his administration.

Furthermore, that era of Augustan peace under an admittedly questionable political regime had fostered new patronage of poetry. This close relationship of the poets to the new society 'tended to make literature tamer in spirit and thought, perhaps also less original in invention, more bounded in its range of human interest'.[39] Virgil was more than the kept poet of a despotic regime; he was the writer who makes us understand why many people praised and supported that regime.

Despite Sellar's praise for Virgil's national outlook, a clear sense of ambivalence surrounded his consideration of Virgil's relationship to Augustus. Sellar provided numerous explanations for Virgil's support for the Caesarian cause based on his childhood in northern Italy in a district generally sympathetic to Julius Caesar. He had himself lost land inherited from his father and received compensation from Augustus. All of the chief features of his character, his lack of sympathy with the old republic, his hatred of conflict, and his desire for peace and stability 'made him a sincere supporter of the idea of the Empire in opposition to that of the Republic'. Although the virtues of piety and stoic endurance could be ascribed to Virgil, Sellar believed it impossible to clear his memory entirely from the reproach of 'undue subservience to power'. His character was deficient in qualities of independence and self-assertion. It was to 'the excess of his feeling of deference to power, and not to any insincerity of nature, that we attribute the language occasionally – as in the Invocation to the Georgics – transcending the limits of truth and sobriety, in which the position of Augustus is magnified'. As Sellar claimed, 'the nobleness of Virgil's nature is not the nobleness of those qualities which make men great in resistance to wrong, but the nobleness of a gentle and gracious spirit'.[40]

Despite these reservations about Virgil's personality, there could be no doubt about the sincerity of his support of Augustus. For Sellar that sincerity in effect cleansed Virgil's character of the accusations

---

[39] Ibid., pp. 81–2, 31.   [40] Ibid., pp. 129, 129–30.

of being simply a kept poet. There could be no doubt that in his era, Augustus was 'pre-eminently the man suited to his age, as an age of restoration and re-organisation, and he was pre-eminently a Roman of the Romans'. He displayed all those qualities of 'industry, vigilance, practical sagacity, authority, dignity, and urbanity' required of great political leaders and governors. In delineating the character of Aeneas rather than looking to the earlier ideal rulers such as Romulus or Numa, Virgil sought to establish a new ideal which would anticipate the future. The function of Aeneas was to furnish Augustus with 'ancestral distinction' rather than a model for action. Sellar contended, 'In thus throwing the halo both of a remote antiquity and of a divine ancestry around Augustus, Virgil helped to recommend his rule to the sentiment of his countrymen.'[41]

Through his epic Virgil had set forth a 'sympathetic comprehension of the imperial idea of Rome in its secular, religious, and personal significance'. Yet Sellar found much lacking in this achievement. He thought it better associated with a work of history rather than of poetry. Virgil had glorified power, civilization, and material greatness. But unlike the highest art, his epic had not enlarged the spiritual sense, purified the notion of happiness, or explored the issues of righteousness in government. For all of his talent and sincerity Virgil had chosen the wrong subject for true artistic and poetic achievement. Sellar concluded,

The idea of imperial Rome is rather that of the enemy than of the promoter of the spiritual life or of individual happiness: it impresses on the mind the thought of a vast and orderly, but not of a moral and humane government ... In the Aeneid, Virgil is really the panegyrist of despotism under the delusive disguise of paternal government.

It was the shortcomings of the imperial ideal itself rather than any failure of Virgil's conception or of his characters that ultimately lowered Sellar's estimation of the Aeneid. The ideal of imperial Rome had perhaps touched the world more profoundly than any other secular ideal, but it did not and could not 'touch the heart, or enlighten the conscience'.[42]

Other contemporary commentators, including J. R. Green and Frederic Myers, directly approved Virgil's support for Augustus. Myers made the most forceful case against accusations that Virgil

---

[41] Ibid., p. 343, 345.   [42] Ibid., pp. 347, 348–9, 349.

had been a timeserving court poet. In the bluntest statement on the matter in all Victorian classical commentary, Myers declared,

So far as Virgil's mere support of Augustus goes, this objection, however natural to the lovers of free government, will hardly stand the test of historical inquiry. For Virgil had not to choose between Augustus and the Republic, but between Augustus and Antony. The Republic was gone for ever; and not Hannibal himself, we may surely say, was a more dangerous foe than Antony to the Roman people. No battle which that people ever fought was more thoroughly national, more decisively important, than the battle of Actium. The name of Actium, indeed, can never waken the glory and the joy which spring to the heart at the name of Salamis. . . But the essence of each battle was in fact the same. Whether it were against the hosts of Susa and Ecbatana, or against 'the dog Anubis' and the Egyptian queen, each battle was the triumph of Western discipline, religion, virtue, over the tide of sensuality and superstition which swept onwards from the unfathomable East.

Virgil had not chosen the government of Augustus in preference to a free republic. It was unfortunate that in certain passsages he acquiesced in the deification of the emperor. But in the key passages referring to the deification of the emperor he was 'more or less closely identified with Rome herself'. The speed with which the worship of the emperor developed did not constitute 'the birth of a merely meaningless servility, but represented what was in fact a religious reform and a return to the oldest instincts of the Roman people'. In the face of the religious inadequacy of spiritual influences that had come from Greece and beyond, the Romans had found it 'necessary to fall back upon a more thoroughly national and primitive conception, and to deify once more the abstraction of the one earthly existence whose greatness was overwhelmingly evident – the power of Rome'.[43]

Furthermore, according to Myers, although Augustus himself was not 'a moral hero', he nonetheless favoured and fostered a restoration of old moral and religious values. However inadequate his reform, it was still responsible for whatever virtue existed in the empire. Virgil contributed directly to this effort of moral reform as the Georgics 'testified at least to the continued life of pure ideas, to the undying conception of a contented labour, of an unbought and guileless joy'. But in the Aeneid Virgil went even further by

---

[43] Myers, *Essays: classical*, pp. 149–50, 154, 155, 157. See also Green, *Stray studies from England and Italy*, p. 246.

appealing to all the ideals, values, and communal associations surrounding Rome itself. In that regard, Myers wrote, 'The Georgics had been the psalm of Italy, the Aeneid was the sacred book of the Religion of Rome.' Myers even thought Virgil's implicit support of Augustus's deification defensible in that it supported older values that were good for national life. The commentator urged,

The Lares of Augustus were at once identical in a certain sense with Augustus himself, and with the public Penates worshipped immemorially in their chapel in the heart of the city. And if, as is no doubt the case, the worship of Roma and the Lares augusti could claim in Virgil its half-unconscious prophet, we may reply that this worship, however afterwards debased, was in its origin and essence neither novel nor servile, but national and antique; and that until the rise of Christianity, . . . it would have been hard to say what other form of religion could at once have satisfied the ancient instincts and bound together the remote extremities of the Roman world.[44]

Myers's comments were early straws in what would soon become a very strong wind of late Victorian classical historical scholarship. By the early twentieth century politics had triumphed over poetics in the British appreciation and evaluation of Virgil. As the political achievement of Augustus received new support and appreciation because of modern suspicions of popular government, the ancient poet who had sung the praises of the emperor came to be read in a new light – the light of authoritarian nationalism – and in that light he found many new admirers.

Just after the turn of the century T. R. Glover, fellow of St John's College, Cambridge, set forth a strong secular defence of Virgil. He declared that 'the Aeneid is one, it is "grand", it interests, it expresses the Roman people, and it rises from time to time to be the utterance of humanity'. For Glover the subject of Virgil's epic was

the birth of a great people, of a great work done to found a great race, of a spirit and temper brought into the world which should in time enable that race to hold sway over the whole world and to be the whole world, with all its tribes and tongues, the pledge and the symbol of its union and its peace.

In the story of Aeneas, Virgil had discovered a

clue to the story of every man, the linking of divine decree with human suffering and service, something to explain waste of life and failure of hope by a broader view of heaven's purposes and earth's needs, a justification of

---

[44] Myers, *Essays: classical*, pp. 150, 151, 152–3, 159.

the ways of God to men, not complete, only tentative, but yet an anodyne and an encouragement in an unintelligible world.

Virgil's originality lay in his 'conscious appeal to a nation, as we understand the word "nation" today, to a people of one blood living within well-defined but broad limits, a people with various traditions all fusing in one common tradition'. Virgil was the poet who 'gave for the first time its literary expression to the triumph of a nation, politically, racially, and geographically one, over the clan and over the city-state'. In doing so, Virgil stood as the poet who expressed in the character of Aeneas a collective nation and the ideal best self of 'the ideal Roman temper'.[45] Behind all these achievements lay the shadow of Augustus who had brought to a world of disorder the benefits of peace, stability, and restoration of traditional values.

Glover's remarks were curious on a number of levels including his uncritically following Virgil's theme in Book 12 of the Aeneid ascribing blood nationhood to the polyglot Augustan empire. There was little or no evidence that the Romans under the Principate looked to Virgil as having set forth their ideal temper. But there was, of course, overwhelming evidence that the Greeks in various ages and cities saw Homer as their common bond, and as having expressed values to which they all subscribed in one way or another. Homer and the Olympic religion did to some extent overcome political and religious localism in Greece, and that role for Homer was well known and widely acknowledged. Glover was simply attempting to appropriate that Homeric role to Virgil.

IV

The difficulties that the Victorians confronted understanding and interpreting Virgil reflected the larger problems they encountered in addressing Roman history, life, and culture. The nineteenth century was truly the era of the triumph of ancient Greece over Rome. This was especially the case in Germany, but only slightly less so in Great Britain. The Victorians knew that Rome and the works of Rome had long loomed large in Western culture. They knew that from the Renaissance through the eighteenth century Roman history and

---

[45] T. R. Glover, *Virgil*, 2nd edn (London: Methuen and Co., Ltd, 1912), pp. 83, 84, 105, 106, 141. Glover entitled the first edition of his work (1904) *Studies in Virgil*, but changed the title of subsequent editions to *Virgil*.

literature had been fundamental to their own intellectual and cultural life. Yet the Romans could not retain a position at the core of Victorian intellectual endeavour. As W. Y. Sellar himself confessed,

Familiarity with Latin literature is probably not less common than it was a century ago, but it is much less common relatively to familiarity with the older [Greek] literature. The attraction of the latter has been greater from its novelty, its originality, its higher intrinsic excellence, its profounder relation to the heart and mind of man.[46]

One of the liabilities of Roman studies was their very continuity with the past; one of the virtues of Greek studies to a century profoundly aware of the changes it was experiencing was their novelty and discontinuity.

All of the British nineteenth-century commentators on Virgil without exception felt they had to admit that Homer was a greater poet. For some it was his position as a more ancient and thus more original poet. For some it was his delineation of character. For some it was the excitement of his narrative. For some it was the very character of the Greek language. Myers declared, 'There never has been, there never will be, a language like the dead Greek. For Greek had all the merits of other tongues without their accompanying defects.'[47] Even the critics who devoted extensive essays or books to Virgil did so from a position of defensiveness and inner doubt. All that they had come to admire in modern poetry as well as ancient tended to be missing in Virgil and in Roman literature in general.

The demise in the appreciation of things Roman also displayed itself in the Victorian attitude toward Roman philosophy. Whereas Cicero had held a place of honour in the eighteenth century, the *Ethics* of Aristotle and the various works of Plato came to the fore from the middle of the nineteenth century onward. George Grote had made the radical utilitarian case for Greek philosophy, and the Anglican scholars had found it necessary to refute him. The scholarly conflict itself, as will be seen in the next essay, served to ignite even wider interest in Greek thought. Roman philosophers seemed useful to neither side of that dispute. Ciceronian public philosophy had been suited to a republic of hereditary senators possessing immense privilege or to an aristocracy facing the emergence of a

[46] Sellar, *The Roman poets of the Augustan age: Virgil*, p. 74.
[47] Myers, *Essays: classical*, p. 133.

tyrannical monarchy. Neither situation obtained in Victorian Britain. By contrast, both Aristotle and Plato portrayed a social and intellectual elite functioning and maintaining itself in the face of democracy. They provided a philosophy for a political elite legitimated by merit and by moral and intellectual superiority.

No less important, no Roman philosopher could provide the kind of surrogate to Christianity that was available in Plato. Many historians, as noted in an earlier essay, believed that the formation of the Roman Empire was a providential event that had unified the Mediterranean world and thus provided the largely unified political and social setting which permitted the original spread of Christianity beyond the borders of Palestine. On the other hand, Victorian commentators did not regard the Roman world as having produced any religion or philosophy that might have significantly contributed to or challenged the spiritual or moral insights of the Christian faith. They considered Roman religion as extremely political, intellectually uninteresting, and lacking in moral power. It was the religion that Christianity had overthrown.

Even at its best the Roman religious and philosophical heritage could not present a true rival to Christianity. In 1863 Matthew Arnold wrote an important and often reprinted essay on Marcus Aurelius, the Roman whom more Victorian intellectuals admired than any other. In that essay, Arnold asserted that Marcus Aurelius had been one of the truly great moralists, acquaintance with whom constituted 'an imperishable benefit'. Furthermore, he described Marcus Aurelius as 'perhaps the most beautiful figure in history' and as 'one of those consoling and hope-inspiring marks, which stand for ever to remind our weak and easily discouraged race how high human goodness and perseverance have once been carried, and may be carried again'. Marcus Aurelius prescribed right actions and assigned to them motives 'which every clear reason must recognise as valid'.[48]

What Arnold found especially attractive in this philosopher's morality was 'its accent of emotion ... [that] reminds one of Christian morality'. This emotional side of the *Meditations* gave to the work and the author a genuinely religious quality and a moral tone that in Arnold's eyes raised his thought above scientific naturalism or utilitarianism. Arnold regarded the most admirable feature of

[48] Matthew Arnold, *Essays in criticism: first series* (New York, The Macmillan Co., 1924), pp. 350, 354–5, 378.

Marcus Aurelius's writing to be his clear yearning for something which he could not attain through mere human means. Arnold declared,

What an affinity for Christianity had this persecutor of the Christians! The effusion of Christianity, its relieving tears, its happy self-sacrifice, were the very element, one feels, for which his soul longed; they were near him, they brushed him, he touched them, he passed them by . . . We see him wise, just, self-governed, tender, thankful, blameless; yet, with all this, agitated, stretching out his arms for something beyond.[49]

The great charm of Marcus Aurelius was not that he was a Roman but rather that he had displayed the kind of spiritual yearning for which Christianity, as Arnold understood it, might have provided sustenance. Not only had he passed by the opportunity, but he had also persecuted the Christians, an action that Arnold sought to mitigate but could not deny.

Since Marcus Aurelius had lived after the coming of Christ, neither the emperor's character nor his thought posed a real alternative to Christianity. Judgements of his worth had to be made by the standard of the Christian faith which he had rejected and persecuted as well as by the standard of Christian morality. For Arnold to state both the attractions of Marcus Aurelius and his shortcomings was to undermine any serious thought of his role as an intellectual or philosophical model even for a liberal Christian such as Arnold. To have seen Marcus Aurelius as supplementing Christianity would have been to deny the full adequacy of the faith. Roman morality at its best was as austere as Christian, but at its worst was just exactly what Christianity had displaced.

The moral and religious situations with the Greeks were quite different. The Greeks, unlike the Romans, had not sinned against the Light, quite simply because their culture had predated the Christian dispensation. It was that situation which allowed the Greeks in contrast to the Romans to loom so beneficently in Victorian thought. In the eyes of even so devoted a Latin scholar as Henry Nettleship the Greeks had performed a unique role in the European development. He once reminded an audience,

Greece was the mother not only of poetry and oratory, but – at least for the European world – of philosophy. And by philosophy I do not mean merely a succession of metaphysical and ethical systems, but the active love of

49 Ibid., pp. 367, 379.

knowledge, the search for truth. Will it be said that this spirit is not now as necessary an element in civilized human life as it ever was? In the long run it would almost appear as if it were mainly this which saves society from degeneracy and decay. The charitable instincts die out in an atmosphere of ignorance, for ignorance is the mother of terror and hatred. The free moral impulse which makes a man a man, which bids him love all good more than he fears death or pain – this is what was cherished in the Greek philosophic schools, the vital element, of which their metaphysical disputes were only the superficial manifestation . . . This is an inheritance as precious as Greek art and literary form; nay, if the continuous life of the nations be regarded, an inheritance even more precious.[50]

This achievement had occurred in the world of learning before the Romans and before the Christian dispensation. It had a perennial value. There was nothing in Roman life, culture, or literature that could match it. What Nettleship praised, of course, were the chief values of late Victorian university intellectuals. They found them alive in the world of ancient Greece largely because they had implanted them there but not in the world of Virgil or of Augustus. They could voice praise for the poetry of the former and the politics of the latter, but never without serious reservation and qualification. In the life work of neither could they find an image or reflection of their best selves.

[50] Henry Nettleship, *Lectures and essays: second series*, ed. F. Haverfield (Oxford: Clarendon Press, 1895), p. 217.

CHAPTER 12

The triumph of idealism in Victorian classical studies

Few topics in nineteenth-century intellectual history have been so neglected as the story of idealism after the death of Hegel. In the work of most historians idealism becomes displaced by science and positivism on the one hand and Marxism on the other. Yet in point of fact, philosophical idealism of different varieties continued to permeate and even dominate numerous areas of thought from the 1840s through World War I not only in Great Britain but also on the European continent and in America. One need only peruse the pages of J. T. Merz's *History of European thought in the nineteenth century* (4 vols., 1896–1914) to begin to appreciate the vast idealist presence. Spokesmen for idealism held chairs in philosophy in virtually all major universities across the Western world, influenced political and social philosophy, blunted the impact of utilitarianism and scientific naturalism, and exercised influence over all schools of early and late century theology. There was no single idealist philosophy, but rather at the close of the century idealism represented an outlook that emphasized metaphysical questions in philosophy, historicist analysis of the past, the spiritual character of the world, the active powers of the human mind, intuitionism, subjective religiosity, the responsibility of individuals for undertaking moral choice and action, the relative or even absolute importance of communities and communal institutions over individual action or rights, and the shallowness of any mode of reductionist thought. Generally idealism in its various modes associated itself with liberal Christianity or religions that eschewed strong institutional or biblical authority. All of these impulses tended to be rooted in post-Kantian German philosophical and theological developments or later interpretations of those developments.

Much of the material for this interpretive essay has been drawn from Frank M. Turner, *The Greek heritage in Victorian Britain* (New Haven: Yale University Press, 1981).

Historians after Merz have found late nineteenth-century idealism a particular problem. The twentieth-century demise of idealist
philosophy in the Anglo-American academy, the new directions
taken by continental philosophy, the general separation of philosophy and theology, the collapse in the broader culture of liberal
Protestantism grounded in idealist theology, the general abandonment of idealism in scientific thought, and the reorientation and
distortion of much intellectual activity resulting from the establishment of the Bolshevik regime in Russia in 1918 led to the neglect by
historians of late Victorian idealism in virtually all of its settings.
T. H. Green and other Oxford idealists have received some attention, but the more general idealist phenomenon has received much
less.[1] It has been too difficult to assimilate idealism into what was
thought or assumed to be a largely uninterrupted development of
positivistic streams of modern thought. So idealism was long
ignored and with it almost a half-century of British intellectual
activity.

By contrast, no area of Victorian intellectual life has received so
extensive scholarly examination as that of science and the emergence
of associated modes of rationalistic thought. This circumstance in
large measure reflects the expansive Victorian scientific activity, the
professionalizing efforts of its protagonists, and the impact of science
and technology on everyday life. Advocates of science and rationalism following the model of the contemporary men of letters rendered their ideas accessible to a larger public in essays of model
prose. Poets, novelists, literary critics, philosophers, theologians,
economists, historians, as well as political and social commentators,
looked to science and rationalistic or positivistic analysis for models

---

[1] Melvin Richter, *The politics of conscience: T. H. Green and his age* (Cambridge, Mass.:
Harvard University Press, 1964); Bruce Kuklick, *The rise of American philosophy: Cambridge,
Massachusetts, 1860–1930* (New Haven: Yale University Press, 1977), pp. 127–403; Stephan
Collini, *Liberalism and sociology: L. T. Hobhouse and political argument in England 1880–1914*
(Cambridge: Cambridge University Press, 1979); Stephan Collini, Donald Winch, and
John Burrow, *That noble science of politics: a study in nineteenth-century intellectual history*
(Cambridge: Cambridge University Press, 1983); Raymond Plant and Vincent Andrew,
Philosophy, politics and citizenship: the life and thought of the British idealists (Oxford: Basil
Blackwell, 1984); Standish Meacham, *Toynbee Hall and social reform 1880–1914: the search for
community* (New Haven: Yale University Press, 1987); Peter R. Nicholson, *The political
philosophy of the British idealists: selected studies* (New York: Cambridge University Press,
1990).

of progressive thought and method.² Until recently historical exploration of the emergence of these naturalistic world views has in many respects exaggerated their impact, led to the neglect of rival outlooks, and made difficult a discernment of which patterns of thought dominated at particular moments in the century.

For the purposes of Victorian intellectual history, it now appears that the decades from the 1840s through the mid-1870s marked a high water mark for critical rationalist thought. Such thinking was associated with the assimilation of the higher criticism of the Bible, the importation of Comtean positivism, the spread of the scientific theory, radical individualism, anti-idealist polemics associated with J. S. Mill, the presence of Owenism and other modes of materialism within working-class culture, and the emergence of scientific naturalism. Most of the influence of these developments had peaked by the mid-1870s. Thereafter in one field after another of Victorian intellectual life the scientific, naturalistic, positivistic, and rationalistic outlooks that had come to the fore in the 1830s and 1840s began to flounder against versions of idealism some as staid as the study of Hegel and others as exotic as theosophy.³ This pattern was, of course, not one of absolute change. Idealism associated with Coleridge and Carlyle and with William Whewell's philosophy of science had flourished earlier in the century. Furthermore, the mid-century advocates of science, positivism, and rationalism were rarely mindless reductionists; and rationalist ideas continued to exert influence

---

² Frank Miller Turner, *Between science and religion: the reaction to scientific naturalism in late Victorian England* (New Haven: Yale University Press, 1974), pp. 8–37; T. W. Heyck, *The transformation of intellectual life in Victorian England* (London: Croom Helm, 1982), pp. 24–154; Roger Cooter, *The cultural meaning of popular science: phrenology and the organization of consent in nineteenth-century Britain* (Cambridge: Cambridge University Press, 1984); James Paradis and Thomas Postlewait, *Victorian science and Victorian values: literary perspectives* (New Brunswick, N.J.: Rutgers University Press, 1985); Peter Allen Dale, *In pursuit of a scientific culture: science, art, and society in the Victorian age* (Madison: University of Wisconsin Press, 1989); Patrick Brantlinger, ed., *Energy & entropy: science and culture in Victorian Britain* (Bloomington: Indiana University Press, 1989). See also the classical statement of the influence of positivistic analysis in Noel Annan, *The curious strength of positivism in English political thought* (London: Oxford University Press, 1959).

³ Peter J. Bowler, *The eclipse of Darwinism: anti-Darwinian evolution theories in the decades around 1900* (Baltimore: Johns Hopkins University Press, 1983); Richard D. French, *Antivivisection and medical science in Victorian society* (Princeton: Princeton University Press, 1975); Coral Lansbury, *The old brown dog: women, workers, and vivisection in Edwardian England* (Madison: University of Wisconsin Press, 1985); J. B. Schneewind, *Sidgwick's ethics and Victorian moral philosophy* (Oxford: Clarendon Press, 1977); Martin J. Wiener, *English culture and the decline of the industrial spirit, 1850–1980* (Cambridge: Cambridge University Press, 1981); W. David Shaw, *The lucid veil: poetic truth in the Victorian age* (Madison: University of Wisconsin Press, 1987).

after the 1870s. Nonetheless, even when qualifications have been made, there can be no doubt that a distinct shift toward idealism did occur from that decade onward and shaped the climate of opinion for virtually all late Victorian intellectual activity.

One of the perhaps unexpected arenas in whch advocates of rationalistic and idealistic outlooks battled against each other was the investigation of the ancient world and most particularly that of ancient Greece. By the close of the nineteenth-century the study of ancient Greek history, literature, and philosophy had become broadly associated with idealist outlooks. The writers who had most deeply influenced this achievement were Matthew Arnold and Benjamin Jowett along with their many disciples and students who taught in public schools and universities throughout Great Britain. This late Victorian image of Greece emphasized community over individualism, ethical idealism over utilitarianism, a reverential if quite liberal sense of religion over either orthodoxy or unbelief, and an often reluctant acceptance of democracy tempered by the belief in the necessity of a well-educated leadership. The institutional foundation for this classical teaching was the Oxford *Litterae Humaniores* programme of study described by one of its Edwardian critics as the curriculum where 'the most characteristic and most influential of Oxford teachers have their scope' and 'the ablest of the students take their degrees'.[4]

Arnold, Jowett, and those who followed in their wake effectively redefined Christianity and liberal Anglican social values into a humanistic ethic grounded as much on Greek experience and philosophy as on distinctly Christian teachings. In 1912 Richard Livingstone of Oxford summed up the thrust of the outlook that informed that course of study:

Greece ... stands for humanity, simple and unashamed, with all the variety of its nature free to play. The Greek set himself to answer the question how, with no revelation from God to guide him, with no overbracing necessity to cramp or intimidate him, man should live. It has been a tendency of our own age to deny that heaven has revealed to us in any way how we ought to behave, or to find such a revelation in human nature itself. In either case we are thrown back on ourselves and obliged to seek our guide there. This is why the influence of Greece has grown so much. The Greeks are the only

---

4 Percy Gardner, *Oxford at the cross roads: a criticism of the Litterae Humaniores in the university* (London: Adam and Charles Black, 1903), p. 19.

people who have conceived the problem similarly; their answer is the only one which has yet been made.[5]

The answer of the Greeks to those questions as they were taught in late Victorian and Edwardian Oxford stood grounded in the ethical idealism of Jowett's interpretation of Plato and the humanistic Hellenism of Arnold. The Greeks had demonstrated that without Christian revelation or the tradition of the Church a people could remain moral and achieve a lasting impact on civilization without resort to utilitarianism, scientific naturalism, positivism, or critical rationalism.

The triumph of this idealist vision of ancient Greece, which remained commonplace for decades throughout the English-speaking world, had been anything but inevitable and would have been difficult to predict at mid-century. Between 1846 and 1865 the historian George Grote had brilliantly articulated an alternative version of the intellectual and political life of Greece. His twelve-volume *History of Greece* (1846–56) and his three-volume *Plato, and the other companions of Socrates* (1865) constituted one of the most impressive scholarly accomplishments of the mid-Victorian age. His writings were read across Europe and America with many of them being translated into both French and German. His works set the scholarly agenda for more than two generations of classicists. By any account Grote must be regarded as one of the preeminent mid-Victorian intellectuals, and he was recognized as such at the time. Had industriousness of research, extent of ancient and modern learning, power of analysis, and tenacity of purpose carried the day, a very different image of Greek life and culture, one totally hostile to idealism and to Christianity, would have dominated the thought of Britain and America by the close of the century. This important clash between the forces of rationalism and idealism for the control of the minds of learned Victorians has been virtually ignored although the cultural stakes proved to be quite high.

I

George Grote's vision of ancient Greece became one of the most significant intellectual paths not taken in the late Victorian age. His voluminous mid-century writings posed to the world of classical

5 Richard W. Livingstone, *The Greek genius and its meaning to us* (Oxford: Clarendon Press, 1912), pp. 247–8.

scholarship the same challenge of critical rationalism that Darwin and the advocates of scientific naturalism posed to contemporary Anglican-dominated science. Grote was a middle-class London banker, a member of the Bentham and Mill utilitarian circle, an associate of other advanced London intellectuals, a founder of University College London, and a parliamentary political radical. His general social and intellectual world mirrored on a somewhat expanded basis the society of London radicals and Unitarians that Darwin had encountered between his return from the voyage of *The Beagle* and his settling in Down. During the early 1840s, like other philosophic radicals who were disappointed with their failure to achieve a programme of radical reform in Parliament after 1832, Grote retired from active political life. He then turned to the writing of Greek history becoming a classical scholar of enormous erudition and of international reputation.[6]

For Grote the writing of Greek history continued the political and intellectual agenda that he had pursued as a young radical hostile to the aristocracy and Church and supportive of democracy and critical rationalism. Grote had long understood the importance of classical studies for influencing and possibly redirecting contemporary English intellectual and political life. In 1826 he had contributed an important article to the *Westminster Review* criticizing William Mitford's conservative eighteenth-century *History of Greece* and deploring its continued domination of the universities. The ongoing influence of Mitford's deeply flawed history demonstrated to Grote that English Greek studies remained 'confined to the technicalities of language, or the intricacies of its metres, instead of being employed to unfold the mechanism of society, and to bring to view the numerous illustrations which Grecian phenomena afford, of the principles of human nature'. Grote thought it not surprising that Mitford's very conservative views 'should be eminently agreeable to the reigning interests in England; nor that instructors devoted to those interests should carefully discourage all those mental qualities which might enable their pupils to look into evidence for themselves, and to deduce just inferences from the Greek authors who are put into their hands'. The young Grote concluded that few works would

---

[6] Harriet Grote, *The personal life of George Grote*, 2nd edn (London: John Murray, 1873); Martin Lowther Clarke, *George Grote, a biography* (London: University of London: Athlone Press, 1962); Joseph Hamburger, *Intellectuals in politics: John Stuart Mill and the philosophic radicals* (New Haven: Yale University Press, 1965).

so prevent future instructors from teaching superficially and uncritically 'than a good history of Greece'.[7] Such a history would provide the occasion to unfold 'the mechanism of society' and 'the principles of human nature' as illustrated in the Greek experience for the instruction of the nineteenth century. Thus from the beginning, in Grote's mind the undertaking of historical writing was to provide a vehicle for changing the present world by educating the next generation in enlightened and critically rational ideas.

Twenty years later having concluded his career in parliamentary politics, Grote began to publish just such a history. In the course of its publication, Grote's self-consciously radical history displaced Connop Thirlwall's eight-volume *History of Greece* (1835–45).[8] Thirlwall had been a Cambridge scholar of considerable distinction and wide learning. His advocacy of university reform and sympathy for Nonconformists brought him much difficulty at Cambridge and eventual elevation by Lord Melbourne to the see of St David's in Wales. However liberal his theology and moderate his politics, Thirlwall was not a radical reformer. He was a moderate Anglican whose general intellectual and religious outlook very much paralleled that of the liberal Anglicans who founded the British Association for the Advancement of Science. Thirlwall drew extensively upon German critical scholarship, but his history was neither politically radical nor intellectually rationalistic. He composed a worthy and learned history of Greece that embodied recent scholarship but that did not significantly challenge the intellectual, theological, or political status quo. For example, he believed there was much confusion and distortion in Greek myths, but that the narratives still contained elements of historical truth. Unlike Mitford, Thirlwall was not overly critical of Athenian democracy, but neither did he defend its virtues. Grote's politics, religion, and historical writing differed markedly from Thirlwall's even though the two writers retained scholarly respect and personal friendship for each other. Drawing upon both Enlightenment rationalism and advanced German philological and historical scholarship, Grote presented an interpretation of Greek society based on radical democra-

---

7 George Grote, 'Institutions of ancient Greece', *Westminster Review*, 5 (1826), 331.

8 Connop Thirlwall, *A history of Greece*, 8 vols. (London: Longman, Rees, Orme, Brown, Green, & Longman and John Taylor, 1835–45); John Connop Thirlwall, *Connop Thirlwall, historian and theologian* (New York: The Macmillan Co., 1936); Turner, *The Greek heritage in Victorian Britain*, pp. 81, 211–12, 278–83.

tic politics, utilitarian ethics, and thoroughly naturalistic science designed to challenge conservative British institutions in general and contemporary Christianity in particular.

As might have been predicted from his remarks of 1826, Grote's history directed against Mitford a long polemic defending the wisdom of ancient and by implication modern democratic institutions. The core of Grote's argument was the contention, counterinstinctual to most of his readers, that through radical democracy Athens had achieved 'constitutional morality' or a respect for the process of government by debate and persuasion. Grote urged that the broad political participation afforded by radical democratic institutions had bred 'a paramount reverence for the forms of the constitution, enforcing obedience to the authorities acting under and within those forms, yet combined with the habit of open speech, of action subject only to definite legal control, and unrestrained censure of those very authorities as to all their public acts'.[9] Rather than political tumult Athenian democracy had fostered a stable public life that secured broad consent, due process, individual liberty, freedom of thought, sound administration, and security of property. The political problems of Athenian history and the alleged failures of its democratic institutions he ascribed to ancient aristocratic and religious influences that inhibited or corrupted the proper functioning of democracy. Although Grote's defence of ancient democracy encountered critics, it set the terms for historical debate on the issue in Britain and throughout Europe for several decades.

Grote's *History of Greece* quite properly attained its primary fame for its last ten volumes which presented his powerful pro-democratic analysis of Greek political development. That situation masked other goals that he pursued which also had very considerable contemporary significance. The first two volumes of *A history of Greece* published in 1846 primarily addressed the subjects of Greek myth, religion, and the Homeric epics. These discussions constituted a major, if generally unrecognized, element in his larger defence of ancient and by implication modern democratic institutions. Whereas earlier historians had blamed the crimes and errors of the Athenians on democratic institutions, Grote in every instance traced them to the residual pernicious influence of myth, religion, and superstition that had originated in earlier eras.[10] In a characteristic

⁹ George Grote, *A history of Greece*, new edn (London: John Murray, 1869), IV, 81.
¹⁰ Turner, *The Greek heritage in Victorian Britain*, pp. 213–34.

Benthamite manner he also argued that sinister aristocratic political interests had drawn upon religious superstition to frustrate the functioning of the democracy and to overturn the virtues of 'constitutional morality'. On other occasions Grote traced politically disastrous or morally repugnant democratic decisions to democratic citizens being temporarily overwhelmed by atavistic religious sentiments.

Grote's interest in the influence of religion represented an example of the ongoing concern of Victorian political reformers and radicals with irrational political behaviour. From his earliest days in the Bentham circle Grote had been hostile to modern religious thought and institutions. Grote was acutely aware of the manner in which religious faith, sentiment, and organizations could frustrate democratic politics. These concerns grew during the years of the composition of *A history of Greece*. The 1840s and 1850s saw a resurgence of religious activity throughout the British Isles in the form of the Tractarian controversy in the Church of England, the Great Disruption in the Church of Scotland, the revival of Roman Catholicism in Ireland, the reestablishment of the Roman Catholic hierarchy in England, the consequent rise of virulent anti-Catholicism, as well as the widespread resurgence of Nonconformity. Religious influences on their own or as used by political manipulators could in the opinion of Grote and other observers prevent democratic citizens from voting and behaving in an independent, rational manner and could thus bring tumult, confusion, and new modes of conservatism to British politics.

Although by conviction highly sceptical of Christianity, Grote was also deeply sensitive to contemporary social pressures toward religious accommodation and he publicly wrote nothing about the Christian faith.[11] Nonetheless, his initial two volumes of *A history of Greece*, dealing with Greek myth and Homer, represent major contributions to the religiously dissolvent mid-century literature associated with Unitarian and radical London intellectual life. Other notable examples of such writings include Charles Hennell's *Inquiry concerning the origin of Christianity* (1838), John Stuart Mill's *System of logic* (1843), G. H. Lewes's *Biographical history of philosophy* (1845) and his philosophical explication in *Comte's philosophy of the*

11 David Berman, *A history of atheism in Britain: from Hobbes to Russell* (London: Croom Helm, 1988), pp. 191–201; George Grote, 'John Stuart Mill on the philosophy of Sir William Hamilton', *Westminster Review*, 85 (1866), 8–9, 16–17.

sciences (1853), Marian Evans's translations of Strauss's *Leben Jesu* (1846) and Feuerbach's *Essence of Christianity* (1854), F. W. Newman's *A history of the Hebrew monarchy* (1847), R. W. Mackay's *The progress of the intellect, as exemplified in the religious development of the Greeks and Hebrews* (1850) and *Sketch of the rise and progress of Christianity* (1854), W. R. Greg's *The creed of Christendom* (1851), and Harriet Martineau's two-volume abridgement of *The positive philosophy of Auguste Comte* (1853). Each of these works, like Grote's, drew upon advanced French and German philosophy and biblical criticism. They addressed themselves to the validity of the historical content of ancient texts, the character of ancient myth, the manner in which human beings passed from religious thinking toward scientific, and the intellectual methods that might make this critical transition possible. All of these works and their authors implicitly or explicitly denied any privileged position to Christian scriptures or sacred history.

Grote's analysis of the Homeric question fitted directly into this liberal and critically radical religious literature. The point of contact was the textual integrity and historical validity of the Bible. In 1795 F. A. Wolf had published his *Prolegomena ad Homerum*. There he contended that the Iliad, as collected and collated during the age of Pisistratus, represented an edited collection of ballads composed hundreds of years earlier in a preliterate age by wandering minstrels. Consequently, according to Wolf, there was no single Homer, and the Iliad was not a work conceived by a single creative artistic mind. Such views also raised the most serious questions about the historical validity of the content of the Homeric narrative. In volume II of *A history of Greece* published in 1846, George Grote very fully explored and embraced Wolfian theories and made his own significant contribution to them. Grote denied the unitary authorship of the Iliad though he thought the evidence less certain for the Odyssey. The specific details of Grote's view of Homer are not germane to this essay, but the general thrust of his analysis like that of other critical theories of Homer directly paralleled advanced German biblical criticism. If the ancient text of Homer and the historical narrative it contained could disintegrate under the scrutiny of scholarly examination, the same was true of the Bible.[12]

---

[12] Turner, *The Greek heritage in Victorian Britain*, pp. 140–54; Anthony Grafton, *Defenders of the text: the traditions of scholarship in an age of science, 1450–1800* (Cambridge, Mass.: Harvard University Press, 1991), pp. 214–43.

Grote's analysis of Greek myth posed even more direct danger to Christianity. In contrast to his English predecessors, Grote argued that no historical facts or information were to be discovered in or behind the myths. Indeed for Grote it was 'essentially unphilosophical' to confuse the materials of legend and epic poetry with those of history. Recognizing that some readers would find his outlook puzzling, Grote explained, that if the reader were to ask

why I do not undraw the curtain and disclose the picture – I reply in the words of the painter Zeuxis, when the same question was addressed to him on exhibiting his masterpiece of imitative art – 'The curtain *is* the picture.' What we now read as poetry and legend was once accredited history, and the only genuine history which the first Greeks could conceive or relish of their past time: the curtain conceals nothing behind, and cannot by any ingenuity be withdrawn. I undertake only to show it as it stands – not to efface, still less to re-paint it.

According to Grote, the narratives of the myths and the Homeric epics had presented 'a past which never was present, – a region essentially mythical, neither approachable by the critic nor measurable by the chronologer'.[13] As such, the myths could provide no trustworthy evidence of early Greek history.

Grote asserted that myths arose during an 'age of historical faith, as distinguished from the later age of historical reason' and constituted 'a popularized expression of the divine and heroic faith of the people' of that epoch. Yet the sincerity of the ancient faith that sustained the myths did not and could not impart any historical reality to their content. Rather than being a mistaken or distorted version of past events, the myths provided 'a quasi-history and quasi-philosophy' which 'filled up the vacuum of the unrecorded past, and explained many of the puzzling incognita of the present'. Had people from the Homeric age been confronted with firm evidence of a modern scientific kind, it would have appeared to them 'not merely unholy and unimpressive, but destitute of all plausibility or title to credence'. Grote's radical historicizing of myth thus both recognized the validity of such thought during a particular era of human history and simultaneously eradicated its validity as a source of later or modern knowledge about the events of that period. Nor did the age of myth deserve the nostalgia of later eras. Of the demise of mythic thought Grote once declared, 'Estimated by a poetical

[13] Grote, *A history of Greece*, I, viii, 43.

standard, the loss has been serious indeed; but it has been far more than compensated by the acquisition of lasting and substantial benefits.'[14]

Grote was concerned to illustrate the confusion that could arise when myth was not fully recognized as myth in later ages. To that end, he analysed the manner in which the Greeks of historical times had attempted to deal critically with their mythic inheritance. He traced this development through the framework of Comte's Law of Three Stages with myth and religion giving way first to metaphysics and next to science. The thought of Xenophanes and Pythagoras illustrated the displacement of a mythic point of view by metaphysical interpretation. Afterwards in the fifth century BC the thought of genuinely enlightened figures with scientific outlooks, including Socrates, Anaxagoras, and Hippocrates, had made clear the 'radical discord between the mental impulses of science and religion'. Thereafter 'positive science and criticism, and the idea of an invariable sequence of events' supplanted earlier religious concepts. Science and religion could no longer stand together, 'but in every particular case the admission of one involved the rejection of the other'.[15]

As a result of this 'anti-mythic vein of criticism' and the associated 'improved tone of sentiment and a newly created canon of credibility', the Greek myths themselves had become the object of rational, scientific scrutiny. Certain fifth-century Greeks attempted either to explain or to reinterpret the mythic inheritance. Through the application of the new canons of evidence and criticism the myths came to be regarded in a manner 'completely foreign to the reverential curiosity and literal imaginative faith of the Homeric man'. The myths were in the process 'broken up and recast in order to force them into new moulds such as their authors had never conceived'. Through this process the myths assumed a new cultural role in Greek life, but they were still not recognized as a mode of thought pertaining to an earlier age of human development. Despite Euripides's scepticism, the general tendency of Athenian tragedy from Aeschylus onward had been 'to uphold an unquestioning faith and a reverential estimate of the general mythical world and its personages, but to treat the particular narratives rather as matters

---

[14] Ibid., viii, 428, 343, 346; George Grote, 'Grecian legends and early history', *Westminster Review*, 39 (1843), 328.
[15] Grote, *A history of Greece*, I, 362, 348.

for the emotions than as recitals of actual fact'. Herodotus and Thucydides had exercised a critical attitude toward the myths, but still used them in their narratives as did later historians in the ancient world. Other Greeks had allegorized the myths in some fashion. Grote explained that this manner of 'distinguishing the interpreted from the literal myth has passed from the literary men of antiquity to those of the modern world' who had consequently continued to extract from the myths 'quasi-historical persons' and 'quasi-historical events' and had thus failed to understand the myths as a particular manifestation of the human mind at a particular stage of human social and intellectual development that was inapplicable at a later stage.[16]

Grote's critical analysis of the character and fate of Greek myth and religion had direct contemporary religious implications. In attacking the historical validity of ancient Greek myth, Grote was also implicitly criticizing the historical validity of the myths that undergirded the Christian tradition. Every part of his analysis of Greek myth had a Christian analogue. In his mind and those of contemporaries, such as David Friedrich Strauss, the narratives of the Bible were products of a mythopoeic age. They represented the mentality of a people at a particular time and place but did not communicate information upon which genuine historical knowledge could be based.[17] Attempts of liberal Christians to produce a more nearly spiritual rather than literal interpretation of the Christian myths no more improved the situation fundamentally than had the work of the ancient tragedians. The same was the case with those Christian writers who attempted to sort out historical truth from historical falsehoods in the mythical narratives. The persistence of a mythic mentality in ancient Athens and a religious mentality in mid-Victorian England each represented intellectual regression and fostered cultural confusion.

Grote's interpretation of ancient Greek philosophy found in volume VIII of *A history of Greece* and in *Plato, and the other companions of Socrates* represented one of the major statements of mid-Victorian philosophic and political radicalism and continued to assert the

[16] Ibid., 364, 375–6, 437.
[17] Grote very carefully published nothing about the narratives of the Bible or early history of the Church. Nonetheless he did directly attack myths and miraculous stories from the Christian Middle Ages in a long chapter entitled, 'The Grecian mythical vein compared with that of modern Europe', ibid., 445–73.

sceptical outlook present in his first two volumes. For Grote the world of fifth-century Athens was one of an ancient enlightenment whose best spokesmen challenged tradition and received ideas. Grote championed the civic skills of the sophists, the logic and science of Socrates, and the searching examinations of received ideas presented by Plato's dialogues. Grote's narrative and analysis constituted a far ranging polemic in defence of free expression, intellectual individualism, science, and critical philosophy. Throughout this analysis Grote's targets were intellectual conformity and complacency, the authority of community opinion, idealism, and residual religion.

Whereas previous scholars had almost uniformly condemned the ancient sophists and associated them with destructive eighteenth-century Enlightenment rationalism, Grote presented them as paid teachers who trained young Athenians in the rhetorical skills required for responsible democratic political activity.[18] Their instruction had taught citizens to value persuasion over coercion and thus in part accounted for the achievement of Athenian 'constitutional morality'. Modern authorities insufficiently appreciated the lively political and intellectual interchange of ancient Athens and consequently had mistakenly accepted at face value ancient hostile accusations directed toward the sophists, including Plato's. By contrast Grote thought the presence of both the sophists and Plato demonstrated that Athens was a place where 'every man could speak out his sentiments and his criticisms with a freedom unparalleled in the ancient world, and hardly paralleled even in the modern, in which a vast body of dissent both is, and always has been, condemned to absolute silence'.[19]

Grote contended that it was wrong to condemn, as did some modern commentators, the sophists for the political ambition of their students while failing to recognize how the skills of persuasion, memory, and speaking taught by the sophists rendered more nearly civil the manner in which those ambitions were pursued. Grote argued that the best way to inhibit evil uses of speech was to assure the possibility for the broadest scope of competent persons presenting various points of view. In Athens the teaching of the sophists had established just such a climate by increasing the number of skilled speakers capable of both setting forth and criticizing a variety of

---

[18] Turner, *The Greek heritage in Victorian Britain*, pp. 268–70, 283–92.
[19] Grote, *A history of Greece*, VIII, 149.

opinions so that the public could be genuinely informed and not merely deceived. Grote asserted that the value of politics by persuasion rather than coercion was 'not less applicable to English than to Athenian politics' and indeed 'to every country where any free scope is left for human energy'. Rather than representing ambition or other political evils, Grote declared that the sophist

represents intellectual and persuasive force, reflecting and methodized so as to operate upon the minds of free hearers, yet under perfect liberty of opposition ... It is this which I am here upholding ... as not only no evil, but (in my judgement) one of the grand sources of good in Athens, and essential to human improvement everywhere else ... Discredit the arguments of the Sophist as much as you can by others of an opposite tendency: but when you discredit his weapon of intellectual and persuasive force, as if it were nothing better than cheat and imposture, manufactured and sold for the use of ambitious men – you leave open no other ascendency over men's minds, except the crushing engine of extraneous coercion with assumed infallibility.[20]

Like John Stuart Mill, Grote associated such uninhibited discussion with human progress and a free, open society. Grote knew from his early radical political acquaintances about the repression of free expression and a free press in Britain itself.[21] During the 1840s and 1850s he witnessed the spread of political oppression across the continent. Grote firmly believed that the real alternative to government through discussion carried on by an ever widening circle of people capable of participating was some form of repressive political regime. For those reasons he would later sharply and harshly criticize the limitations on thought and discussion that appeared in Plato's political philosophy.

Grote to the surprise of most readers drew Socrates into the company of the sophists as epitomizing one who opened all questions to free, probing discussion. One of Socrates's particular contributions to the better use of open discussion was his role in establishing the methods of inductive discourse which according to Grote were carried further by Aristotle in ancient times and then recast by J. S. Mill in the modern era.[22] By pioneering the path to understanding

[20] Ibid., 161fn, 162fn.
[21] See Joseph Hamburger, 'Religion and *On Liberty*', in Michael Laine, ed., *A cultivated mind: essays on J. S. Mill presented to John M. Robson* (Toronto: University of Toronto Press, 1991), pp. 139–81.
[22] Turner, *The Greek heritage in Victorian Britain*, pp. 292–309.

what is and is not scientifically discoverable, Socrates had come to
the 'conviction that the scientific and the religious point of view
mutually excluded one another, so that where the latter began the
former ended'. Like Bentham and his followers, Grote's Socrates set
forth to employ his reason so as to disturb the moral and intellectual
complacency of his fellow Athenians in hope of transforming those
citizens into critical self-conscious thinkers on moral, political, and
religious issues. In *Plato, and the other companions of Socrates* Grote
directly presented Socrates as epitomizing the radical intellectual
individualism of Mill's *On liberty*. For both Mill and Grote the
primary enemy of independent, probing thought was 'orthodox
sentiment among the ordinary public' which constituted a 'perpetual drag-chain, even if its force is not absolutely repressive, upon
free speculation'. Socrates had directed the negative, sceptical force
of his conversations against this sentiment whenever it displayed
itself in the form of 'false knowledge, or confident unreasoned
belief'.[23] Socrates had thus become the great antagonist of King
Nomos in Athens.

Grote emphasized the radically negative philosophic qualities that
he believed had originated with Socrates because he thought such
scepticism continued throughout Plato's work. Grote contended that
the Socrates of numerous Platonic dialogues had introduced into
philosophy 'a complete revolution in method' by placing negative
criticism at the fore of his procedure. The result as it displayed itself
in certain of Plato's dialogues was 'philosophy, or reasoned truth,
approached in the most polemical manner, operative at first only to
discredit the natural, unreasoned intellectual growths of the ordin-

[23] Grote, *A history of Greece*, VIII, 227; George Grote, *Plato, and the other companions of Socrates*
(London: John Murray, 1865), I, ix. The year after publishing *Plato, and the other companions
of Socrates* Grote made the following observation in regard to arguments in Mill's *Examination
of the philosophy of Sir William Hamilton*: 'Mr. Mill announces his resolution to determine for
himself, and according to his own reason and conscience, what God he will worship, and
what God he will not worship. For ourselves, we cordially sympathize with his resolution.
But Mr. Mill must be aware that this is a point on which society is equally resolved that no
individual shall determine for himself, if they can help it. Each new-born child finds his
religious creed readily prepared for him. In his earliest days of unconscious infancy, the
stamp of the national, gentile, phratric, God, or Gods, is imprinted upon him by his elders;
and if the future man, in the exercise of his own independent reason, acquires such
convictions as compel him to renounce those Gods, proclaiming openly that he does so – he
must count upon such treatment as will go far to spoil the value of the present life to him,
even before he passes to those ulterior liabilities which Mr. Mill indicates in the distance.'
Grote, 'John Stuart Mill on the Philosophy of Sir William Hamilton', 8–9. As a footnote to
the passage, Grote referred to the execution of Socrates. I am indebted to Joseph
Hamburger for bringing this reference to my attention.

ary mind, and to generate a painful consciousness of ignorance'.[24] He contended that such dialogues remained essentially incomprehensible without the recognition of the function of the Socratic negative dialectic. This emphasis upon the sceptical character of many of the Platonic dialogues was a unique and innovative contribution of Grote's analysis. In this regard, Grote's discussion stood in sharp contrast to that of both earlier English writers and contemporary continental commentators.

Grote vigorously denied that there existed any single Platonic philosophy. Rather he insisted that Plato's thought had gone through a series of not even necessarily connected or internally consistent stages. There were the dialogues of 'search', such as the *Hippias*, the *Protagoras*, the *Gorgias*, and the early Socratic dialogues, in which Plato displayed a critical and often sceptical mentality. Grote admired the manner in which those dialogues attacked and cast doubt upon inherited customs and ideas. But Grote deplored the dialogues of 'exposition', which included the *Republic* and the *Laws*.[25] There he found an illiberal, anti-democratic political and social theory that repressed private life and individual action in the name of the external authority of the state and of an intuitive theory of knowledge incompatible with scientific understanding. These latter elements of Plato Grote consistently criticized.

Throughout his volumes on Plato, Grote championed the sceptical strains and emphasized the necessary independence of the individual intellect. He repeatedly supported the Protagorean doctrine of Homo Mensura or man the measure of all things against Plato's criticism. In one of the most memorable passages in his voluminous writings, Grote declared,

Whoever denies the Protagorean autonomy of the individual judgement, must propound as his counter-theory some heteronomy, such as he (the denier) approves. If I am not allowed to judge of truth and falsehood for myself, who is to judge for me? ... If you pronounce a man unfit to be the measure of truth for himself, you constitute yourself the measure, in his place: either directly as lawgiver – or by nominating censors according to your own judgement ... You can only exchange one individual judgement for another. You cannot get out of the region of individual judgements, more or fewer in number: the King, the Pope, the Priest, the Judges or Censors, the author of some book, or the promulgator of such and such doctrine. The

[24] Grote, *Plato, and the other companions of Socrates*, I, viii, ix.
[25] Ibid., 210–17, 237–80.

infallible measure which you undertake to provide must be found in some person or persons – if it can be found at all: in some person selected by yourself – that is, in the last result, *yourself*.[26]

In Grote's view the good parts of Plato led to scepticism and the unleashing of individualism while the bad parts led to repressive, illiberal regimes where the individual was sacrificed to the community. Plato sobered by Socratic scepticism needed to be turned against Plato drunk on dogmatism. In this regard Grote's analysis of Platonic philosophy carried out in the context of the ancient world the attack on idealism that characterized Mill's *Examination of Sir William Hamilton's Philosophy* (1865) and the later portions of his *Autobiography* (1873).

With the publication in 1865 of *Plato, and the other companions of Socrates* George Grote had contributed fifteen substantial volumes on the religious, literary, political, and intellectual history of ancient Greece displacing the works of both Mitford and Thirlwall. It is difficult to overestimate the quality, vigour, and extent of this interpretive achievement in its own day. Nothing comparable existed in the English language, nor would any future English classical scholar achieve so capacious a coverage and analysis of the subject. Grote's studies had received extensive reviews throughout the Victorian journals. Furthermore, in 1865 there existed no substantial alternative examination of ancient Greek political and intellectual history. Had Grote gone unanswered, his rationalistic analysis would have carried the day. The coverage of the ancient Greek world available to students and other readers throughout the English-speaking world would have championed democracy, political and intellectual individualism, scepticism, empiricism, positivism, and science while degrading aristocracy, religion, custom, community authority, and idealism.

Yet such was not to be the case. Although both Oxford and Cambridge awarded Grote honorary degrees, their dons refused to teach the Greek world as he had presented it. The late Victorian university vision of Greece did not come to embrace the values and outlooks of Jeremy Bentham, John Stuart Mill, Auguste Comte, and the contributors to advanced continental philology, religious criticism, and mythography. Rather point by point Grote's interpretation of Greek religious and intellectual life was ignored, refuted, or

[26] Ibid., II, 358–9.

assimilated so as to rid it of its inherent radicalism. His rationalistic Socrates became a kind of quaint mid-Victorian period piece. His philosophically inconsistent Plato did not become the Plato of the universities. Although critics and commentators accepted much of Grote's defence of Athenian democracy, they accommodated themselves to both ancient and modern democracy on grounds other than Grote's. Indeed, perhaps only more impressive than the scholarship of George Grote was its failure to capture the minds and imaginations of the learned British world.

Most of the refutation and displacement of Grote occurred at the hands of Anglican critics and scholars. It is significant and worth noting in this regard that Anglicans never displayed toward Grote the personal hostility or animosity that they often directed against one of their own who embraced advanced or radical ideas. Grote was not a cultural apostate. He was a self-confessed political and intellectual radical who had intended to confront directly the dominance of the aristocracy and the Church. Without any apology Grote stood as part of that radical London culture against which Anglican intellectuals battled for most of the century. Intellectual and religious criticism from such an outsider raised less inherent anxiety than that posed by persons, such as Darwin or Newman, emerging from the Anglican fold itself. Grote did not raise self-doubt in Anglican university scholars. His ideas presented a target of a relatively familiar kind to be attacked and refuted, but not to be legitimized by interior angst.

II

From the late 1840s onward much Victorian scholarship on Greek religion, literature, and philosophy represented an attempt – largely successful – within the Anglican universities to erect barriers against the influence of Grote's writings. Grote became the ever present negative force against which the Anglicans directed their energies. The Anglican insiders stood determined to resist the intrusion of the radical outsider. His views and interpretations were not refuted, they quite simply were not permitted to contest the terrain for the minds of the late Victorian and Edwardian generations. Yet it was Grote who set the terms of the debate, and the interpretations of the ancient world enunciated by Anglican scholars and critics more often than not directly reversed those of Grote.

The response to Grote's views on Homer and Greek myth were part of the more general Anglican attempt to resist the intrusion of critical biblical studies. The scriptures remained central to both Anglican and Nonconformist Christianity. Challenges to the privileged status of scripture and of sacred history received sharp rebukes throughout the century. As early as the 1830s Thomas Arnold expressed anxiety over the future of critical biblical studies to his friend Richard Whately, Archbishop of Dublin:

The higher Criticism of the Pentateuch, and the other historical Books of the Old Testament will not I fear be attempted in England in my Time; – I know no Man who has the knowledge & peculiar talent to fit him for such a Work, together with the moral & spiritual Requisites besides; and if there were such a Man, I do not think that the English Public would receive his Results more favourably than the Inquisition did Galileo.[27]

The experience of those who sought to explore publicly the higher criticism of the scriptures during the next fifty years proved Arnold right. The leaders of the Anglican Church including those of a moderate theological and political outlook stood determined to resist the inroads of what they regarded as destructive critical methods into biblical scholarship. That determination touched classical studies as well.

There existed a clear recognition on the part of scholars across the spectrum of Anglican opinion, as well as among Nonconformists, that the extension of critical philological methods to classical Greek or Roman subjects could wreak havoc in biblical scholarship and sacred history. Such philology could present the Bible, as well as Homer, as a text written by numerous hands under diverse historical circumstances. The validity of the narratives of sacred history could come into question. Furthermore, comparative philological and anthropological methods could recognize affinities and parallels between Christian and non-Christian myths thus dissolving the claims to divine revelation of the former. Religious ideas and moral values also regarded as uniquely Judeo-Christian might be discovered to have arisen independently elsewhere in the ancient world and to have influenced the Hebrews and the early Church. Anglican authorities and opinion in the Church and the universities actively discouraged the pursuit of such critical studies of either the Bible or the Greek and Roman world.

27 Undated letter from Thomas Arnold to Richard Whately in The Brotherton Collection, Leeds University Library.

Fear of persecution among university scholars should not be ignored as a factor preventing the assimilation of Grote's interpretation of Homer and myth. The hostility and legal persecution directed toward contributors to *Essays and reviews* (1860) dissuaded venturesome scholarship and writing in the Church of England and the universities far longer than has generally been recognized.[28] Writers occupying any position of security within the Anglican or other religious worlds could be persecuted or have their lives made miserable for voicing even moderately liberal theological ideas let alone advanced critical ones. In this regard scholars of the ancient world unlike the scientists who were moving toward a more thoroughly naturalistic interpretation of nature lacked an institutional setting that allowed genuine or even relatively free expression of thought.

An example taken from late in the century will illustrate the situation. The emergence of anthropological analysis of religion made it difficult, if not impossible, for Victorian scholars to continue to ignore the similarities to Christianity of pagan practices whether Greek or Roman. James Frazer recognized the dangers inherent in clearly drawing the parallels and consciously chose to remain silent about the implications for Christianity of *The golden bough*. In a letter posted to his publisher in November 1889, shortly before he submitted the manuscript of the first volume of that work, Frazer wrote,

I shall soon have completed a study in the history of primitive religion which I propose to offer to you for publication. The book is an explanation of the legend of the Golden Bough, as that legend is given by Servius in his commentary on Virgil ... This is the base outline of the book which, whatever may be thought of its theories[,] will be found, I believe, to contain a large cadre of very curious customs, many of which may be new even to professional anthropologists. The resemblance of many of the savage customs and ideas to the fundamental doctrines of Christianity is striking. But I make no reference to this parallelism, leaving my readers to draw their own conclusions, one way or the other.[29]

The letter is remarkable for the candour of the proposed absence of

---

[28] I. Ellis, *Seven against Christ: a study of 'Essays and reviews'* (Leiden: E. J. Brill, 1980).

[29] James G. Frazer to Macmillan, 8 Nov. 1889, Macmillian Co. Archives, British Library, Add. MSS 55134, fo. 10. (Reprinted with the permission of the Master and Fellows of Trinity College, Cambridge.) See Robert Ackerman, *J. G. Frazer: his life and work* (Cambridge: Cambridge University Press, 1987), pp. 188–90, for an account of Frazer's later confrontation with religious difficulties.

candour. The particular example cited was from a Roman religious rite, but Frazer knew there were practices in Greek religion that would open similar parallels to Christianity that many readers would regard as dissolvent of the latter faith. Frazer and others recognized that any free and open discussion of similarities between the Greeks and Romans and the later Christians would open him or any other author to possible criticism and even persecution. Frazer's contemporary and soon-to-be Cambridge colleague William Robertson Smith had experienced a formal denominational trial for heresy in Scotland for his advanced views of Hebrew scripture based on anthropology. Frazer, who continued to exercise caution even after the turn of the century, saw no need to court similar trouble.

It is difficult to know for certain that such apprehensions over persecution had blocked the full appropriation of Grote's theories of Homer during the middle decades of the century. What is certain is that no single section of his writings received so little notice by contemporary reviewers and later commentators as Grote's exploration of Wolfian theories of Homer published in 1846. This refutation by silence cannot have been accidental because contemporary reviewers did discuss his equally critical theory of myth which appeared at the same time. The Wolfian Homeric Trojan horse allegedly constructed by Pisistratean editors and filled with hidden biblical critics was not about to be permitted within the walls of the universities or the mainstream of British culture.

British classical commentators were certain that the critical exploration of Homer would necessarily lead to similar doubt about the scriptures. English scholars had been aware of Wolf's theories by at least the 1820s when questions concerning it appeared on Cambridge University examinations. The examiners, however, framed the questions so as to elicit answers describing the inadequacies of Wolf's arguments. Two decades later a reviewer reminded readers, 'The doctrine revived and developed by Wolf as to Homer, was an offset from the determined warfare against the Bible which throughout the last century occupied so many of the liveliest intellects in Europe.' In 1854 E. B. Pusey, Regius Professor of Hebrew at Oxford, whose name was by then the byword for high church religious orthodoxy, declared of critical German philological scholarship, 'The scepticism as to Homer ushered in the scepticism on the Old

Testament.'³⁰ Later commentators, such as John Stuart Blackie of Edinburgh and J. P. Mahaffy of Trinity College, Dublin, also noted the parallels between Homeric and biblical criticism and resisted or tempered any approval of critical approaches to Homer for fear of the impact on the Bible. As a consequence of these concerns, British classical university scholars of Anglican and other religious persuasions had virtually nothing to do with critical approaches to Homer until after the repeal of the Oxford and Cambridge religious tests in 1871 and the gradual assimilation thereafter of biblical criticism into the universities. The limits of free expression about biblical scholarship set the parameters for classical explorations as well.

The reception of Grote's views on myth proved much friendlier than his discussion of Homer because later interpreters could and did blunt the critical, radical edge of his analysis. Grote had drawn upon a Viconian concept of a prehistoric age in which the imagination dominated and then upon a Comtean interpretation of intellectual development from that era toward one of rational understanding and scientific analysis. Many of Grote's readers, as well as later mythographers, rejected these theories of history and embraced instead a German idealist notion of the ongoing spiritual education of the human race from an early age of religious misunderstanding toward later periods of religious enlightenment and spiritual development. Whereas Grote had presented the reinterpretations of the mythic heritage in fifth-century Athens as leading to confusion about the myths and to confusion in Greek thought generally, later writers saw those ancient reforms as part of a larger effort whereby human beings had expanded and refined their spiritual and ethical knowledge and sensibilities.

While commenting upon the ancient reformers of the mythic inheritance, liberal Christians quite consciously drew attention to the affinities they found in the ancient world to their own modern efforts at theological reorientation. On one occasion F. D. Maurice, the most important liberal Anglican theologian of the mid-century, discussed the ancient Greek questioning of their inherited religious traditions. Some had begun to look to the religion of Egypt for spiritual insights while others had turned to unbelief. But according

³⁰ John Gibson Lockhardt, 'Homeric controversy', *Quarterly Review* (American edn), 87 (1850), 236; Edward Bouverie Pusey, *Collegiate and professorial teaching and discipline in answer to Professor Vaughn's strictures* (Oxford: J. H. Parker, 1854), p. 62. See Turner, *The Greek heritage in Victorian Britain*, pp. 140–54.

to Maurice, 'the wisest' of those Greek thinkers had attempted to show their fellow citizens

that their consciences and reason did demand something which they did not create for themselves; that all faith and reverence and worship, the words which they spoke – their own existence – their very doubts and questionings, pointed to a deep, eternal ground, which could not be a visible phantom, nor a theory, nor an abstraction – which must be *the* Being.[31]

Maurice here as in other of his writings saw the enlightened Greeks as participating in a more general human recognition of religious truth. Such in his view was similarly the position of the moderate Anglican who resisted the contemporary attraction of Roman Catholicism, the modern equivalent to Egypt, or the path of unbelief. Drawing upon intuitive knowledge from their inner selves, religiously minded persons would inevitably be drawn to a recognition of the presence of the divine in the world.

Other Anglican writers presented the religiously reforming dramas of Aeschylus and Sophocles as working through one kind of religious dispensation toward another. They suggested that the situation resembled in some respects the effort whereby St Paul had expanded Christianity from a religion pertaining to the Jewish dispensation into one that embraced the entire world. F. A. Paley observed,

To reconcile the old law of inexorable justice with the newer law of mercy, seems to have been the leading idea of Aeschylus. To improve humanity by holding up to admiration the qualities of justice, fortitude under affliction, sympathy with distress, firmness in duty, and generally, all practical goodness was the cherished object of Sophocles.

E. H. Plumptre, a major Victorian translator of Sophocles, described the mission of the dramatist in words that might have been applied to almost any contemporary nineteenth-century liberal Protestant:

The work of Sophocles ... was the task, finding the mythology of Homer in possession of the mind of the people, to turn it, as far as it could be turned, into an instrument of moral education, and to lead men upwards to the eternal laws of God, and the thought of His righteous order.[32]

[31] Frederick Denison Maurice, *The religions of the world and their relations to Christianity* (London: John W. Parker, 1847), p. 17.
[32] F. A. Paley, *The tragedies of Aeschylus*, re-edited with an English commentary (London: Whittaker and Co., 1855), p. xix; E. H. Plumptre, tr., *The tragedies of Sophocles* (New York: George Routledge and Sons, n.d.), p. xciv.

It had, of course, been exactly such reinterpretations of the ancient mythic inheritance that Grote believed had confused later Greek thought and undermined ancient democratic politics. The liberal Anglican theologians and biblical commentators regarded such moderate reinterpretations as necessary to sustain Christianity in the face of new scientific knowledge and moral sensibilities.

Other theories of myth not distinctly theological in origin but compatible with a moderate Christianity or liberal spirituality and a generally idealist view of life also directly challenged Grote's rationalist analysis. The most famous and pervasive of these during the 1870s and 1880s was F. Max Mueller's solar theory. This liberal Christian German philologist, who was friendly with the major liberal Anglicans, settled at Oxford where he was showered with prestigious honours. He produced volume after volume in which he interpreted virtually all ancient myths from India to Greece as representing some aspect of the sun. Much earlier nineteenth-century philology had appeared hostile to religion, but Mueller's analysis served to provide evidence of an upward religious evolution whereby ancient peoples could be seen as having attempted to achieve true spiritual knowledge. As he wrote near the end of his life,

What ... I consider as the most important outcome of Comparative Mythology is the conviction which it leaves in our minds that the ancestors of the Aryan races were not mere drivelling idiots, but that there was a continuous development in the growth of the Aryan mind as in the growth of the surface of the earth ... It is to me the same relief to know that the gods of Greece and India were not mere devils or the work of devils or fools, but that they also, even in their greatest degradation, had a rational meaning and a noble purpose.[33]

To trace the origins of Greek myth to speculations about the sun was to illustrate that human beings were essentially spiritual creatures. The myths with all their crudity, sexuality, and violence might not contain any historical information, but the psychology inherent in

---

[33] F. Max Mueller, *Contributions to the science of mythology* (London: Longmans, Green, and Co., 1897), pp. 21–2. See also Richard Dorson, 'The eclipse of solar mythology', in Thomas A. Sebeok, ed., *Myth: a symposium* (Bloomington, Ind.: Indiana University Press, 1974), pp. 25–63; Turner, *The Greek heritage in Victorian Britain*, pp. 104–15; Linda Dowling, *Language and decadence in the Victorian fin de siècle* (Princeton: Princeton University Press, 1986), pp. 61–77; J. B. Bullen, *The sun is god: painting, literature and mythology in the nineteenth century* (Oxford: Clarendon Press, 1989), *passim*.

the process of making myths from interpreting the sun demonstrated that human beings from their earliest appearance had sought spiritual truth and manifested spiritual yearnings. The rest of human history was the realization of that search for higher, truer, and purer religion. Mueller's theory encountered enormous criticism, but within the world of university and Anglican scholarship it exerted broad influence and long prevented any reductionist theory of myth from receiving wide acceptance.

Writers more concerned with aesthetics than theology often embraced Grote's views only to squeeze from them the particular critical vitality that Grote had infused into them. Grote's historicist theory of myth deeply influenced the mythography of John Ruskin, Walter Pater, and J. A. Symonds. These writers readily accepted Grote's view that myth related to the childhood of the race and exemplified the activity of the human imagination. But while Grote had explicitly rejected any nostalgia for a mythopoeic age, these later writers enthusiastically embraced that nostalgia. In some respects this treatment paralleled contemporary scientific writers who accepted the concept of evolution but rejected Darwin's deterministic mechanism of natural selection in favour of some idealist or theistic mode of organic change.

Walter Pater, for example, a scholar and critic deeply read in German philosophy, presented Greek myths as the product of the *human* imagination rather than of the imagination of the Greeks living in a particular time and place. Instead of drawing Grote's conclusion that myths were fundamentally empty of meaning outside their own epoch, Pater believed the myths presented artistic and aesthetic ideals that could become meaningful in the modern world. Pater argued that the much loved myth of Demeter and Persephone illustrated

the power of the Greek religion as a religion of pure ideas – of conceptions, which having no link on historical fact, yet, because they arose naturally out of the spirit of man, and embodied, in adequate symbols, his deepest thoughts concerning the conditions of his physical and spiritual life, maintained their hold through many changes, and are still not without a solemnising power even for the modern mind, which has once admitted them as recognized and habitual inhabitants; and, abiding thus for the elevation and purifying of our sentiments, long after the earlier and simpler races of their worshippers have passed away, they may be a pledge to us of the place in our culture, at once legitimate and possible, of the associations, the conceptions, the imagery, of Greek religious poetry in general, of the poetry of all religion.[34]

For Pater the myths represented moments of perennial expression of the human imagination and situation. The images, emotions, and narratives of the myths could authentically resonate with human beings today as well as for those who had lived over two millennia earlier. Pater's aesthetic sense of the imagination and religiosity was fundamentally antinomian. It was equally dissolvent of Grote's progressive Comtean rationalism on the one hand and any mode of teleological human religious development on the other. In that regard Pater's idealism was equally corrosive to both Victorian rationalism and Christianity.

Except for Mueller's solar theory all of this mid- and late Victorian mythography owed much to Grote, but each of them took only part of what he had offered. No later Victorian classical commentator actually pursued his total rejection of the historicity of the mythic age. The archaeology of the last three decades of the century, and most especially the excavation of Troy, undermined the historical agnosticism of Grote's position. Many commentators accepted his concept of the age of myth as being one of imagination, but none spurned the imagination as he had done. All were interested in the emergence of the human mind from the age of imaginative myth, but none believed that development to have been the wholeheartedly desirable journey toward scientific enlighten- ment that Grote had portrayed. In other words, the idealism of those who were concerned about human spiritual development, of those who treasured the role of the imagination over the understanding, and of those who could not believe that Helen had never looked from the walls of Troy toward the dark ships overcame the reductionist rationalism that informed Grote's mythography. Simultaneously with the refutation and recasting of Grote's analysis of Greek religion and literature there occurred the construction of an alternative idealist vision of Greece.

---

[34] Walter Pater, *Greek studies*, ed. Charles L. Shadwell (New York: The Macmillan Co., 1903), 155–6. See also Carolyn Williams, *Transfigured world: Walter Pater's aesthetic historicism* (Ithaca: Cornell University Press, 1989), pp. 103–10, 238–58.

III

Grote's remarkable body of scholarship constituted an Anglican nightmare of classical studies gone awry just as scientific naturalism constituted an Anglican nightmare of misdirected scientific pursuits. Yet whereas the advanced scientists through the aggressive establishment of independent professional institutions ultimately won a distinct place for themselves in Victorian intellectual life, Anglican classicists, who were culturally if not always theologically conservative, continued to control Oxford and Cambridge. Their students and sympathizers tended to dominate the late Victorian provincial and Scottish universities. From those positions classicists, at first Anglican but later in the century drawn from other Christian denominations as well, who were hostile to the ideas and values of Grote enunciated an idealist version of ancient Greece that captured teaching and shaped scholarship well into the twentieth century.

After 1865 when Grote had completed his major publications, Matthew Arnold, Benjamin Jowett, and their followers steadily challenged his implicit position within both English and Scottish university circles as the primary authority on the moral and intellectual character of Greek thought and philosophy. Although the Hellenism of Arnold and Jowett is relatively familiar, its mission in preventing the wider permeation into British culture of Grote's radical, rationalist, democratic interpretation of Greece has not been recognized even though there is a direct chronological relationship.[35] Their vision of Hellenism was directly rooted in idealist philosophy and in turn served to establish philosophic idealism as one of the chief intellectual bonds of the late century university-educated generation. This idealism functioned in a fashion similar to the bond provided by Anglicanism in the pre-reformed university setting. Early in the century Anglicanism had served intellectually

---

[35] I have elsewhere dealt extensively with the reception and criticism of Grote's political analysis of Athenian democracy. It should be noted that during the second half of the century criticism of Athenian democracy and of radical democracy in general was not rare in English histories of Greece even if their authors accepted much of Grote's analysis. His own view of radical democracy was quite utopian whereas later writers even when sympathetic to democracy were less uncritically enthusiastic than Grote had been. These later historians virtually ignored the close relationship that Grote had attempted to draw between politics and religious culture in Athens. In that respect, Grote came to be regarded later in the century strictly as a political historian when he had always understood politics as part of and inseparable from the broader culture. See Turner, *The Greek heritage in Victorian Britain*, pp. 213–63.

and socially to protect the universities from the intrusion of political and religious radicalism. The spirituality inherent in late century philosophical idealism provided to university-educated men by then recruited across a broad spectrum of religious beliefs and social backgrounds a similar bulwark against the dissolvents of radical individualistic politics, religious scepticism, reductionist empiricism, and scientific naturalism.

Arnold's vision of Greece articulated in *Culture and anarchy* (1869) and in a previous series of major literary essays stood in direct opposition to Grote's positivistic, individualistic interpretation which so clearly paralleled the political views of John Stuart Mill. Arnold regarded those latter outlooks as contributing to contemporary cultural and political anarchy that necessarily ensued when individuals did as they pleased. It was the rejection of traditional values and national institutions on the part of both political radicals and religious Nonconformists that Arnold sought to counter by his appeal to Greece. Virtually all of Arnold's ideas about Greece and Hellenism originated with early nineteenth-century Germans and their ideal of the cultivation of the moral self in the context of a strong community or state. He cast on to the scales the weight of modern idealism imposed on ancient Greece to combat the influence of modern rationalism that Grote had imposed on the same culture. In effect Arnold refused to leave the terrain of the ancient world uncontested.

Arnold trimmed from his discussions various irrational elements of the Greek experience about which he was knowledgeable in order to present a more pristine and stable image of Greek life.[36] In his various writings on Hellenism, Arnold ascribed to fifth-century Greece an ethical outlook and respect for existing institutions largely analogous to the moderation associated with liberal Anglicanism. Arnold contrasted such Hellenism with both the narrow moral strictness of the Nonconformists and the expansive individualism of political liberals. Arnold's Greeks were sane, rational, playful, and moral without being priggish. Echoing other religious liberals, Arnold believed that Hellenism had been most exquisitely embodied in the drama of Sophocles and in Greek literature before the emergence of Euripides's critical scepticism. In contrast to Grote,

[36] Warren D. Anderson, *Matthew Arnold and the classical tradition* (Ann Arbor: University of Michigan Press, 1965), pp. 30–49; David J. DeLaura, *Hebrew and hellene in Victorian England: Newman, Arnold, and Pater* (Austin: University of Texas Press, 1969), pp. 171–91; Turner, *The Greek heritage in Victorian Britain*, pp. 17–36.

Arnold contended that those particular Greek writers with their reverence for the mythic inheritance and for tradition had grasped many of the deeper mysteries and values of human life which Christianity had explored more profoundly. The character of Greek life and morality demonstrated for Arnold that polite, civil values might be maintained as an alternative to rampant critical individualism even when Christianity was not present. Furthermore, the experience of Greece also displayed vital aspects of human nature that could not be gleaned from the narrower morality of Christian scripture. Both the morality of the Greeks and of the Bible each tempering the other were necessary for the full development of human beings. The Greeks had also understood the importance of the shared community values religious and otherwise against which Grote's Socrates in ancient Athens and J. S. Mill in contemporary Britain had so strenuously objected. Arnold in effect praised in both ancient and contemporary society the role of the spirit of King Nomos so detested by Grote and Mill.

Arnoldian Hellenism as articulated throughout the 1860s provided the immediate and generally unrecognized backdrop for the introduction of Plato as a major philosophical figure in British education and university life. Plato became a genuinely familiar figure to Victorian intellectuals only from mid-century onward. Grote's *Plato, and the other companions of Socrates* was the first extensive commentary on the philosopher to be written in Great Britain. But it was not Grote who brought Plato to the centre of university life or of general British intellectual activity. The construction of a Plato for the English-speaking world was the accomplishment of Benjamin Jowett, Regius Professor of Greek at Oxford and later Master of Balliol College. As one of the much persecuted authors of *Essays and reviews*, Jowett came to recognize during the early 1860s that neither the high church party nor the evangelicals in the Church of England would permit an interpretation of scripture that took into account the critical difficulties posed by modern scholarship. Without such a new reading of scripture, he believed that traditional Christian moral values and the kind of society they had fostered among the upper British social classes might not survive the mid-century intellectual assault arising from utilitarianism, historical criticism, and scientific naturalism.[37]

---

[37] Peter Hinchliff, *Benjamin Jowett and the Christian religion* (Oxford: Clarendon Press, 1987).

Foiled in his effort to sustain Christian morality on the basis of liberal theology, Jowett turned to the philosophy of Plato to provide a surrogate. A faith in the spiritual character of the universe, a traditional sense of what was right and wrong, and a conventional understanding of what was fitting and unfitting all of which some persons could achieve on the grounds of traditional Christian teachings and the scriptures, Jowett attempted to sustain through an appeal to the idealism of Plato. Jowett and others after him reinterpreted Christianity to mesh with Plato and Plato to mesh with Christianity and both to mesh with polite Anglicanism, moderate social hierarchy, a strong state, and a sense of shared community. The affinities between the classical projects of Jowett and Arnold were clear and usually attracted the same followers.[38]

In 1871, the year before Grote's death, Jowett published *Dialogues of Plato, translated into English with analyses and introductions*. A second edition with modest revisions appeared in 1875 and a third with more extensive changes, in 1892. Jowett's translations of Plato supplanted Grote's commentary just as Grote's *History of Greece* had Thirlwall's. In this new battle of the books Anglican idealism won out over the challenge of rationalist utilitarianism. In contrast to Grote's volumes, Jowett's provided introductions, commentary, paraphrase, and translations. The writings of Plato in English immediately stood encased in a whole system of translated text, paraphrase, and commentary not unlike that found in annotated editions of the scriptures in English. In both instances the commentary served to contain, conceal, and control internal elements or external interpretations that might prove embarrassing or offensive to the reverent reader or commentator. The language and rhetoric of Jowett's translations contained echoes of those of the Bible and the Book of Common Prayer. The introductions, analysis, and commentary prefacing each translation sometimes addressed philosophical or epistemological issues; other times they provided the occasion for meditations on moral or political issues. To the extent that readers studied the introductions rather than the dialogues themselves, they imbibed as much of the thought of Jowett as they did of Plato. It is not insignificant that until the third edition published in 1892 no annotation distinguished Jowett's analysis and commentary from his

---

[38] One of the clearest examples of a writer who was dually attracted to Arnold and Jowett was Percy Gardner. This Oxford scholar wrote criticism of ancient art that embodied Arnoldian Hellenism and religious works that drew upon liberal Anglicanism.

paraphrase of Plato which prefaced the translation proper of each dialogue.

The quarrel of Jowett and Grote over Plato was not merely one between scholars but rather one between two fundamentally different moral and political visions that had clashed throughout Victorian intellectual life for the privilege of replacing traditional Christian outlooks and values. The rivalry of intellectual orientation that Mill had so starkly portrayed in his essays on Bentham and Coleridge reasserted itself almost three decades later in these rival Platonic commentaries. Jowett initially claimed to approach Plato from an historicizing standpoint arguing that the ancient philosopher must be interpreted according to the conditions of his own day and not judged by later standards. In opposition to Grote, Jowett urged that it was his own intention,

> to represent Plato as the father of Idealism, which is not to be measured by the standard of utilitarianism or any other modern philosophical system. He is the poet or maker of ideas, satisfying the wants of his own age, providing the instruments of thought for future generations. He is no dreamer, but a great philosophical genius struggling with the unequal conditions of light and knowledge under which he is living. He may be illustrated by the writings of moderns, but he must be interpreted by his own, and by his place in the history of philosophy. We are not concerned to determine what is the residuum of truth which remains for ourselves. His truth may not be our truth, and nevertheless may have an extraordinary value and interest for us.[39]

Although Jowett boldly asserted this historicist position, he had every intention of making Plato relevant for modern readers. Whereas Grote had used commentary on Plato to introduce the ideas of Bentham, Comte, and Mill to wider circles, Jowett used his commentaries to introduce the thought of Kant and Hegel. In other words, just as Grote had sought to make Plato conform to Enlightenment rationalism, Jowett sought to make him conform to German idealism.

Empiricism, utilitarianism, naturalism, radical individualism, and scepticism represented for Jowett varieties of philosophical and moral worldliness that failed to take account of the presence of evil in

---

[39] Benjamin Jowett, *The dialogues of Plato, translated into English with analyses and introductions*, 3rd edn, rev. and corr., 5 vols. (Oxford: Oxford University Press, 1924), I, xi. All quotes are taken from this edition of Jowett's work. Unless indicated in the footnote or text the material quoted appears in the first edition.

human life. They posed shallow solutions to the deeper issues of the human condition and ignored fundamental spiritual questions and concerns. Jowett attempted to use Plato to unmask the inadequacies of those outlooks and to establish an ethic resembling that of Christianity but founded on a universalistic rather than a particularistic Christian foundation. Jowett mixed Kantian, Hegelian, and Platonic ideas into a kind of liberal Christian potpourri of unselfish morality. In Jowett's pages Plato came to the fore as the defender of a proto-Christian ethic of duty based on intuition. According to Jowett, Plato had spurned any form of utilitarianism and had taught duty, self-sacrifice, the pursuit of ideals higher than ourselves and higher than those of the world. Plato had insisted that 'in some sense or other truth and right are alone to be sought, and that all other goods are only desirable as means towards these'.[40] Such an intuitive unselfish ethic had, of course, long been regarded as one of the key messages of Christianity and of Anglican morality, but for Jowett Plato became its new proponent and defender.

Despite his claims to historicism, Jowett repeatedly removed Plato from the confines of ancient Athens. Plato emerged, like the founders of the great religious traditions, as a voice relevant to problems of all ages. Plato was always seen as addressing universal evils and wrongs that appeared perennially throughout human history rather than the particular shortcomings of Athenian politics and society. For example, Jowett took the specific evils that Plato had associated with the Sophists and broadened them to embrace a whole series of general human shortcomings. Jowett claimed,

The great enemy of Plato is the world, not exactly in the theological sense, yet in one not wholly different – the world as the hater of truth and lover of appearance, occupied in the pursuit of gain and pleasure rather than of knowledge, banded together against the few good and wise men, and devoid of true education. This creature has many heads; rhetoricians, lawyers, statesmen, poets, sophists. But the Sophist is the Proteus who takes the likeness of all of them; all other deceivers have a piece of him in them. And sometimes he is represented as the corrupter of the world; and sometimes the world as the corrupter of him and of itself.[41]

It was against this many faceted sophistry that could manifest itself in any time and place, a sophistry reminiscent in Jowett's prose of the Christian concepts of worldliness and sin, that Plato's philoso-

---

40 Ibid., II, 295 (small revision after the 1st edn).
41 Ibid., IV, 287 (some revision after the 1st edn).

phy had taken its stand in fifth-century Athens and could again in Victorian Britain.

The combat against moral evil justified for Jowett many of the more repressive elements in Plato's politics. Jowett did not really see them as repressive, but rather as devices that prevented the eruption of larger wrongs or extreme individualism. In Jowett's eyes Plato's emphasis on community, a political elite, and limitations of thought and expression constituted not an illiberal political philosophy, but wise and vigilant protection of good taste and of a common sense of morality. Jowett complacently saw Plato's expulsion of the poets as related to the achievement of a polite moral society. He contended,

Plato does not seriously intend to expel poets from life and society. But he feels strongly the unreality of their writings; he is protesting against the degeneracy of poetry in his own day as we might protest against the want of serious purpose in modern fiction, against the unseemliness or extravagance of some of our poets or novelists, against the time-serving preachers or public writers, against the regardlessness of truth which to the eye of the philosopher seems to characterize the greater part of the world.[42]

Jowett thus appealed to the apprehensions of his readers that without protectors of good taste and propriety the traditional moral and political values of the society would collapse. The protection of those outlooks was not censorship nor evidence of repression, but quite simply the necessary role of an educated elite that sought to protect what was good, true, and beautiful in its own sight.

Jowett was also very much at one with the entire British idealist tradition stemming from Coleridge and Carlyle that emphasized the importance of the power of the state to prevent the excesses of personal selfishness and commercialism.[43] Jowett like others of his generation saw the authority of the state as a force that could prevent disorder and that might also be a force for social progress. He associated such authority as did Plato with a particular kind of leadership. In 1875 Jowett explained in the introduction to the *Gorgias*,

---

[42] Ibid., III, clxiv.
[43] Jowett's comfort with a relatively powerful state may have been in part rooted in his experience of religious persecution. During the persecutions arising from *Essays and reviews* the secular courts had provided relief by not convicting those who were brought before them. Furthermore, during the 1870s the secular authorities cooperated with ecclesiastical leadership in attempting to curb what Jowett and others of his outlook regarded as the excesses of ritualism.

A true statesman is he who brings order out of disorder; who first organizes and then administers the government of his own country; and having made a nation, seeks to reconcile the national interests with those of Europe and of mankind. He is not a mere theorist, not yet a dealer in expedients; the whole and the parts grow together in his mind; while the head is conceiving, the hand is executing. Although obliged to descend to the world, he is not of the world. His thoughts are fixed not on power or riches or extension of territory, but on an ideal state, in which all the citizens have an equal chance of health and life, and the highest education is within the reach of all, and the moral and intellectual qualities of every individual are freely developed, and the 'idea of good' is the animating principle of the whole. Not the attainment of freedom alone, or of order alone, but how to unite freedom with order is the problem which he has to solve.[44]

Plato thus took his place in the long tradition of thinkers that had appreciated the necessity of balancing freedom and order which so many intellectuals of Jowett's generation saw as fundamental to the increasingly democratic British scene. In this respect, Jowett's praise of the state and the necessity of strong leadership paralleled the contemporary comments on Julius Caesar and Augustus.

The general target of late century Oxford Platonism from Jowett onward was radical individualism associated with selfish commercialism on the one hand and political liberalism on the other. Oxford Christians hated it on ethical grounds; Oxford idealists, because it clashed with their vision of the importance of community. Grote had championed such individualism throughout his discussion of Socrates and of the Socratic scepticism he regarded as fundamental to Plato's philosophy. He also regarded it as fundamental to the exercise of proper democratic life. Jowett and his followers such as Richard Nettleship and Ernest Barker were among those figures who transformed the political vocabulary of early Victorian liberalism and radicalism into that of the new liberalism of community and collectivism. Old words were literally given new meanings. Richard Nettleship, while commenting on Plato, told his students,

There is no such thing as an individual in the abstract, a human being literally independent of all others. Nor, conversely, is there such a thing as a community which is not a community of individuals, or a common life or interest which is not lived or shared by men and women. Nor is individuality, in the true sense of the word, diminished by participation in this common life or interest ... When a man so completely throws himself into the common interest that he can be said to live for others, he does not lose

44 Ibid., II, 308–9.

his individuality; rather his individuality becomes a greater one. In this sense it may be said that what Plato had in view was not the abolition of individuality, but the raising of it to the highest possible pitch through *esprit de corps*.

According to Nettleship, Plato had contended that the 'test of a man's goodness and of his greatness is the extent to which he can lead a common life ... or can identify himself with, and throw himself into, something not himself'.[45] Here Nettleship was combining Plato's idea of his guardians with the public school ethic and with the ideal of the individual realizing himself through community that was associated with Victorian medievalism, the Nonconformist chapel, and the temperance movement as well as political idealism.

In Jowett's reading of Plato there was little or no room for radical Socratic scepticism as Grote had presented it. In the wake of Jowett's commentary Grote's image of Socrates as a scientific, rationalist figure and the best of the sophists generally faded from British classical commentary. Liberal Anglicans had from the 1830s seen Socrates as a figure who sought to reform religion and morality in a constructive or even reverent spirit rather than destructively. In occasional essays of unsystematic character R. D. Hampden, W. A. Butler, F. D. Maurice, Connop Thirlwall, and A. P. Stanley interpreted the Platonic Socrates as a figure of true religious reverence and import. According to these liberal Anglicans Socrates had opposed the intellectual evils of the ancient sophists whom they equated with modern rationalists or utilitarians. In Thirlwall's words, Socrates had believed in 'man as a rational being – capable of distinguishing truth from error, and of giving an intelligent preference to that good which most properly belongs to his nature, over every other end'. Socrates for Stanley, in an essay written in reply to Grote's analysis, represented a 'Prophet of the Gentile world' who had the capacity to transport one 'from the glories of Hellenic heathenism into the sanctities of Biblical religion'.[46] Socrates's

---

45 Richard Lewis Nettleship, *Lectures on the 'Republic' of Plato*, ed. Godfrey R. Benson (London: Macmillan and Co., 1937), pp. 177, 299–300. On the redefinition of the language of early Victorian liberalism, see Gertrude Himmelfarb, *Poverty and compassion: the moral imagination of the late Victorians* (New York: Alfred A. Knopf, 1991), pp. 245–66.
46 Thirlwall, *A history of Greece*, new edn (London: Longman, Brown, Green, and Longmans, 1847), IV, 533–4; A. P. Stanley, *Lectures on the history of the Jewish church: third series* (New York: Scribner, Armstrong and Company, 1877), pp. xix, 218. See also Turner, *The Greek heritage in Victorian Britain*, pp. 268–73.

combination of probing intellect with sincere religious devotion mirrored the very intellectual stance that liberal Anglicans hoped to make their own in science, the classics, and other arenas of intellectual activity. Similar sentiments were found in Jowett's discussions of Socrates. Jowett presented Socrates as a teacher who had challenged the moral complacency of the sophists.

As the century passed, attitudes towards Grote's rationalistic Socrates became much more complicated and generally critical. To the extent that Socrates had challenged Athenian democracy in a radically individualistic manner, he encountered measured criticism from writers such as Gilbert Murray, J. B. Bury, Ernest Barker, and T. R. Glover all of whom championed the influence of the community over disruptive individuals. These writers in a sense agreed with Grote's interpretation of Socrates, but critcized the individualism that Grote had admired.

Still other scholars denied Socrates's rationalism and portrayed him as an ancient idealist.[47] Such views particularly flourished in Scotland. Scholars such as John Burnet and later A. E. Taylor essentially rejected Grote's image and interpreted Socrates as a kind of ancient mystic. For Burnet and Taylor ancient philosophy had not arisen as part of an effort to reach rational enlightenment, but rather from the need to address issues arising from a religious instinct. Indeed Socrates's mission had exhibited a reaction to rationalism rather than an assertion of it. For these idealist philosophers Socrates illustrated the necessary complementary relationship of philosophy, science, and religion. Rather than standing as the father of Western science, Socrates emerged by the close of the nineteenth and the early years of the twentieth centuries as a philosopher who had touched upon truths only properly developed under the dispensation of Christianity interpreted from the standpoint of philosophic idealism. Socrates as the Millite individualist championing science, questioning tradition, and challenging King Nomos almost passed from the scene in scholarship of British universities. Socrates had not imbued Plato particularly or philosophy generally with a sceptical turn of mind but rather had fostered an appreciation for the instincts that best realized themselves in ancient Pythagoreanism, religion, and idealist philosophy.

47 Turner, *The Greek heritage in Victorian Britain*, pp. 309–21.

IV

Well before the close of the century George Grote's critical rationalist challenge to classical scholarship in Great Britain stood effectively repulsed. His corpse rested with honour in Westminster Abbey,
and his works resided on numerous library shelves. But his rationalistic project of the 1840s had failed. Grote's scholarship remained one
of the monuments of Victorian intellectual life, but it entered only
marginally the lasting consciousness of the Victorian learned world.
His interpretation of Greece found no champions who established
the kind of lasting institutional setting of the Oxford *Litterae Humaniores*. The domination of political and philosophical discourse by
philosophic idealism that Grote and Mill had so feared and so long
combated came to pass. Scholars, dons, and students did not look to
fifth-century Greece as an example of a rational, critical enlightenment but rather of political, religious, and ethical idealism.

This situation represents almost the exact reverse of what occurred
contemporaneously within the world of Victorian science. In a very
real sense science and the classics constituted counterpoints to each
other. In both venues liberal Anglican university scholars confronted
radical London-based intellectuals who intended to introduce ideas,
methods, and scholarly goals that would overturn Anglican values
and outlooks, as well as Anglican social and cultural dominance. But
in contrast to the Anglican clergymen-scientists whose influence
steadily diminished from the third quarter of the century onward,
Anglican or idealist classical commentators largely succeeded in
deflecting the intrusion of rationalism and positivism within classical
scholarship. They retained a dominant position in university education and guided such education and most especially that of Oxford
toward an understanding of the ancient Greek world that preserved
moderate Anglican values, philosophic idealism, and polite Christian attitudes outside a specifically Christian ecclesiastical, institutional, or cultural setting.

As with the contemporaneous Victorian conflict between science
and religion, both ideas and institutional arrangements determined
the outcome of the struggle among classical scholars. The Anglican
idealists succeeded in large measure because the chief location of
classical studies and teaching remained the universities which even
after the reforms of the mid-century continued to be dominated by
Anglicans. Within university classical studies Anglicans of moderate

religious values retained the very kind of influence they lost in Victorian scientific institutions and also to a considerable measure in the Church of England itself. More rationalistically minded classical scholars who might have attacked the idealist Anglican version of Greek scholarship attained no independent institutional base as did the advanced naturalistically minded scientists who flourished outside the universities within institutions increasingly free of clerical and Anglican influence.

Furthermore, Grote and his work were representative of the mid-Victorian generation of institutionally independent scholars and historians. They were writers either of independent means or of positions in the church or government bureaucracy. From the 1860s onward fewer and fewer scholars or intellectuals without a firm attachment to a university or other educational or research institution could exercise influence over intellectual activity. There was little room for the amateur scholarship that had been the by-word of the mid-century Victorian intellectuals. Grote as an independent scholar had trained no followers to continue his work, whereas Jowett trained a whole generation of both students and faculty successors. Finally because in the late century universities the teaching ideal largely triumphed over the research ideal, the universities generated little new scholarship to challenge the image of Greece that had come to dominate within them by the late 1880s. Nor did the dons of that generation necessarily even appreciate the scholarly research of Grote.

Within the universities the idealist version of Greece embodied in the *Litterae Humaniores* also encountered only a minimal religious opposition even though the mixing of Greek and Christian values involved not uncontroversial assumptions about Christianity.[48] The absence of criticism reflects the changed institutional arrangements in Oxford. Parliament's abolishing of religious tests in 1871 removed religious affiliation and thus religious orthodoxy as issues involved in university appointments except for the Theology Faculty. The more

---

[48] The most important such challenge might have arisen from the publication of Edward Hatch's *The influence of Greek ideas and usages on the Christian church*, ed. A. M. Fairbairn (London: Williams and Norgate, 1890). This Oxford scholar drawing upon Harnack criticized the residuum of Greek ideas in the historical dogmas of Christianity. He contended this Greek presence had distorted the original simple Gospel message. Hatch's was really an argument for the radical reform of Christianity rather than of the modern understanding of Greece. Although his work became a classic in the field of theology and religious studies, it appears to have exercised no influence over the modern mixture of Christian and Greek values in the *Litterae Humaniores*.

orthodox members of the university, most especially those associated with the high church, regarded that reform as having finally transformed Oxford into a distinctly secular rather than an Anglican society. Fearing a total separation of collegiate life from religious influences, the high church party established its own Oxford institutions in the hope of preserving their outlook. The most important of these were Keble College founded in 1870 and Pusey House established in 1884. Evangelicals at Oxford primarily institutionalized themselves in certain of the city's churches rather than in university or collegiate institutions. The establishment of a separate Theology Faculty examining for its own degrees also separated religious education from general university life. Since Jowett's Hellenism only marginally touched these new institutions or religious training proper, the self-consciously religiously orthodox pursued their goals in their own institutions largely indifferent to the *Litterae Humaniores* which symbolized simply one more element in the life of a university separated from religious and theological concerns.

The resistance to critical rationalism within the world of Victorian classicism stands as an important reminder that whole areas of Victorian intellectual life remain unexamined and underappreciated. The impact of science, naturalism, empiricism, utilitarianism, and the like have received enormous coverage in the historical literature. The great gap is the full exploration of the various modes of idealism that functioned as a major force of cultural resistance to rationalism. There may have been no single impulse that more fully permeated Victorian intellectual activity. Yet its presence, influence, and impact have yet to receive their proper recognition. In the wake of the rise of analytic philosophy at the turn of the century idealism has generally failed to command the attention of historians.[49] If, however, one had been dwelling in virtually any English-speaking university in 1900, it would have seemed almost inconceivable that idealist philosophies would not dominate twentieth-century intellectual life. How and why those idealist philosophies came to and remained so strongly at the fore of British intellectual life are issues still to be fully explored as is why their seemingly impregnable position so quickly eroded during the first three decades of the twentieth century.

[49] Peter Hylton, *Russell, idealism, and the emergence of analytic philosophy* (New York: Oxford University Press, 1990).

Index

Achilles, 292
Acton, Lord, 42
Aeneas, 292, 295, 300–5, 314, 317
Aeschylus, 303, 333, 345
Agamemnon, 305
Agassiz, L., 18
agnosticism, 20, 82
Airy, G., 203
American scholars and secularist thesis, 4–7
Anaxagoras, 333
Andrade, E. N. Da C., 282–3
Anglican culture, 46–8, 72, 349–50
Anglo-Catholicism, 50–4, 83
Anti-Catholicism, 26, 83, 191, 195–6
antivivisectionists, 206–7
apostolic succession, 27
Aristophanes, 288
Aristotle, 288, 318–19, 336
Armstrong, H., 211–12, 215–16
Arnold, M., 40, 42, 49, 70–1, 152, 308; critical of Nonconformists, 29, 33; on Lucretius, 267; Hellenism of, 287, 310, 325–6, 349, 350–2; on Marcus Aurelius, 319–20
Arnold, T., 245–7, 341
Arnstein, W., 26
Athenian democracy, 288, 329
Augustus, 236, 244, 356; Ferguson on, 244; Merivale on, 251; Edwardian views of, 257–9; Syme on, 260–1; Virgil and, 291, 295, 297, 299–301, 306, 312–16, 321, 356; Myers on, 315
Austen, J., 47
Ayrton, A. S., 208

Babbage, C., 40, 177, 203
Bacon, F., 124–5
Baconianism of everyday life, 124
Baden-Powell, R., 211
Bailyn, B., 233

Bain, A., 40
Bainbridge, W. S., 2
Balfour, A., 171, 199, 217
Barber, B., 175
Barker, E., 356, 358
Barton, R., 21
Bateson, W., 215–16
Baynes, T. S., 262
Belfast Address, 21, 83, 141, 153, 196–7, 270–1, 280, 289
Bell, C., 11, 113–14, 118
Benn, A. W., 73, 135, 175, 281
Bentham, J., 327, 337, 339, 353
Berman, M., 203
Bernal, J. D., 227
Bernard, C., 17
Blackie, J. S., 344
Blackwell, T., 236–8, 292
Blake, W., 66
Bolingbroke, Lord, 233
Bonaparte, Napoleon, 248–9
Bovey, H., 214–15
Bowler, P., 19, 117
Boyle, R., 102
Bradlaugh, C., 133, 152
Bradley, A. C., 284
Brent, R., 25
Brewster, D., 60
Bridgewater treatises, 47, 76, 111–16, 178
Briggs, Asa, 15, 125, 199
British Association for the Advancement of Science, 21, 48, 55, 57, 60, 77, 177, 180, 183–4, 186–7, 198, 202–3, 206, 215, 217–18, 270–1, 328
British Science Guild, 217–21, 223
Brock, W. H., 218
Brontë, C., 40
Brooke, J. H., 18
Browning, R., 40
Buchan, J., 258

362